Geopolitics and Governance
in North Africa

Edinburgh Studies on the Maghreb

Series Editors: Allen James Fromherz and Matt Buehler

International Advisory Board
- Amira Bennison
- Aomar Boum
- Francesco Cavatorta
- Mounira M. Charrad
- Irene Fernández-Molina
- Jonathan Hill
- Frédéric Volpi
- Katja Žvan Elliott

Books in the series (published and forthcoming)

Geopolitics and Governance in North Africa: Local Challenges, Global Implications
Sarah E. Yerkes (ed.)

Thami al-Glaoui: Morocco's Greatest Pasha
Orit Ouaknine-Yekutieli

International Influences on Tunisian Democratisation
Pietro Marzo

edinburghuniversitypress.com/series/estm

Geopolitics and Governance in North Africa

Local Challenges, Global Implications

Edited by Sarah E. Yerkes

EDINBURGH
University Press

Edinburgh University Press is one of the leading university presses in the UK. We publish academic books and journals in our selected subject areas across the humanities and social sciences, combining cutting-edge scholarship with high editorial and production values to produce academic works of lasting importance. For more information visit our website: edinburghuniversitypress.com

© editorial matter and organisation, Sarah E. Yerkes, 2023, 2025
© the chapters their several authors, 2023, 2025

Edinburgh University Press Ltd
13 Infirmary Street,
Edinburgh, EH1 1LT

First published in hardback by Edinburgh University Press 2023

Typeset in 10/12 Source Serif Pro by
Cheshire Typesetting Ltd, Cuddington, Cheshire

A CIP record for this book is available from the British Library

ISBN 978 1 3995 0369 3 (hardback)
ISBN 978 1 399 50370 9 (paperback)
ISBN 978 1 3995 0371 6 (webready PDF)
ISBN 978 1 3995 0372 3 (epub)

The right of Sarah E. Yerkes to be identified as editor of this work has been asserted in accordance with the Copyright, Designs and Patents Act 1988 and the Copyright and Related Rights Regulations 2003 (SI No. 2498).

Contents

List of Figures vii
List of Contributors viii
Acknowledgements xi

   Introduction 1
   Sarah E. Yerkes

1. From the Shores of Tripoli: The Global Implications of Libya's Post-2011 Governance Travails 12
Frederic Wehrey and Jacqueline Stomski

2. Egypt's Waxing Challenges and Waning Power 42
Michele Dunne

3. Moroccan Politics: Defensive at Home, Assertive Abroad 74
Mohamed Daadaoui

4. Tunisia's Unfinished Revolution: Addressing Regional Inequality 101
Sarah E. Yerkes

5. Mauritania: The Multi-dimensionality of its Enduring Challenges 135
Fatima Hadji

6. Plus ça change, plus c'est la même chose: The Herculean Task of Civilianising the Algerian State 168
Anouar Boukhars

7. Gender Imbalances across North Africa 194
Sarah E. Yerkes

8. North Africa in the World 234
   Sarah E. Yerkes and Maha Sohail AlHomoud

Bibliography 273
Index 325

Figures

2.1	Egypt's Population, 1960–2020	45
2.2	Fertility Rates in Egypt, 1960–2019	46
4.1	Regional Indicators in Tunisia	112
7.1	Global Gender Gap Index Scores, 2021	196
7.2	Women, Business and the Law Index Scores, 2021	197

Contributors

Maha Sohail AlHomoud was a 2021–22 James C. Gaither Junior Fellow in the Middle East Program at the Carnegie Endowment for International Peace. She conducted research on Tunisia, Egypt and the Gulf States, focusing on domestic and foreign policy, climate change and US policy orientations in the region. Her research interests include authoritarianism, oil-dependent states and economic diversification, legal and social reform, nationalism and state-society relations. Maha is an alumna of the University of Washington in Seattle, with a bachelor's degree in Political Science and a concentration in Political Economy, with Honours.

Anouar Boukhars is a non-resident fellow in the Middle East Program at the Carnegie Endowment for International Peace and a professor of Countering Violent Extremism (CVE) and Counter-Terrorism (CT) at the Africa Center for Strategic Studies (ACSS), National Defence University, Washington DC. His publications have appeared in the *Journal of Conflict Studies, International Political Science Review, Middle Eastern Studies, African Security Review, European Security, Journal of the Middle East and Africa, Counter Terrorism Centre Sentinel, World Politics Review, Al Jazeera Centre for Studies, Orient* and *Terrorism Monitor*. Boukhars is the author of *Politics in Morocco: Executive Monarchy and Enlightened Authoritarianism* (2010) and co-author of *Salafism in the Maghrib: Politics, Piety, and Militancy* (2019). He is also the co-editor of *Perilous Desert: Insecurity in the Sahara* (2013) and *Perspectives on Western Sahara: Myths, Nationalisms and Geopolitics* (2013). The views expressed are his and not an official policy or position of the National Defense University, Department of Defense, or US Government.

Mohamed Daadaoui is a professor of Political Science and Chair of Political Science, History, and Philosophy and Rhetoric at Oklahoma City University. He has authored *Moroccan Monarchy and the Islamist Challenge* (2011). Daadaoui is a specialist of North African politics. Mohamed's articles have appeared in the *Journal of Middle Eastern Studies, Journal of North African Studies, Hudson Institute, Washington Post*'s *Monkey Cage, Foreign Policy, Huffington Post*, the blog *Sada* of the Carnegie Endowment for International Peace, the *Middle East Institute, Jadaliyya* and *Muftah*. He has provided commentary to local and international media outlets such as Oklahoma's local PBS affiliate, C-Span and Al-Jazeera English. Daadaoui is also the author of a blog on the Maghreb region called *Maghreb Blog*. He is currently working on a Historical Dictionary of the Arab Uprisings and a manuscript on Islamism in Morocco and Tunisia.

Michele Dunne is a non-resident scholar in the Middle East Program of the Carnegie Endowment in Washington DC, where her work focuses on political and economic change in Arab countries, particularly Egypt, as well as US policies towards the region. During a twenty-year career at the US Department of State, she served as Director for Egypt and North Africa on the National Security Council staff, as political officer in the US Embassy in Egypt and Consulate General in Jerusalem, and as member of the Secretary of State's Policy Planning Staff. She holds a PhD in Arabic language and linguistics from Georgetown University, where she also served as visiting assistant professor.

Fatima Hadji is a senior programme officer at the National Endowment for Democracy (NED), covering Maghreb programmes. Before joining the NED, she was a senior programme officer at the National Democratic Institute where she worked in the Middle East and North Africa division. Hadji holds a PhD from the School of Conflict Analysis and Resolution at George Mason University.

Jacqueline Stomski is an independent researcher specialising in Security Sector Governance and Reform (SSG/R) and the politics of mobility policies in conflict and post-conflict environments. She was a 2020–21 James C. Gaither Junior Fellow in the Middle East Program of the Carnegie Endowment for International Peace, where she contributed to research on Libyan SSG/R, armed group identities and US security policies toward the Middle East and North Africa. She holds a bachelor's degree in Arabic Studies from the University of Maryland, College Park, and is a 2020 graduate of the Arabic Flagship Program Capstone Year, in Meknes, Morocco.

Frederic Wehrey is a senior fellow in the Middle East Program at the Carnegie Endowment, focusing on armed conflict, security sectors and politics in North Africa and the Gulf. His work has appeared in the *New York Review of Books*, *TIME Magazine*, *The New Yorker* and other publications. He is the author of *The Burning Shores: Inside the Battle for the New Libya* (2018), which the *New York Times* called 'the essential text on the country's disintegration'. His first book, *Sectarian Politics in the Gulf* (2013), was chosen as 'Best Book on the Middle East' by *Foreign Affairs* magazine. Together with Anouar Boukhars, he co-authored *Salafism in the Maghrib: Politics, Piety, and Militancy* (2019). A former US military officer, he holds a doctorate in international relations from the University of Oxford.

Sarah E. Yerkes is a senior fellow in the Middle East Program of the Carnegie Endowment for International Peace and a globally recognised expert on North Africa. She has published numerous book chapters, reports, articles and op-eds on the Middle East and North Africa, with a focus on state-society relations and governance. She is a former member of the State Department's Policy Planning Staff, where she covered North Africa and spent time at the Pentagon, advising the Joint Chiefs of Staff. She holds an MA in Middle Eastern Studies from Harvard University and a PhD in Government from Georgetown University.

Acknowledgments

We would like to express our deep gratitude to the many people who assisted during the research and writing process. First, we wish to thank the Open Society Foundations, Carnegie Corporation of New York and Global Affairs Canada for their generous support of the research and field work that went into this book.

We would also like to thank Marwan Muasher, Michele Dunne and Amr Hamzawy for their stewardship of the Middle East program of the Carnegie Endowment for International Peace and their tremendous support of this project. We also benefitted tremendously from the research assistance of Nesrine Mbarek and Khulood Fahim. An extra special thanks to Maha AlHomoud for her tireless efforts in reviewing draft after draft of the book and providing thoughtful feedback and camaraderie throughout.

We are also indebted to the many scholars, analysts and activists who participated in two workshops to help frame the book – one in Tunis in February 2020 and one held virtually in October 2021. Thank you also to the many individuals who shared their time and insight with us during multiple trips to North Africa.

Finally, we are grateful for the support of Emma House and the Edinburgh University Press team.

Introduction

Sarah E. Yerkes

In 2011, North Africa caught the world's attention when ordinary citizens took to the streets to demand change. From Tunis to Cairo to Tripoli, North Africans succeeded in removing from power dictators who had ruled for decades, silencing the opposition, capturing state wealth and sowing division. The uprisings commonly known as the Arab Spring unleashed a decade of instability and disorder throughout much of the Middle East North Africa (MENA) region. Today, North Africa – defined here as Algeria, Egypt, Libya, Mauritania, Morocco and Tunisia – is a dynamic region facing several social, economic and political challenges, many of which were exacerbated by the COVID-19 pandemic, with implications for the stability of the broader MENA region and beyond. From global power competition and the broken international order on display in Libya, over rising socio-economic inequality and marginalisation across Tunisia, as well as the climate change and population growth that, along with the continued fight over the Grand Ethiopian Renaissance Dam, will worsen Egypt's water insecurity, to the decline of Algeria's hydrocarbons-based economies that has added further fire to the ongoing protests, each North African state – whether individually or collectively – is on the precipice of change. Furthermore, the region's geostrategic location at the nexus of Africa, Europe and the Middle East means that what happens in North Africa has broad ramifications outside of the region. And the changing geopolitical dynamics – whether the rise of Russia and China and the decline of US influence, or the intra-regional conflicts in the Middle East – has serious implications for how each country responds to the challenges at home.

A common thread running through all the region's major challenges is the broken social contract. A decade after the Arab Spring began, North Africa is in the midst of a transformation. The factors that led to the Arab Spring have not gone away. Most of the social, economic and political factors that brought people onto the streets in 2010–11 are worse today, and in the wake of the COVID-19 pandemic, regional governments have been exposed for their failure to deliver the effective governance (including adequate healthcare, social safety nets and stability) that the people demand. These governance failures have led to protests in some cases and violent extremism in others, and they have contributed to the growth of the region as both a transit point as well as a point of origin for migration from Africa to Europe.

Each North African country has undergone or is undergoing a transformation that is reshaping its political and social trajectory. In Tunisia, the events of July 2021 saw the democratically elected president seize power from the parliament and the judiciary and roll back much of the decade-long progress of the country's democratic transition. Although seen as hopeful and inspiring to the rest of the world for much of the period from 2011 to 2021, Tunisia's transition has failed to fully benefit large parts of the population. The country continues to grapple with profound social inequalities as the government struggles to overcome rapidly growing polarisation and determine a clear economic path that will satisfy a variety of opposing political actors and bring economic growth and stability. At the same time, Tunisia is facing dire economic fallout from COVID-19, at a time when its relationship with traditional allies is changing and greater influence from actors such as China and Russia is rising across North Africa. Various regional actors – particularly Saudi Arabia and the United Arab Emirates (UAE) – have taken advantage of Tunisia's dire economic situation and precarious political situation to exert influence there. Mauritania is also undergoing a political and economic transition that could usher in a more stable and profitable future but faces the curse of oil-rich economies. Sarah Chayes and Sarah Peck explain that oil wealth can 'distort a country's economic fundamentals, fuel corruption, and create conditions that trigger conflict'.[1] Mauritania continues to grapple with major issues such as who controls rents, how to maintain stability and security, and what a socially equitable and environmentally sustainable future looks like. The country is dealing with a legacy of authoritarianism and instability that is not easy to overcome. And a host of environmental problems – water shortages, pollution and the encroachment of the Sahara on agricultural lands – all threaten to create more instability.

Libya and Egypt offer particularly vivid examples of how global challenges are reshaping these countries and by extension impacting North Africa with clear implications for Sub-Saharan Africa, Europe and the rest of the Middle East. Egypt, long a major regional player, has undergone a political transformation that is reshaping not only its own future but also that of the region. The repressive military regime is facing grave security, economic and climate challenges that have reshaped its role into one of less influence but greater interventionism. President Abdel Fattah al-Sisi's government's failure to adequately address the rapidly growing population and concomitant water shortages have led to Egypt's decline as a regional leader. As a result, Egypt is forced to rely increasingly on external actors for support. In Libya, the civil war has transformed the country into a regional area of influence and proxy conflict with broad ramifications. Since 2011, Libya has attracted regional and global powers – particularly Qatar, Turkey, the UAE and Russia – seeking to expand their influence through both direct military intervention as well as political jockeying and the use of media. The instability brought about and perpetuated by foreign interference has led to a massive migration crisis and allowed a particularly dangerous affiliate of the Islamic State to flourish, directly impacting the security of Libya's neighbours and threatening Western interests.

In each North African country, governments and civil society actors continue to grapple with how and whether to promote gender equality. While some states have made attempts at empowering women, significant gender gaps remain across all domains, from political participation over education to employment. Gender inequality has implications well beyond the moral imperative of providing equal access to opportunities and an equal voice to all citizens, regardless of their gender. Governments across the world have used gender inequality to sow division within society, and gender inequality at the national level can trickle down to the workplace and the home, contributing to strains in family life. On the political level, gender inequality can lead to less female-friendly policies, and many scholars have found that the level of equal access to political participation is correlated with higher economic growth and prosperity.[2] There are also several studies confirming a link between gender equality in education and economic growth.[3]

This book examines the major internal and external challenges facing each North African state and provides recommendations to local actors and the international community to address them effectively. It offers field-based analysis of the dynamics at play in each state in the region, as well as cross-cutting analysis of how the inclusion or exclusion of women adds to the challenges at the local level across the region. The volume also seeks to understand the role of international actors – both Western donors (the United States and Europe) and global powers (Russia and China), as well as regional actors (such as Saudi Arabia, the United Arab Emirates and Qatar), in addressing the region's internal and external challenges.

Why North Africa?

North Africa is a dynamic and consequential region on the precipice of tremendous change, yet one that is often overlooked. As Irene Fernandez-Molina argues, 'North Africa tends to fall in the cracks of conventional geopolitical categories, which might contribute to its invisibility and its positional in-betweenness (physically and in terms of identity). North Africa struggles not to be seen as the little brother of the Middle East'.[4] The impact of the internal dynamics of North African states can be felt well beyond the borders of the region. For Europe, North Africa is a near neighbour, as well as an important economic partner and gatekeeper for the growing number of Sub-Saharan (and North African) migrants seeking to reach Europe's shores. In 2020, North Africans made up more than 40 percent of migrant flows to Europe (42,417 migrants out of a total of 99,475 arrivals); as of October 2021, North Africans made up one-third of migrant flows to Europe (32,258 out of 121,463).[5] As Haim Malka argues, '[i]rregular migration of North African citizens to Europe is a barometer of the region's socio-economic and political environment.

Higher flows of migrants indicate more challenging political and economic conditions in the Maghrib'.⁶

Instability in North Africa has a direct effect on Europe. Europe relies on North African security forces to fight terrorism in the region and in the neighbouring Sahel. Algeria is one of the European Union's top gas suppliers, meaning that disruption to energy flows, which have been the repeated targets of terrorist groups, harms Europe. North African states have also traditionally played an important role in negotiating peace agreements between MENA actors. Egypt, in particular, has been a key player in negotiating between Hamas and Israel. Furthermore, given the large North African diaspora communities in France, Belgium, Denmark, Spain and the Netherlands, amongst others, some scholars argue that North Africa is both a domestic and a foreign policy concern for Europe.⁷ In Africa writ large, Lidet Tadesse Shiferaw notes that North Africa, home to the continent's largest economies, is flexing its muscles, as many North African states are 'strategically expanding their presence and seizing economic opportunities in Africa, while securing strategic foreign policy goals'.⁸ For example, Algeria uses the platform of the African Union to promote its approach towards counter-terrorism and to advocate on behalf of the Sahrawi cause.⁹ And Morocco has sought to expand its economic relationships across the continent as part of its effort to position itself 'as Europe's gateway to Africa'.¹⁰

While the United States is less geographically tied to North Africa, the region is consequential to a host of US interests, from national security over energy to global power competition. Like Europe, the United States sees several North African states as security exporters and relies on countries such as Morocco, Algeria and Tunisia to tackle violent extremism before it spills over their borders. However, North Africa has traditionally been overshadowed by other areas or issues pertaining to the MENA region, such as Iran, the Israeli-Palestinian conflict, or US economic interests in the Gulf. Amid American neglect, both Russia and China have expanded their presence in North Africa, threatening US and European interests and investment. The Arab Spring forced an uptick in US interest and engagement in the region, particularly in Egypt and Tunisia, as the Obama administration sought to shore up support for democratic transitions and civil society actors to stave off further instability. But that support was both insufficient and short-lived: within a short time after the fall of both Hosni Mubarak and Zine el Abidine Ben Ali, North Africa was once again relegated to second-tier status within the MENA region. Nevertheless, the grievances that fuelled the Arab Spring remain salient across the region today. Thus, as Thomas Hill and Sarah Yerkes argue, failing to prioritise North Africa is 'particularly dangerous today, at a time when many regional economies are performing worse than in 2010 and high levels of corruption, unemployment and relative deprivation persist, leaving North African citizens angry, frustrated and hopeless'.[11]

Survey of the Book

The authors in this volume examine each North African state in detail, highlighting the big challenges facing each country and how ineffective governance as well as international interference have exacerbated these challenges. They also address some broader, cross-regional trends, including persistent gender inequality. The volume concludes with a look at the role that various foreign actors have played in the region.

Chapter One unpacks how Libya's post-2011 conflicts are the product of broader global trends that include growing multipolarity, American retrenchment, European disunity, military adventurism by rival Middle Eastern states and a breakdown of international norms and multi-lateral institutions (reflected in the diminished authority of the United Nations and recurring contempt for the UN arms embargo). Frederic Wehrey and Jacqueline Stomski explore how Libya's political fragmentation, dearth of formal institutions and oil wealth have long acted as a magnet for predatory middle and great powers. They argue that, despite being on the margins of US policy concerns for nearly a decade, Libya is increasingly exerting an outsized influence on the political and security landscapes of Africa, Europe, the Mediterranean Basin and the greater Middle East. Libya is the gateway for the largest African migration flow in modern history, which has tilted European politics to the right; it is the site of the world's most internationalised civil war, with no fewer than ten outside states intervening militarily; it was home to the Islamic State's most lethal affiliate outside of Iraq and Syria and remains fertile ground for transnational jihadism; it has the largest proven oil reserves in Africa and continues to influence global markets; and its economic and security spill-over poses a significant threat to the Arab world's only democracy (Tunisia) and its most populous state (Egypt). Having analysed the global ripple effects of Libya's dissolution since 2011, the chapter concludes with a forward-looking assessment of how emerging international challenges could both exacerbate and temper the country's conflicts: the global plunge in oil demand, the economic aftershocks of the COVID-19 pandemic and climate change.

In Chapter Two, Michele Dunne discusses two critical challenges facing Egypt – massive population growth and water scarcity. She describes how these challenges have had an impact on Egypt's changing influence on the Middle East, Africa and the world. This nation of 100 million, which sits on a land bridge between Africa and Asia, has had a strong effect on others in the region, including in the tumultuous decade of 2010–20, which saw an attempted democratic transition brought to a crashing halt by a military coup, ushering in unprecedented repression. Egypt has seen its traditional Arab leadership role eclipsed by Gulf States and its position in Africa diminished relative to that of rivals such as Ethiopia and Sudan. The next decade is likely to be no less dramatic, as Egypt faces massive challenges related to rapid population growth coupled with diminishing water and food security – partly due to climate change – in addition to the economic and health effects of the pandemic. The chapter examines how Egypt's current military-dominated government is addressing such challenges and the global as well as regional repercussions of those choices, and it asks whether the nation can reinvent itself to face a new era.

In Chapter Three, Mohamed Daadaoui explores how regional and domestic dynamics are reshaping the narrative of Morocco's stability and political future. The country continues to struggle with deep social and economic inequalities that it seeks to address through a series of policy prescriptions within the framework of decentralisation. With mixed results, Morocco has nonetheless pursued an aggressive foreign policy to expand its influence in Sub-Saharan Africa, perceiving an opening in the retreat of two major regional powers – that is, Algeria during the transitional year of the Hirak protests and Libya after the end of the Qadhafi regime. Furthermore, Morocco's relationship with its traditional allies – the Gulf, the African Union and the United States – has changed gradually over the years, yielding a new set of challenges and opportunities for the country. Morocco's response has so far been a more assertive and confident foreign policy agenda that looks to integrate the country more forcefully into an economically rising African continent. The chapter explores how these trends play into the country's stability and security within a dynamic North Africa.

As Tunisia ends the first decade of its democratic transition and enters an era of political instability and uncertainty, in Chapter Four Sarah E. Yerkes examines the governance consequences of regional marginalisation in Tunisia and analyses central and local government efforts at addressing this issue. Regional disparities, brought about in part by an official Ben Ali-era policy of favouring the coastal governorates, left the country deeply divided and fuelled the 2010–11 revolution. Tunisia began an official decentralisation process in May 2018, but four years later little progress has been made to devolve power from the central state to local authorities, and President Kais Saied's July 2021 power grab put the decentralisation process on hold. The Coronavirus outbreak has further polarised the country, with more than half of the governorates lacking access to intensive care facilities at the start of the pandemic and contributing to further socio-economic inequality. The chapter assesses the successes and failures of the decentralisation process to date and offers recommendations for local actors and international donors to improve governance at the local level and to level the playing field for the traditionally neglected interior and southern regions to prevent instability in the future.

After decades of instability and insecurity, Mauritania has been moving toward a more secure and stable government. In Chapter Five, Fatima Hadji examines several challenges facing Mauritania – challenges that prevent and threaten its socioeconomic growth, democratic development and stability. She looks at the legacy of authoritarianism and instability as well as the enduring economic and sociopolitical crises that have mired Mauritania's history for decades. Mauritania experienced nine military coups between 1978 and 2009, and today the military continues to exert a major influence on the political space, as well as the economy and the security sector. Like many other countries in the world, Mauritania is also dealing with environmental problems that are threatening its population, natural resources and stability including water shortages, pollution and the encroachment of the Sahara on agricultural lands. As Hadji explains, the growing environmental threats have the potential to overshadow any effort that Mauritania is making to overcome its economic and sociopolitical challenges.

In Chapter Six, Anouar Boukhars looks at the prospects for political and economic reform in Algeria in the wake of the wave of popular protests known as the Hirak movement, which helped end Abdelaziz Bouteflika's twenty-year rule. He examines the relationship between Algeria's military and civilian leadership and evaluates how former President Bouteflika – with varying degrees of success – attempted to reign in Algerian security and intelligence forces. Boukhars describes the current crisis facing Algeria's leaders, amplified by the COVID-19 pandemic, which, combined with low oil and gas prices, hit the country hard. With the government unable or unwilling to meet the demands of the Hirak movement, public anger is growing. Faced with tighter budgets and prospects of resurgence of protests, Algeria's new rulers must adapt. The crisis represents an opportunity to implement greater political openness, to move beyond hydrocarbons and to reinvigorate Algeria's vibrant role in the crises that threaten its neighbourhood – namely, those in Libya and Mali. This chapter offers a guide to the currents that will likely shape Algeria's future.

Chapter Seven takes a cross-regional look, analysing how gender imbalances impact governance across North Africa. While several states in the region have made broad public attempts at empowering women, gender gaps remain in everything from political participation over education to employment. Sarah E. Yerkes evaluates the status of gender equality in each country of the region and examines the efforts at addressing gender inequality – whether by national governments, local officials, local civil society actors, or international donors, as well as impediments to gender equality and the role of Islamist parties and movements in impeding or, at times, promoting gender equality. This chapter provides a crosscutting view and explains how failure to adequately address gender inequality has implications for stability and security both within and outside of North Africa.

The final chapter, Chapter Eight, takes a broad look at North Africa's relationship to other regions. As Sarah E. Yerkes and Maha Sohail AlHomoud explain, North Africa sits at the nexus of Europe, Africa and the Middle East. Each of these global regions has influenced and has been influenced by the domestic challenges within North Africa. This chapter assesses the role of Europe (as well as the United States), Sub-Saharan Africa, the Middle East and the global powers China and Russia in addressing – or exacerbating – the region's governance challenges. It examines both the way in which North African countries approach the geopolitical landscape and the way in which outside actors are shaping the region.

Notes

1. Sarah Chayes and Sarah Peck, 'The Oil Curse: A Remedial Role for the Oil Industry', *Carnegie Endowment for International Peace*, 30 September 2015, https://carnegieendowment.org/2015/09/30/oil-curse-remedial-role-for-oil-industry-pub-61445.
2. Laura Cabeza-García, Esther Del Brio, and Mery Oscanoa-Victorio, 'Gender Factors and Inclusive Economic Growth: The Silent Revolution', *Sustainability* 10, no. 2 (6 January 2018): 121.
3. Stephan Klasen and Francesca Lamanna, 'The Impact of Gender Inequality in Education and Employment on Economic Growth: New Evidence for a Panel of Countries', *Feminist Economics* 15, no. 3 (1 July 2009): 91–132.
4. I. Fernandez Molina and M. H. de Larramendi, eds., *Foreign Policy in North Africa: Navigating Global, Regional and Domestic Transformations* (New York: Routledge, 2020), 2–4.
5. 'Displacement Tracking Matrix', *International Organization for Migration*, n. d, https://migration.iom.int/europe/arrivals?type=arrivals.
6. Haim Malka, 'Turbulence Ahead: The North African Maghrib in 2019', *Centre for Strategic and International Studies*, 11 January 2019. https://www.csis.org/analysis/turbulence-ahead-north-african-maghreb-2019.
7. Kristin Archick and Derek E. Mix, 'The United States and Europe: Responding to Change in the Middle East and North Africa,' *Congressional Research Service Report for Congress*, 12 June 2013, https://www.files.ethz.ch/isn/165485/210923.pdf.

8. Lidet Tadesse Shiferaw, 'Peace and Security in Africa: Drivers and Implications of North Africa's Southern Gaze,' *European Centre for Development Policy Management,* October 2019, https://ecdpm.org/publications/peace-security-africa-drivers-implications-north-africas-southern-gaze/.
9. Shiferaw, 'Peace and Security in Africa'.
10. Shiferaw, 'Peace and Security in Africa'.
11. Thomas Hill and Sarah Yerkes, 'A New Strategy for US Engagement in North Africa', *United States Institute of Peace* and *Carnegie Endowment for International Peace,* February 2021, http://carnegieendowment.org/files/HillYerkes-ANewStrategyforUSEngagementinNorthAfrica-Feb2021.pdf.

1

From the Shores of Tripoli: The Global Implications of Libya's Post-2011 Governance Travails

Frederic Wehrey and Jacqueline Stomski

For millennia, the African territory encompassed in the modern state of Libya has been a place on the margins of global history. The very name itself, *Libia*, was used in Antiquity by the Egyptians and later the Greeks to denote the region on the western edges of the known world, a place of desolation and barbarity, inhabited, in many literary accounts, by fantastical beasts.[1] In the ensuing centuries, waves of conquerors and empires governed it lightly and ambivalently, focusing their energies mostly on maintaining chains of garrisons, outposts and entrepots along the trading routes that linked the Mediterranean Basin to the African interior. By the nineteenth century, the geopolitical profile of the region had increased, with the ruling Ottoman Empire devolving significant power to the local suzerains of the so-called Barbary States.[2] Through the first half of the twentieth century, the territory of Libya continued to acquire greater strategic significance: from the Italo-Turkish War – which witnessed the first ever use of the airplane for military purposes – and continuing through the Second World War, during which tank battles raged across vast swathes of Cyrenaica (eastern Libya).[3] Traditional narratives minimise the role of Libyan elites in this mostly European contest of the early and mid-twentieth century, although more careful historians have highlighted how local notables, tribal chieftains and guerrilla commanders skilfully played outside patrons against one another.[4]

While the 1969 officers' coup heralded a new era under Muammar Qadhafi, Libya continued to flit at the margins of both major events of the world and the Middle East. Despite Qadhafi's efforts to parlay Libya's oil wealth and his support to militants and insurgents across the globe into geopolitical power, he was unable to consolidate meaningful clout. Since 2011, the seminal events of the 17 February Revolution and the UN-mandated, NATO-led military intervention have spawned more than one effort to re-appraise and, in some cases, inflate Libya's global significance. The first of these is a retrospective, framing Qadhafi's decision to abandon weapons of mass destruction (WMDs) in return for re-integration into the global economic order as a major world event: a validation of diplomacy's potential to 'tame' a 'rogue' regime with a mix of 'sticks' and incentives. Some voices have relatedly pointed to the 2011 toppling of Qadhafi, after he had relinquished his WMD programme in return for what he expected would be regime survival, as reinforcing North Korea's unwillingness to relinquish its own nuclear arsenal.[5] Both these arguments are rife with errors: the process of dismantling Libyan WMDs began before the 2003 Iraq invasion, and Qadhafi's programme was so nascent and rudimentary that he did not have much to 'surrender', making parallels to North Korea's calculus ludicrous.[6]

The second, more accurate and undeniable global impact attributed to post-2011 Libya concerns the tenet of the so-called 'responsibility to protect' (R2P) and, later, the norms of embargo enforcement and the very credibility of the United Nations. Here, US proponents of intervention in Libya, often citing the failure of the West to act during the Rwandan genocide, believed that in early 2011 they were acting nobly to forestall another mass slaughter.[7] When those fears turned out to be overblown – and when by 2012 the post-intervention nation-building project collapsed into what President Obama called a 'shit-show' – Libya became associated with the death knell of liberal interventionism, arguably deterring the American administration from more forcefully acting against President Assad's regime in Syria.[8]

These macro-level narratives will continue to be centred in future historians' debates and cited by polemicists or former policy-makers to justify partisan positions. Even as Libya has faded from mainstream news coverage in the decade after the fall of Qadhafi, it continues to serve as a bellwether, harbinger, catalyst and laboratory for several global and regional trends. To be sure, this country of nearly seven million still has little agency in the major dramas of Middle Eastern politics, but as the site of several spill-over trends it merits closer examination, and looking at localised political and governance travails with a view towards appreciating their regional and global impacts adopts a new significance.

Since 2011, Libya has become an arena for regional and great power rivalry, waged through political influence, media narratives and direct military intervention, including an unprecedented use of drones and foreign mercenaries. It has emerged as the thoroughfare for one of history's largest and deadliest flows of human migration – hundreds of thousands of irregular migrants, many from Sub-Saharan Africa, traverse the territory en route to the perilous Mediterranean crossing – thrusting the liberal European order into a wrenching moral and political crisis. Similarly, Libya's post-revolutionary security crisis paved the way for the establishment of the most lethal affiliate of the Islamic State outside of Syria and Iraq, which projected its terror and influence well beyond the borders of the North African state.

This chapter will explore these global implications of Libya's post-2011 path by linking local governance challenges to larger macro trends concerning state sovereignty, international norms and the future of conflict. It surveys the contours of regional and great power intervention during and after the fall of Qadhafi, interrogates common narratives surrounding the migration crisis and unpacks how armed conflict and terrorism have spilled over Libya's borders. In addition to these negative, heavily securitised dimensions, it will address how Libya is both affecting and grappling with several non-traditional global challenges, including changing patterns of global hydrocarbon demand and climate change. The goal in doing so is to accurately situate Libya as a country of consequence within the Maghreb and the Mediterranean basin, but also, on the global stage, taking stock of both its instrumentalised significance and its actual impact, in a way that avoids the polemics and partisanship that have too often dominated commentary and scholarship on this North African state.

The Arena: Libya as a Site of Regional and Great Power Competition

External powers have long infringed on local sovereignty in Libya to prevent competitors from gaining influence, even as these powers, ironically, have often dismissed the geopolitical significance of Libya. Beginning with the Ottoman exit in 1912, internal Libyan conflicts have been shaped by external designs. Although the Ottomans declared the region wholly autonomous and denied Italian claims to the territory, the lack of international consensus on the region's sovereign power was made murkier by the maintenance of Ottoman officials in Libya.[9] The ensuing clashes for authority solidified the emergence of Libya as an arena for great power competition and created a legacy that continues to enable foreign manipulation of Libyan sovereign realities.

From the interwar period until Libyan independence in 1951, outside powers exploited Libya as a strategic outpost from which they could spread control across the North African region. As the colonial era began to crumble on the margins of the First World War, the British and French – desperate to secure Egyptian, Tunisian, Sahelian and Sub-Saharan African colonies – turned to Libya as a rampart for regional stability.[10] Simultaneously, Italo-Ottoman competition for opportunities to expand their reach from Libya underscored Libya's geostrategic potential.[11] What ultimately became Libya's transition from Ottoman to Italian administration depended on micro-allegiances – on a city-by-city or clan basis – enabling external powers to manipulate domestic concepts of national identity to their own ends, often dividing Libyans.[12] Prior to the post-colonial definition of Libya's modern borders, external powers valued Libyan territory as a platform from which they could protect or project influence.

While the Second World War was an inflection point in many aspects of the Libyan narrative, external powers continued to use Libya as a gambit in their foreign policies for geostrategic gains. The Second World War revived the intra-Libyan disputes of the First World War and the interwar period: local leadership divided on foreign allegiances left state sovereignty dangerously ambiguous.[13] In the war's aftermath, the British and French were once again primarily concerned with their regional interests: security of the Libyan-Egyptian border and Saharan holdings.[14] However, once Moscow voiced interest in administering Tripolitania, the Allied Powers mobilised to prevent foreign control of Libyan territory with the 1951 UN process.[15] This Western-led endeavour to safeguard

Libya's geostrategic potential from the Soviets was nominally disrupted by mass Libyan protests in 1949, tanking a UN proposal to divide Libya.[16] The United Nations ultimately in 1951 installed a constitutional monarchy under King Idris Al-Senussi. This UN-designed government was, according to scholar Lisa Anderson, an inefficient 'complex picture of dependence', enabling British and American military expansion in Libya to prevent Russian access to the region.[17] The international failure in designing a Libyan state is overshadowed by Libya's comparative geostrategic importance in the Cold War.

The 1969 toppling of the sclerotic Libyan king by disgruntled Libyan army officers and Captain Muammar al-Qadhafi's ascension to power ushered in significant geopolitical shifts. Libya exited the US-led post-war orbit, warmed to the Soviet Union and attempted to align itself with the ideological currents of the Arab world – especially the pan-Arabism and anti-imperialism of neighbouring Nasser-ruled Egypt – that had permeated Libya and electrified Captain Qadhafi and his fellow officers. Yet, in the following decades, despite Qadhafi's best efforts, Libya continued to linger on the margins of the major events of the world and the Middle East, even after the discovery and exploitation of its oil reserves (the largest in Africa). To be sure, Qadhafi used this hydrocarbon wealth to support a vast array of guerrilla movements in far-flung corners of the globe, ranging from Irish republicans to South Pacific separatists. Yet, the increasingly mercurial leader never converted this militant patronage, nor his menacing reputation, to real geopolitical clout that would guarantee his regime's survival. Even the Soviet Union, despite selling him massive quantities of arms, never regarded him as a reliable client, as it did with some other Sunni Arab states.

By the mid-2000s these Arab states, led by Saudi Arabia, had completely isolated Libya from the regional order. To counter his lack of allies, Qadhafi had begun pivoting his country's gaze to the African interior in the late 1990s, portraying Libya as inextricably bound to Sub-Saharan Africa. In practice, this re-orientation was epitomised by vast investment projects across the continent and the continued funding of African rebellions. But among the Libyan elites constituting Qadhafi's government apparatuses, the 'African turn' was never popular, nor did it yield tangible benefits for the country. Ultimately, this posture failed to ensure Qadhafi's longevity as Libya's 'Brother Leader'. Certainly, a few fellow despots – such as Zimbabwe's Robert Mugabe and Uganda's Yoweri Museveni – came to his defence amid the 2011 revolution, but more welcomed his departure.[18]

Post-2011, conflicts wedge Libyans between rival regional and global powers – all competing to dominate and manage Libya's future. Outside competition for primacy in Libya began with both the 2011 NATO-led intervention and the concurrent manifestation of the Emirati-Qatari rivalry through weapons flows and military support to anti-Qadhafi factions on the ground – who would later advance competing notions of political order for the post-Qadhafi state. Although the period between late 2011 to 2014 was largely devoid of overt foreign military intervention, international manoeuvring foreshadowed what would become globalised engagement in Libya's conflict(s). In Tripoli's 2011 liberation, both intra-Libyan and Qatari-Emirati tensions played out with rival armed groups seizing strategic pieces of territory within the capital – ports, airport, ministries and bases – which they later sought to use to gain political influence. After Tripoli's liberation, foreign powers continued to maintain unique lines of political, military and media support for increasingly fractured political elites and armed groups who were basing their legitimacy on these strategic territorial holdings. Compounding Libya's security sector challenges to post-conflict stabilisation and nation-building, the enduring legacy of Qadhafi's regime – which failed to bequeath Libyans a basic democratic experience or functioning institutions, save, perhaps, the oil sector – fuelled an increasingly detrimental political deadlock. Concurrently, political and social divisions that predated the revolution – as a result of divide-and-rule policies, which were catalysed by 2011's fighting and by the regime's selective use of force against certain communities – rose to the fore. Tensions and open violence surfaced between towns, regions, and ethnic and linguistic minorities, especially between the vestiges of the regime and younger revolutionaries, over access to Libya's economic and political spoils.[19]

Western and UN attention focused on shepherding the country toward national legislative elections in summer 2012 to replace the moribund and unelected National Transitional

Council. In retrospect, elections were accorded outsized importance as a 'success marker' by Western diplomats and policy-makers. Washington attached excessive deference to local sovereignty and a 'Libyan-led' transition – and since Libyan revolutionary political leaders wanted elections as soon as possible, Washington was in no position to delay them, despite the risks.[20] A similar deferral to risky and ill-informed Libyan decisions occurred on the financial front: Western policy-makers unfroze Libya's assets and avoided what they saw as an overbearing supervision or control of how those assets were spent. The deleterious effects of the Western hands-off approach started as early as late 2011, when Libya's transitional government starting channelling funds to armed groups, sky-rocketing the number of militiamen on the state payroll. This action seeded much of Libya's later security turmoil, but at the time Libya lacked a legal institutional framework for exerting control over national financial assets that would have made escrow-type management of resources possible, and Western policy-makers avoided intervention, citing sacrosanct principles of national economic sovereignty. This inaction allowed Libya's financial institutions, especially the Central Bank of Libya, to become the site of increasingly fierce struggles for international influence.[21]

As instability persisted, Libya's media landscape proved an especially toxic forum for interference. In tandem, competing satellite television stations owned or supported by Qatar, the UAE and Turkey disseminated disinformation and partisan reporting. Social media became an increasingly contested space, marked by the massive deployment of 'electronic armies' of Twitter trolls, bots and 'franchised' accounts that posed as locals but were often proxies for foreign powers.[22] Increasingly, these powers worked through Libyan interlocutors, brokers and fixers who often resided in Istanbul, Doha, or Dubai, which created an additional layer of arbitration as these Libyan actors added their own agendas to those of their foreign patrons.[23] After the July 2013 Saudi- and Emirati-backed coup against the Muslim Brotherhood in Egypt, the burgeoning war of narratives hardened as a front in Libya's conflict. Committed to preventing the emergence of an Islamist-dominated Libya – which it feared could deploy the country's vast oil resources to support Islamists elsewhere in the region – the Emirates, along with Egypt, became especially maligned meddlers in Libya, wielding material weapons, the media and political influence.

With the eruption of civil war in May 2014, marked by Khalifa Haftar's launch of Operation Dignity on Benghazi and the countervailing Libya Dawn Movement by his Islamist and revolutionary opponents in Tripoli, behind the scenes international interference shifted to overt military support with increased arms flows, airstrikes, advisors and special operations raids. By late 2014, Libya hosted a classic proxy war, with outside powers working through competing Libyan factions on the ground: Egypt, the UAE, Saudi Arabia and Jordan-backed Haftar's anti-Islamist Dignity faction, while Turkey, Qatar and, initially, Sudan backed his opponents. Although often framed through binary axes of 'Islamists versus anti-Islamists' or 'revolutionary versus counter-revolutionary', the motives of the foreign protagonists were in fact more multi-faceted and complex: an array of economic, geostrategic and ideational concerns drove their actions.

In late 2015, the UN-brokered Skhirat peace agreement aimed to bridge the factional divides of the civil war and to establish a new unity government in Tripoli. In practice, it simply reverted the nature of global jockeying back to political influence and media meddling, while facilitating build-up for the next round of violent conflict. Rejecting the Government of National Accord, Haftar continued to consolidate power in eastern Libya through the vanquishing of his Islamist, jihadist and factional opponents in the city of Benghazi – a victory achieved through robust foreign military support from the Emirates and from French intelligence operatives. Having won the East, he set his sights on seizing national power – an ambition that was encouraged and materially supported by foreign powers – the Emirates, Egypt, France and Russia, who saw in the aspiring Libyan authoritarian the potential for not only stability, but also critical influence.

Haftar's April 2019 attack on Tripoli set in motion what would become the most internationalised civil war in the Middle East and possibly the world, with at least eight countries – Egypt, UAE, Saudi Arabia, Russia, France, Turkey, Chad and Qatar – militarily intervening, either directly or indirectly.[24] These interventions carry significance on a global scale, which may be apparent only in hindsight: from 2019 to 2020, Libya witnessed the largest combat deployment of armed drones ever, including one that may have conducted the first-ever autonomous attack on human ground targets.[25] However, the technological and science-fiction qualities of the fighting should not be overstated – Libya's war was still a fiercely human affair, waged by young Libyan men and, especially, by thousands of poorly paid mercenaries from Eurasia, Africa and the Middle East.[26]

Momentous shifts in the global order permitted this military free-for-all. Above all else, American retrenchment, disinterest and, under the Trump Administration, blatant partisanship for Haftar and his backers provided a green light for escalating intervention and attendant human rights abuses.[27] The erosion of global norms on embargo enforcement and the diminishing credibility of the United Nations itself only reinforced the impunity of the meddlers: the UN Security Council repeatedly failed to pass a cease-fire resolution, and at least two sitting members – Russia and France (and to a lesser extent the United States) – provided diplomatic cover to the most lethal of Libya's interveners, the UAE. US deference to Emirati support for Haftar's campaign – out of the belief that the Emirates' support on other US files such as Iran was too vital to jeopardise over a state of comparatively less import – emboldened the UAE to facilitate and enable the entrenchment of Russian military forces on NATO's southern flank, thus planting conditions for great power competition on the African continent. Similarly, as the French worked in tandem with the Emirates to support Haftar's counter-terrorism efforts in the Sahel, rebels of the Chadian Front for Change and Concord in Chad (FACT), harboured by Haftar and allegedly trained by Russian Wagner troops, ultimately helped precipitate the death of France's long-time strongman president in Chad, Idris Deby.[28]

Beyond these macro-level trends of regional and great power rivalries, post-2011 Libya became a site of increasing instrumentalisation of spill-over threats by Western powers, who unilaterally engaged with Libyan elites and armed groups on the ground to contain and eradicate those threats. These self-interested interventions often ran counter to these same powers' professed aims of institution-building and armed group disarmament – and their consequences for Libya's sovereignty and cohesion have been profound.

The Incubator: Libya as an Accelerator and Conveyor of Transnational Instability and Terrorism

Since Qadhafi's regime collapsed in late 2011, the travails of the transitional period – especially the post-2012 slide to violence – have been underpinned by international narratives of state failure, flanked by fears of arms, smuggling and terrorism proliferation. In assessing these spill-over effects across the region – and their instrumentalisation by foreign powers – it is important to situate the origins of Libya's militarisation and securitisation prior to the 2011 revolution. With the regime slogan 'power, wealth and weapons in the hands of the people', Qadhafi distributed stockpiles of weapons across Libya.[29] These munitions seeded conditions ripe for a 'people's war', leaving material easily accessible and as clear targets in the instance of popular uprising. Prior to the outbreak of the modern Libyan conflict, civilian firearm possession was rare, with an estimated 400,000 to 1,000,000 firearms – mostly old Kalashnikovs – documented in citizen hands.[30] The rapid escalation of the first civil war led to a dramatic redistribution of this equipment. By the end of 2011, it is unlikely that these weapons and associated ammunition from Qadhafi-era stockpiles represented even a simple majority of the weapons in Libya.[31]

Threats of arms proliferation beyond Libyan borders were grossly exaggerated after the 2011 revolution.[32] To be sure, weapons and fighters did flow outward, especially as Qadhafi-era border management – often reliant on tribal co-option and some permissiveness rather than water-tight control – collapsed.[33] The most critical outflows from Libya occurred between 2012 and 2013, when equipment such as anti-aircraft guns and rockets arrived in conflict arenas, qualitatively enhancing insurgent groups' military capabilities.[34] In Mali, this spill-over contributed to civil war – although this exogenous impact is often inflated by Malian officials in an attempt to deflect attention from their own corrosive governance as a contributing factor to the state's collapse. In January 2012, Tuareg fighters leaving Libya for Mali introduced advanced weaponry (notably heavy machineguns, 23mm cannons and essential munitions) to a separatist movement, generating the initial momentum for the rebels.[35] Elsewhere, Libyan arms such as 14.5mm antiaircraft guns and multi-barrel rocket launchers helped opposition forces in Sinai to mount effective resistance to Egyptian forces.[36] Libyan arms and fighters also went to Syria (some with alleged CIA assistance), where some combatants helped spawn a nucleus of the Islamic State that would return to Libya in 2014. Taken together, the first two years of post-Qadhafi Libya were distinguished by the channelling of weapons and fighters out of the country. By late 2013 and early 2014, the flow had reversed, with external powers' military interventions in Libya's civil war pouring in material and personnel.[37]

As Libyan institutions fragmented and security conditions worsened, Libya's potential to host and export militant extremism emerged as another major concern for external powers. Here, again, it is critical to look at continuity with the pre-revolutionary period. Qadhafi's material and financial support to global militants challenged the broader international order and cultivated narratives in the popular imagination about Libya's friendliness to extremist ideology that lingered well after the dictator's demise.[38] But domestic extremists were major contributors to Libya's trajectory during and after the Qadhafi regime. A new generation of Islamist militants, who would assume prominent military roles during the 2011 revolution, were radicalised in part by Qadhafi's iron-fisted response to Islamist dissent in the 1990s, epitomised by collective punishment strategies in Derna, Benghazi and especially the 1996 Abu Slim Massacre. Furthermore, Western instrumentalisation and indirect abetment fostered the rise of Libyan extremism. After 'coming in from the cold', Qadhafi positioned himself as a counter-terrorism ally to the West, enjoying substantial support from America's Central Intelligence Agency (CIA) and the United Kingdom's Secret Intelligence Service (also known as MI6), who overlooked abuses in his prisons (which were breeding new strains of radicalism that would eventually threaten the West). Moreover, this excessive focus on bilateral intelligence cooperation on counter-terrorism with Libyan security services left little will or bandwidth among Western intelligence agencies for gathering information that might have anticipated the rupture of 2011. Western intelligence agencies and especially the CIA were thus caught completely off guard by the scale of the protests and the revolution.[39]

During the revolution, Libyan Islamists with experience on foreign jihadist battlefields played increasingly prominent roles on the frontlines. After the fall of Qadhafi, some supported the transition to politics and elections over continued militancy or even anti-Americanism (one group of former jihadists in the town of Derna even provided bodyguard protection for visiting US diplomats).[40] But by the summer of 2012, Western intelligence agencies were detecting growing violence against ex-regime foreign targets by younger, more radical jihadists, especially Ansar al-Sharia, who were 'exporting' radicalism through the channelling of weapons, fighters and humanitarian aid to Mali, Syria, Gaza and other conflict zones.[41] Militants aligned with Ansar conducted the infamous 2012 attack on the US diplomatic mission in Benghazi that killed Ambassador J. Christopher Stevens and three other staff members – a seminal event prompting further retrenchment of US policy and solidifying counter-terrorism as the most prominent lens through which Libya was viewed. The subsequent deterioration of security in Benghazi after the American departure from the Eastern city – a mix of jihadist violence and tit-for-tat vendettas – contributed to the 2014 outbreak of civil war.

That civil war forced the evacuation of nearly all foreign embassies and, as noted, created openings for foreign intervention, thus further widening Libya's fissures. Unsurprisingly, a new wave of jihadism exploited those fissures and Libya's collapse of governance. In 2014, the return of Libyan fighters from Syria and the establishment of the Islamic Youth Shura Council in the eastern town of Derna heralded the start of the Islamic State in Libya, which soon spread to Benghazi, Sabratha, Sirte, parts of Tripoli and the Fezzan. Foreign influences were certainly instrumental: an array of arriving ideologues, advisors, judges, trainers and foot soldiers from Syria, Iraq, Sudan, Egypt, Algeria, Yemen and West Africa proved crucial in its initial seeding and spread.[42] Yet, Libyans and the specificities of the Libyan context were also pivotal in determining the extent of the terrorist groups' penetration into Libya's complex social and political landscape. Some existing jihadists or Islamist militants, such as those from Ansar al-Sharia or the Libya Shield, defected to the Islamic State in 2014, out of ideological solidarity in some cases, but also because they believed that the rebranding and foreign military and media support would be crucial in the battle against Khalifa Haftar.[43]

In Western capitals, the presence of the Islamic State and its increasingly lethal attacks in Tunisia and in the heart of Europe prompted mounting alarm. Officials, especially in the United States, initially believed that the shared threat from the Islamic State might unite Libya's disparate factions. For their part, Libyan armed group leaders, eager for Western patronage, quickly realised that marketing themselves to the West as counter-terrorism partners was a sure-fire way to gain attention and legitimacy. In particular, Haftar and his propaganda outlets and foreign backers increasingly played up his counter-terrorism credentials, labelling all his opponents as al-Qaida or ISIS.[44] 'I am fighting terrorism on your behalf', he told one of the authors of this chapter in a 2014 interview. Through such narratives, conveyed even in mainstream Western outlets, foreign audiences were led to believe that Libya's conflict was being waged along a binary axis between Islamist radical militias and 'secular' forces, while local realities reflected a much more complex and multi-polar conflict, between revolutionary and counter-revolutionary forces, classes, regions, families and even neighbourhoods.

Between 2016 and 2018, a mélange of local armed groups engaged in military conflict with the Islamic State across Libya, often for self-interested political or economic motives, and sometimes using 'counter-terrorism' to go after rivals.[45] In doing so, they engaged with foreign powers and received varying degrees of assistance, from hands-on battlefield support by special operations forces over airstrikes to limited intelligence-sharing. The most damaging effects of this international counter-terrorist intervention to Libya's cohesion and future stability were felt in eastern Libya, where French and Emirati forces' successful operational support to Haftar's campaign in Benghazi emboldened him to expand his power. The Obama Administration in 2014 resisted formally embracing Haftar as a counter-terrorism ally, even though some clandestine contact continued. Meanwhile, in 2016, the main thrust of America's intervention occurred against the Islamic State in Libya's central base in Sirte. Here, the United States provided very limited material and intelligence support to counter-Islamic State militias, who nominally tied themselves to the Government of National Accord (GNA) – the 'unity' government whose 2015 formation was partially occasioned by Washington's need to establish a 'legitimate' governing partner for counter-terrorism cooperation.[46]

By 2018 and 2019, the Islamic State had all but vanished from the Libyan scene, although roving bands of militants operating in the Fezzan sometimes staged attacks. By one metric, foreign counter-terrorism efforts, especially by the United States and its partners, could be deemed a success: the campaign had been conducted largely through Libyan forces, backed by US airpower, intelligence and special operations forces, with no loss of American equipment or personnel. And, yet, the hoped-for payoff in using the threat of terrorism as a means to bridge Libya's political divides, between Haftar and his opponents in Western Libya, completely failed. This was epitomised by Haftar's refusal to join the mostly Misratan-led operation against the Islamic State in Sirte; while his foes in Misrata were preoccupied with anti-ISIS combat, Haftar was consolidating his control in the oil crescent.[47] Moreover, the aftermath of foreign-backed, Libyan-led counter-terrorism operations altered the political order and social hierarchies of several Libyan locales, creating new points of tension that have yet to abate. The fragmentation of local powers in the fight against IS (and IS's intensification of Libya's conflict) critically damaged the capacity of local Libyan institutions to resolve the disputes at the core of Libya's conflict – thereby further prolonging an already protracted fight.

The Thoroughfare: Libya as a Node and Conduit in Global Migration

Just as the threats of terrorism and the Islamic State have produced both genuine spill-over effects and a ready-made narrative for outside powers to justify their interventions, so too have post-2011 flows of irregular migrants across and beyond Libya's territory. Here, again, internal governance dynamics affected this global challenge: Qadhafi's migration management – often cynical and exploitative – gave way to new hyper-localised actors controlling and profiting from migratory movements. After the 17 February revolution, Libyan elites and armed groups responded to Europe's 'counter-migration' marketplace, by relying on the retrenched system of monetised transactional politics governing Mediterranean crossings, positioning themselves as coastguards and wardens of horrific migrant detention centres.

The north-south routes followed by today's smuggled migrants have been migratory routes since Antiquity. The Qadhafi regime managed, rather than controlled, these flows; but, as noted by Emanuela Paoletti, '[r]ising levels of cross-border mobility seem[ed] to coexist with trends that consolidated the state's authority of its territory'.[48] Libyan labour demands and trans-Saharan routes crystallised in the 1990s with sustained demand for labour-seeking migrants on southern Libyan oil fields.[49] In this same decade, what would become Europe's aggressive anti-migrant stance began with the securitisation of the Adriatic route (connecting Albania and Italy), ultimately transforming Libya into a major transit state through the inadvertent elevation of the Sicilian route (connecting Libya and Italy).[50] And as the Sicilian route rose in political and economic prominence, Qadhafi, long isolated by Western and Arab powers, welcomed Sub-Saharan migrants to work in Libya and permitted (or established) profit-generating mechanisms around the central route. However, Italy's interests in border security – and the fundamental need for cooperation with Qadhafi – factored into the international community's realignment with Libya. To facilitate enhanced cooperation on migration security, Rome championed Libya's re-engagement with the international community as relations between Qadhafi and European powers thawed at the beginning of the twenty-first century.[51] Italy's Libyan engagement over the interceding decade seeded the already fertile situation for what would become known as Europe's migration crisis. Prior to his 2011 fall, Qadhafi proved a difficult partner in migration-management for Europe. Libyan-Italian migration cooperation was based on a secretive 2003 document which reportedly facilitated the exchange of liaison officers, trained Libyan border officers and positioned Rome to fund the construction of several immigrant detention centres in Libya.[52] While accusing Qadhafi of 'dumping' unwanted migrants on Italy, in 2003 alone Rome spent 5.5 million Euro on Libyan migration management, which granted Italy the privilege to expel unwanted migrants to Libya.[53] Despite Qadhafi's lack of cooperation, the Berlusconi government advocated for lifting the European arms embargo on Libya, hoping to entice Qadhafi to become a more cooperative partner. Ultimately, Italy's sustained rhetorical emphasis on the threat of migration forced the EU to lift the arms embargo, easing Libya's return to the international community.

Throughout the beginning of the twenty-first century, Europe (and Italy especially) depicted itself as threatened by massive waves of unwanted and undocumented migrants to justify cooperation and collaboration with Qadhafi's regime, despite massive human rights concerns. Notably, data show that the reality of unwanted migration to Italian soil between the 1990s and 2011 was largely overplayed, but, more importantly, disembarkations (reflecting migrants successfully transiting the Sicilian migration route by sea) represented only a fraction of arrivals in this period, with the majority of undocumented immigrants in Italy entering legally and overstaying their visas.[54] While many criticise the European Union's role in extraterritorially managing this migratory route in the early 2000s, opponents of this rhetoric point to Qadhafi as exploiting European fears of migration (and related crime and terrorism) and harnessing this potential to consolidate considerable financial and material resources. In 2011, entrenched anti-migration rhetoric empowered EU powers to act decisively in the face of emerging unrest in Benghazi. Italy had long sought to capitalise on the threats of a 'biblical exodus' posed by migrants in Libya.[55] Latching onto this familiar rhetoric, from the onset of violence connected to the 17 February revolution, EU leadership (and citizenry) were convinced of the need for a dramatic reaction to what was then a localised conflict.

Indisputably, the full outbreak of the Libyan conflict precipitated massive migratory movements. An estimated 600,000 Libyans and 800,000 foreign nationals fled Libya between February and November 2011.[56] In response to what seemed to be an unfolding humanitarian crisis, European leaders leaned heavily on NATO, precipitating the R2P intervention, and on multi-lateral international organisations to protect their interests and further their policy agendas, rather than to advance humanitarian protections for the extremely vulnerable populations in Libya.[57] However, as these interventions established Western standards of migration management, they 'transformed the local and regional patterns of exchange and territorial order', according to scholars James Ferguson and Akhil Gupta.[58] The 'humanitarian' intervention illustrates not only the successful export of European migration management approaches, but also the extra-territorialisation of European borders. Multi-lateral agencies conceptualised Libya into three key frontier zones: the political borders of the Schengen Area, the north and west coasts of the African continent as buffer zones and the Sahara as an ungovernable area.[59]

The effects of these aggressive EU policies are by no means restricted to the securitisation of the Sicilian route over the past twenty years, as they have also detrimentally painted migration as an affliction, driving anti-migrant sentiments across the Sahel, Libya and Europe. While migration has emerged as a critical policy point for Libyan, Sub-Saharan and European stake-holders alike, none of these players has formulated an ethical, sustainable response that moves beyond containment.[60] Irregular migration plays a vital role in all regional economies. In both Libya and southern Europe, irregular migration is 'a fundamental resource for economic development', providing vital energy to the service and construction sectors.[61] This reality is often obscured by European rhetoric distracting from the demand aspects of migration and fecklessly painting Libya as only a country of transit, not destination. Libyan demand for irregular migrant labour, like European, is well-documented and will prove essential in the state's ultimate reconstruction. But European anti-migrant sentiment has not only resulted in dramatic political clashes in Europe. In Libya, the expansion of xenophobic anti-migrant rhetoric, as pushed by European citizens and leaders, illustrates North African states' willingness to adopt European discourse and leadership.

The Exporter: Libya's Changing Role in Global Oil Markets

Another feature of Libya which links domestic turmoil to global influence is its role as an oil exporter. Prior to the 2011 revolution, Libya was the second-largest energy producer in North Africa, producing 1.8 million barrels per day of high-quality crude oil and gas.[62] Observers and investors feared the ripple effects of Libya's revolution on global oil prices, based on speculation about the spread of instability to other key producers.[63]

However, that spread did not materialise, and while global demand dipped slightly around the onset of the revolution due to the devastating tsunami in Japan, this fall in demand paired with a Saudi increase in production, which largely insulated oil prices from Libyan production-induced fluctuation.

Oil has long been an outsized determinant of many of Libya's governance pathologies: as a so-called 'rentier state', Libya exhibits many facets of the 'oil curse' – such as a bloated public sector, the absence of productive private enterprise and massive corruption. 'I wish you had discovered water instead of oil', King Idris was reported to have told American oil executives upon the 1962 discovery of oil in the Kingdom of Libya. 'Water makes men work; oil makes men dream'.[64]

He might have also added that oil makes men fight. Throughout Libya's post-revolutionary period, oil has been a driver and accelerant of conflict. The dispersal of oil wealth to young men in armed groups, beginning under Qadhafi as a massive rent distribution scheme, continued with hundreds of thousands of young men employed in the state security sector (often in 'hybrid' armed groups that are only nominally affiliated with the government).[65] Adding to that are the attempts of armed groups to seize and control oil facilities as leverage against the central government, to outmanoeuvre their rivals and, in some cases, to try and sell Libyan oil illicitly on the global market.

Here, global norms of sovereignty and legitimacy have prevailed. There is of course smuggling of refined products, namely subsidised fuel, via sea and overland, but the illegal sale of crude oil beyond Libya's borders has been limited by adherence to norms and, occasionally, outright intervention, like the 2014 dispatch of US Navy Seals to stop a vessel under North Korean flag, the *Morning Glory*, from illegally transhipping Libyan oil.[66] And yet, the operation, while successful, dealt a fatal blow to the political legitimacy of then Libyan Prime Minister Ali Zeidan, who was seen before constituents and the world as being unable to exercise sovereignty over his country's most precious resource. His resignation was in part spurred by the *Morning Glory* episode.[67]

Beyond this American intercession, Libyan energy reserves and their potential impacts on energy markets have also served as a backdrop for international engagement and a justification for proxy intervention. Competing global and regional powers have sought to harness Libya's oil wealth for the provision of infrastructure, energy and arms contracts, or to prevent that wealth from being channelled to ideological opponents, as in the case of the UAE today. Sub-state actors have parlayed this international interest in hydrocarbons into power and autonomy. Local militias have offered their services to Italian oil companies to guard facilities while, perhaps more ominously, the Libyan militia leader Ibrahim Jathran, head of a self-styled oil protection force controlling the Sirte Basin oil facilities, was approached by Russia, offering arms in return for letting Moscow market the crude oil. Yet, here again the presence of a counter-vailing great power – namely, the United States – and the principle of state sovereignty prevailed: Jathran declined the offer in favour of the recognised government of Tripoli. As a result, Russia supported another local client, Haftar, who wrested the central oil facilities from Jathran's control in 2016.[68]

Throughout the post-Qadhafi period, foreign perceptions of the threat of oil profit extortion – perpetuated by non-state armed groups and fanned by geostrategic competition – has encouraged further competition for resource control. Between 2016 and 2019, Libyan petroleum exports accounted for roughly 3 percent of global energy supplies.[69] While this figure is minimal in global terms, energy production remains the backbone of the Libyan economy. Since the discovery of oil, the significance of fuel exports has fluctuated little, ranging between 96 and 100 percent of total Libyan merchandise exports.[70] Although Libya's potential for market influence is often exploited as a reason for global attention, data and history reflect the relatively inconsequential nature of Libyan hydrocarbons. For example, following the onset of civil unrest in 2011 it took investors roughly two weeks to recalibrate and accept that Libyan oil would not return to global markets at the same levels.[71]

On the eve of Qadhafi's fall, Italy was the primary importer of Libyan petroleum, importing 35.6 percent (crude oil, gas and refined oil) alone.[72] Overall, petroleum imports accounted for 15 percent of Italian imports in 2010, 3.37 percent of which were sourced from Libya.[73] Libyan hydrocarbons are strategic to the extent that the high-quality crude oil and LNG are well positioned to reach lucrative (and demanding) European markets. To US policy-makers, these reserves still offer a viable alternative to European dependence on Russian hydrocarbons. However, as the international community has already illustrated, Libyan reserves are merely an 'extra' that will likely decline in importance with the oil sunset.

The Desert: How an Arid Libya is Grappling with Climate Change

The looming end of the oil era presents enormous socio-economic challenges to Libya in terms of transitioning to non-oil sources of revenue. This will certainly compound growing alarm surrounding Libya's climate change resiliency and worsening water shortages. Libya is one of the driest countries in the world; over 90 percent of its territory is desert.[74] More than 60 percent of Libya's population lives along the Jefara Plain, dependent on groundwater resources that are already unable to meet the burgeoning urban demand.[75] Added to this is the spectre of rising sea levels due to climate change. Although this by itself does not pose a direct threat to the unconfined aquifer that serves as the main water source for this area, growing and unregulated demands from Libyan agriculture – which, across the country, accounts for 85 percent of Libya's water consumption – and urbanisation are leading to an increase in seawater intrusion, contaminating the underground water supply.[76]

The control of water has long been wielded as a tool of governance throughout Libya's history, just as water scarcity has long been a governance challenge. The ancient civilisations of Libya's interior all developed infrastructures to harness water from rainfall and oases to support urban populations and agriculture. Borrowing from the Egyptians, the Garamantian people of the Fezzan developed an elaborate system of irrigation canals – the *foggara* or *qanat* – which bolstered an expansion of their Saharan proto-state.[77] The Romans and Greeks adopted similar practices for their colonies in Cyrenaica.[78] But the twentieth century saw Libya deviate from these ancient technologies with the discovery of a hitherto untapped supply of water: in 1953, oil engineers uncovered massive underground aquifers in the expansive Fezzan. Decades later, Qadhafi undertook an ambitious pipeline scheme known as the Great Man-Made

River to harness this supply and bring water to Libya's populated north. Yet, the mega project was always clouded by an aura of unreality, exaggerated expectations and propaganda. The dictator's corruption and divide-and-rule policies prevented it from attaining its lofty goals. But, most crucially, the project transformed water management into a governance stratagem, a spoil to reward loyal constituencies while shutting out less favoured tribes and communities, such as the Amazigh (Berbers) in the western Nafusa Mountains, who were denied access to the pipelines of the Great Man-Made River.[79]

Since the 2011 overthrow of the dictator, water management has been afflicted by similar dynamics of poor governance and weaponisation. In the capital of Tripoli, successive weak governments have been unable to protect critical water supplies, accelerating the degradation of existing reserves.[80] Moreover, local factions have often exploited vulnerable infrastructure, especially the Great Man-Made River, as a source of leverage against rivals or the central government.[81] Illustrating this, foreign news outlets reported remarkable scenes of Tripoli residents digging for water through paved concrete in 2017, after an armed group south of the capital turned off the flow to pressure the weak government into releasing a leader imprisoned by a rival militia.[82] The shortages were repeated in 2019–20, during Haftar's attack on the capital.[83] Taken together, these shortages underscore the deleterious compounding effects that misgovernance and particularly political conflict – exacerbated by foreign intervention – have on natural resources and especially water scarcity. The worsening effects of climate change will cast these effects into sharper relief.

Among the countries in the Maghreb, Libya is not the one most vulnerable to climate change, but the effects are still dire and already evident. The mean precipitation during rainy seasons is decreasing in parts of the country; simultaneously, the mean temperature, drought and heatwave intensity have all increased dramatically.[84] West of the capital, the agricultural areas stretching to the Tunisian border are acutely vulnerable to climate change, since they depend on rain for irrigation.[85] Given this regional variance in climate change effects across Libya, local responses via financially and politically empowered municipal leadership will be critical – a governance imperative that has dramatically fallen flat since the 2011 revolution.

Climate change is also likely to add an additional layer of socio-economic and governance challenges to an already daunting list of afflictions in the country. Heavy rainfall is expected to increase in parts of Libya in the spring and autumn (likely causing flooding), while drought spells will likely become more frequent and lengthier.[86] As illustrated in other drought-prone conflict zones reliant on rain-irrigated agriculture, droughts can become a lethal intensifying factor in precipitating civil conflicts.[87] Looking ahead to Libya's sensitivity in the remainder of this century, Libya remains dangerously reliant on cereal grain imports and notably has the lowest agricultural production per capita in the region.[88] Not only will Libya be unable to meet domestic irrigation demand by the end of the century, but the global impacts of climate change will likely raise food prices.[89] This emerging scenario of predicted food insecurity aligns with the literature that connects negative downturns in agriculture production (and more generally food availability) to an increase in violence perpetuated by groups dependent on agriculture and by those already experiencing inequalities or marginalisation.[90] Existing literature also indicates a correlation between decreased food security and increased social unrest; regardless, as we have seen in Libya already, instability acutely affects a state's adaptive capacity and resiliency.

Conclusion

For much of its modern history, Libya itself has not exerted agency over the major events of the globe or the Middle East. And yet, by the twentieth century, its geostrategic location and oil reserves began to change its global relevance. The territory became the site of successive interventions by foreign powers – to project influence, extract resources and deny their rivals' access or dominance. The post-2011 period saw the emergence of new, more securitised narratives, related to the spill-over of instability, arms, terrorism and migrants. To be sure, these afflictions were real, but they were also instrumentalised by regional and global powers in their pursuit of geopolitical and ideological agendas. In tandem, outside powers continued to intervene in the hopes of capturing Libya's oil wealth, either through directly marketing it or by obtaining favourable contracts for weapons and infrastructure. The sum total of this interference has been the attenuation of Libya's sovereignty and the empowerment of sub-national, highly local actors – often influenced by foreign powers.

Yet, the process is hardly unidirectional. Libya is often described as a passive vehicle for outsiders' ambitions and actions, with little attention to the role of the Libyans themselves. Still, Libyan elites, notables, tribal chiefs and resistance leaders have proven skilful in soliciting foreign backing, manipulating support and playing outsiders against each other – a dynamic that is especially apparent in the current round of civil war.

What becomes apparent, then, is the need to link the country's internal political dynamics with regional and global events. As in many states, the COVID-19 pandemic has further exposed critical gaps in Libyan governance and emphasised the role of hyper-local actors in the Libyan public service delivery. Against both this backdrop and in many previous instances, the impact of highly localised events in Libya – the actions of specific towns or armed groups – cannot be understated. This localisation has had an outsized impact by accelerating, tempering or channelling foreign interventions, and it has posed challenges in determining the extent of external spill-over effects, such as irregular migrant flows or terrorism. In the face of this strong micro-level cohesion and the absence of a unifying centre, local-level agency and governance will prove vital in addressing the impending global challenges that are already being felt in the country: the looming end of the 'rentier' era and the impact of climate change. In both instances, the malignant effects of these natural resource challenges are not predetermined but rather exacerbated by human factors – mismanagement, poor governance and political conflict. In particular, highly centralised control and endemic corruption across the entire political spectrum have worsened the misery of Libyans in the country's far-flung locales, resulting in both oil and water being weaponised and leveraged against civilian populations. All of this speaks to the urgency for better and more inclusive local governance and an end to open conflict – a salient imperative that Libyan elites should support by putting aside self-destructive enrichment and rivalries and one in which foreign states should similarly assist by desisting from self-serving interventions.

Notes

1. For example, to situate Libya in Greek empire-building and mythology, see Claude Camale, *Myth and History in Ancient Greece: The Symbolic Creation of a Colony* (Princeton: Princeton University Press, 2003). For an overview of Libya in Roman mythology, see Matthew Leigh, 'Lucan and the Libyan Tale', *The Journal of Roman Studies* 90 (2000): 95–109.
2. For an overview of the role of US forces in the First Barbary War, see Richard Bordeaux Parker, *Uncle Sam in Barbary: A Diplomatic History* (Gainesville: University Press of Florida, 2004).
3. For an exploration of nationalisms affecting Libya during the Italo-Turkish War, see Jonathan McCollum, 'Reimagining Mediterranean Spaces: Libya and the Italo-Turkish War, 1911–1912', *Diacrone* 23 (2015), https://journals.openedition.org/diacronie/2356#quotation.
4. Ali Abdullatif Ahmida illuminates the agency of Libyans in manipulating colonial, war-time and post-colonial balances of power; see Ali Abdullatif Ahmida, *Forgotten Voices: Power and Agency in Colonial and Post-Colonial Libya* (Abingdon: Taylor & Francis, 2013).
5. Megan Specia and David E. Sanger, 'How the "Libya Model" Became a Sticking Point in North Korea Nuclear Talks', *The New York Times*, 16 May 2018, sec. World, https://www.nytimes.com/2018/05/16/world/asia/north-korea-libya-model.html.
6. For insights into the closure of Libya's nuclear programme, see Målfred Braut-Hegghammer, *To Join Or Not to Join the Nuclear Club: How Nations Think about Nuclear Weapons: Lessons from the Middle East* (n. p.: Middle East Studies at the Marine Corps University, 2013). On the comparison between Qadhafi's and North Korea's nuclear programmes, see Frederic Wehrey, 'Testimony in "The Crisis in Libya": Next Steps and U.S Policy Options', in *Hearing before the Committee on Foreign Relations of the United States Senate, 115th Cong*, 2017, https://www.govinfo.gov/content/pkg/CHRG-115shrg40164/html/CHRG-115shrg40164.htm.
7. Anne-Marie Slaughter, 'Why Libya Sceptics Were Proved Badly Wrong', *The Financial Times*, 24 August 2011, https://www.ft.com/content/18cb7f14-ce3c-11e0-99ec-00144feabdc0#axzz1W1l269ak.
8. On Obama's 'shit-show' comment, see his 2016 interview in *The Atlantic*: Jeffrey Goldberg, 'The Obama Doctrine', *The Atlantic*, 10 March 2016, https://www.theatlantic.com/magazine/archive/2016/04/the-obama-doctrine/471525/. On the impact of Libya on Obama's calculus in Syria, see Missy Ryan and Gillian Brockell, 'A War Fought, a War Avoided: Libya and Syria Tested Obama's Core

Values', *Washington Post*, 3 June 2016, https://www.washingtonpost.com/graphics/national/obama-legacy/intervention-libya-and-syrian-crisis.html.
9. See Mehmed V, 'Imperial Firman Granting Autonomy to Tripoli and Cyrenaica', translated in William Henry Beehler, *The History of the Italian-Turkish War, September 29, 1911, to October 18, 1912* (Annapolis: Advertiser-Republican, 1913).
10. Lisa Anderson, '"They Defeated Us All": International Interests, Local Politics and Contested Sovereignty', *The Middle East Journal* 71, no. 2 (2017): 229–47.
11. Initial First World War competition was for Misrata, to protect supply chains and broaden influence.
12. Tripolitania first mobilised alongside the Ottomans, while from Cyrenaica the Sanussis capitalised on an opportunity for autonomy (with French and British support). Furthermore, from Misrata the Muntaisr clan allied with the Italians.
13. Anderson, 'They Defeated Us All', 234.
14. The British still saw the Sanussi leadership as the best guarantor of Egypt's security, while the French sought direct control of the Fezzan to protect Saharan interests.
15. For an overview of UN and international engagement in crafting Libyan sovereignty, see Ann Dearden, 'Independence for Libya: The Political Problems', *The Middle East Journal* 4, no. 4 (October 1950): 395–409.
16. 'Foreign Relations of the United States, 1949, Western Europe, Volume IV', *Office of the Historian*, https://history.state.gov/historicaldocuments/frus1949v04/d317.
17. Anderson, 'They Defeated Us All', 238.
18. Alex De Waal, 'The African Union and the Libya Conflict of 2011', *Reinventing Peace*, 19 December 2012, https://sites.tufts.edu/reinventingpeace/2012/12/19/the-african-union-and-the-libya-conflict-of-2011/.
19. Wolfram Lacher, *Libya's Fragmentation: Structure and Process in Violent Conflict* (London, Bloomsbury, 2020).
20. Frederic Wehrey, *The Burning Shores: Inside the Battle for the New Libya* (New York: Farrar, Straus, & Giroux, 2018), 74.
21. Jalel Harchaoui, 'Libya's Looming Crisis for the Central Bank', *War on the Rocks*, 1 April 2019, https://warontherocks.com/2019/04/libyas-looming-contest-for-the-central-bank/.
22. Khadeja Ramali, 'A Light in Libya's Fog of Disinformation', *Africa Center for Strategic Studies*, 9 October 2020, https://africacenter.org/spotlight/light-libya-fog-disinformation/.
23. Wolfram Lacher, 'Magnates, Media, and Mercenaries: How Libya's Conflicts Produce Transnational Networks Straddling

North Africa and the Middle East', *Project on Middle East Political Science*, June 2020, https://pomeps.org/magnates-media-and-mercenaries-how-libyas-conflicts-produce-transnational-networks-straddling-africa-and-the-middle-east.
24. Frederic Wehrey, 'This War Is Out of Our Hands', *Center for New America Studies*, September 2020, https://www.newamerica.org/international-security/reports/this-war-is-out-of-our-hands/.
25. 'Final Report of the Panel of Experts on Libya Established Pursuant to Resolution 1973 (2011)', United Nations Security Council, 8 March 2021, https://reliefweb.int/report/libya/final-report-panel-experts-libya-established-pursuant-resolution-1973-2011-s20174666, 17.
26. Luca Raineri, 'Robot Fighting: Libya and the Wars of the Future', *Security Praxis*, 13 December 2019, https://securitypraxis.eu/robot-fighting-libya/.
27. Samer Al-Atrush, Jennifer Jacobs, and Margaret Talev, 'Trump Backed Libyan Strongman's Attack on Tripoli, U.S. Officials Say', *Bloomberg News*, 24 April 2019, https://www.bloomberg.com/news/articles/2019-04-24/trump-libya-haftar-tripoli?sref=QmOxnLFz.
28. Declan Walsh, 'Where Did Chad Rebels Prepare for Their Own War? In Libya', *The New York Times*, 22 April 2021, https://www.nytimes.com/2021/04/22/world/africa/chad-rebels.html.
29. Gemma Bowsher, P. Bogue, and P. Patel, 'Small and Light Arms Violence Reduction as a Public Health Measure: The Case of Libya', *Conflict and Health* 12, no. 29 (2018): 1–9.
30. Nicholas Marsh, 'Brothers Came Back with Weapons: The Effects of Arms Proliferation from Libya', *PRISM* 6, no. 4 (2017): 78–97.
31. Marsh, 'Brothers Came Back with Weapons', 80.
32. Although Libyan arms have appeared in other conflict contexts, they are not documented to have qualitatively enhanced militant capacity. Even one of the most fundamental international concerns – the proliferation of man-portable air defence systems (MANPADS) from Qadhafi-era stockpiles – is unfulfilled.
33. Peter Cole, 'Borderline Chaos? Stabilizing Libya's Periphery', *The Carnegie Endowment for International Peace*, 2012, https://carnegieendowment.org/files/stablizing_libya_periphery.pdf.
34. Marsh, 'Brothers Came Back with Weapons', 80.
35. Within three months the Tuareg separatists, propelled by these critical arms acquisitions from Libya, were in control of large swaths of northern Mali, the Libyan munitions having enabled the seizure of advanced material by Malian forces.
36. 'Letter Dated 15 February 2013 from the Panel of Experts on Libya Established Pursuant to Resolution 1973 (2011) Addressed to the

Security Council', *United Nations Security Council*, 9 March 2013, https://www.securitycouncilreport.org/atf/cf/%7B65BFCF9B-6D 27-4E9C-8CD3-CF6E4FF96FF9%7D/s_2013_99.pdf, 33.
37. Andrew Rettman, 'Libya Is Test of EU Geopolitics, Ex-UN Inspector Says', *EUobserver*, 25 February 2020, https://euobserver.com/foreign/147536.
38. Anderson, 'They Defeated Us All', 239–40.
39. Wehrey, *The Burning Shores*, 20.
40. Frederic Wehrey's interview with a US diplomat, Washington DC, June 2016.
41. Aaron Y. Zelin, 'When Jihadists Learn How to Help', *The Washington Post*, 7 May 2014, https://www.washingtonpost.com/news/monkey-cage/wp/2014/05/07/when-jihadists-learn-how-to-help/.
42. Yehudit Ronen, 'Libya: Teetering Between War and Diplomacy the Islamic State's Role in Libya's Disintegration', *Diplomacy and Statecraft* 28, no. 1 (2017): 118–23.
43. Frederic Wehrey, 'When the Islamic State Came to Libya', *The Atlantic*, 10 February 2018, https://www.theatlantic.com/international/archive/2018/02/isis-libya-hiftar-al-qaeda-syria/552419/.
44. Wehrey, 'This War Is Out of Our Hands', 20.
45. Emadeddin Badi, 'Exploring Armed Groups in Libya: Perspectives on SSR in a Hybrid Environment', *Geneva Center for Security Sector Reform*, 23 November 2020, https://www.dcaf.ch/exploring-armed-groups-libya-perspectives-ssr-hybrid-environment.
46. Frederic Wehrey, 'Libyans Are Winning the Battle Against the Islamic State', *Foreign Policy*, 30 June 2016, https://foreignpolicy.com/2016/06/30/libyans-are-winning-the-battle-against-the-islamic-state/; Frederic Wehrey, 'Winning the Peace: Armed Groups and Security Sector Challenges', *Brookings Institution* and *Crisis Response Council*, 3 July 2021, https://www.youtube.com/watch?v=JenfLeN-Mv4&feature=emb_title.
47. Instead, Haftar focused on consolidating control over petrol resources at Ras Lanuf, Es-Sidra and Zueitina.
48. Emanuela Paoletti, 'Power Relations and International Migration: The Case of Italy and Libya', *Political Studies* 59 (2011): 269.
49. Hein De Haas, 'The Myth of Invasion: The Inconvenient Realities of African Migration to Europe', *Third World Quarterly* 29, no. 7 (2008): 1307.
50. Derek Lutterbeck, 'Migrants Weapons and Oil: Europe and Libya After the Sanctions', *Journal of North African Studies* 14, no. 2 (2009): 170.
51. Some argue that Libya's return to the international community was largely facilitated by European shock over the unregulated

migration along the Sicilian route. On this theory, see De Haas, 'The Myth of Invasion'.
52. 'Immigrazione, Italia e Libia Insieme per Pattugliare le Coste Libiche', *La Repubblica*, 27 December 2007.
53. Lutterbeck, 'Migrants, Weapons and Oil', 172.
54. Paoletti, 'Power Relations and International Migration', 279–80.
55. 'Italy Warns of a New Wave of Immigrants to Europe', *Spiegel International*, 24 February 2011, https://www.spiegel.de/internat ional/europe/libyan-crisis-italy-warns-of-a-new-wave-of-immigr ants-to-europe-a-747459.html.
56. These figures do not include the at least 200,000 internally displaced people documented in the same period, or the individuals who left Libya of their own accord. Julien Brachet, 'Policing the Desert: The IOM in Libya Beyond War and Peace', *Antipode* 48, no. 2 (2016): 272–73.
57. The IOM, the existence of which predates the Libyan conflict, did not dramatically shift their objectives or policies in Libya with the conflict (despite receiving emergency funding to deal with the rising threat of migrants). In practice, the IOM remained focused on 'the control of migrants and their systemic removal from Europe's southern borders'. IOM involvement in Libya's conflict has harmfully reframed the fields of intervention, illustrating that some humanitarian spaces are seen as untouchable by laws. Brachet, 'Policing the Desert', 272, 282.
58. James Ferguson and Akhil Gupta, 'Spatializing States: Toward an Ethnography of Neoliberal Govermentality', *American Ethnologist* 29, no. 4 (2002): 981–1002.
59. Brachet, 'Policing the Desert', 276.
60. De Haas, 'The Myth of Invasion', 1312.
61. De Haas, 'The Myth of Invasion', 1315.
62. 'Libya Is a Major Energy Exporter, Especially to Europe', *U.S. Energy Information Administration*, 12 March 2011, https://www.eia.gov/todayinenergy/detail.php?id=590.
63. Violetta Gaucan, 'Japan and Libya: Different Impacts on World Markets', *Journal of Knowledge Management, Economics and Information Technology* 1, no. 2 (2011): 6.
64. Wehrey, *The Burning Shores*, 10.
65. Frederic Wehrey and Peter Cole, 'Building Libya's Security Sector', *Carnegie Endowment for International Peace*, 6 August 2013, https://carnegieendowment.org/2013/08/06/building-libya-s-secu rity-sector-pub-52603; Badi, 'Exploring Armed Groups in Libya'.
66. Frederic Wehrey, 'Bleeding Fuel', *Diwan*, 14 June 2017, https://carnegie-mec.org/diwan/71223; Fred Barbash, 'Navy SEALs

Board Mystery Tanker Morning Glory Near Cyprus: No One Hurt, Pentagon Says', *The Washington Post*, 17 March 2014, https://www.washingtonpost.com/news/morning-mix/wp/2014/03/17/navy-seals-board-tanker-morning-glory-near-cyprus-no-one-hurt-pentagon-says/.
67. Wehrey, *The Burning Shores*, 191.
68. Jo Becker and Eric Schmitt, 'As Trump Wavers on Libya, an ISIS Haven, Russia Presses On', *The New York Times*, 17 February 2018, https://www.nytimes.com/2018/02/07/world/africa/trump-libya-policy-russia.html.
69. 'List of Products Exported by Libya, State Of', n. d., https://www.trademap.org/Product_SelCountry_TS.aspx?nvpm=1%7c434%7c%7c%7c%7c2709%7c%7c%7c4%7c1%7c1%7c2%7c2%7c1%7c1%7c1%7c1%7c1.
70. 'Fuel exports (% of merchandise exports) – Libya', *World Bank*, 2018, https://data.worldbank.org/indicator/TX.VAL.FUEL.ZS.UN?locations=LY.
71. Gaucan, 'Japan and Libya', 1–10.
72. 'Libya', *Observatory of Economic Complexity*, 2010, https://oec.world/en/profile/country/lby?yearSelector1=exportGrowthYear16.
73. 'Italy', *Observatory of Economic Complexity*, 2010, https://oec.world/en/profile/country/ita?yearSelector2=importGrowthYear16; 'What Does Italy Import?' *Observatory of Economic Complexity*, 2010, https://oec.world/en/visualize/tree_map/hs92/import/ita/all/show/2018/.
74. Hussein Aqeil, James Tindall, and Edward Moran, 'Water Security and Interconnected Challenges in Libya', *TinMore Institute for Water Security*, November 2012, http://www.tinmore.com/pdf/WS121027_WaterSecurityLibya.pdf.
75. A. M. S. Gejam, 'Climate Change and Sea Level Rise Impacts on Seawater Intrusion at Jefara Plain, Libya', *Nature and Science* 14, no. 3 (2016): 75–81.
76. Gejam, 'Climate Change and Sea Level Rise', 75–81.
77. Andrew Wilson, 'Foggara Irrigation and Early State Formation in the Libyan Sahara: The Garamantes of Fazzan', *Schriftenreihe der Frontinus-Gesellschaft* 26 (2005): 223–34.
78. Mohamed Omar M. Abdrbba, 'Water Supply Systems in Cyrenaica during the Greek and Roman Periods: Cyrene in Context', *Libyan Studies* 50 (2019): 99–105.
79. Malak Altaeb, 'Water Politics in Libya: A Crisis of Management Not Scarcity', *Arab Reform*, 29 June 2021, https://www.arab-reform.net/publication/water-politics-in-libya-a-crisis-of-management-not-scarcity/, 75.
80. Gejam, 'Climate Change and Sea Level Rise'.

81. Jean Marie Takelou, 'Libya: Vandalism Threatens Large Man-Made River That Supplies the Country', *Afrik21*, 4 August 2021, https://www.afrik21.africa/en/libya-vandalism-threatens-large-man-made-river-that-supplies-the-country/.
82. Aidan Lewis and Ulf Laessing, 'Libyans Dig for Water in Latest Test for Capital's Residents', *Reuters*, 2 July 2019, https://www.reuters.com/article/us-libya-security-tripoli/libyans-dig-for-water-in-latest-test-for-capitals-residents-idUSKBN1CW2SH.
83. Ulf Laessing and Ahmed Elumami, 'In Battle for Libya's Oil, Water Becomes a Casualty', *Reuters*, 2 July 2019, https://www.reuters.com/article/us-libya-security-water-insight/in-battle-for-libyas-oil-water-becomes-a-casualty-idUSKCN1TX0KQ.
84. Janpeter Schilling and Lisa Krause, 'Climate Change Vulnerability, Water Resources, and Social Implications in North Africa', *Regional Environmental Change* 20, no. 15 (2020): 3.
85. In comparison with forecasts for its regional neighbours, Libya's exact sensitivity is difficult to predict due to a lack of data.
86. Schilling and Krause, 'Climate Change Vulnerability'.
87. Janpeter Schilling and Lisa Krause, 'Climate Change and Conflict in Northern Africa', *Oxford Bibliographies*, 20 November 2019, https://www.oxfordbibliographies.com/view/document/obo-9780199363445/obo-9780199363445-0090.xml.
88. 'OECD-FAO Agricultural Outlook 2018–2027', *OECD/FAO*, 3 July 2018, https://www.oecd-ilibrary.org/agriculture-and-food/oecd-fao-agricultural-outlook-2018-2027_agr_outlook-2018-en.
89. Schilling and Krause, 'Climate Change Vulnerability', 8.
90. For a leading example of research into the relationship between climate change and violence, see Michael Brzoska, 'Weather Extremes, Disasters, and Collective Violence: Conditions, Mechanisms, and Disaster-Related Policies in Recent Research', *Current Climate Change Reports* 4 (2018): 320–29.

2
Egypt's Waxing Challenges and Waning Power

Michele Dunne

Introduction

With a population well over 100 million and a civilisation going back more than 5,000 years, Egypt's footprint in the Middle East and North Africa is large. Located on a land bridge between Africa and Asia, Egypt has played a consequential and at times dominant regional role as recently as the mid-twentieth century and as far back as ancient times. In the late twentieth and early twenty-first century, however, Egypt has seen its traditional Arab leadership role gradually eclipsed by the Gulf States and its position in Africa diminished compared to that of rivals such as Ethiopia. Signs of these changes include Egypt's deference on many issues to Gulf States – for example, the surrender of two Red Sea islands to Saudi Arabia and of the struggle with Ethiopia over Nile waters.

While Egypt's large population and strategic location astride key bodies of water (the Suez Canal, the River Nile, and the Mediterranean and Red Seas) keep it ever-relevant, paradoxically it is these very same factors – people and water – that are making the Egyptian state increasingly dependent on external financing and more of a follower than a leader in regional affairs. A rapidly growing population along with inadequate economic reforms has led to a high youth unemployment rate. These factors, combined with political stagnation during the thirty-year presidency of Hosni Mubarak, made Egypt vulnerable to the wave of popular uprisings across the Arab world that began in late 2010 and resulted in the fall of Mubarak. In the decade since, Egypt experienced a military-led transition leading to the election of an Islamist-majority parliament and president, a coup abruptly ending the attempt at a democratic transition and a form of military rule under President Abdel Fattah al-Sisi that is far more brutal, authoritarian and rapacious than it was under Mubarak.

Amid political chaos and a state that is ever more overtly dominated by the military, the Egyptian government has become less and less capable of addressing the needs of its population. Its economy faltered during the failed democratic transition and subsequently fell ever more heavily under the sway of the military, which directed resources towards massive arms purchases and the construction of mega-projects rather than job generation and labour force development, both of which are crucial to addressing Egypt's economic challenges. Meanwhile, challenges to the country's water supply multiplied, at a time when Egypt was ill-equipped to address them. Not only did a burgeoning population place larger demands on the fresh water supply, but by 2021 climate change and the construction of the Grand Ethiopian Renaissance Dam (GERD) turned a growing water shortage into a crisis.

These challenges left Egypt heavily dependent on external political patrons such as the Gulf States and international financial institutions. In some ways, Sisi appears to have constructed this situation deliberately, understanding that not only his arms purchases but also his extensive borrowing would give important powers such as the United States, China and France (as well as the International Monetary Fund and the European Bank for Reconstruction and Development) a stake in his regime's survival. After all, if Sisi were to fall, as did Mubarak, how likely is it that all those lenders will be repaid? But Egypt's heavy dependence on external powers and assistance is a consequence of its massive internal challenges rather than any deliberate strategy. Because of that dependence, Egypt is constantly in a balancing act – simultaneously trying to convince its benefactors to act in the Egyptian regime's interests, while also dealing with demands from external players that Egypt is not always willing to meet.

The next decade is likely to be no less dramatic for Egypt, as the country faces massive challenges related to its abundance of people and dearth of water. How is Egypt's current military-dominated regime addressing such challenges, and what are the global as well as regional repercussions of those choices? How do the country's internal challenges affect its ability to influence others in the Arab and African regions? Are there ways in which Egypt can turn its challenges into advantages as it faces a new era?

Egypt's Twin Challenges: Super Abundance of People, Scarcity of Water

Egypt faces two interrelated challenges – dramatic population growth and a diminishing amount of available water – which are driving its decline as a regional leader. Egypt's large population and high growth rate put tremendous pressure on water consumption, food production, health, education, job creation and ultimately on political stability. Growing demands for food and water mean that the country will have to rely increasingly on imports to avoid declining living standards and even malnutrition. The education system is under significant strain as it must serve millions more youths than it was set up to handle and was already in a situation that leaves young adults unprepared to compete in the global labour market. The domestic job market can generate nowhere near the number of positions needed to absorb new entrants annually, and the Gulf countries that have traditionally absorbed excess labour have begun to nationalise their work forces. Further, gender inequality has incalculable costs for Egyptian society, as women remain vastly underemployed, contributing to early marriage and childbearing.

While the Egyptian government is aware of these challenges, it has adopted ineffective strategies to address them. The military-dominated regime's prioritisation of vanity projects over concrete policies and programmes to address unemployment, education and other domestic needs has dangerous consequences for the Egyptian people.

Demography

As the early phases of the record-setting COVID-19 pandemic unfurled across the world in February 2020, Egypt set a record of its own, officially crossing the threshold of a population of 100 million people.[1] It was a threshold that Egypt had hoped not to cross so soon, but it became inevitable as earlier progress in controlling population growth was reversed starting in about 2007 – well before the 2011 uprising.

The fact that fertility rates (the average number of children born per woman) in Egypt started rising again in 2007 after falling gradually for decades was puzzling, as once countries begin a downward trend, they generally stay on it.[2] From nearly seven children per woman in the 1960s (when infant mortality was high) to three children per woman in the early 2000s, the fertility rate ticked back up from 2007 onwards, reaching an average of 3.5 children per woman by 2014 and then falling slightly to 3.3 by 2021.[3] Such rates are more than 50 percent above the replacement rate of 2.1 children per woman. The World Population Review calls Egypt's rate of increase 'extremely progressive', noting that, in a country the size of Egypt, this is adding at least two million people per year.[4]

While sometimes associated anecdotally with Egypt's 2011 uprising or with the brief political ascendance of the Muslim Brotherhood (2012–13), the actual causes of Egypt's rising fertility appear to lie elsewhere. First, the government of Egypt and international donors began to shift their focus away from population control and towards other development issues

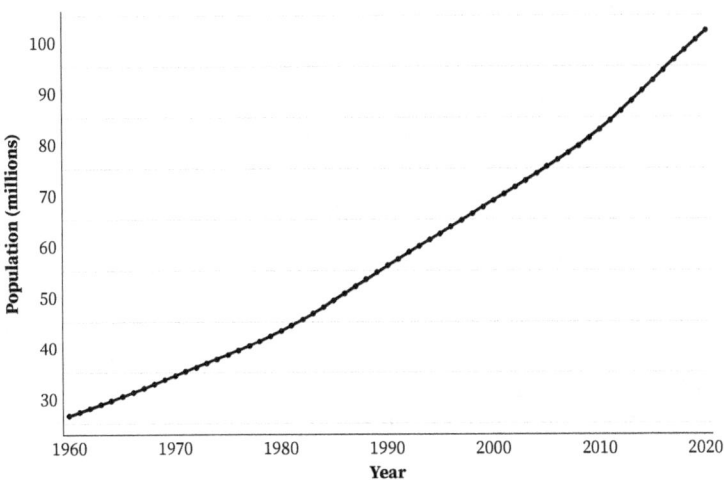

Figure 2.1 Egypt's Population, 1960–2020

'Egypt Population 2021', World Population Review, 2021, https:/worldpopulationreview.com/countries/egypt-population

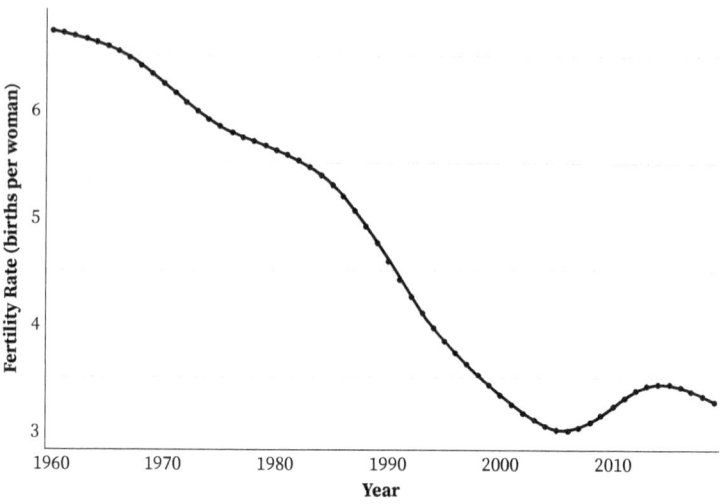

Figure 2.2 Fertility Rates in Egypt, 1960–2019
'Egypt Fertility Rate 1950–2021,' Macrotrends, 2021,
https://www.macrotrends.net/countries/EGY/egypt/fertility-rate

beginning in about 2007–8. Notably, the US government began phasing out the mass distribution of contraceptives in Egypt around that time, as part of a broader draw-back of economic assistance.[5]

Second, demographers noted a trend in Egypt: women with higher levels of education, who typically postpone marriage and childbearing longer than less educated women (and therefore often bear fewer children overall), started having children at a young age once again. This appeared to be due to the paucity of jobs for young women, including university-educated women, as public-sector opportunities were reduced and insufficient private-sector opportunities created. A 2020 Rand study described 'vastly disproportionate' challenges for women workers in Egypt, who face very high unemployment, inequitable wages, costly childcare and many other obstacles.[6] The International Labour Organisation found in 2015 that young women were five times more likely to be unemployed than young men.[7] A study by noted labour specialists Ragui Assad and Caroline Krafft found in 2014 that some 75 percent of young women were not participating in the labour force, with that rate rising to 90 percent among women without higher education.[8]

Egyptian government officials, including President Sisi, began taking public note of population control as a problem, particularly since 2018. The approach so far has been hortatory and punitive, with a 'Two is Enough' public relations campaign aimed at low-income participants in the *Takaful* and *Karama* government cash transfer programmes, with plans to institute eventual cuts to benefits for families with more than two children. In February 2021, Sisi gave a speech in which he criticised Egyptians for having too many children (as he had criticised them in the past for eating too much and exercising too little), explicitly linking demographics to the possibility of unrest: 'You are burdening yourself, your children and the country with a matter too great for its capacity [. . .] and then you revolted, and go out on the streets, and destroy your country? And the series plays again: destruction on top of destruction'.[9] USAID and the European Union have responded to Sisi's concerns, resuming assistance for population control in recent years.

Yet, it remains unclear whether the Egyptian government's approach is of the appropriate scale or targeted at the key factors – unavailability of contraceptives and jobs for women – to be effective against population growth. While Sisi has stressed that 'there is no solution but birth control in Egypt',[10] access to contraception has been uneven at best, with frequent and widespread shortages, in addition to rising prices that put them beyond the reach of lower-income women, pointing to a long-term problem only made worse by the pandemic. A former deputy health minister told an Egyptian publication in 2018 that millions of women in Upper Egypt lacked access to contraception, while a Reuters journalist in 2019 following up on the new 'Two is Enough' campaign during a spot-check found that clinics were out of contraceptives.[11] Meanwhile, a 2021 UN study found widespread interruptions in the supply of contraceptives during the pandemic, as well as women having to weigh spending on increasingly expensive birth control against other family needs.[12]

This inconsistent approach to providing contraception is in stark contrast to strategies adopted by countries that have succeeded in bringing down birth rates. The Islamic Republic of Iran, for example, starting in the late 1980s implemented a strategy that made contraception universally available and free or inexpensive, producing condoms and other supplies in the country.[13] Combining contraception with other incentives and disincentives (such as diminished benefits for larger families), the programme succeeded in reducing fertility rates in the country from 6.5 children per women in the mid-1980s to 2.0 by 2005.[14] Iran's example illustrates that it is possible for a state to implement a population growth reduction strategy based on simple, voluntary methods and without dependence on foreign donors – something that Egypt has not done.

Economy

Another way to control population growth in Egypt is through increasing employment opportunities for women, part of a much broader set of economic problems. Egypt's economy has long failed to provide inclusive prosperity for its people, struggling with several interlinked challenges, including generating jobs for a growing population, balancing the roles of the public and private sectors and spreading wealth beyond the elite. The government of late President Hosni Mubarak won plaudits from international donors and financial institutions in the 2000s for its privatising reforms and admirable growth rate, but the failure to spread prosperity beyond a favoured elite led to cries of 'Bread, Freedom and Social Justice' during the massive 2011 revolution that brought an end to Mubarak's rule.

The ensuing political instability – two years of a chaotic democratic transition under military leadership, the 2013 military coup and years of repression and resistance – was costly for the economy, which then suffered further due to a collapse of tourism during the 2020–21 pandemic. By 2018, official government statistics showed that nearly one-third of the population lived in deep poverty (less than $1.30 per person per day), sharply increasing from just under 28 percent three years earlier.[15] And yet, despite the undeniable economic costs of the pandemic and the political crises during the decade before 2021, at the end of that period Egypt was again struggling with the same underlying issues: how to create jobs, balance the public and private sectors, and spread prosperity beyond the elite?

Creating jobs for a population growing at more than two million people annually is a tall order that the Egyptian economy has been unable to fill, leading to high unemployment, especially among women as well as educated men. There is a persistent mismatch between the skills possessed by new entrants to the labour force and the jobs available to them, leading to widespread under-employment – people working fewer hours than they would like and/or in jobs well below their aspirations. One study found that an average of 10 percent of Egyptians were under-employed, with that number closer to 20 percent among less educated workers.[16]

Among the reasons, according to labour economists, are declining opportunities in the public sector and weak demand for labour in the formal private sector, which tends to be heavily invested in unproductive sectors such as energy and real estate rather than in manufacturing and agriculture.[17] The failure to invest in labour-intensive modes of production has been a long-term problem in Egypt, according to the World Bank, and is due to government policy choices not designed to promote employment and productivity but rather to 'protect insider privileges'.[18]

Young Egyptians end up seeking jobs in small and medium-sized enterprises in the informal private sector, which in many cases offer poor pay, sub-standard working conditions and little job security. According to the International Labour Office, Egypt has seen a sharp rise in 'precariousness' and a 'drastic decline in job quality' since 2015, even amidst what appeared to be reasonably robust annual economic growth of 4 to 5 percent annually before the pandemic.[19] Young women are particularly vulnerable to the vagaries of the labour market, as they are subject to discrimination as well as family demands that make it difficult for them to accept jobs with long hours or commutes. Unemployment among women aged between fifteen and twenty-four who were participating in the labour force was 43 percent in 2018, compared to 28 percent for men in the same age cohort. A disproportionately large percentage of young women are not involved in any form of education, training or employment, which in turn results in young marriage, early child-bearing and high fertility rates.[20]

Water: Population, Climate and GERD Threaten Security

Egypt is facing a trifecta of threats to its water and food security from population growth, climate change and increased water use by upstream Nile states. Egypt presents a water paradox. On the one hand, as Herodotus said, Egypt is the 'gift of the Nile,' a millennia-old riparian civilisation that always relied on ample water to bring forth plentiful crops, and on river transport to keep parts of a large empire connected. Ancient Egyptians either invented irrigation or at least were among its earliest users, with evidence of flood irrigation going back as far as 8,000 years.[21] And until quite recently, Egyptians continued to use Nile water freely, as though its abundance would never end.

At the same time, Egypt is one of the most water-dependent countries in the world, second only to Kuwait in global rankings from the World Bank.[22] Nearly all the fresh water that Egypt uses falls as rain outside its borders, mostly in the highlands of Ethiopia. Egypt uses the vast majority – estimated by various sources at 77–86 percent – of its water for agriculture, much of which is still done through open canals, which waste a great deal through evaporation as well as leakage.[23] There have been many water management schemes by governments over the years, the biggest one being the construction of the Aswan High Dam in the 1960s, as well as increased wastewater reprocessing, efforts to change the crop mix (for example, reducing the cultivation of rice) and desalination (primarily for residential and industrial rather than agricultural use). The government announced a four-pronged strategy to improve water management in July 2021 (improving water quality, rationing, distribution, developing resources and training workers to raise awareness), but it was unclear how successful this strategy would be in addressing what is quickly becoming a crisis.[24]

Per capita water figures for Egypt are now below UN thresholds of water poverty and expected to reach absolute scarcity by 2025. In addition to increased demands from population growth, climate change is making the Nile's flows less predictable due to more variable annual rains.[25] At the same time, temperatures are rising significantly, especially in summer, and the little rainfall that Egypt itself receives is diminishing.[26] Rising seas associated with climate change also are compromising the agricultural lands, as well as the fresh water supplies of the Nile River Delta.

As if these threats to Egypt's water supply were not enough, the country also faces a strong challenge from Ethiopia regarding the share of the Nile to which Egypt has long considered itself entitled. For centuries, Egypt was politically and economically stronger than its downstream neighbours. Egypt managed to claim a significant share of Nile water in agreements reached in 1929 and 1959, which included Sudan (with a much smaller share than Egypt) but not Ethiopia.[27] Moreover, Egypt benefited from underuse of the Nile by its southern neighbour, in fact using part of Sudan's allotted share as well as its own.[28]

In the half century since the 1959 agreement, however, Ethiopia's economic and political weight has grown gradually, and regional power dynamics have shifted in its favour. In 2011, Ethiopia began building the Grand Ethiopian Renaissance Dam (GERD), despite Egyptian objections. For Ethiopians, the GERD is a project of paramount importance; hydroelectric power is seen as essential for developing the economy and raising standards of living. Partly due to Egyptian objections, Ethiopians had to raise most of the funds for the dam themselves (China also financed part of the project, perhaps as much as one-third of the total cost), and the project has become a source of national pride, in some ways paralleling Egypt's own experience with the Aswan Dam in the 1960s.[29] By 2019 the dam was largely complete, and Ethiopia began filling its basin during the rainy seasons of summer 2020 and 2021, despite vigorous objections from Egypt.

For Egypt, the GERD has become a long-running nightmare. Despite Ethiopian protestations that the dam will not affect the volume of water reaching downstream countries, Egypt has legitimate concerns on that score. There is no denying that Ethiopia and Sudan intend to use more Nile water for hydropower as well as irrigation as they develop their economies. A 2021 technical study showed that the GERD basin filling could reduce Nile waters reaching Egypt by as much as one-third for at least several years.[30] Egypt is already undergoing severe water stress, with the repeated re-use of agricultural water diminishing its quality and concentrating pollutants. The study also considered possible knock-on effects of significantly diminished food production and employment in Egypt, although it made clear that it was still possible for mitigating measures – slower basin-filling by Ethiopia, better water management by Egypt, development of a cooperative regime for Nile management – to avert the worst outcomes.

As of this writing, however, Ethiopia has begun filling the dam basin without agreeing to a specific schedule and has resisted establishing a cooperative management scheme for the Nile. Of particular concern to Egypt is the likelihood of multi-year droughts due to climate change, with Ethiopia unilaterally making decisions about water storage and release. Sudan, however, has worries about flooding in heavy rainfall years, a situation that Egypt would be better able to manage due to the Aswan Dam. While cooperative arrangements among the three countries, including the coordinated operation of the GERD and the Aswan Dam particularly when rains are scarce or heavy, would benefit all involved, even attempts to carry out the needed scientific studies have failed so far.[31]

While the GERD issue grabs headlines, it is important to recall that Egypt would be facing a water crisis even without that added stress, due to population growth. The demands of the Egyptian population outpaced the volume of Nile water available as early as the 1970s, and ever since then Egypt has had to import virtual water – that is, a significant portion of its food because it did not have enough water to grow what it needed.[32] Because of continued population growth, projections are that, by the end of the 2020s, Egypt will need to import annually a volume of virtual water (in the form of food it cannot produce due to lack of water) greater than the volume of actual water it has historically withdrawn from the Nile.[33] This will be quite expensive and create additional vulnerabilities for a population already under stress, as well as for a government heavily indebted. As Catherine Nikiel and Elfatih Eltahir conclude, if Egypt does not address population growth and water use promptly, '[i]t will soon serve as an ecological cautionary tale with implications for the entire region'.[34]

Egypt's Governance Challenges: Elite Decision-making Harms the Greater Good

The inability of the Egyptian state to meet the needs of its population in the decades before the 2011 uprising, as well as the years after the 2013 coup, is tied to the very nature of the state itself. Put simply, the Egyptian state is not set up for citizen input into policy-making, which naturally leads to decisions not designed to meet citizens' needs. Rather, decisions are largely driven by the interests of a small ruling elite – for example, the ruling party/military/business elite under Mubarak and, since 2013, a military-dominated regime with a group of less empowered private sector cronies. Focused on retaining power and extracting wealth, these elites have tried to make only those political, legal and economic concessions to the broader public that are necessary to preserve the peace – a strategy that has failed dramatically on a few occasions, notably during the 2011 uprising against Mubarak.

The sharpest manifestation of elite dominance has been the treatment of those who dare to oppose or criticise the rulers. Human rights conditions were already poor under Mubarak and during the brief democratic opening but have become abysmal under Sisi. After the 2013 coup, Sisi escalated the use of repressive methods well known in Egypt, including torture, unfair trials and lengthy pre-trial detention against opponents such as the Muslim Brotherhood and secular opposition groups (including the April Six Youth Movement, Revolutionary Socialists and others), journalists and civil society activists.[35] He introduced or greatly increased the use of brutal practices previously rare in the country, including forced disappearance, extrajudicial killing and denial of critical medical treatment in prison.[36] Just weeks after the coup, forces under Sisi's command carried out several mass killings of hundreds of protesters, traumatic events that remain taboo for discussion in Egypt.[37]

While such abuses are dramatic and resonate widely in society, there are also more subtle but pervasive ways in which governance by an exclusive elite has harmed Egypt. Elite dominance has meant a tragic waste of human capital, as mass education has been a low priority and many talented and even well-educated Egyptians have been barred from making meaningful contributions to public policy if they lacked elite connections. As explained by veteran Egypt observer Robert Springborg, the state is narrowly focused on its own survival above all, and that has meant that 'the three branches of government could not develop infrastructural power with which better to perform their duties'.[38] He also noted that 'political and civil society, shackled by intrusive manipulation and outright repression, could not serve as areas within which public brainpower could be developed and drawn upon by the state better to discharge its functions'.[39]

The lack of citizen input into public policy is one form of brain drain; another is the wasted economic potential of many Egyptians who are unemployed or employed far below their capabilities. There is also a large-scale external brain drain, in the form of many Egyptians who have gone abroad, making brilliant scientific or political achievements – such as Nobel laureates Ahmed Zewail and Mohamed ElBaradei – that would not have been possible at home. Governance under the current military-dominated regime, as opposed to the mixed military-civilian regime under Mubarak, has skewed decision-making and resource allocation further.

This is not an entirely new problem. As noted in the World Bank report cited above, the state has since the 1970s consistently made policies that favoured the interests of the few Egyptians who made their money in energy, real estate, or construction, over the interests of the many who would have benefited from policies that favour larger, more sophisticated industrial and agricultural sectors. Since 2013, however, this problem has become more acute, as the ruling elite is more narrowly comprised of military officers, with civilians present but in more subservient roles than in the past. Therefore, the interests of the elite are more narrowly defined.

Skewed State Budget Priorities

Since 2013, Sisi has concentrated resources and policy efforts in directions that serve his own political interests, as well as those of the military elite that supports him. Two areas of particular focus have been grandiose construction projects and weapons purchases. Such priorities are meant to build Sisi's reputation domestically and his support internationally, as well as to enrich the senior military officers who support him. At the same time, the opportunity costs of such projects are immense, as they divert scarce resources from the pressing needs of the broader population, while also causing a sharp rise in external debt.

There have been numerous mega-sized construction projects announced during the Sisi era; many have not come to fruition, but two important projects that have are the Suez Canal expansion and the construction of a new administrative capital in the desert east of Cairo. Each has been enormously expensive: the Suez Canal expansion costs $8 billion (much of it raised in a public bond), and the new capital is projected to cost approximately $58 billion.[40]

The Suez Canal expansion involved digging a 23-mile-long channel parallel to the original canal to allow more ships to pass at the same time. Several factors increased the cost of the project and diminished its returns. First, Sisi was determined to complete the expansion in his first year after becoming president, so as to show his ability to get things done, which meant that Egypt paid a premium for the construction. Second, the project was undertaken without studying feasibility, and it turned out that (even before the pandemic) there was not enough demand to justify the expansion and certainly not to generate the projected increase in revenues. In the five years following the canal expansion, revenues increased a mere 4.7 percent.[41] Moreover, an embarrassing incident in May 2021 – in which the container ship *Ever Given* became lodged sideways in the canal for six days, creating a cascade of shipping delays worldwide – showed that it might have made more sense to deepen and widen the original canal to accommodate today's large ships, rather than to dig a new passage.[42]

Much larger and more expensive than the Suez Canal expansion is the construction of a new administrative capital in the desert, twenty-eight miles east of Cairo, the sprawling and heavily populated city that has served as Egypt's capital for a thousand years. Launching the project in 2015, Sisi promised a massive, ultra-modern city for bureaucrats, diplomats and military officers far from the traffic jams of Cairo. Construction began in earnest in 2017, with estimated costs for the first seven-year phase of construction varying from $24 to $58 billion. There has been little transparency about where the funds would come from – not to mention the water. What has been clear from the intended prices of housing and the planned transportation links is that the new city is meant to serve and house primarily elite and some mid-level bureaucrats and military officers. It will be tightly controlled by a military hub and not accessible to most Egyptians (particularly any who might someday attempt another popular uprising).[43]

As of this writing, it is not entirely clear when the new capital would be inhabited and whether it would take off as a true alternative to Cairo; other communities constructed in the desert have floundered. In any case, the capital is one of many public projects that either ignore the needs of the poor who live in other governorates or attempt to displace them in order to make way for housing or commercial developments for the rich.[44] As Ursula Lindsey notes, '[t]he government finds it easier to finance blank slate development and promote real estate speculation in the desert than to invest in infrastructure that would serve the urban majority'.[45] Easier yes, and more profitable, as nearly all desert land belongs to the state and the military, which generate large profits from selling or developing that land. Real estate is one of several sectors in which Sisi has increased the grip of the military on the economy.[46]

In addition to grandiose projects such as the capital and the canal, weapons purchases have consumed inordinate resources under Sisi, even though Egypt is not at war or facing likely attack. While the most important threats to security in Egypt come from domestic militant groups (currently based primarily in Sinai) and the long land border with Libya, much of the state's military spending is on high-prestige items such as fighter jets, which are rarely used. For the period from 2015 to 2019, Egypt emerged as the third-largest importer of weapons in the world, spending at least $12 billion and more than tripling its purchases of the previous five years.[47] Sisi also diversified sources, making large purchases from France, Russia, Germany, Italy and the United States. As Maged Mandour points out, this diversification strategy has helped Sisi create an international safety net, in which foreign powers become heavily invested in the perpetuation of his rule because they are involved in massive arms contracts with – and in some cases have also lent heavily to – his regime.[48]

Weapons purchases, as well as offset or joint production arrangements, also are a source of enrichment for senior military officers, Sisi's most important source of support.[49] Thus, the benefits to Sisi and his circle of military supporters are clear, but the opportunity cost to Egyptian citizens of billions in funds that might have been spent on their needs is obscured. Additionally, the scope of state spending on the military is not known, as Egypt's military budget is a state secret, kept separate from the rest of the executive branch budget and not subject to parliamentary or other civilian review.

Sisi's lavish spending on mega projects and weapons is particularly troubling because it has been accompanied by a massive rise in foreign debt. Egypt's external debt as of mid-2021 was $134.8 billion, almost three times what it had been in 2015 ($49.8 billion), and some 90 percent of the gross domestic product.[50] Part of that was some $20 billion in new borrowing related to the pandemic, but even before the pandemic, by the end of 2019, Egypt's external debt amounted to $112.7 billion, well more than double its level in 2015. Analysts have deemed this level of external debt sustainable for the short term because much of it is long-term debt and/or owed to Gulf States that are unlikely to exert pressure. However, according to the Economist Intelligence Unit, it is not clear that Egypt can handle this level of debt over the medium to long term.[51]

Effects on Egypt's Regional and Global Role

Problems related to a rapidly growing population and diminishing water – and the choices made by Egyptian leaders that have left Egypt more and more indebted to foreign powers – have made Egypt increasingly vulnerable and less able than in the past to lead on the regional level. This situation is painful for Egyptians, who take pride not only in their civilisation's leadership in the ancient world, but also in more recent chapters such as the leading role of Egyptian intellectual and social pioneers in the nineteenth and twentieth centuries, Gamal Abdel Nasser's ideological leadership in Arab and African circles in the 1950s and 1960s, and the international fame garnered by Anwar Sadat for making peace with Israel in the late 1970s. The thirty-year-long Mubarak era was one of slow decline in regional influence, as Egypt's internal problems multiplied. There was a brief period of Egyptian fame on the international scene (and renewed cultural influence in Arab circles) during the 2011–13 attempt at a democratic transition, and foreign policy was probably the most successful aspect of the brief presidency of Mohamed Morsi, who succeeded in garnering global support for the nascent democracy. Sisi has also had an assertive foreign policy since becoming president following the 2013 coup. It has become increasingly clear, nevertheless, that the hand of cards that Egypt now holds is not a strong one, however cleverly Sisi and his diplomats might try to play it.

Egypt's dual challenges of super-abundant population and increasingly scarce water have driven as well as constrained its influence in the Middle East as well as Africa. The relative advantages that Egypt once enjoyed over its Arab and African neighbours in terms of education and economic development have faded away over a long period, with a more dramatic collapse in the cataclysmic decade since the 2011 uprising.

Struggling in the Arab World against an Empowered Gulf

Several episodes highlight how Egypt has lost influence relative to the Gulf States, particularly as Egypt's need for external financing has grown. During the brief presidency of Mohamed Morsi, many Egyptians objected to what they saw as excessive influence from Qatar, which promised some $8 billion in assistance and a further $18 billion in investments.

After the July 2013 coup, Saudi Arabia, the United Arab Emirates (UAE) and Kuwait provided more than $20 billion in bank deposits, soft loans and petroleum grants to Egypt, assistance that made it possible for Sisi to stabilise the country's finances.[52] Since then, Egypt has needed approximately $10 billion per year in external financing, with the Gulf States continuing to be important contributors alongside international financial institutions and other donors. And the Gulf States, particularly the UAE and at times Saudi Arabia, have done more than opening their wallets, showing strong political and diplomatic support for Sisi. UAE leader Mohammed Bin Zayed, for example, visited Sisi in Cairo in early September 2013, just weeks after the mass killings that made Egypt's new de facto leader (at that time, still defence minister) a pariah internationally.[53]

At times, Sisi has been able to compensate Gulf leaders for their largesse with vague statements about his nation's commitment to Gulf security, but that has not always been enough. Egypt's subservience to the Gulf States was brought home in spring 2016, in an episode that stunned the country's citizens. When Saudi King Salman visited Cairo in April of that year, he came bearing the promise of a $16 billion investment fund for Egypt. In return, Egypt relinquished sovereignty over two islands in the Red Sea, Tiran and Sanafir, to Saudi Arabia, which has longed claimed them. The islands were small and uninhabited; yet their surrender provoked one of the greatest crises of Sisi's tenure so far. Egyptians had been taught for decades that the islands, which Israel had occupied from 1967 until 1982, belonged to them and that Egyptian soldiers had died trying to protect them. Moreover, the islands are strategically significant, as they flank the Straits of Tiran; whoever holds them controls access to the Gulf of Aqaba and therefore to the Israeli and Jordanian ports of Eilat and Aqaba, respectively. Despite protests, lawsuits and criticism from Sisi's political opponents and even many of his supporters, the transfer went ahead.[54]

A second episode that illustrated how the Gulf States had outflanked Egypt regionally was the normalisation of relations between the UAE and Israel in August 2020. Bahrain, Morocco and Sudan also established relations with Israel around the same time, but it was the high-profile Emirati normalisation that caused alarm in Cairo. First, the UAE positioned itself as Israel's partner of choice in the region for economic and technical cooperation, something that Egypt had never be able to achieve, due partly to public opposition (not a concern for the UAE, which has a tiny and wealthy population) and partly to Egyptian officials' suspicions that Israel would dominate such a relationship. Second, the Abraham Accords laid out a process by which the UAE would join with Israel and the United States to draw up a 'Strategic Agenda for the Middle East', usurping a role that Egyptians had long considered to be theirs.[55]

Worst of all for Egypt, the Trump administration rewarded the UAE for the accords with a mammoth arms sale including F-35 fighter jets and advanced drones. Egypt had sought F-35s (as well as F-15s) for years to upgrade its air power but had been denied due to opposition from the US Congress and Israel.[56] The whole affair was a bitter pill for the Egyptians, but they had to swallow it due to Cairo's financial and political dependence on the UAE; there was no official protest against the United States, and the normally vociferous commentators in Cairo's government-affiliated media were largely silent.[57]

A third episode in which Egypt appeared to be following (rather than leading) the Gulf States was the Saudi and Emirati decision in January 2021 to end a boycott of Qatar, which had been going on since 2017, apparently in a bid to pave the way for good relations with US president-elect Biden. Egypt did sign the early January agreement but perhaps under duress – just a few weeks prior, Egypt had been continuing to pursue with enthusiasm its long-running propaganda war against Qatar, claiming (falsely in this case) that Qatar was funding foreign think-tanks to criticise Egypt's human rights record.[58]

While these episodes show that Egypt in recent years has often been a follower more than a leader when it comes to the Gulf, and at times even been manipulated by the Gulf, this is not to say that Egypt has lost all agency. When it comes to deploying its army, Egypt has retained the right of refusal. Egypt apparently refused a Saudi request to send ground troops to fight in the Saudi/UAE military intervention in Yemen in 2015, instead limiting its involvement to naval support in the Bab al-Mandab.[59] Egypt had fought a long, damaging war in Yemen in the 1960s, during which it lost some 10,000 soldiers; hence, returning to that terrain would have been nightmarish for its military leaders as well as citizens. Egypt also said no to Trump's proposed 'Middle East Security Alliance', sometimes nicknamed the 'Arab NATO', according to which Egyptian troops would have been under joint Arab command. Sisi played along when the idea was first proposed in 2017 but eventually withdrew quietly from the project in 2019, which Egyptians saw as driven by Saudi interests such as combating Iran (which Egypt does not consider a direct threat).[60]

Libya was another issue with which Egypt had to struggle to meet its own critical interests against Gulf imperatives. Egypt has a long, porous land border with Libya, as well as many labourers in the country, and the civil war there has brought many security challenges, including the movement of weapons and militants. When Libya's civil war erupted in May 2014, Egypt backed renegade general Khalifa Haftar with some enthusiasm, joining a camp led by the UAE and supported inter alia by Saudi Arabia, Russia and France. But Haftar disappointed militarily as well as politically, and by the time he launched a campaign to take Tripoli in April 2019, Sisi was less confident of his success than were Haftar's UAE and Russian backers. By early 2020, Turkey had been drawn into the conflict, supporting the UN-backed Government of National Accord against Haftar – and defeating Haftar's forces by early June.

The Turkish victory in Libya was a near-disaster for Sisi, as Turkey had been a major regional rival since the 2013 coup

(Erdoğan was a strong Morsi supporter). There were tense weeks during summer 2020 during which Egypt had to consider taking on Turkey militarily to avoid having Turkish forces on its western border, but in the end the two nations backed away from a conflict. Sisi shifted Egypt's policy concerning Libya to one more amenable to a diplomatic solution instead of a Haftar military victory, a change that led to some tension with the UAE.[61] Once again, as with Yemen, Libya was a case in which the Egyptian military could have been drawn into a conflict in which it might not have prevailed – and therefore Sisi acted, uncharacteristically, in a way at odds with the preferences of his Gulf patrons. Not only did his choice avoid a conflict with Turkey, but it also improved the possibility that Egypt would be able to benefit from reconstruction contracts in Libya, should the situation stabilise.

Another way in which Egypt has attempted to assert its independence from Gulf patronage is through a recent economic alliance with Jordan and Iraq, echoing the close cooperation that the three countries had enjoyed during the 1980s. Iraqi leader Saddam Hussein's 1990 invasion of Kuwait disrupted that cooperation, forcing Egypt to make a clear choice between an alliance with the Gulf (and the United States) or with Iraq. There is no reason to expect such a difficult choice now, however, and the three countries see overlapping interests in several spheres: reducing dependence on Saudi Arabia for Egypt and Jordan, creating leverage with Iran for Iraq and allowing all three to capitalise on the economic benefits of reconstructing Syria when that possibility arises.[62]

Struggling in Africa against an Empowered Ethiopia

If the ways in which Egypt has had to struggle against Gulf patrons have occasionally been uncomfortable for Egyptians, Egypt's inability to stop Ethiopia from building and filling the GERD has been nothing short of alarming. Although the advantages of a dam for Ethiopia had been identified decades ago, Egypt was able to use its international relationships to discourage donors from supporting such a project. That strategy gradually lost steam in the 2000s, as Ethiopia began to gather the financing and diplomatic support within Africa to move forward with the project, which it did with alacrity in 2011, breaking ground just two months after Mubarak's fall. Ethiopia and other Nile states had also signed a Nile Basin Initiative in 2010, which Egypt and Sudan refused to join because it did not acknowledge their allocations under the 1929 and 1959 agreements.[63]

Although Egyptians were strongly preoccupied with internal affairs from 2011 to 2013, the GERD still received attention. Egypt repeatedly tried to assert the continued salience of the 1929 and 1959 agreements, asserting that, whatever Ethiopia did with the GERD, Egypt must continue to receive its full water allotment – an argument completely refused by Ethiopia, which was not a party to the agreements.[64] Many tense episodes ensued, including in June 2013 (mere weeks before he was deposed) a hint at military options from Morsi, who said: 'We are not propagators of war, but we will not allow our water security threatened'.[65]

After Sisi became president in 2014, he initially pursued a somewhat conciliatory approach to the GERD. His most important step was to sign a March 2015 Declaration of Principles with the leaders of Ethiopia and Sudan, which in effect acknowledged Ethiopia's right to build the dam while also pledging cooperation and coordination on the dam's operation.[66] Unfortunately for Egypt, the agreement's vague wording and lack of enforcement mechanisms allowed Ethiopia to largely ignore it and to proceed towards completing and filling the dam on its own.[67] Sisi also focused on building diplomatic and security ties within Africa, which had badly deteriorated from their heyday in the 1960s under Gamal Abdel Nasser. While other North African states (particularly Morocco and Algeria) were also devoting more attention to relations with other African states, for Egypt this had become a matter of life and death.[68] Sisi concentrated his efforts on states in East Africa surrounding Ethiopia, including Eritrea, Djibouti, Somalia, Somaliland and Uganda, even flirting with establishing military bases in some of them.[69] He has worked hard to get the support of Kenya as well, signing a technical agreement on defence issues with the country in summer 2021.[70]

Most important of all for Egypt was Sudan, a country which historically has been under strong Egyptian influence, but which began to chart a less reliable course after 2011. Much to the shock of the Egyptians, Sudan's position on Nile issues fluctuated. At times it sided with Egypt in arguing to preserve the 1929 and 1959 agreements; at other times it sided with Ethiopia due to the strong economic ties that had developed between the two nations during the 2000s. Sisi began to cultivate Sudanese strongman Omar al-Bashir (despite Bashir's Islamist ties) as an ally against Ethiopia and even bolstered his regime against increasing protests in 2018–19 – which then put Sisi on the wrong side of the Sudanese public when Bashir was overthrown in April 2019.

Sisi and the allied Gulf States (Saudi Arabia and UAE) tried to promote the fortunes of senior Sudanese military leaders as opposed to civilians in the transition, with Ethiopian leader Abiy Ahmed positioning himself as the champion of civilian-led democracy.[71] Egypt worked hard at improving relations with the transitional Sudanese government, and Sudanese-Ethiopian relations have since deteriorated due to the reignited Fashaga border conflict as well as damaging floods in Sudan related to the GERD in 2020. Suffice it to say, however, that for Egypt Sudan is no longer a docile, reliable ally: their relationship is one that requires constant tending.

Sisi's diplomatic moves in Africa helped him win the presidency of the African Union (AU) for a one-year term beginning in February 2020, but he was unable to parlay the position into any significant advantage for Egypt versus Ethiopia. His tenure was marred by two events in which his disregard for human rights provoked widespread criticism in Africa: the first was the holding of the African Commission on Human and People's Rights in Egypt in April 2019 amidst repressive conditions there, and the second was Sisi's unsuccessful attempt to prevent Sudan from being suspended from the AU after a massacre of Sudanese protesters in June.

Egypt has also lobbied its patrons – particularly the United States, the Gulf States and Israel – for help on the GERD issue. US President Donald Trump strongly took Egypt's side, although without any ultimate positive effect. Trump sponsored tripartite negotiations on the Nile in Washington in January and February of 2020, but Ethiopia walked out. In response, the Trump administration suspended $130 million in economic aid to Ethiopia, in an effort to force the country to accommodate Egypt, and the president even suggested in public remarks in October 2020 that Egypt could be forgiven for using military force against the dam.[72] His successor, President Joseph Biden, has taken a much lower-profile approach but has appointed an experienced diplomat as envoy to the Horn of Africa, including the GERD, with the prospect that less biased US involvement might be more successful. The GERD issue, as of this writing, remains at the top of the Egyptian agenda in bilateral relations with the United States.

When it comes to engaging the Gulf States as well as Israel concerning the GERD, the picture for Egypt has been even more complicated. While Saudi Arabia and the UAE have no desire to see Egypt run out of water, at the same time they have made significant investments in agriculture in Sudan and Ethiopia to enhance their own nations' food security. Moreover, the two nations have many complex security as well as economic interests at stake in the Horn of Africa, an arena where they struggle for influence against Iran, Turkey and Qatar.[73] In mid-2021, Saudi Arabia began to take Egypt's side against Ethiopia more actively, while the UAE remained neutral.[74]

Egypt has also tried to draw the United Nations Security Council into the GERD dispute, after the many rounds of diplomacy by the African Union registered no progress. In July 2021, as Ethiopia began a second season of filling the dam basin without agreement from the other parties, Tunisia sponsored a UNSC resolution calling for a binding agreement to be reached within six months under UN/AU auspices.[75] However, the draft resolution did not garner enough support from major players (including the United States, Russia and France) and did not result in any change to the diplomatic framework.[76] Instead, the Democratic Republic of Congo, as president of the African Union, pledged to take the talks forward once again.

Over the past decade, Egypt has gradually adjusted its negotiating posture towards Ethiopia – from insisting on the old water-sharing allotments, over trying to prevent Ethiopia from filling the dam basin until a new agreement was reached, to pleading for cooperative arrangements among the states concerned to manage Nile flow, particularly during drought years – thus lowering its sights and adopting more achievable goals. The fact that three presidents – Mubarak, Morsi and now Sisi – have tried everything from honeyed diplomacy in Africa over increasingly frantic diplomacy at the international level to vague threats of military force, all to no avail, is an uncomfortable demonstration of Egypt's diminished strategic weight.

Somewhat paradoxically, Egypt's diminished weight also increases the possibility that it might at some point take the enormous risk of using military force (for example, bombing the dam turbines) to force a higher level of international diplomatic attention to the problem and compel Ethiopia to reach an agreement.[77] After the failed attempt at an UNSC resolution, former Egyptian Foreign Minister Nabil Fahmy came to the ominous conclusion that 'sooner or later confrontation seems inevitable, unless we see a sudden and unexpected change in Ethiopia's position'.[78]

The difficult position in which Egypt finds itself regarding the Nile water is partly an unavoidable result of other countries, in this case Ethiopia, becoming more developed economically and more powerful militarily than they once were. At the same time, Egypt is as vulnerable as it is to any changes in Nile flow due to the state's failure to deal effectively with rapid population growth and wasteful water use practices. That failure has played out over decades, but it has become even more apparent during the Sisi era, with a regime spending lavishly on new play-things, including weaponry and the new capital.

Conclusion: Can Egypt Regain its Influence?

During a July 2021 conference in Germany, Egyptian Minister of Water Mohamed Abdel Aty warned European interlocutors that a failure to side with Egypt on the GERD could lead to a water crisis in which Egyptian youth start to migrate to Europe in large numbers and even join terrorist groups there.[79] It was a classic Egyptian too-big-to-fail threat, an attempt to turn a weakness into a strength by warning of the consequences that state failure in Egypt could have for the rest of the world. Sisi and his Foreign Minister Shoukry have used the same tactic repeatedly with patrons and creditors from the United States, Europe, the Gulf and the IMF.

Such tactics have worked for some time, but are unlikely to work indefinitely, particularly as the world gradually shifts away from an economy fuelled by oil and gas. The Gulf States already show many signs of focusing their attention closer to home and will be able to do much less for Egypt – whether in terms of largesse, investment or absorbing excess labour – in future years than they have in the past. The United States likewise is slowly, fitfully re-orienting its priorities away from the Middle East.

There might still be ways, however, in which Egypt can turn what is now one of its vulnerabilities – its large population – into a strength. As oil and gas recede in importance, Arab states will need to generate prosperity through human capital and technology. Here, Egypt has a chance to regain its comparative advantage over the coming decades, but only if the government makes major shifts. First, there would have to be a concerted, comprehensive programme to reduce population growth so that any gains that Egypt makes will not be overwhelmed immediately. Second, Egypt would need a revolution in water usage, particularly in agriculture, as well as cooperative mechanisms with upstream Nile states, to ensure water and food security. Third, Egypt would need large investments in its educational systems at all levels to improve the preparedness of its labour forces.

Finally, the Egyptian state would need to adopt a new way of dealing with its citizens, treating them as an asset to be developed rather than a liability or threat and allowing them the freedoms necessary so that they can contribute to solutions to the country's challenges. If that were to happen someday, Egypt might well regain its place as a political, economic and cultural leader in the Middle East and Africa.

Notes

1. 'Egypt's Population Officially Hits the 100 Million Milestone', *Ahram Online*, 11 February 2020, https://english.ahram.org.eg/NewsContent/1/64/363276/Egypt/Politics-/Egypts-population-officially-hits-the--million-mil.aspx.
2. Max Roser, 'Fertility Rate', *Our World in Data*, 2014, https://ourworldindata.org/fertility-rate.
3. 'Egypt Fertility Rate 1950–2021,' *Macrotrends*, 2021, https://www.macrotrends.net/countries/EGY/egypt/fertility-rate.
4. 'Egypt Population 2021', *World Population Review*, 2021, https://worldpopulationreview.com/countries/egypt-population.
5. Joy Riggs-Perla et al., 'Egypt Health and Population Legacy Review', *USAID*, March 2011, https://pdf.usaid.gov/pdf_docs/PDACR591.pdf.

6. Louay Constant et al., *Barriers to Employment That Women Face in Egypt: Policy Challenges and Considerations* (Santa Monica: RAND Corporation, 2020); Lena Masri, '"Two Is Enough", Egypt Tells Poor Families as Population Booms', *Reuters*, 20 February 2019, https://www.reuters.com/article/us-egypt-population/two-is-enough-egypt-tells-poor-families-as-population-booms-idUSKCN1Q91RJ.
7. 'Skills Mismatch and Underemployment: How to Boost Employment of Young Women and Men in Egypt', *International Labour Organization*, 2015, https://www.ilo.org/wcmsp5/groups/public/---africa/---ro-abidjan/---sro-cairo/documents/publication/wcms_499397.pdf.
8. Caroline Krafft and Ragui Assad, 'Why the Unemployment Rate Is a Misleading Indicator of Labour Market Health in Egypt', *Economic Research Forum Policy Perspective*, 1 January 2014, https://erf.org.eg/publications/why-the-unemployment-rate-is-a-misleading-indicator-of-labor-market-health-in-egypt/.
9. 'Sisi Links Political Unrest to Population Growth in Public Address Calling for Birth Control', *Mada Masr*, 17 February 2021, https://www.madamasr.com/en/2021/02/17/news/politics/sisi-links-political-unrest-to-population-growth-in-public-address-calling-for-birth-control/.
10. 'Sisi Says Egypt's Population Growth Needs to Fall to 400K Annually for 10 Years', *Egypt Independent*, 10 March 2021, https://egyptindependent.com/sisi-says-egypts-population-growth-needs-to-fall-to-400k-annually-for-10-years/.
11. '2 Million Egyptian Women Have No Access to Contraceptives: Officials', *Egypt Today*, July 11, 2018, https://www.egypttoday.com/Article/1/53760/2-million-Egyptian-women-have-no-access-to-contraceptives-officials.
12. Nahla Abdel Tawab et al., 'Effects of COVID-19 Pandemic on Fertility in Egypt', *USAID* and *Evidence*, 2021, https://www.un.org/development/desa/pd/sites/www.un.org.development.desa.pd/files/undesa_pd_2021_egm_session_v_nahla_abdel-tawab.pdf.
13. 'The Islamic Republic of Iran's Flavoured Condoms, Free Vasectomies, and Gender Reassignment Surgery', *HuffPost*, 18 June 2014, https://www.huffpost.com/entry/the-islamic-republic-of-i_2_b_5481323.
14. Richard Cincotta and Karim Sadjadpour, 'Iran in Transition: The Implications of the Islamic Republic's Changing Demographics', *Carnegie Endowment for International Peace*, December 2017, https://carnegieendowment.org/files/CP324_Iran_in_Transition_Final.pdf.

15. '32.5% of Egyptians Live in Extreme Poverty: CAPMAS', *Egypt Today*, 1 August 2019, https://www.egypttoday.com/Article/1/734 37/32-5-of-Egyptians-live-in-extreme-poverty-CAPMAS.
16. Krafft and Assaad, 'Why the Unemployment Rate Is a Misleading Indicator'.
17. Ragui Assaad, Caroline Krafft, and Shaimaa Yassin, 'Job Creation or Labour Absorption? An Analysis of Private Sector Job Growth in Egypt', *Middle East Development Journal* 12, no. 2 (2 July 2020): 177–207.
18. 'More Jobs, Better Jobs: A Priority for Egypt', *World Bank*, June 2014, https://documents1.worldbank.org/curated/en/9268314682 47461895/pdf/884470EG0repla00Box385343B00PUBLIC0.pdf.
19. L. Fedi, M. Amer, and A. Rashad, 'Growth and Precariousness in Egypt', *International Labour Organisation*, 2019, https://www.ilo.org/wcmsp5/groups/public/---ed_emp/documents/publication/wcms_735169.pdf.
20. 'Egypt's Debt Sustainability', *Economic Intelligence Unit*, 27 July 2020, http://country.eiu.com/article.aspx?articleid=669932250.
21. R. E. Sojka, D. L. Bjorneberg, and J. A. Entry, 'Irrigation: An Historical Perspective', in *Encyclopaedia of Soil Science*, ed. by Rattan Lal, 1st edition (New York: Marcel Dekker, 2002), 745–49.
22. 'Country Profile: Egypt', *FAO AQUASTAT Reports*, Food and Agriculture Organization of the United Nations, 2016, https://www.fao.org/3/i9729en/I9729EN.pdf.
23. 'Country Profile: Egypt'.
24. Asmaa Ansar, 'الرى: وضع استراتيجية قومية حتى ٢٠٥٠ لحل كافة المشكلات والأزمات [Ministry of Water Resources and Irrigation: National Strategy in Place Until 2050 to Solve All Problems and Crises]', *Youm7*, 26 July 2021, https://www.youm7.com/story/2021/7/26/الرى-تم-وضع-استراتيجية-قومية-حتى-2050-لحل-كافة-المشكلات/5399182.
25. 'Water Accounting in the Nile River Basin: Remote Sensing for Water Productivity', *Food and Agriculture Organization of the United Nations* and *IHE Delft Institute for Water Education: WaPOR Water Accounting Series*, 2020, https://www.fao.org/3/ca9895en/ca9895en.pdf.
26. 'Egypt: Current Climate: Climatology', *World Bank*, 2020, https://climateknowledgeportal.worldbank.org/country/egypt/climate-data-historical.
27. 'FACTBOX: Nile River Agreements and Issues', *Reuters*, 27 July 2009, sec. Environment, https://www.reuters.com/article/us-egypt-nile-factbox-sb/factbox-nile-river-agreements-and-issues-idUSTRE56Q3MD20090727.

28. Catherine A. Nikiel and Elfatih A. B. Eltahir, 'Past and Future Trends of Egypt's Water Consumption and Its Sources', *Nature Communications* 12 (23 July 2021): art. no. 4508.
29. 'Strategic Analysis: Repercussions of Chinese Investments in the Nile River Basin', *MAX Security Solutions*, n. d., https://www.max-security.com/reports/strategic-analysis-reprecussions-of-chinese-investments-in-the-nile-river-basin/; John Mukum Mbaku, 'The Controversy over the Grand Ethiopian Renaissance Dam', *Brookings Institution: Africa in Focus*, 5 August 2020, https://www.brookings.edu/blog/africa-in-focus/2020/08/05/the-controversy-over-the-grand-ethiopian-renaissance-dam/.
30. Essam Heggy, Zane Sharkawy, and Abotalib Zaki Abotalib, 'Egypt's Water Budget Deficit and Suggested Mitigation Policies for the Grand Ethiopian Renaissance Dam Filling Scenarios', *Environmental Research Letters*, 11 June 2021, https://doi.org/10.1088/1748-9326/ac0ac9.
31. Alya El Markaby, 'Q&A: Unpacking the Environmental and Economic Impacts of the GERD with Engineer Mohammed Basheer', *Mada Masr*, 25 August 2021, https://www.madamasr.com/en/2021/08/25/feature/politics/qa-unpacking-the-environmental-and-economic-impacts-of-the-gerd-with-engineer-mohammed-basheer/.
32. Tony Allan, 'The Concept of Virtual Water', *World Energy 46: Water Stories. Eni S.p.A.*, 20 March 2020, https://www.eni.com/static/en-IT/world-energy-magazine/water-stories.html#slide11.
33. Nikiel and Eltahir, 'Past and Future Trends'.
34. Nikiel and Eltahir, 'Past and Future Trends'.
35. 'Egypt 2021', *Amnesty International*, n. d., https://www.amnesty.org/en/location/middle-east-and-north-africa/egypt/report-egypt/; '"We Do Unreasonable Things Here": Torture and National Security in al-Sisi's Egypt', *Human Rights Watch*, 5 September 2017, https://www.hrw.org/report/2017/09/05/we-do-unreasonable-things-here/torture-and-national-security-al-sisis-egypt.
36. 'Egypt Investigates Evidence of Extrajudicial Executions by Egyptian Army in North Sinai', *Amnesty International*, 5 August 2021, https://www.amnesty.org/en/latest/news/2021/08/egypt-investigate-evidence-of-extrajudicial-executions-by-egyptian-army-in-north-sinai/; Sherif Azer, '"Behind the Sun": How Egypt Denies Forced Disappearances', *The Tahrir Institute for Middle East Policy*, 30 April 2018, https://timep.org/commentary/analysis/behind-the-sun-how-egypt-denies-forced-disappearances/; '"What Do I Care If You Die?" Negligence and Denial of Health Care in Egyptian Prisons', *Amnesty International*, 25 January 2021, https://www.amnesty.org/en/documents/mde12/3538/2021/en/.

37. 'All According to Plan: The Rab'a Massacre and Mass Killings of Protestors in Egypt', *Human Rights Watch*, 2014, https://www.hrw.org/sites/default/files/reports/egypt0814web_0.pdf.
38. Robert Springborg, *Egypt*, 1st edition (Cambridge and Medford: Polity Press, 2017), 161.
39. Springborg, *Egypt*, 161.
40. Heba Habib and Erin Cunningham, 'Egypt's "Gift to the World" Cost $8 Billion and Probably Wasn't Necessary', *The Washington Post*, 6 August 2015, https://www.washingtonpost.com/news/worldviews/wp/2015/08/06/egypts-gift-to-the-world-cost-8-billion-and-probably-wasnt-necessary/.
41. 'Egypt's Suez Canal Revenues up 4.7% in Last 5 Years – Chairman', *Reuters*, 6 August 2020, https://www.reuters.com/article/egypt-economy-suezcanal-idUSL8N2F84GW.
42. Kit Chellel, Matthew Campbell, and K Oanh Ha, 'Six Days in Suez: The Inside Story of the Ship That Broke Global Trade', *Bloomberg*, 24 June 2021, https://www.bloomberg.com/news/features/2021-06-24/how-the-billion-dollar-ever-given-cargo-ship-got-stuck-in-the-suez-canal.
43. Michele Dunne, 'Sisi Builds a Green Zone for Egypt', *Current History* 117, no. 803 (1 December 2018): 355–58.
44. Maged Mandour, 'The Sinister Side of Sisi's Urban Development', *Carnegie Endowment for International Peace: Sada*, 10 May 2021, https://carnegieendowment.org/sada/84504.
45. Ursula Lindsey, 'The Anti-Cairo', *Places Journal*, March 2017, https://placesjournal.org/article/the-anti-cairo/?cn-reloaded=1.
46. Yezid Sayigh, 'Praetorian Spearhead: The Role of the Military in the Evolution of Egypt's State Capitalism 3.0', *London School of Economics Middle East Centre*, January 2021, http://eprints.lse.ac.uk/108516/2/PraetorianSpearhead.pdf.
47. Pieter D. Wezeman et al., 'Trends in International Arms Transfers, 2019', *SIPRI Arms Transfers Database*, March 2020, https://sipri.org/sites/default/files/2020-03/fs_2003_at_2019.pdf.
48. Maged Mandour, 'Dollars to Despots: Sisi's International Patrons', *Carnegie Endowment for International Peace: Sada*, 19 November 2020, https://carnegieendowment.org/sada/83277.
49. Jodi Vittori, 'Mitigating Patronage and Personal Enrichment in US Arms Sales', in *From Hardware to Holism: Rebalancing America's Security Engagement with the Arab States*, ed. Michele Dunne and Frederic Wehrey, *Carnegie Endowment for International Peace*, 18 May 2021, https://carnegieendowment.org/2021/05/18/from-hardware-to-holism-rebalancing-america-s-security-engagement-with-arab-states-pub-84520.

50. Doaa A. Moneim, 'Egypt's External Debt up to $134.8 Bln in Q3 FY2020/21: CBE', *Ahram Online*, 11 July 2021, https://english.ahram.org.eg/NewsContent/3/12/416983/Business/Economy/Egypt%E2%80%99s-external-debt-up-to--bln-in-Q-FY-CBE.aspx.
51. 'Egypt's Debt Sustainability'.
52. 'Gulf Aid to Egypt since 30 June More than $20 Billion: El-Sisi', *Ahram Online*, 6 May 2014, https://english.ahram.org.eg/NewsContent/1/64/100653/Egypt/Politics-/Gulf-aid-to-Egypt-since--June-more-than--billion-E.aspx.
53. Alice Fordham, 'Mohammed Bin Zayed Visits Cairo to "Stand by Our Brothers in Egypt"', *The National News*, 1 September 2013, https://www.thenationalnews.com/world/mena/mohammed-bin-zayed-visits-cairo-to-stand-by-our-brothers-in-egypt-1.477295.
54. 'Tiran and Sanafir: Developments, Dynamics and Implications', *The Tahrir Institute for Middle East Policy*, 9 August 2017, https://timep.org/wp-content/uploads/2017/08/Tiran-and-Sanafir-Developments-Dynamics-and-Implications-web.pdf.
55. 'Abraham Accords Peace Agreement: Treaty of Peace, Diplomatic Relations and Full Normalization Between the United Arab Emirates and the State of Israel', *US Department of State*, 15 September 2020, https://www.state.gov/wp-content/uploads/2020/09/UAE_Israel-treaty-signed-FINAL-15-Sept-2020-508.pdf.
56. Ali Dizboni and Karim El-Baz, 'Understanding the Egyptian Military's Perspective on Su-35 Deal', *Washington Institute for Near East Policy: Fikra Forum*, 15 July 2021, https://www.washingtoninstitute.org/policy-analysis/understanding-egyptian-militarys-perspective-su-35-deal.
57. Haisam Hassanein, 'Normalization Is Making Cairo Uncomfortable', *The Washington Institute for Near East Policy*, 19 August 2020, https://www.washingtoninstitute.org/policy-analysis/normalization-making-cairo-uncomfortable.
58. Mohamed Sabry, 'Egypt Thaws Relations with Qatar after Long-Running Feud Read More', *Al-Monitor*, 8 January 2021, https://www.al-monitor.com/originals/2021/01/egypt-qatar-gulf-rift-reconciliation-muslim-brotherhood.html.
59. Adhan Youssef, 'Egypt's Pledge to Send Troops Was Not in Context of Yemen War: Saudi General', *Daily News Egypt*, 18 April 2017, https://dailynewsegypt.com/2017/04/18/egypts-pledge-send-troops-not-context-yemen-war-saudi-general/.
60. Yasmine Farouk, 'The Middle East Strategic Alliance Has a Long Way to Go', *Carnegie Endowment for International Peace*, 8 February 2019, https://carnegieendowment.org/2019/02/08/middle-east-strategic-alliance-has-long-way-to-go-pub-78317.

61. Khalil Al-Anani, 'Egypt's Changing Policy in Libya: Opportunities and Challenges', *Arab Centre Washington DC*, 21 January 2021, https://arabcenterdc.org/resource/egypts-changing-policy-in-libya-opportunities-and-challenges/.
62. Katherine Harvey and Bruce Riedel, 'Egypt, Iraq, and Jordan: A New Partnership 30 Years in the Making', *Brookings Institution: Order from Chaos*, 2 July 2021, https://www.brookings.edu/blog/order-from-chaos/2021/07/02/egypt-iraq-and-jordan-a-new-partnership-30-years-in-the-making/.
63. Mwangi S. Kimenyi and John Mukum Mbaku, 'The Limits of the New "Nile Agreement"', *Brookings Institution: Africa in Focus*, 28 April 2015, https://www.brookings.edu/blog/africa-in-focus/2015/04/28/the-limits-of-the-new-nile-agreement/.
64. 'Exchange of Notes Between Her Majesty's Government in the United Kingdom and the Egyptian Government on the Use of Waters of the Nile for Irrigation', *International Water Law Project*, 7 May 1929, https://www.internationalwaterlaw.org/documents/regionaldocs/Egypt_UK_Nile_Agreement-1929.html; 'Agreement between the Republic of Sudan and the United Arab Republic for the Full Utilization of the Nile Waters', *Food and Agriculture Organization of the United Nations*, 8 November 1959, https://www.fao.org/3/w7414b/w7414b13.htm.
65. Ramadan Al-Sherbini, 'Mursi Warns Ethiopia over Nile Dam', *Gulf News*, 11 June 2013, https://gulfnews.com/world/mena/mursi-warns-ethiopia-over-nile-dam-1.1195550.
66. 'Agreement on Declaration of Principles between The Arab Republic of Egypt, The Federal Democratic Republic of Ethiopia and the Republic of the Sudan on The Grand Ethiopian Renaissance Dam Project (GERDP)', *Food and Agriculture Organization of the United Nations*, 23 March 2015, https://leap.unep.org/content/treaty/agreement-declaration-principles-between-arab-republic-egypt-federal-democratic.
67. Kimenyi and Mbaku, 'The Limits of the New "Nile Agreement"'.
68. Anthony Dworkin, 'A Return to Africa: Why North African States Are Looking South', *European Council on Foreign Relations*, 3 July 2020, https://ecfr.eu/publication/a_return_to_africa_why_north_african_states_are_looking_south/.
69. 'Egypt's Hope for a Military Base in the Horn of Africa Is Waning', *Egypt Watch*, 24 August 2020, https://egyptwatch.net/2020/08/24/egypts-hope-for-a-military-base-in-the-horn-of-africa-is-waning/.
70. 'Kenya, Egypt Sign Defence Deal as Cairo Moves to Consolidate Its Position on Ethiopia Dam', *Middle East Monitor*, 27 May 2021, https://www.middleeastmonitor.com/20210527-kenya-egypt-si

gn-defence-deal-as-cairo-moves-to-consolidate-its-position-on-ethiopia-dam/.
71. Michele Dunne, 'Fear and Learning in the Arab Uprisings', *Journal of Democracy* 31, no. 1 (January 2020): 189–92.
72. 'Suspension of US Aid to Ethiopia Is Yet Another Example of Trump's Disregard for Africa', *The Conversation*, 27 September 2020, https://theconversation.com/suspension-of-us-aid-to-ethiopia-is-yet-another-example-of-trumps-disregard-for-africa-146460; 'Trump Warns Ethiopia of Egyptian Attack on Dam', *The Independent*, 24 October 2020, https://theconversation.com/suspension-of-us-aid-to-ethiopia-is-yet-another-example-of-trumps-disregard-for-africa-146460.
73. Nima Khorrami, 'Deadlock on the Nile', *Carnegie Endowment for International Peace: Sada*, 22 July 2020, https://carnegieendowment.org/sada/82344.
74. Mohamed Saied, 'Could Israel Help Egypt Break Nile Dam Deadlock', *Al-Monitor*, 20 July 2021, https://www.al-monitor.com/originals/2021/07/could-israel-help-egypt-break-nile-dam-deadlock.
75. 'Egypt's FM Receives DRC Counterpart in Cairo to Discuss Resumption of GERD Talks', *Egypt Today*, 16 September 2021, https://www.egypttoday.com/Article/1/107883/Egypt's-FM-receives-DRC-counterpart-in-Cairo-to-discuss-resumption.
76. Nabil Fahmy, 'The Renaissance Dam after the Security Council', *The Cairo Review of Global Affairs*, Summer 2021, https://www.thecairoreview.com/essays/the-renaissance-dam-after-the-security-council/.
77. Charles W. Dunne, 'The Grand Ethiopian Renaissance Dam and Egypt's Military Options', *Arab Centre Washington DC*, July 30, 2020, https://arabcenterdc.org/resource/the-grand-ethiopian-renaissance-dam-and-egypts-military-options/.
78. Fahmy, 'The Renaissance Dam after the Security Council'.
79. Ibrahim Ayyad, 'Egypt Warns Europe against Illegal Immigration amid Nile Dam Impasse', *Al-Monitor*, 9 July 2021, https://www.al-monitor.com/originals/2021/07/egypt-warns-europe-against-illegal-immigration-amid-nile-dam-impasse.

3

Moroccan Politics: Confident at Home, Assertive Abroad

Mohamed Daadaoui

In the post Arab Spring era, after uprisings unseated the authoritarian regimes in Tunisia and Egypt, the MENA region continues to undergo massive changes. As I have argued, 'between Syria's crackdown and Libya's quagmire, the Arab spring seems stalled and the momentum for further regime change' all but gone.[1] While demands for socio-economic and political reforms have continued, not all MENA regimes have used violence to push back on those demands. Morocco has been able to rely on the popular appeal of its monarchy to deal with its protest movement, through 'a calibrated political strategy of sheepish reforms, while also benefitting from the fledgling opposition movement's lack of coherence and organization'.[2] Domestically, the monarchy in Morocco continues to be confident in its carefully managed style of governance and engineered electoral contests that add legitimacy to the political system. Regionally, the monarchy advances a robust foreign policy that centres around the perennial conflict in the Western Sahara involving Algeria as a regional foe and buoyed most recently by US recognition of Morocco's claims on the territory. Morocco's domestic politics have been shaped by three different interrelated events that show-cased the supremacy of the regime in managing the political arena and its ability in placating the different opposition forces. The events of the Arab uprisings, the Hirak protests and the ascent of the Islamist Party of Justice and Development (PJD) have each challenged the regime domestically and forced it to adopt different strategies of cooptation and confinement. Foreign policy issues centred around the Western Sahara conflict have also served to distract from the domestic challenges and unite Moroccans around a nationalist consensus.

This chapter analyses the Moroccan regime's confidence at home, as displayed in its handling of each of the three challenges of the 'Moroccan' Arab Uprisings and the 20 February Movement, the Hirak protests and the resurgence of the Islamist PJD's popularity at the polls. In addressing each of these challenges, the Moroccan regime has been the sole authority in an increasingly authoritarian edifice. However, protests in the last decade have also unmasked a new kind of dilemma for the monarchy: the failure of the regime's dual strategy of appearing above the political fray, while at the same time managing the political system and opposition forces. Confidence at home has empowered a robust foreign policy that centres on the issue of the Western Sahara as a lynchpin for Moroccan foreign relations, as well as a consensus-building nationalist issue enabling the regime to further consolidate the regime supremacy above all political reproach and to manage domestic challenges.

Morocco's Spring: Monarchical Exceptionalism or Advantage?

A decade after the uprisings commonly known as the Arab Spring, the record of revolutionary success is mixed. Whereas Tunisia is engaged in its own post-revolutionary institutional experiments, Syria, Libya and Yemen have descended into civil war, while Egypt briefly flirted with bringing duly elected Islamists to power, only to later reverse course in a coup d'état and subsequent repression under President Abdel Fattah al-Sisi. While several Arab states underwent revolutionary tumult, the region's monarchies in the Gulf, Jordan and Morocco have largely managed to survive the protests there.

Eleven years after the onset of the Arab Spring, monarchies appear to have 'an "advantage" that they possess over republican states in the Middle East and North Africa'.[3] The exception is the Kingdom of Bahrain, which has experienced the most tumultuous upheavals among the Arab monarchies, following a sustained period of protests and tremendous state violence. Its sectarian society fomented the pace and intensity of the protests against the minority Sunni monarchy of King Hamad bin 'Issa al-Khalifa. Despite this, 'the Arab authoritarian states all used, in one way or another, the similar strategies from the same menu of autocratic manipulation'.[4]

Monarchies possess an advantage over republican authoritarian states, which goes beyond 'institutional manipulation and vastly cosmetic changes'.[5] Thus, rather than describing a crisis of authoritarianism, it is more accurate to identify a 'republican' authoritarian crisis and a monarchical advantage. It is therefore not surprising that the Maghreb's only monarchy, Morocco, 'proved more resilient than many had expected and has largely outlasted and outmanoeuvred the beleaguered February 20th movement'.[6]

This monarchical advantage goes back to the colonial period and the arbitrary nature with which European colonial masters established most of the republican states. While republics were created in an arbitrary manner, monarchies, such as Morocco, had political orders that pre-dated the edifice of the modern state constructed by either French or British colonialism. Therefore, most Arab monarchies relied on pre-colonial regime coalitions – religious, tribal, clan and so on – to build their modern states. These state structures, like those in Jordan and the Gulf States, have withstood the test of time. Most Arab republican states, conversely, 'were either colonially created states, or were subjected to military coups that disrupted pre-existing regime orders as was the case in Algeria, Egypt and Iraq'.[7]

The monarchy's 'advantage' plays out in in its religious and traditional guise, 'and the resulting manipulation of its symbols of power facilitates authoritarian rule in most of the Arab monarchies'.[8] This is evident in Jordan, where the combination of the Hashemite lineage of the monarchy as well as tribal manipulation have been crucial in facilitating the regime's grip on power. In the Gulf sheikhdoms, who benefit from oil rents, the distribution of those rents, along with tribal and clan relationships, have kept the regimes afloat. And in Morocco, the legacy of French colonialism, which strengthened monarchical rule by subduing former lawless territories outside the dominance of the monarch and made them part of a centralised modern state, allowed the monarchy to grow more autocratic after independence in 1956.

The Moroccan regime's stability since independence is due to a combination of 'symbolic, historical and coercive means', all of which come under the authority of the *Makhzen*. The state in Morocco can therefore be seen as the product of two systems – rational-temporal and symbolic-religious – which dually exist in the face of modern challenges to regime stability. The modern *Makhzen*, roughly translated as the main Moroccan power structures and power-holders, was initially supported by French colonial state modernisation, but over time it has adopted new constitutional and administrative structures. It simultaneously retained its historical and symbolic rigour as well as its authority. The symbiosis of traditional and modern manifestations of power are still hallmarks of the monarchy's exercise of authority in Morocco.

The monarchy employs a ritualisation of the political process in the country to consecrate the king's status as the arbiter and guarantor of order and stability. This process relies on rituals and symbols of socio-religious importance to society, such as ceremonies, spectacles and public performances. The regime therefore 'reproduces legitimacy. However, these symbols are not independent as the monarchy helps shape the way they are perceived in society'.[9] The monarchy's symbols of sharifian lineage, commandment of the faithful and *bay'ah* (annual pledge of allegiance to the king) are codified in the Moroccan political system; they are tied to and used by the regime to elevate it as an arbiter above the political scene. In this case, political authority in Morocco lies with those who control dominant narratives, in addition to dominant political and economic structures.[10]

The dual nature of the monarchy as both a modern and traditional form of authority created through colonial administration is difficult to challenge by any other oppositional discourse, making for a robust edifice of authoritarian rule based on patronage and specific institutionalised rituals of powers.[11] Thus, the monarchy benefits from the culture of dissonance created by the modern manifestations of old traditions of power.[12]

As I have argued, the 'symbolic, traditional, tribal or religious capital associated with monarchical regimes subsumes all other features of authoritarian rule'.[13] Morocco's strategy towards the 20 February movement is useful in this case.

Relying on his 'socio-cultural capital', King Mohammed VI was able to 'slow the momentum' of the protest movement of 20 February, 'by offering a semblance of reforms' and co-opting political opposition forces.[14]

The 20 February Movement: The Regime's Institutional Management and Discursive Methods of Control

In his research on social movements and street politics in the Middle East, Asef Bayat develops the concept of 'non-movements' to conceptualise other forms of activism and protests that have not been traditionally part of the 'Western' genealogy of the Social Movement Theory. For Bayat, non-movements are 'collective actions of non-collective actors; they embody shared practices of large numbers of ordinary people whose fragmented but similar activities trigger much social change, even though these practices are rarely guided by an ideology or recognizable leaderships and organizations'.[15] In this respect, agency in non-movements is a key variable promoting change in the Middle East without conforming to an overarching ideology or organisational frame. Such agency is fragmented in the movement and everyday practices of 'millions of subaltern, chiefly the urban poor, Muslim women and youth'.[16] These 'quiet' everyday acts by 'big numbers' of ordinary people, albeit fragmented and lacking in strategy, do in fact challenge the existing norms and rules in society.[17] However, regime frames can hinder the capabilities of social movements by interrupting their cycle of contention and weakening the movement's framing processes.

In the case of the 20 February movement in Morocco, a protest movement that launched its own massive demonstrations in most major cities during the events of the Arab uprisings, the cycle of contention was disrupted early on by the regime's institutional management strategies of control – notably the state's constitutional reforms and legislative elections – while the monarchy's discursive methods exposed the lack of an alternative cultural frame – hindering the discursive framing of the protest movement. An alternative cultural frame could have challenged that of the regime's and articulated a sovereign alternative capable of demystifying the regime. The 20 February movement was led by tech-savvy youth activists using the social media platforms of Facebook, Twitter and YouTube, where the activists released the movement's founding document that called for a democratic constitution, the recognition of Amazigh as an official language and the release of prisoners of conscience.[18]

In a nationally televised speech on 8 March 2011, King Mohammed VI promised to 'undertake a comprehensive constitutional reform'.[19] Days later, he established a blue-ribbon royal commission entrusted with the task of proposing a new constitution unveiled and endorsed by the monarch in June 2011.[20] Despite opposition from the 20 February movement, the new constitution was approved in a national referendum by an overwhelming majority of 98.5 percent of votes.[21]

Despite the state narrative, the 2011 referendum and subsequent legislative elections were hardly revolutionary and fell short of the specific demands for democratic reforms, rule of law and end to corruption that the protesters championed. The new constitution featured several changes to the relationship between regime and state in Morocco, as it nominally empowered the prime minister in policy-making and appeased the Amazigh movement's quest for recognition of their cultural and identity rights.[22]

The monarchy, however, still retained its ubiquitous discretionary powers, which in effect could suspend the law-making function of the legislative body of the parliament. The monarchical prerogative in dissolving the parliament and the government, albeit with the consent of the government, limits the principle of the separation of powers. Similarly, the king maintains authority over the military, foreign policy and Islamic affairs, given his claim to be the commander of the faithful. This royal religious title, and the monarchy's claim to sharifian lineage, also set the monarch as an inviolable figure in Morocco, where *lèse-majesté* laws prohibit any criticism of the monarchy.[23]

Constitutional and institutional state reforms, albeit 'in great measure cosmetic',[24] managed to interrupt the momentum and cycle of contention of the 20 February movement. However, it is the movement's lack of a contentious cultural frame that proved its most pronounced weakness vis-à-vis the regime's cultural capital.[25] In addition to the regime's cosmetic constitutional changes and curated elections, the beleaguered movement was also beset by the regime's superior cultural frames that effectively impeded the movement's success in its articulation of narratives alternative to the monarchy. Despite some slogans denouncing the monarchy as 'rotten' and calling for the downfall of the regime of Mohammed VI, the protest movement did not manage to articulate a strong discourse alternative to that of the monarchy, especially in its traditional and religious appeal.[26]

The mistakes of the 20 February movement were also compounded by its lack of organisation and coherent strategy of protests. Its centrifugal and leaderless structure meant that the movement increasingly found it difficult to organise coordinated large-scale protests. The results of the referendum and the legislative elections also 'dealt the movement a major blow and severely restricted its ability to mount a significant challenge to the corrupt undemocratic foundations of the state in Morocco'.[27]

The 'coup de grâce' for the 20 February movement was delivered with the legislative election of 2011.[28] The elections failed to live up to the hype as a landmark institutional breakthrough in Morocco, as they effectively closed the cycle of contention for the protest movement at the national level. However, they ushered in the rise of peripheral local protest episodes that feature different dynamics of organisation, mobilisation and strategies. Ideological fissures amplified the 20 February movement's weakness, lack of consistent contestation strategy, internal disorganisation, state penetration and co-optation. In many ways the monarchy's apparent 'success' in weathering the tempest of the Arab revolts is also a function of the weakness and manipulation of local protest movements. Despite its failure, the movement managed a slight discursive silver lining, as it has elevated the anti-regime narrative to include dissent in areas previously considered taboo by the state in Morocco, notably the boycotts of products made by companies associated with the king's economic holdings and even the status of the monarchy's dominant role in politics.[29] It has also provided an impetus for the proliferation of protests in Morocco, changing the collective consciousness of Moroccans' demands towards the regime.

From Centre to Periphery: The Proliferation of Protests in Morocco

After more than two decades on the throne, Mohammed VI and the Moroccan monarchy are no longer immune from societal reproach. The Arab uprisings' 20 February movement and subsequent social protests have 'managed to lift the veil of fear and to demystify the monarchy'.[30] These protests have led to the decentralisation of social protests, moving from urban centres to peripheral regions in Morocco that share common political and economic grievances, often triggered by accidental events. The Hirak protests in 2016, the protests in the remote Amazigh village of Imider that lasted uninterrupted from 2011 to 2019, the water shortage demonstrations in the Sahara desert town of Zagora in 2017, the coal mine protests in the northeastern border town of Jerada in 2018 and the unprecedented 2018 economic boycott of Morocco's dairy, mineral water and fuel distribution oligopolies that have close ties to the regime –all of these are acts of civil dissent which have become quotidian performances of resistance against *hogra* (Moroccan for extreme injustice) that is seen as rampant in the *Makhzen*'s entrenched authoritarian edifice.[31]

These 'non-movements' of peripheral protests in various regions of Morocco are rarely guided by an ideology or led by recognisable leaderships and structures; most importantly, they have challenged the monarchy's ability to simultaneously position itself outside of politics while manipulating the political system. The monarchy's constant manipulation of the political party scene and civil society has removed the buffer between the royal institution and the people and has exposed the palace to direct scrutiny. The monarchy's increasing inability to deal with social unrest, as was evidenced by the Hirak protests in the Rif, has made it more prone to the use of old oppressive methods of control.[32]

Hirak Protests in the Rif

The tragic death of a fish vendor, Mohsin Fikri, in the northern Riffian city of al-Hoceima in October 2016 sent thousands of protesters to the streets in several major cities in Morocco. Fikri was illegally selling fish on the street; thus, his merchandise was confiscated and thrown into a garbage truck. The thirty-one-year-old vendor then jumped into the garbage compactor to retrieve his fish, where he was subsequently crushed to death. Social media went ablaze with indignation and calls for mobilisation under the hashtag #t'han mou (an expletive meaning 'crush his mother'), reportedly the final words that Fikri heard from the police officer who ordered the truck driver to operate the garbage compactor with Fikri in it. Almost immediately after the tragic killing of Fikri, protests erupted across Morocco, spreading from al-Hoceima to Marrakesh and Rabat.[33] Moroccans expressed their outrage and uploaded videos and photos of ongoing protests. Many internet users uploaded live videos of the protests on their Facebook accounts.[34] To placate increasing public anger and the protests that engulfed the entire country, high-level officials travelled to the scene of the crime where they pledged to fully investigate and hold those involved accountable. King Mohammed VI dispatched the Ministry of the Interior and pledged a 'careful and in-depth' investigation.[35]

The significance of the demonstrations is that they erupted in al-Hoceima in the Rif region, which has a long and tumultuous history with the regime. In the 1920s, its talismanic leader, Abdelkrim al-Khattabi, declared independence of the Rif, which was short lived due to Spanish colonisation. In the 1950s, the Rif would be subject to state repression after a violent rebellion was put down by then Crown Prince Moulay Hassan. Al-Hoceima also witnessed multiple casualties in the 2011 Arab uprisings protests, which turned more violent in nature than elsewhere in Morocco and took on a more pronounced anti-monarchy position. The spontaneous collective reaction to the most pernicious aspects of *Makhzen* power – namely, injustice, corruption and daily denigration of Moroccans – soon was channelled by Nasser Zefzafi as a symbol of the movement in al-Hoceima, while protesters in front of the parliament in Rabat chanted 'Mohsin was killed, and the *Makhzen* is responsible'.[36]

Moroccans have long lamented the *hogra* that is seen as rampant in the *Makhzen*'s entrenched authoritarian edifice. Despite widely praised constitutional changes in 2011 and two legislative elections that buttressed Islamist PJD gains, Morocco has regressed in civil liberties. The press remains beset with limitations, while corruption, nepotism and a lack of accountability are still chief grievances among most Moroccans. According to the Arab Barometer V in 2019, 71 percent of Moroccans view the state as corrupt, and 80 percent say that *wasta* (nepotistic connections) is important for obtaining employment.[37]

Moroccans' daily life and the growing wealth gap provide the starkest reminder of *hogra*. Moroccans see the luxury cars, opulent palaces and other ostentatious accoutrements of wealth of the *Makhzen*'s members. These sharply juxtapose the lives of the oligarchs with the systematic subjugation and impoverished existence of many Moroccans. Some of the slogans in al-Hoceima crystallised that profound sense of deprivation. What Moroccans crave is fundamental change to government, through rule of law and gradual shifts in the distribution of political power. They know full well that the monarchy is immune from any reproach and that deep, meaningful reforms must start with the structure of the leviathan *Makhzen*.

Fikri's death drew comparisons to Mohamed Bouazizi, the Tunisian fruit seller who self-immolated in 2010, thus sparking the Arab Spring uprisings. However, that Fikri's death did not turn into a Bouazizi-like moment for Morocco is largely due to the perceived covert ethnic Amazigh nature of the Hirak protests which brandished slogans of 'Rif Revolution' and 'Arab Colonialism', alienating the the rest of the country by making the protests almost purely Amazigh in nature. Several Rif protesters also waved 20 February movement flags, symbolically invoking the continuity of the movement and its grievances against state corruption and injustice. The regime managed the manifestations by offering some sort of conciliatory approach to the demands of the protesters while working to limit the damage to the structure of the political order. There again the regime displayed its dual strategy of discursive and institutional management, exemplified in the king's silence and refusal to address the protests directly, his July 2017 speech where he launched a searing critique of the Moroccan political class and his cabinet re-shuffle in October 2017, barring five former ministers from ever taking official duties again. The unprecedented move by the Moroccan sovereign was presented as an attempt by the palace to introduce some government accountability. However, the sacking of government ministers is merely the latest example of the increasing royal emasculation of the political class, and an astute deflection from the palace's own responsibility in the current socio-political malaise in Morocco.[38] The royal management of the Hirak protests also reveals a growing dilemma that may have tremendous ramifications for the kingdom. These protests and the Islamist challenge during the tenure of the populist Prime Minister Benkirane have also unmasked a new kind of dilemma for the monarchy.

The monarchy, in turn, has had to adjust to the pressures of new forms of activism during 'Morocco's Spring', which would usher in a revival of the old authoritarian habits of institutional and constitutional constraints, as the regime engaged in old tactics such as re-shuffling cabinets and holding electorally engineered legislative elections. The resulting recycling of political parties and coalitions is necessary to maintain the façade of competitive political participation. Thus, as in the past, sham opposition would be given the reins of quasi-political authority. In 2012, it was the turn of the Islamist Party of Justice and Development (PJD) at the helm of the government, which served as a counter-weight to the exuberant 20 February movement protesting in the streets of Morocco.

Faced with a carefully crafted regime based on a traditional-modern institutional symbiosis, opposition parties and the 20 February movement have largely been limited in their effects.[39] While unsuccessful in their aim for deep socio-economic and political reforms, the 20 February movement and 'subsequent social protests managed to lift the veil of fear and to demystify the monarchy'.[40] The rise of spontaneous organic forms of political and social activism is a hallmark of the current activism scene in Morocco.[41]

These 'non-movements' of peripheral protests in various regions of Morocco are rarely guided by an ideology or led by recognisable leaderships and structures. Even the figure of Nasser Zefzafi in the Rif is almost as accidental as the events leading to the year-long Hirak protests following Fikri's death. Zefzafi's interruption of the Friday prayer and sermon in a mosque in the city of al-Hoceima in 2017 was a spontaneous, not calculated, expression of anger and desperation against a hegemonic cultural and political discourse of domination. Therein lies the novelty of current social activism in Morocco and elsewhere: protests emanate from the shared experiences of large numbers of ordinary people lamenting common socio-economic grievances.[42]

A New King Dilemma

The monarchy in Morocco is facing a new kind of dilemma: how to maintain control over both the political system and opposition forces, while also publicly distancing itself from the political machinations inside the kingdom. The dilemma was clearly manifested in the king's strategies towards the populist leadership of Abdelilah Benkirane and the Islamist PJD, as well as in the monarchy's role in sabotaging Benkirane's attempts to form a government in the aftermath of the 2016 legislative elections. The monarchy is ill at ease when managing the political system, and its discourse is increasingly accusatory, deflecting the blame for the socio-economic plight of the country on the political elite. In the king's throne day speech of July 2017, for instance, the monarchy laid the blame for the political paralysis in Morocco everywhere else but the monarchical regime. In his speech, King Mohammed VI delivered a strongly worded opprobrium to the political elite, chiding them for a lack of creativity and for hiding behind the palace. In doing so, the king cast his institution above and outside the political elite, as if Morocco were a true constitutional monarchy, where the regime is at a distance from the travails of politics.[43] The king possesses vast discretionary powers and is in charge of security and foreign policy. Legislation is located within the parliament but subject to monarchical veto.

In his speech, the king did not offer any words or vision that would appease the Rif protests, which had been going on for a year at that time. Instead, the king later issued an amnesty for some of the Hirak prisoners. The king's decree to sack government ministers came a few months after Morocco had undergone a political crisis, which hindered the ability of former Prime Minister Benkirane to form a government due to a political gridlock, a *blocage* in Moroccan parlance, manufactured by royalist political parties. For five months, royalist parties whose participation in the coalition government was necessary for the Islamists PJD refused to join, perhaps in an attempt to sabotage a Benkirane-led government.[44] Then the *blocage* show-cased the supremacy of the regime vis-à-vis the political class, where popularity and populism are reserved for the monarchy, and not any one political leader such as Benkirane.

In the throne day speech of July 2017, the king lamented: 'The evolution witnessed in Morocco in the political domain and in the area of development has not led to the kind of positive reaction you would expect from political parties, leaders and government officials when dealing with the real aspirations and concerns of Moroccans'.[45] The monarch excoriated those politicians whose 'mentalities have not evolved' to match said evolution. But unlike what the speech leads us to believe, the monarchy is not a passive actor in the Moroccan state edifice. It is well-entrenched in the system and has for decades fostered a patronage system that is as inimical to transparency and accountability as it is conducive to venal practices which are rampant everywhere in the Moroccan state and its institutions.[46]

The discontent of the king paradoxically is a result of decades of monarchical control over the political system and its management of the party scene.[47] The regime has emptied the political party scene of any significance and created a political vacuum. In his throne speech, King Mohammed VI rightly bemoaned this 'regrettable and dangerous vacuum' but misdiagnosed its causes. The omnipotent monarchy has weakened the political class and has for decades stoked intense rivalry among political parties, which the king in the speech criticised for 'a win-lose rationale to preserve or expand their political capital at the expense of the homeland'.[48]

But this strategy has run its course. While it has sustained the monarchy in the past, the monarchy's constant control over the political sphere is ill-devised in the post-Arab uprisings, where the protests of the 20 February movement and the current Hirak movement in al-Hoceima have somewhat demystified the monarchy. The duality between regime and state that the palace has woven for decades to shield its edifice from any reproach may be running its course.[49] The monarchy's consistent attempt to face new challenges to the state with old autocratic tools shows significant fissures as the political *blocage* and the Hirak movement in the Rif starkly highlighted.

Street demands would have been absorbed by civil society and channelled through institutional mechanisms, if the

Makhzen, at the behest of the palace, had not impoverished the political scene and emasculated its most promising actors. The king's scathing criticism of the political elite is in fact a critique of his *Makhzen*, long characterised by institutional manipulation of political forces, as it was the case of the Islamist PJD in the post-Arab uprisings' era.[50]

The Rise and Fall of the PJD Islamists

The legislative elections of November 2021 saw the plurality victory of the Islamist Justice and Development Party (PJD) and the appointment of its head Abdelilah Benkirane as prime minister. Many were hopeful that the electoral victory of the former opposition and Islamist party would be a prelude to meaningful political and economic reforms. Such hopes were quickly dashed, as the work of the government continues to be undermined by the palace's own shadow government of personal advisors.[51]

In October 2016, the PJD won a plurality of seats in the legislative elections and appeared well on its way towards a second consecutive term at the helm of the Moroccan government. But all was not well for the party's leader, Benkirane, as he sought coalition parties to join the government. Most of the parties that the PJD approached either declined to join or ignored Benkirane's offers of cabinet portfolios. After an unprecedented five months of post-election gridlock, King Mohammed VI dismissed Prime Minister Designate Benkirane.

A palace communiqué lauded Benkirane's service to the country, his 'effectiveness, competence and self-sacrifice', adding that the king would task another member of the PJD to form the government.[52] Benkirane accepted the royal decision in an austere tone: 'This is our king and he came to a decision under the framework of the constitution, which I've always expressed support for [. . .] I'm going to perform ablution, pray and continue working on the ground'.[53] The king further cornered the PJD and tasked Saadeddine Othmani, former secretary-general of the PJD and current head of the party's national council, with forming the new government.

Benkirane's intransigence in the face of the royalist bloc is unlikely to be undermined by Othmani, who was briefly minister of foreign affairs in Benkirane's first government and is seen as a consensus-building politician. But the removal of the beleaguered Benkirane was only the first phase in the regime's overall attempt to re-order the political landscape in Morocco, and a setback to the pace of reforms of the post-Arab uprisings. The political *blocage* was orchestrated by a *Makhzen* determined to regain control over the political party scene five years after the protests of the Arab uprisings. But the choice of Othmani also showed that the gridlock was more about Benkirane than about the PJD. Several forces were at work behind the scenes to lay the foundations for a post-Benkirane political environment dominated by more docile royal parties and more pliable PJD leadership. As in the past, the regime sought new reconfigurations of the Moroccan political scene, made up mainly of royalist parties.

The meteoric electoral ascent of the PJD under Benkirane may have irked the state enough to thwart the second experiment of the PJD post-Morocco Spring. The electoral success of the PJD gave it the confidence that, in the absence of state electoral interference, it could win more elections due to its formidable grass root mobilisation. The party has not always yielded to the *Makhzen* and has grown in confidence, perhaps too much so for the palace. During the election campaign of 2016, the populist Benkirane advanced his party as the voice of the people, in direct contrast to the palace-loyal parties – the PJD straddled the fence, acting loyal to the palace while also criticising the political system for *tahakoum* – that is, political manipulation. Benkirane's style and tone thus became his downfall with the regime.[54]

The PJD may also be a victim of its own initial success in articulating a nuanced discourse on social and economic changes and subsequent reforms that have advanced Benkirane and his party in some corners as a possible peer to the regime in Morocco. But in Morocco the regime is peerless, and whenever opposition forces grow in stature they are weakened by a resourceful and robust political order. The legislative elections of 2011 and 2016 legitimised the state's strategy to placate the Moroccan Spring's street anger and were an attempt to tame the PJD as an opposition and reformist force. The PJD was not supposed to win two consecutive elections, especially as the state mobilised the Party of Authenticity and Modernity (PAM) and other parties against it. The PJD with its populist leader Benkirane simply became a thorn in the side of the *Makhzen*.

The PJD could also have initially mobilised behind the 20 February movement in 2011 but chose to pursue participation in the elections to enhance its political standing in Morocco's limited electoral system. In doing so, the PJD adopted a 'third way' by joining the political system in partnership with the palace and the promise of deeper reforms, without risking the instability of uncontrolled popular protests.[55]

The abrupt end to the Benkirane era was a harbinger of things to come, as it began the process of drawing the curtain on the palace's experiment allowing for an Islamist, PJD-led government after the 2011 Arab uprisings. In a system where all parties submit to the will of the regime, Moroccan governments have historically been weakened by the monarchy's far-reaching prerogatives and constitutional powers. Patronage and clientelist practices are endemic within the state and facilitate the co-optation of the political and economic elite. Opposition forces are severely restricted in their ability to mount a significant challenge to the foundations of the state in Morocco.

Amidst limited options, the PJD's return to the opposition may be its best path forward to salvage its standing in the political party system and with its own rank and file. Rejecting the king's offer would lead to new elections, which the party can win again if the state does not interfere. But once in the doldrums of the opposition halls, the PJD also risks losing its electoral momentum and could face the same fate as the Social Union of Popular Forces (USFP), the once dominant opposition party which, like the PJD in 2011, made the cardinal sin of taking a bite of the state's low-hanging fruit of government power within tight institutional constraints.

This strategic miscalculation would prove costly in the September 2021 legislative elections where the PJD sustained a resounding defeat in the polls, winning an abysmal thirteen seats in parliament, down from 125 in 2016 and 107 in 2011. The PJD was relegated to the opposition with the plurality victory of the royalist part of the Rally of National Independents (RNI) led by former Minister of Agriculture Aziz Akhanouch. The gradual weakening of the PJD and its subsequent defeat in the September 2021 elections are an indication of the regime's meticulous control of the political system, which is intentionally fragmented into 'divided structures of contestation' (SOCs).[56] In divided SOCs, the monarchy allows select political opponents to take part in the political system while excluding others. These spheres of political contestation condition government-opposition relations and dictate the rules of the game that the opposition plays within the formal political system. The resulting recycling of political parties and coalitions is necessary to maintain the smoke-screen of political participation. The Moroccan monarchy has a 'long tradition of managing opposition parties through co-optation and confinement, allowing opposition parties some stake in power, while the monarchy and the palace shadow government are positively in power'.[57]

Regime control of policy agenda is even more apparent in foreign policy where the monarchy reigns supreme with vast discretionary powers, through one of its main sovereignty ministries of foreign affairs, in addition to the overall domain of foreign policy-making, which has largely been dominated by Morocco's perennial issue of the Western Sahara conflict – a conflict that serves as a lynchpin for Morocco's foreign policy and its relations with regional and international powers.

The Western Sahara Conflict: Morocco's Perennial Issue

The Western Sahara has been object of intense litigation and military conflict since the area's Spanish decolonisation in 1975. The territory was then divided between Morocco and Mauritania, without the consent of the local population. Subsequently, the Sahrawi people, led by the POLISARIO Front (Spanish acronym for the Popular Front for the Liberation of Saguia al-Hamra and Rio de Oro) and supported by Algeria, launched a war of secession and in the process established the Sahrawi Arab Democratic Republic (SADR) in 1976.[58]

Mauritania relinquished its southern territory of the Western Sahara in 1978, which Morocco immediately annexed. Guerrilla warfare ensued against Morocco for a decade, during most of the 1980s. The end of the Cold War and the collapse of the Soviet Union gave the United Nations an opportunity to force both parties to sign a cease-fire and accept the terms for an UN-sponsored referendum for self-determination. However, since 1992 the United Nations have been unsuccessful in implementing the referendum due to conflicting claims put forward by both Morocco and the POLISARIO Front, especially in relation to the identification process for residents of the Western Sahara.[59] While Morocco claims historical links to the territory, the POLISARIO argues for self-determination, stating that they are a people different from the Moroccans to the north and thus have a legitimate right to secede from Morocco.

The impetus for a referendum has somewhat diminished, largely because of Morocco's autonomy plan of 2007, which would make the Western Sahara a semi-autonomous region under Moroccan sovereignty.[60] But the referendum in the Western Sahara has been beset by two issues: difficulty in determining voter eligibility and Morocco's historical ties to the region. The concept of self-determination has long dominated discourses on the Western Sahara conflict. As such, the conflict's resolution has depended on identifying who qualifies as Sahrawi and, thereby, is eligible to vote in the referendum. Modern conceptions of self-determination lack the basic parameters for defining a 'people' entitled to self-determination or autonomy. As with most conflicts, the dizzying number of UN resolutions on the Western Sahara conflict fail to demarcate the contours of identity, while clearly positing self-determination as a *sine qua non* to self-governance.[61]

The Western Sahara conflict has recently witnessed a marked departure from issues of self-determination, identity determinants and the historicity of the region. These nascent narratives are arguably influenced by the mounting threat of radical Islamism in the region and renewed interest from international powers. Consequently, recent academic and media attention has framed the Western Sahara quagmire almost primarily as a struggle against Moroccan authoritarianism and its inherent 'tension between a rule of law and respect for human rights and that of global geopolitics'.[62] While it is difficult to argue against the robust authoritarianism that still controls the main protagonists in the conflict, including the POLISARIO Front, as I have argued, 'these emerging narratives do not advance our understanding of the complex nature of the conflict and offer only a partial reading' into the conflict.[63]

Furthermore, these authoritarianism-based accounts unduly eschew Morocco's important historical claims because of its abuses of human rights and undemocratic state system. In other words, the fact that Morocco is an authoritarian state does not delegitimise its claims to the territory.

The conflict has so many complex dimensions that a new focus on regime types and political comportment of the state will not help advance it towards a comprehensive solution. Narratives on authoritarianism also place much more emphasis on Morocco's autocratic regime as an impediment to the resolution of the conflict, with little or nothing to say about equally, if not more, repressive regimes in Algeria and the POLISARIO-controlled camps in Tindouf, in southwestern Algeria.[64]

The concept of self-determination is an important dimension of the conflict, but its modern application through the United Nations has de-emphasised the historical territorial claims of Morocco in the Western Sahara. Modern self-determination theory in its two broad categories – that is, classical and secessionist – neglects the colonial legacy of the territory, the problem of identity determinants and the difficulty of identifying the indigenous peoples of the territory due to its emphasis on a rather rigid positivist legal framework of identification.[65]

The nascent anti-authoritarian narratives espouse these shortcomings and provide a limited historical account of the conflict. They set the Spanish colonial rule of the region as a starting point for the history of the conflict. Hence, the story goes that, after the Spanish had left the territory in 1975, Morocco – taking advantage of a highly contentious and ambiguous opinion from the International Court of Justice which states that Morocco had some historical ties in the form of allegiance to some of the Sahrawi tribes – mobilised a popular march to annex the Western Sahara. This reading of history treats the region prior to Spanish colonisation as *terra nullius*, a 'no man's land' devoid of any vestiges of political order or forms of governance.[66]

Such historical reading is misleading. Prior to Spanish rule in 1902, local Sahrawi tribes, while enjoying a great deal of autonomy, did have historical ties in the form of allegiance rites to various Moroccan monarchs, as recognised in the 1975

ICJ advisory opinion.[67] This is what Morocco's autonomy plan offers the Sahrawis in the region: a return to a historical reality and modicum of governance for the local population under nominal rule by Morocco. The POLISARIO Front and Algeria summarily rejected the plan and demanded a full withdrawal of Morocco from the territory, as well as a return to a self-determination plebiscite.[68]

Algeria's involvement highlights another important dimension of the conflict. Beyond self-determination and identity construction, the conflict in the Western Sahara is geopolitical as well. Regional stability in the Maghreb and the Sahel regions further complicate the Moroccan-Algerian entente, especially considering the threat of radical Islamist terrorism in the Sahel region with the deteriorating security situation in Libya and Tunisia. Self-determination without a calibrated process of constructive negotiations may embolden other secessionist claims in the region and create a power struggle in much of the southern parts of the Maghreb region.[69] In fact, the doctrine of *uti possidetis* in international law was specifically formulated in the nineteenth century to put an end to the nature of irredentist conflicts potentially destructive to regions and states.[70]

The conflict in the Western Sahara has raged, but has been largely ignored for almost four decades, and there seems to be no end in sight. All parties have held steadfast to their intransigent positions as Morocco's foreign and military complex is dominated by the stale-mated conflict in the Western Sahara.

The Western Sahara as a Lynchpin for Morocco's Foreign Policy

The Western Sahara conflict has influenced Morocco's foreign policy-making as the kingdom has fervently sought regional and international recognition. As a lynchpin issue for Morocco's foreign policy, the conflict has dictated Morocco's relations with regional and international partners. Morocco's overture to Africa and the vast investment in key African countries is meant to draw wider acceptance of Morocco's claim on the Western Sahara. Similarly, Morocco's tensions with traditional allies in Europe has been dictated by resistance to Morocco's side in the conflict, at times to the detriment of the strong economic ties between the European Union and Morocco. In 2019, the EU was Morocco's largest trade partner, with 64 percent of its goods going to EU markets.[71]

Morocco has repeatedly quarrelled with Europe over the Western Sahara, especially with Germany and Spain, as Europe sought to press Morocco on issues of self-determination. In May 2021, Morocco was furious with Spain's hosting the leader of the POLISARIO front, Brahim Ghali, for medical reasons. In response to what Morocco perceived as a 'test of friendship', the kingdom allowed scores of Moroccans, adults and children, to cross the border into Spanish territory in the northern Moroccan enclave of Ceuta.[72] Morocco has at times used the card of illegal immigrants as pressure point for the EU. The tensions further heightened when Morocco suddenly suspended all cooperation with the German embassy in Rabat in March 2021, citing 'deep disagreements'.[73] This may be due in part to Germany's strong reaction to the US recognition of Morocco's sovereignty over the Western Sahara, but also the German snub of Morocco in an international meeting about Libya. EU-Moroccan relations further deteriorated after an EU court ruled that EU-Morocco trade deals including farm and fish products were null and void because of a lack of consent from the people of the Western Sahara.[74]

As those tensions rocked European-Moroccan relations, the kingdom has had its own Asia pivot, as it has pursued an intentional strategy to mitigate over-reliance on traditional European partners. In this vein, Morocco has courted foreign investments from Asia, especially China, as the country continues to market itself as a strategic, secure African trade hub. China has been keen to strategically position its goods and economic reach closer to Europe and has invested heavily in Morocco's infrastructure, including Morocco's $10 billion Tanger Med Port, dubbed the largest port in Africa.[75]

Most strikingly, Morocco has invested heavily in Africa, seeking greater diplomatic and political influence in the African Union, where the Western Sahara issue is largely dominated by Algeria's stance. Morocco's Africa strategy culminated in the kingdom's re-joining the African Union in 2017, after more than three decades of absence due to the African Union's recognition of the Sahrawi Arab Democratic Republic, as official representatives of the POLISARIO Front in the Western Sahara in 1984. Under the direction of King Mohammed VI, Moroccan investment in Africa reached its zenith in the period between 2008 and 2018, increasing by 68 percent, as Moroccan exports to western African countries tripled.[76]

Morocco has been quite confident in seeking a greater leadership role in regional conflicts such as the Libyan peace process, despite tensions with the European Union. However, Morocco's steady and bold foreign policy reached its peak with the US recognition of Morocco's sovereignty over the Western Sahara in December 2020. In a final act of the Trump administration's foreign policy, President Donald Trump announced that Morocco and Israel had reached a deal to normalise relations, making the kingdom the fourth Arab country to establish relations with Israel as part of the administration's 'Abraham Accords'. In exchange, the United States recognised Morocco's sovereignty claims, upending decades of US policy towards the Western Sahara. Under the Biden administration, the United States has reviewed Trump's policy and has so far maintained the tripartite deal with Morocco and Israel, publicly and privately encouraging the UN process to push for conflict resolution in the Western Sahara under the umbrella of the autonomy plan put forth by Morocco in 2007. However, the Biden administration has made no efforts to establish a US consulate in the Western Sahara and has ceded the policy space back to the United Nations, in an attempt to distance itself from the Trump position. Nevertheless, the Trump-era recognition of Moroccan claims to the Western Sahara has further bolstered Morocco and given it impetus to solidify its positions on key regional issues and to stand up to major international allies in Europe.

Conclusion

Morocco's confidence at home in successfully placating the challenges of the post-Arab uprisings' era was most clearly manifested in its strategies towards the 20 February movement, the Hirak protests and the resurgence of the Islamist PJD popularity at the polls. In doing so, the Moroccan regime has further consolidated its foothold in an increasingly authoritarian edifice. But the protests of the Moroccan 'Spring' have also emboldened a public consciousness and a political culture of protests, which have exposed a new dilemma for the monarchy: the inability of the regime to maintain its authority as an arbiter over the political system, while at the same time managing the political system and opposition forces. Confidence at home has also fuelled an assertive foreign policy that centres on the issue of the Western Sahara as a lynchpin for Moroccan foreign policy and a consensus-building nationalist issue enabling the regime to remain, for now, immune from any substantive challenge to its enduring status in Moroccan politics.

Notes

1. Mohamed Daadaoui, 'Whither the Arab Spring in Morocco', *Muftah*, 19 August 2011, https://muftah.org/whither-the-arab-spring-in-morocco/#.Yyjk8nbMK38.
2. Daadaoui, 'Whither the Arab Spring in Morocco'.
3. Mohamed Daadaoui, 'A Moroccan Monarchical Exception?' *Foreign Policy*, 14 December 2012, https://foreignpolicy.com/2012/12/14/a-moroccan-monarchical-exception/.
4. Daadaoui, 'A Moroccan Monarchical Exception?'
5. Daadaoui, 'A Moroccan Monarchical Exception?'
6. Daadaoui, 'A Moroccan Monarchical Exception?'
7. Daadaoui, 'A Moroccan Monarchical Exception?'
8. Daadaoui, 'A Moroccan Monarchical Exception?'
9. For a full account and analysis of rituals of power in Morocco, see Mohamed Daadaoui, *Maintaining the Makhzen: Rituals of Power and the Islamist Challenge* (New York: Palgrave, 2011).
10. James Scott, *Domination and the Art of Resistance* (New Haven, CT: Yale University Press, 1990), 39.
11. Daadaoui, 'A Moroccan Monarchical Exception?'
12. Daadaoui, 'A Moroccan Monarchical Exception?'
13. Daadaoui, 'A Moroccan Monarchical Exception?'
14. Daadaoui, 'A Moroccan Monarchical Exception?'
15. Asef Bayat, *Life as Politics: How Ordinary People Change the Middle East* (Amsterdam: Amsterdam University Press, 2013), 14.
16. Bayat, *Life as Politics*.
17. Bayat, *Life as Politics*, 20.
18. Mohamed Daadaoui, 'Morocco's "Spring" and the Failure of the Protest Movement', *HuffPost*, 24 February 2016, https://www.huffpost.com/entry/moroccos-spring-and-the-failure-of-the-protest-movement_b_9287158.
19. King Mohammed VI's Speech, 8 March 2011. Translated by the author.

20. Mohamed Daadaoui, 'Of Monarchs and Islamists: The "Refo-Lutionary" Promise of the PJD Islamists and Regime Control in Morocco', *Middle East Critique* 26, no. 4 (2 October 2017): 355–71.
21. 'Morocco Approves King Mohammed's Constitutional Reforms', *BBC*, 2 July 2011, https://www.bbc.com/news/world-africa-13976480.
22. Marina Ottaway, 'The New Moroccan Constitution: Real Change or More of the Same?' *Carnegie Endowment for International Peace*, 2011, https://carnegieendowment.org/2011/06/20/new-moroccan-constitution-real-change-or-more-of-same-pub-44731.
23. Mohamed Daadaoui, 'Islamism and the State in Morocco', *Hudson Institute*, 29 April 2016, http://www.hudson.org/research/12286-islamism-and-the-state-in-morocco.
24. Irene Fernandez Molina, 'The Monarchy vs. the 20 February Movement: Who Holds the Reins of Political Change in Morocco?' *Mediterranean Politics* 16 (2011): 435–41.
25. Daadaoui, 'Morocco's "Spring" and the Failure of the Protest Movement'.
26. Daadaoui, 'Morocco's "Spring" and the Failure of the Protest Movement'.
27. Daadaoui, 'Of Monarchs and Islamists'.
28. Daadaoui, 'A Moroccan Monarchical Exception?'
29. Daadaoui, 'Morocco's "Spring" and the Failure of the Protest Movement'.
30. Mohamed Daadaoui, 'Maghreb Blog', n. d., http://www.maghreblog.com/.
31. 'Morocco: Imider Amazigh Movement Decides to Dismantle Protest Camp after 8 Years', *Nationalia*, 9 September 2019, https://www.nationalia.info/brief/11245/morocco-imider-amazigh-movement-decides-to-dismantle-protest-camp-after-8-years; Ilhalm Al-Talbi, 'Water Shortage in the Maghrib: Morocco's Thirst Revolution', *Goethe Institut: Perspectives*, March 2021, https://www.goethe.de/prj/ruy/en/watlife/21718884.html; Saad Guerraoui, 'Jerada, the Graveyard of Clandestine Miners in Eastern Morocco', *The Arab Weekly*, 15 February 2018, https://thearabweekly.com/jerada-graveyard-clandestine-miners-eastern-morocco. For an analysis of the boycott, see Mohammed Masbah, '"Let It Spoil!" Morocco's Boycott and the Empowerment of "Regular" Citizen', *Aljazeera Center for Studies*, 14 November 2018, https://studies.aljazeera.net/en/reports/2018/11/181114115931285.html.
32. Daadaoui, 'Maghreb Blog'.
33. Aida Alami, 'Protests Erupt in Morocco Over Fish Vendor's Death in Garbage Compactor', *The New York Times*, 30 October 2016, sec.

World, https://www.nytimes.com/2016/10/31/world/middleeast/protests-erupt-in-morocco-over-fish-vendors-death-in-garbage-compactor.html.
34. Mariam Elmaslouhi, 'Protests Erupt in Morocco Following Fish Vendor's Brutal Death in Garbage Compactor', *Global Voices*, 31 October 2016, https://globalvoices.org/2016/10/31/morocco-protests-fish-vendors-death/.
35. 'Affaire Mouhcine Fikri: Le roi intervient', *L'Economiste*, 30 October 2016, https://www.leconomiste.com/flash-infos/affaire-mouhcine-fikri-le-roi-intervient.
36. 'Morocco Vows to Punish Culprits as Protests Rage over Fishmonger's Death', *Middle East Eye*, 1 November 2016, https://www.middleeasteye.net/news/morocco-vows-punish-culprits-protests-rage-over-fishmongers-death.
37. 'Morocco Country Report', *Arab Barometer* V, 2019, https://www.arabbarometer.org/wp-content/uploads/ABV_Morocco_Report_Public-Opinion_Arab-Barometer_2019.pdf.
38. Mohamed Daadaoui, 'The King's Dilemma in Morocco', *Al Jazeera Online*, 6 November 2017, https://www.aljazeera.com/opinions/2017/11/6/the-kings-dilemma-in-morocco.
39. Daadaoui, 'Of Monarchs and Islamists'.
40. Daadaoui, 'Maghreb Blog'.
41. Daadaoui, 'The King's Dilemma in Morocco'.
42. Daadaoui, 'Maghreb Blog'.
43. Daadaoui, 'Maghreb Blog'.
44. '5 Months of Government "Blockage" – What Was It All For?', *Morocco World News*, 31 March 2017, https://www.moroccoworldnews.com/2017/03/212561/5-months-government-blockage.
45. 'Full Text of King Mohammed VI Speech on the Throne Day', *Morocco World News*, July 2017, https://www.moroccoworldnews.com/2017/07/224848/full-text-king-mohammed-vi-speech-throne-day.
46. Daadaoui, 'Maghreb Blog'.
47. Daadaoui, 'Maghreb Blog'.
48. 'Full Text of King Mohammed VI's Address to the Nation Marking Morocco's Throne Day', *Morocco on the Move*, 31 July 2017, https://moroccoonthemove.com/2017/07/31/full-text-king-mohammed-vis-address-nation-marking-moroccos-throne-day/.
49. Daadaoui, 'Maghreb Blog'.
50. Daadaoui, 'The King's Dilemma in Morocco'.
51. Daadaoui, 'A Moroccan Monarchical Exception?'
52. 'Morocco Press Agency (MAP) Press Release', *MAP*, n. d., http://www.mapexpress.ma/ar/actualite/.

53. Samia Errazzouki, 'Morocco's King Replaces PM Benkirane Amidst Post-Election Deadlock', *Reuters*, 15 March 2017, https://www.reuters.com/article/us-morocco-politics-idUSKBN16M3A9.
54. Yassine Majdi, 'Qu'est-ce que le "tahakoum"?' *TelQuel*, 7 July 2016, https://telquel.ma/2016/07/07/quest-ce-tahakoum_1504927.
55. Marina Ottaway, 'Morocco: Can the Third Way Succeed?' *Carnegie Endowment for International Peace*, 31 July 2012, https://carnegieendowment.org/2012/07/31/morocco-can-third-way-succeed-pub-48968.
56. Ellen Lust-Okar, *Structuring Conflict in the Arab World: Incumbents, Opponents, and Institutions* (Cambridge: Cambridge University Press, 2007), 170–73.
57. Mohamed Daadaoui, 'Morocco's King Just Named a New Prime Minister, in Case You Forgot Who's in Charge', *Washington Post*, 20 March 2017, https://www.washingtonpost.com/news/monkey-cage/wp/2017/03/20/moroccos-king-just-named-a-new-prime-minister-in-case-you-forgot-whos-in-charge/.
58. Mohamed Daadaoui, 'The Western Sahara Conflict: Towards a Constructivist Approach to Self-Determination', *The Journal of North African Studies* 13, no. 2 (1 June 2008): 143–56.
59. Daadaoui, 'The Western Sahara Conflict'.
60. Mohamed Daadaoui, 'Morocco's Unmissed Opportunity in the Western Sahara', *Arab Center Washington DC*, https://arabcenterdc.org/resource/moroccos-unmissed-opportunity-in-the-western-sahara/.
61. Mohamed Daadaoui, 'On Stephen Zunes' Statement about Morocco, Israel, and the Western Sahara', *Maghreb Blog*, 11 September 2012.
62. Samia Errazzouki and Allison L. McManus, 'Roundtable Introduction: Beyond Dominant Narratives on the Western Sahara', *Jadaliyya*, 3 June 2013, https://www.jadaliyya.com/Details/28716/Roundtable-Introduction-Beyond-Dominant-Narratives-on-the-Western-Sahara.
63. Mohamed Daadaoui, 'The Western Sahara Conflict: On Authoritarianism and Self-Determination', *Muftah*, 25 June 2013, https://muftah.org/the-western-sahara-conflict-on-authoritarianism-self-determination/#.Yyjps3bMK38.
64. 'Off the Radar: Human Rights in the Tindouf Refugee Camps', *Human Rights Watch*, 18 October 2014, https://www.hrw.org/report/2014/10/18/radar/human-rights-tindouf-refugee-camps#.
65. Daadaoui, 'The Western Sahara Conflict: On Authoritarianism and Self-Determination'.

66. Daadaoui, 'The Western Sahara Conflict: On Authoritarianism and Self-Determination'.
67. 'Advisory Opinion of the International Court of Justice', *International Court of Justice*, 16 October 1975, https://www.icj-cij.org/public/files/case-related/61/061-19751016-ADV-01-00-EN.pdf.
68. Daadaoui, 'The Western Sahara Conflict: On Authoritarianism and Self-Determination'.
69. Daadaoui, 'The Western Sahara Conflict: On Authoritarianism and Self-Determination'.
70. A territory remains with its controlling party at the end of conflict unless otherwise stated by a treaty or agreement.
71. 'Morocco Trade Picture', *European Commission*, n. d., https://ec.europa.eu/trade/policy/countries-and-regions/countries/morocco/index_en.htm.
72. Anna Palacio, 'Spain-Morocco Tensions: How the EU Can Make Progress on Western Sahara', *European Council of Foreign Relations*, 17 June 2021, https://ecfr.eu/article/spain-morocco-tensions-how-the-eu-can-make-progress-on-western-sahara/.
73. 'Morocco Stops Cooperation with German Embassy', *Middle East Monitor*, n. d., https://www.middleeastmonitor.com/20210303-morocco-stops-cooperation-with-german-embassy/.
74. 'EU Court Annuls EU-Morocco Trade Deals over Western Sahara Consent', *Reuters*, 29 September 2021, https://www.reuters.com/world/europe/eu-court-annuls-eu-morocco-trade-deals-over-western-sahara-consent-2021-09-29/.
75. Irwin-Hunt, Alex, 'A Signal for Morocco's Development', *FDI Intelligence*, 23 December 2020, https://www.fdiintelligence.com/article/79117.
76. Yasmina Abouzzohour, 'Progress and Missed Opportunities: Morocco Enters Its Third Decade Under King Mohammed VI', *Brookings Institution*, 29 July 2020, https://www.brookings.edu/research/progress-and-missed-opportunities-morocco-enters-its-third-decade-under-king-mohammed-vi.

4
Tunisia's Unfinished Revolution: Addressing Regional Inequality

Sarah E. Yerkes

Introduction

Regional disparities, which have plagued Tunisia since independence but were exacerbated by an official Ben Ali-era policy of favouring the coastal governorates, left the country deeply divided and fuelled the 2010–11 revolution. Tunisia began an official decentralisation process in May 2018, but four years later little progress has been made to devolve power from the central state to local authorities. The 2020 Coronavirus outbreak further divided the country, with more than half of the governorates lacking access to intensive care facilities at the outset of the pandemic. This chapter examines the causes and consequences of regional socio-economic inequality, including protest and violent extremism; assesses the successes and failures of the government's efforts at addressing this issue; and offers recommendations for local actors and international donors to improve governance at the local level and to level the playing field for the traditionally neglected interior and southern regions, in an effort to prevent instability in the future.

Regional marginalisation has been destabilising for Tunisia, leading to anger and frustration which has manifested in protest – most notably the 2010–11 revolution – as well as aided violent extremist recruitment, and it has led to increased regular and irregular migration and suicide. As Larbi Sadiki argues, '[w]hile politicians pay lip service to regional development, the gap continues to widen between power holders' declaratory policies and local communities' expectations'.[1] Sadiki points to three forms of marginalisation simultaneously taking place in Tunisia:

First, it consists of regional estrangement from the body politic qua marginalisation, as the country's South and West are relegated to a marginal status. The second level is economic and developmental estrangement from value-making. This hinders the ability to create goods and services and find employment. The third aspect is human estrangement, whereby people are separated from national wealth and distributive justice. Here estrangement is a loss of agency and the potential for self-regeneration qua worthiness, identity and belonging.[2]

Understanding the history of regional marginalisation in Tunisia and its manifestation today is crucial to addressing the political, social and economic challenges facing the country and, in turn, their impact on the broader MENA region as well as the West. The vast socio-economic differences between the centre (or the capital and other coastal enclaves) and the peripheries (or the interior and southern regions) matter not just for Tunisians, but also have a direct impact on Europe, by contributing to the growing number of North African migrants trying to reach Europe's shores. They matter for North Africa more broadly, as Tunisians outside of the centre are forced into the informal economy and, at times, into the arms of extremist recruiters. And they matter for Western governments and NGOs who seek to support the success of Tunisia's democratic transition. Additionally, one of the reasons why scholars failed to predict the 2011 revolution is their tendency to ignore the periphery, often taking a top-down approach that is mostly focused on the capital. By ignoring the periphery, scholars are both contributing to the centre-periphery divide and missing important dynamics about areas in which 'the presence of the state is limited, highly contested or intertwined with forms of power and governance'.[3] As Daniela Huber and Lorenzo Kemal argue, '[t]he major lesson that we can learn about peripheries and their role in the Arab Spring' is that 'the seeds for changing the face of politics and polities are within the peripheries themselves'.[4]

The Problem: Regional Marginalisation

Regional marginalisation is neither a new problem in Tunisia, nor an accidental one. The first Tunisian president following independence, Habib Bourguiba, intentionally cut off certain regions of the country as a way to punish his main political rival, Salah Ben Youssef, and his followers, known as Youssefists. Bourguiba's followers, known as Bourguibists, were concentrated in the coastal region, subscribed to a Francophile ideology and were staunchly secular. Youssefists, conversely, were concentrated in the south and interior regions, subscribed to a Pan-Arab ideology and were, for the most part, staunchly anti-colonial. The confrontation between the Bourguibists and the Youssefists was violent, peaking with an armed insurrection in 1956 in the interior against the French and the newly independent Tunisian state. A French military operation eventually subdued the Youssefists, and Ben Youssef was sentenced to death in absentia in December 1956 and assassinated in Frankfurt in 1961.

As Intissar Kherigi argues, even today there is a feeling that regional inequalities are not 'spontaneously produced by market forces or globalization', but rather are due to 'a systematic policy of marginalization of certain regions'.[5] Thus, she notes, 'regional inequalities were baked or built into the process of state-building'.[6] And pre-independence, French colonial authorities created structures and policies, such as investing in infrastructure in the northern and coastal regions, that set up the disparities that have plagued independent Tunisia.[7] Thus, while the independent Tunisian state adopted a form of decentralisation, the type of decentralisation put in place in 1956 is 'pure fiction' according to Neji Baccouche, who argues: 'Centralization was a political choice which addressed the need of rebuilding a united state which was able to fight against an ancient tribal system'.[8] Regional marginalisation was relatively easy to enforce under Tunisia's highly centralised state structure. In the post-independence period, little attention was paid to local affairs with the focus, instead, on building national unity. The 1959 constitution has only one article discussing local rule, stating only 'the advice [that] municipal and regional councils manage local affairs, within conditions provided by law'.[9]

Following the French prefecture system, Tunisia was divided into twenty-four regions, which were then divided into municipalities. But all real power was maintained at the central state level. The president of Tunisia appointed a governor (*wali*) who was responsible for overseeing regional affairs and chaired the regional council. While the governor was not allowed to vote in the regional council, in practice the governor's decisions were directly transmitted back to Tunis, leaving local authorities relatively powerless.[10] The physical creation of the regions further disempowered local actors. Many of the regions had arbitrarily drawn boundaries, with some regions and municipalities created to divide politically troublesome areas, rather than out of any sort of development or relational considerations. And more than 50 percent of Tunisia's territory was non-municipalised, meaning that the inhabitants were not represented by local officials. Furthermore, local authorities reported to the Ministry of the Interior – a feared entity – leaving them powerless.

By intentionally marginalising certain areas, Bourguiba's government's actions led to more, not less instability. As the centre, particularly the capital, became more modernised and affluent, the periphery was left behind, resulting in an unequal distribution of wealth and state attention. A further factor contributing to marginalisation has been nation-building efforts, particularly following independence. It was crucial for the Bourguiba government to promote unity and prioritise Tunisian identity over local identity, in order to both centralise power and eliminate the threat from local actors who might undermine the national project.[11] As Laryssa Chomiak argues, this played out particularly within parliament, where opposition figures were under-represented, making it difficult for the legislature to address 'the grievances of marginalised and unemployed populations'.[12]

Tunisia, like many other countries in the region at the time, followed a corporatist model, wherein governments provide services to the people in exchange for their quiescence. As Mona Harb and Sami Attalah argue, '[t]he corporatist model was necessary in the post-colonial era to consolidate independent power and thrived on the narrative that the strong central state was essential to shield against threats to sovereignty and promote stability'.[13] However, the corporatist model eventually failed in Tunisia, due in part to demographic changes as well as poor economic conditions that made it difficult for governments to provide adequate services to their citizens.[14] Furthermore, citizen empowerment spurred on by globalisation, access to information and the growth of the internet raised the concept of relative deprivation, particularly for those who lived outside the core and made citizens less willing to remain silent in the face of what they interpreted as marginalisation.

This deliberate stratification of coast and interior persisted under Bourguiba's successor Zine el Abidine Ben Ali. Under Ben Ali, two-thirds of public investment were allocated to coastal regions, and clientelist networks regulated access to employment in state-owned companies in the interior regions (that is, the Gafsa Phosphate Company). Security services, the police force and customs officials kept the border economy under tight control. A system of patronage also exacerbated competition among tribal networks in the region, resulting in increased conflict over employment and welfare between social groups.[15] Additionally, while neo-liberal policies, particularly Ben Ali's structural adjustment programme, encouraged 'foreign investment, created a flexible workforce and lowered taxes on businesses', the economic growth was not evenly distributed, concentrating wealth in the centre and away from the periphery.[16]

Some efforts were made to distribute a certain amount of wealth or establish development projects in marginalised regions, but these were short-lived. Between 1995 and 1998, the Caisse, a national solidarity fund, implemented development projects in Sidi Bouzid and in poorer regions. However, these projects came to a halt after 2000, when Ben Ali and his inner circle used the funds to 'sustain their economic activities'.[17] While both the Bourguiba and Ben Ali governments sought to marginalise the peripheral regions to thwart competitors to state power, these efforts back-fired in some cases. This encouraged residents of the peripheral regions to turn to alternative sources of power, such as kinship networks and other local actors, for service provision.[18] Civil society organisations played (and continue to play) the role of an alternative to the state when the central government was (is) either unable or unwilling to provide for those in the periphery in sufficient measure.[19] Furthermore, marginalisation led to both protest and, at times, violent extremism. Not surprisingly, the areas of Tunisia that have traditionally produced the most violent extremists are those that have been marginalised by the state.

And 'in 2014, 67 percent of all Tunisian migrants detained by Libyan authorities hailed from Tunisia's centre and south'.[20]

The clear favouritism for some regions can be seen in the allocation of the state's budget. For example, 'in the Ben Ali regime's final budget before it fell, 82 percent of state funds were dedicated to coastal areas, compared to only 18 percent for the interior'.[21] Some scholars have found this form of dissonance to be sufficient to fuel large-scale expressions of discontent, even when traditional factors of political destabilisation such as a youth bulge and an ongoing democratic transition are absent.[22] The Ben Ali government further exacerbated the centre-periphery divide in Tunisia by prioritising tourism, more prevalent in the coastal regions, as the country's primary economic driver over agriculture and industry, more prevalent in the interior.[23] And while the interior regions have been crucial to Tunisia's economy, particularly through their natural resources, the centre has often exploited those resources, leaving the regions rich in natural resources under-developed and fuelling discontent.[24] As Sadiki argues,

> The country became mired in skewed 'metropolis-satellite' interactions: its centre would exploit capital and resources from its peripheries, blocking any capacity for economic self-sufficiency or self-renewal. This locked the peripheral regions into a dynamic that exacerbated, rather than eliminated, underdevelopment.[25]

This phenomenon is most visible in the interior region of Gafsa, part of Tunisia's mining basin, home to the Gafsa Phosphate Company (GPC). As part of Ben Ali's structural adjustment programme, the GPC underwent a gradual restructuring in 1986, including closing the underground mines and focusing on above-ground exploitation, leading to a 75-percent decrease in personnel by 2006.[26] This decision angered the residents of Gafsa, as the Tunisian state failed to implement concomitant economic diversification plans or development projects to offset this loss, thus leading the majority of the population to feel that, relative to the Sahel and other regions, where Tunisia's political and economic elites secure their rents, the government has not allocated sufficient resources and attention to the mining basin.[27]

In 2006, while revenues from exports of the phosphates mined in Gafsa were increasing dramatically, there was simultaneously a tremendous loss in jobs. GPC sub-contractors, who made up much of the Gafsa workforce, continued to earn low wages and work under precarious conditions, with the sky-rocketing revenues benefitting the coastal elites and those outside of Tunisia. This, combined with frustration over hiring preferences for friends and relatives of the GPC head Amara Abbassi, sparked a revolt on 5 January 2008. The revolt lasted for six months and took on various forms of dissent: hunger strikes, demonstrations, sit-ins and disruptions of economic activity in phosphate extraction areas, iron ore washing plants and railway tracks. Riots, carried out primarily by high school students and other youth, targeted police and government representatives. Tires were burned on main roads to block entry to the towns. The protesters – first unemployed university graduates and then eventually temporary workers, high school students and the families of phosphate mine workers who had suffered accidents – demanded jobs and a fair distribution of phosphate revenues to the local area. The protests eventually subsided after the army was deployed in Redeyef on 7 June 2008 and the leaders of the protest movement were arrested.

Gafsa continued to experience large-scale strikes and protests following the 2010–11 revolution, also related to unemployment and the central government's insufficient attention to the plight of local residents. In January 2017, hundreds of protestors clashed with police forces while demanding employment on the anniversary of the revolution. In March 2018, protestors burned a police station, demanding jobs and development after two months of protests across Gafsa. And in May 2020, hundreds of university graduates engaged in protests, demanding employment. Protestors halted phosphate output by staging sit-ins at the Gafsa Phosphate Company. Protests continued throughout 2020, halting the entire phosphate output in Gafsa in November 2020. And in January 2021, employees of Gafsa's public administrative institutions held a general strike to demand the implementation of the earlier agreements calling for jobs and development programmes for the region.

In addition to experiencing regional marginalisation, minority groups such as Black Tunisians and Amazigh also suffered in other ways. This marginalisation trend dates to the Bourguiba era, where, as Ahmed Gwirah, President of the Taoujout Association for the Preservation of the Amazigh Villages, told *Al-Monitor*: 'The situation for us in Taoujout was better under the French. They built a lot for us, including two wells. They also built the roads connecting us [to the outside]. That's development'.[28] Amazigh marginalisation was tied to the Ben Youssef-Bourguiba rivalry, as many Amazigh lived in the mountain villages that were also home to Ben Youssef supporters.[29] Thus, Gwirah says that '[t]he real marginalisation started after independence', pointing to the case of the village of Zraoua, which the Tunisian authorities destroyed after independence, cutting off water and power and forcibly moving the inhabitants to a new town in the plains as a way to control them and integrate them into the Arabic-speaking population.[30] The punishment of the areas identified with Ben Youssef thus continues today. Kherigi notes that a member of a municipal council in Jemna described the ongoing marginalisation faced by his region in the following way: 'This area was historically allied with the Youssefists against Bourguiba – we went against the central state, and we have been punished'.[31]

Marginalisation Backfires: The Tunisian Revolution

Given the history of centre-periphery relations in Tunisia, it was not surprising that the protests that would unseat Ben Ali in 2010 started in the interior. When Mohammed Bouazizi, a fruit-seller who suffered from the same broken social contract and corruption that plagued so many in the interior, set himself on fire, his act of hopelessness, despair and frustration about the authorities resonated with Tunisians across the Sidi Bouzid governorate, as much as throughout the marginalised regions.

The protests that would become the revolution began on 17 December 2010, in Sidi Bouzid; however, three days later, youth in Kasserine, Gafsa and Sfax held solidarity protests, and activists from Tunis and other regions began to travel to Sidi Bouzid to join the protests there. The first large-scale protests held in Tunis in solidarity with Sidi Bouzid took place on 25 December, steadily growing over the following days. The protests escalated following Bouazizi's death from his burns on 4 January 2011, with Ben Ali stepping down ten days later.

As former Minister of Local Affairs and the Environment Riadh Mouaker noted, work on decentralisation had started even before the constitution was written and was one of the earliest priorities of revolution.[32] Yet, the socio-economic conditions and regional disparities that led to the 2010–11 uprising have not been adequately addressed, meaning that the grievances are still there. This is clear from protest numbers. In May 2017, marginalised areas in Tunisia 'bore witness to 1,533 protests', fuelled by unemployment, low levels of development and the unequal distribution of wealth. Despite the focus that newer governments have placed on regional development and decentralisation, they have yet to respond adequately to the calls of the protestors.[33]

A Decade after the Revolution: Persistent Regional Disparities Mean Poor Governance

A decade after the revolution, the Tunisian government has failed to address the root causes of marginalisation, leaving a massive socio-economic gap between the privileged coastal areas and the southern and interior regions. These economic disparities were not confined to regional divides. An Oxfam study found that in 2017 more than 40 percent of the national income was held by the richest 10 percent of the population. And the inequalities were exacerbated by austerity policies championed by the IMF, which led to a significant drop in the share of education and health spending in the public budget. Between 2011 and 2019, the share of public spending devoted to education fell from 26.6 to 17.7 percent and to health from 6.6 to 5 percent.[34]

The wealth gap was a key driver of the 2010–11 revolution, and something that the transitional government vowed to address. Article 12 of the 2014 Tunisian Constitution states that the government would seek social justice, sustainable development, equitable distribution of national wealth and resources and that it would implement a form of 'positive discrimination' to benefit the most impoverished regions.[35] Nevertheless, regional disparities persist, particularly between the wealthy coastal regions and the traditionally marginalised interior and southern regions, resulting in poor governance and concomitant frustration there, which frequently manifests in large-scale protests against local and national officials and contributes to instability.

Part of this is due to a massive disparity in state spending. While some progress has been made in rectifying the lop-sided nature of spending under Ben Ali, in 2013, two years after the revolution, eighteen municipalities still held 51 percent of the state's municipal budget, while 246 held the remaining 49 percent.[36] This results in dramatic differences in the quality and availability of social services, such as education and healthcare, and in infrastructure, such as roads and waste management.

Virtually all social services reflect this incredibly lop-sided development that took place under Ben Ali. In the sphere of education, despite a nationally unified curriculum, the success rates in the first session of the Baccalaureate exam vary widely between regions, with nearly three times as many students in coastal areas passing the exam as those in the marginalised regions. In 2019, only 16 percent of students passed the exam in Kasserine and 20 percent in Kebili, compared to 43 percent in Monastir and 49 percent in Sfax.[37] Additionally, the location of universities is heavily concentrated in the Greater Tunis and Centre-East regions, with sixty-three and fifty-six universities there, respectively, compared to sixteen in the Centre-West and thirteen in the South-West. A 2015–16 study further found that the net enrolment rate for students aged between twelve and eighteen ranged from 92 percent in Ben Arous and 90.6 percent in Tunis to 66.8 percent in Kasserine and 66.5 percent in Kairouan.[38] And while the number of primary schools per 10,000 persons was relatively high in the marginalised regions – 8.66 in Sidi Bouzid and 8.34 in Kairouan (but zero in Kasserine), in comparison to only 4.74 in Tunis – the number of private schools is much higher in Tunis – 10 per 10,000 people – and very low in the marginalised regions (1.27 in Sidi Bouzid, 1.11 in Kairouan and 0.48 in Kasserine); this reflects a difference in access to the higher-quality education that is found in private schools.[39]

Access to medical care is another area where there exists tremendous disparity. In 2019, the number of hospital beds per 1,000 inhabitants varied from 4 in Tunis to less than 1 in Ariana and Ben Arous.[40] And while there were 3.4 doctors per 1,000 inhabitants in 2019 in Tunis, no other region had close to that number. In twelve out of twenty-four regions, there was less than 1, and the second-highest region was Sfax at 1.9.⁴¹ Furthermore, in Ben Arous, the average distance to a regional hospital is eight kilometres, compared to fifty-nine in Tataouine. The average distance to a general hospital or university hospital ranges from two kilometres in Tunis to 333 kilometres in Tozeur.⁴²

Other indicators follow similar trends. Unemployment in 2019 in the South-West (24.6 percent) and South-East (23.9 percent) was more than twice as high as in the Centre-East (10.2 percent) and North-East (10.5 percent).⁴³ Moreover, in 2020 the number of internet subscriptions per 100 inhabitants in Tunis (20.4) was more than four times that of Kasserine (3.9) and Sidi Bouzid (4.8).⁴⁴

Poor Governance Leads to Lack of Trust

These indicators manifest themselves in two important ways: lack of trust in local officials and high levels of frustration with the formal political structures. This frustration plays out in several forms: regular protests about the budget; other forms of non-violent resistance such as labour strikes and shut-downs aimed at countering what is perceived as foreign exploitation of local resources; extremist recruitment; rising suicide rates; and migration – both regular and irregular. In a 2018 survey of regions, residents rated their satisfaction of ninety-five indicators in nine domains (institutions and governance, infrastructure and urbanisation, health, education, IT use, financial inclusion, the job market, business dynamism and innovation), revealing the way in which the regional differences impact the people on the ground. While none of the regions performed particularly well, Tunis performed best at 5.15 (on a scale of zero to ten, with ten meaning very satisfied and zero meaning not at all satisfied), followed by Sfax at 4.5. At the low end are Tozeur at 2.04 and Kebili at 1.7.⁴⁵

These numbers correlate with levels of trust in government – both national and local. In a December 2019 survey conducted by the International Republication Institute, 56 percent of Tunisians rated their government's performance as 'very bad' or 'somewhat bad'.⁴⁶ And 68 percent of respondents said the government was doing a bad job of providing services.

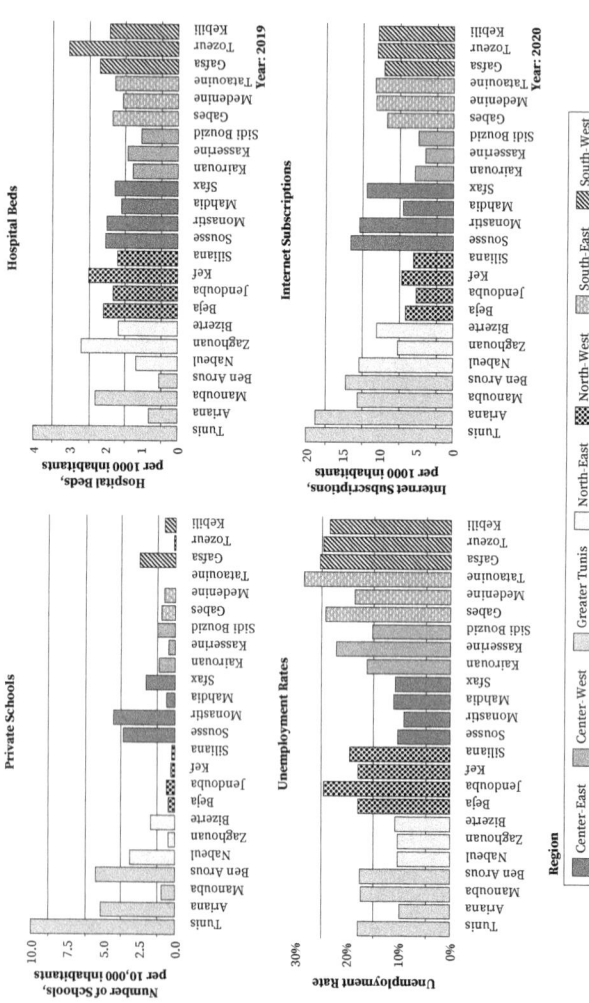

Figure 4.1 Regional Indicators in Tunisia

'La Discrimination Positive: Un principe constitutionnel à concrétiser pour la promotion de l'emploi décent dans les régions,' Organization Internationale du Travail, 2017; 'Annuaire Statistique de La Tunisie: 2015-2019' (National Institute of Statistics, 2021), http://ins.tn/sites/default/files/publication/pdf/annuaire-2019%20avec%20lien_1.pdf; 'Indicateurs de l'emploi et Du Chomage: Deuxieme Trimestre 2019' (National Institute of Statistics, August 2019), http://ins.tn/sites/default/files/publication/pdf/Note_ENPE_2T2019_F2.pdf; 'Annual Report of Infrastructure Indicators: 2020' (National Institute of Statistics, 2020), http://www.ins.tn/sites/default/files/publication/pdf/infrastructure%202020.pdf

Parliament was rated extremely poorly, with 75 percent of respondents saying that parliament did 'nothing' to address the needs of people like them.⁴⁷ In an October 2020 survey by Tunisia Survey, 78 percent of respondents said that they did not have confidence in Speaker of Parliament Rachid Ghannouchi, and 61 percent of respondents stated that they were unsatisfied with President Kais Saied because he did not have a clear programme.⁴⁸

One reason for the low level of trust in the national government is a lack of representation. People in the traditionally marginalised areas do not see national officials from their towns and regions. As one civil society actor from Sidi Bouzid argued, no one in positions of national power is from Sidi Bouzid; thus, it feels like no one is speaking for them.⁴⁹ Additionally, due to both lack of resources and lack of will, members of parliament do not often return to their home districts, leaving citizens disconnected from the central state. While visiting the small town of Kesra in the Siliana Governorate (with a population of less than 3,000 people), there was a rumour that one of the members of parliament was in town. Local activists called around to try to get an audience with her but were unable to find her or confirm whether she was in fact there. This reflects the everyday frustration that residents outside the capital feel when it comes to connecting with those who are elected to represent them.⁵⁰

Poor Governance in Action: The Kamour Protests

Another outcome of poor governance and regional marginalisation consists of popular protest. One recent example is the 2017 Kamour protests in the southern governorate of Tataouine, one of the country's most marginalised regions with the highest levels of unemployment nationally, at around 30 percent.⁵¹ Tataouine is also home to oil and gas fields that contribute to 40 percent of Tunisia's oil production and 20 percent of its gas production.⁵² On 5 April 2017, employees of the oil companies in Tataouine held a general strike in support of twenty-four workers laid off by the Canadian oil company Winstar. As one Tataouine resident, twenty-five-year-old Mahmoud Abdelhour argued, '[i]t was the straw that broke the camel's back', after what local workers perceived as a series of injustices.⁵³ Thus, a few days later, sixty-four protesters began a sit-in on the road used by oil trucks. As Sufian Al-Nasry, one of the demonstrators said, '[p]eople going out to the street, that was a natural result of an accumulation of oppression and a feeling of injustice because of the state's failure to honour its obligations towards its children'.[54]

While the region is home to major oil extraction facilities, few local citizens are employed in the hydrocarbons industry, and the profits rarely reach the local population. Thus, the protesters began by demanding jobs. The Kamour protests grew over the next two months, reaching more than 1,200 people – mostly young and unemployed men from around the region.[55] As twenty-two-year-old Fethi Boufalegha said, '[i]t's not money we are demanding, but development. Oil, salt, phosphate, water and all natural resources must have a return for Tunisia, but we're convinced that our riches have been confiscated by a national elite corrupted by foreign capital'.[56] Another protester, twenty-six-year-old Abdelhaim Katouch stated:

> Youth here have only one ambition: to work in the desert [for the oil companies], but the decision-makers prefer to recruit foreigners or graduates from Sfax, Tunis and the big cities. For thousands of positions, only a few hundred are given to young people from Tataouine.[57]

This was not the first of such protests. Uprisings against the private sector, as well as the local and national government over exploitation of the region's natural resources and the unfair distribution of wealth spring up regularly. One of the larger post-revolutionary protests was the 2015 '*Winou el Petrole* (Where is the Oil)' campaign, which also caught international attention, as protesters in Tunis and the south clashed with the government over its lack of transparency regarding oil revenues and the desire for more of those profits to be funnelled towards local development. But the Kamour protests in many ways were different from past protests. First, the Kamour protesters had very specific demands that they sought from the government – that 20 percent of the oil and gas revenues be invested in Tataouine, that the private oil and gas companies create at least 4,500 jobs for residents of the region and that the Tunisian government invest $40 million in infrastructure and development in the region. While the protesters did not see all their demands being met, the final agreement promised around $30 million dollars a year for a Development and Investment Fund for the region and would provide 1,500 jobs in the oil and gas companies, as well as 500 in the environmental and reforestation sectors.

The protesters also gained tremendous leverage over the state by blocking access to the oil and gas facilities, thereby directly harming the Tunisian economy and costing the state significant funds each day that the protests continued. They also sought the same transparency as in the earlier 'Where is the Oil' campaign, asking for more public information about the oil and gas contracts. Another way in which the protests were different is that they did not work with the UGTT until the final phase, where they relied on the UGTT leadership to help negotiate with the state. The Kamour protests were also unique when compared to earlier iterations, in that they succeeded in securing an agreement with the national and local government (the minister of employment and the governor of Tataouine), signed by the UGTT secretary-general and a representative of the protesters.[58]

However, the Kamour protesters' demands did not materialise, as the Tunisian government did not implement the agreement. Thus, the same issues resurfaced in mid-2020, with protesters demanding the implementation of the 2017 Kamour Agreement. The context for the 2020 protests was quite different, with the expectations of the young protesters raised by President Kais Saied, elected in late 2019 with the support of the youth. President Saied visited Tataouine in January 2020 to meet with activists, but he told them to create their own destinies and not wait for the state to improve conditions on the ground, which angered many of the youth.[59] Furthermore, the protests came on the heels of the COVID-19 pandemic lockdown that had sent the Tunisian economy on a downward trajectory.

The 2020 protests were also more violent than the 2017 version, with security forces clashing with protesters in the streets. The violence grew after police arrested one of the protest leaders, Tarek Hadded, on 20 June 2020, for unknown reasons. Over the following days, police employed tear gas, and the Ministry of Defence deployed the military to protect the oil and gas facilities. As one young protester argued, '[w]hat hurts us most is that God has given us everything, but effectively we have nothing'.⁶⁰ He went on to say that the residents of Tataouine are lacking training and experience and are therefore considered unqualified to work in the oil and gas facilities. But the state and the companies offer no options for training, leaving the region's young people without a path forward.

On 3 July 2020, the UGTT began a general strike in Tataouine over the failure to implement the 2017 Kamour Agreement covering all public sector institutions and public service, with the goal of cutting off the oil and gas fields to force the government's hand.⁶¹ The strike came after protesters rejected an offer negotiated by Prime Minister Elyes Fakhfakh. As Prime Minister Hichem Mechichi inherited the Kamour crisis when he took office, he continued the negotiations, and on 8 November 2020 the government finalised an implementation of the Kamour Agreement, announcing a series of measures designed to boost investment employment in the region and to restart oil and gas production.⁶² These new measures include creating a new local council in Tataouine, dropping charges against Kamour protesters arrested for demonstrating and enacting a series of measures to boost the local economy, including creating a development fund for Tataouine and hiring 1,000 new workers in the region.⁶³ However, protesters continued to gather in late November 2020 following protest leader Dhaou El-Ghoul's arrest, which activists said violated one of the Kamour Agreement's provisions – that all charges would be dropped against protesters.

COVID-19 Exacerbates Things

The issue of regional marginalisation and the disparities between the coast and the interior were exacerbated by the outbreak of COVID-19 in early 2020. At the most basic level, healthcare inequalities were brought into stark relief. More than half of the governorates (thirteen out of twenty-four) did not have any intensive care beds at the outset of the pandemic.⁶⁴ And the pandemic saw an increase in medical brain drain, with medical specialists leaving Tunisia for Europe and North America at a higher rate than prior to the pandemic.⁶⁵ This had already been an issue, but the president of the Tunisian union of private doctors, Samir Chtourou, said: 'Coronavirus has increased the pace of emigration'.[66]

The COVID-19 crisis led to a more general economic disaster across Tunisia. The economy contracted 8.8 percent in 2020, and the country's gross domestic product shrank by 3 percent in the first quarter of 2021, compared to the first quarter of 2020.[67] Unemployment increased to 18.4 percent in the third quarter of 2021, up from 15 percent at the beginning of 2020.[68] This is a dramatic increase from 13 percent in 2010 – one of the major factors that led to the revolution. Women and youth experienced even greater rates of unemployment – at 24.9 and 40.8 percent, respectively.[69] The number of poor and vulnerable Tunisians also increased during the pandemic, from 16.7 to 20.1 percent.[70]

Afef Hammami Marrakchi, Professor at the Sfax Faculty of Law, noted that the local authorities were ill-equipped to handle the pandemic.[71] She argues:

> The role of local authorities will need to be restored in this new context of recovery: they have been subject to insufficient oversight, which has led to numerous difficulties in local management. Many positions that are essential to the proper functioning of municipal authorities or local public services, such as director of the local council, director of local tax collection services or architects and town planners in the departments that issue construction or demolition permits, remain vacant or occupied by insufficiently qualified civil servants.[72]

The international community stepped up in the wake of the pandemic, pledging more than $2.4 billion to assist Tunisia in its response. This started with a $55 million pledge from Italy at the end of March 2020, the Islamic Development Bank pledging $280 million in early April 2020, followed by $745 million from the IMF, the European Union pledging $649 million, the World Bank pledging three separate gifts of $15 million, $20 million and $175 million, the WHO offering $1 million in equipment in May 2020, the African Development Bank pledging $202 million, $89 million from France, $4.7 million from Japan and $171 million from Germany. But while cash infusions are important to staunch the economic bleeding, they are insufficient to address the long-term structural causes of marginalisation. Once vaccines became available, several countries donated vaccines to Tunisia. The United States is the largest donor as of December 2021, with 2,635,890 donated doses, followed by Italy with 1,500,000. Other donors include Algeria (250,000), Austria (50,000), Belgium (150,000), China (600,000), Denmark (484,800), France (1,464,170), Greece (100,000), Latvia (50,400), Romania (425,000), Saudi Arabia (1,000,000), Serbia (40,000), Spain (276,000), Turkey (50,000) and the United Arab Emirates (501,000).[73]

Attempts to Address Marginalisation: Official Decentralisation

The most comprehensive way in which the Tunisian government has sought to address marginalisation is the official decentralisation process. Decentralisation, which is constitutionally mandated per the 2014 Constitution, is overseen by the Ministry of Local Affairs and the Environment and began, *en force*, with the May 2018 Municipal Elections – Tunisia's first-ever democratic local elections. Decentralisation was a crucial part of the vision of the drafters of the 2014 Constitution who said that 'the end of despotism must go through decentralisation' and that true democracy would come in the form of local government working with the citizens on a daily basis.[74] Nevertheless, as one decentralisation expert has pointed out, decentralisation is not a popular project, and the manner in which the Constitution defines decentralisation is rather broad, leaving room for substantial discretion by government officials to implement it in different or more limited contexts than what is truly needed.[75] Additionally, there is a sense among some that decentralisation is an elite project. A former municipal delegate in Sidi Bouzid said that decentralisation is an imperative, not a choice, remarking that '[w]e have to be cautious about local democracy because democracy is a mechanism that doesn't always bring the best [. . .] The citizen becomes the policy maker'.[76]

Devising the decentralisation process began just months after the revolution, in July 2011, and was led by Mokhtar Hammami, a bureaucrat who had served in the Ministry of the Interior – the body originally in charge of decentralisation and eventually taken over by the Ministry of Local Affairs and the Environment. To develop the decentralisation plan, Hammami and his team held thirty-six workshops and seminars, with academics and experts, including international experts from twelve countries.[77] The result is an extensive plan that lays out a twenty-seven-year process for achieving full decentralisation. But much of the process has been shrouded in secrecy. In conversations with both civil society activists and parliamentarians in the months leading up to the 2018 Municipal Elections, numerous people lamented the inability to access the twenty-seven-year plan. Even some parliamentarians tasked with drafting the legislation to implement it stated that the ministry refused to share the plan with them.[78]

While the main principles of decentralisation are included in articles 131–42 of the 2014 Tunisian Constitution, the details are hashed out in the Local Authorities Code (Organic Law Number 2018–29), passed in parliament just days before the 2018 Municipal Elections. The sixty-four-page document explains the role of local authorities relative to the central government and is based on consultation with civil society and local actors from across the country. However, many civil society activists felt that the consultative process was neither adequate nor comprehensive. The officials who drafted the Local Authorities Code only devoted three days to consultations – half a day to consult with the judiciary, half a day to consult with civil society and half a day each for six regional consultations. Furthermore, the draft of the code was only posted on the public website for three days before the consultations began, leaving little time for outside entities to review it, and most of the half-day sessions were taken up with the presentation of the code, giving each civil society organisation (CSO) only one minute to comment on the proposed legislation.

The implementation of the Local Authorities Code has been hampered by a variety of factors. First, because the law was passed just days before the 6 May 2018 Municipal Elections, most of the 7,200 people elected to local office had not had time to adequately review the code prior to assuming their positions. Second, the decentralisation process created eighty-six new municipalities to ensure that the entire country was covered, as required by law. As a result, 18 percent of Tunisians found themselves in brandnew municipalities, with no previous governing experience. And 58 percent became part of extended municipalities, whose boundaries were stretched to accommodate additional citizens and territory but without a concomitant increase in financing. Most importantly, the code is an Organic Law, meaning that its implementation requires the passage of numerous Implementing Laws. More than two years after the law's passage, many of the approximately forty implementing laws had not been published. The COVID-19 pandemic further halted the decentralisation process, particularly in the healthcare sector. On 26 March 2020, then Prime Minister Fakhfakh declared that 'in times of crisis, decisions must be centralised'. And a government circular (number 2020–9) requires officials at the local and national levels to coordinate with the central state on any measures meant to prevent the spread of COVID-19.[79] President Kais Saied's 25 July emergency decree further consolidated power into the hands of the president and froze the parliament, making it impossible for any further legislative action. His 22 September 2021 decree (Decree 117), which froze most of the constitution, continued the July freeze of the parliament, giving the president the power to appoint a government and oversee it without interference, thus putting any hopes of decentralisation on hold. Furthermore, Saied's cabinet, appointed in October 2021, removed the post of minister of local affairsand the 2022 Constitution barely mentions local affairs and offers no details on whether local officials are independent from the central state.

Moreover, the decentralisation process has proven to be inadequate to devolve power by electing municipal officials but leaving the powerful regional governments in the hands of governors appointed by the central state. This creates an awkward power structure. While municipal councillors are elected by the people to represent their district, in practice their decisions can be overturned or ignored by the centrally appointed regional governors who answer to the central government, in violation of the principle of administrative autonomy as described in the 2014 constitution. Thus, more than four years after the municipal elections, Tunisia is still lacking a 'a strong legal framework for decentralization that clearly delineates power and responsibility between the national and local levels'.[80] As decentralisation expert Kherigi notes, 'decentralization is not purely a question of putting elected local councils in place and giving them new functions. It requires rethinking the entire institutional architecture in which those councils are embedded'.[81] As one newly elected municipal councillor said, 'inclusive governance is not as easy as you think – the whole country is a big pilot project, and we just need to be patient and make it work'.[82]

Decentralisation has had some positive outcomes. In part due to lower barriers to entry, Tunisia now has higher numbers of women and youth in local government than in national government. And it has empowered some local actors to make decisions regarding their own communities. Additionally, prior to Saied's 2021 coup, the Tunisian process put a strong emphasis on participatory democracy, with the 2014 constitution stating the following:

> Local authorities shall adopt the mechanisms of participatory democracy and the principles of open governance to ensure the broadest participation of citizens and of civil society in the preparation of development programs and land use planning, and follow up on their implementation, in conformity with the law.[83]

But decentralisation can also perpetuate regional disparities, as it relies on structures already in place. Decentralisation can bring more diversity of leadership and forms of service-provision, which can be good for innovation, but it can also lead to a further gap between localities, with the high performers continuing to perform well and the traditionally marginalised regions left behind. Furthermore, the decentralisation process is not necessarily well-equipped to address long-standing patrimonial networks. One report notes:

> The fundamental nature of the public sector does not automatically change when a public sector is 'decentralized' by severing the bottom tier of the state bureaucracy from the top layers if, at the same time, the 'big man' at the top of the central government pyramid is merely supplemented by smaller 'big men' at the top of each local government pyramid.[84]

And opponents of decentralisation argue that decentralised political systems are easier to corrupt, as there are increased layers of officialdom that could be influenced. Additionally, one need corrupt only one segment of the government to consequently corrupt the whole structure. A 2000 study by Transparency International, using their Corruption Perception Index (CPI), found that federal states are often more corrupt than non-federal states, as 'restraints by one [state] level merely increase the pickings of the other', which means that 'subnational officials invariably engage in corrupt practices that will undermine the state'. The report argues that non-federal states limit the possibilities of corruption.[85] Furthermore, local governmental bodies are generally easier to corrupt, as they are typically less developed than national-level bodies. Within local bodies, 'officials are typically less well trained and less well paid', because employees who have better skills and are better performers often seek employment at the national level. Thus, the report argues, 'national structures would tend to be more transparent and accountable to the citizenry'.[86]

Finally, the decentralisation process suffers from the curse of high expectations. As one report notes, promises to reduce regional disparities and inequality are at risk of remaining unfulfilled, and the decentralisation process itself may heighten tensions instead of relieving them.[87] As Kherigi argues, . . .

> A key fear among many, from politicians and bureaucrats to ordinary citizens, is that decentralization is a means for the central state to withdraw from its traditional functions and transfer responsibility for service provision to under-resourced and over-burdened local governments. Yet, the demands for freedom, dignity and social justice voiced by the Arab uprisings require the central state to be more present in peripheries, not less.[88]

Positive Discrimination and Transitional Justice

Another way in which the government has attempted to address regional disparities is through positive discrimination. A form of affirmative action, this policy requires the central government to provide traditionally marginalised regions with higher levels of funding, as an attempt to level the playing field. The concept of positive discrimination was enshrined in the 2014 constitution, which stated: 'The state shall seek to achieve social justice, sustainable development and balance between regions based on development indicators and the principle of positive discrimination'.[89] The goal of positive discrimination is to provide equitable, rather than equal resource distribution from the central state. Proponents of positive discrimination argue that, because the central state was largely responsible for creating the disparities between regions, the state has an essential responsibility to fix the problem that it created. Furthermore, addressing regional inequities is an integral part of the democratic transition. As one Ennahda MP argued, '[y]ou cannot build democracy without [creating] this process of positive discrimination to give more attention to the poorer classes'.[90]

The need for some sort of redistributive process is clear. In 2013, two years after the revolution, eighteen municipalities (or 7 percent) held 51 percent of the resources of the entire country, while the additional 246 (or 93 percent) held the remaining 49 percent of resources.[91] And given this starting point, Tunisia cannot depend on the municipalities themselves to correct the imbalance. Rather, as Prud'homme argues, '[r]edistribution of income should remain a responsibility of the central government [. . .] attempts by local governments to redress income disparities are likely to be unfair'.[92] Simply raising the level of income of marginalised regions will not be sufficient to reverse decades of discrimination. Further complicating the picture, municipalities have seen a sharp decline in their resources since 2011; today, public-sector salaries take up a massive chunk of municipal budgets, with some municipalities seeing wage bills that exceed their total budgets. In one of the more extreme cases, in the municipality of Guettar in Gafsa in the years after the revolution, salary costs were more than 200 percent of the municipal budget.[93]

A third way in which the government has attempted to address regional inequality is through the official transitional justice process. Tunisia's transitional justice process was unique in many regards, including by introducing the concept of collective transitional justice through the use of victim regions. As part of the official transitional justice process, entire regions could submit their case alongside individual claims of victims. The concept of 'victim regions', used during the transitional justice process, was an attempt at both recognising and addressing the systemic marginalisation of geographic areas. During the transitional justice process, the

Truth and Dignity Commission (Instance Vérité et Dignité, or IVD) received 220 dossiers filed on behalf of regions, villages and districts that suffered systematic marginalisation, out of 62,720 total complaints.[94] Complaints by victim regions sought restitution through four mechanisms: recognition of marginalised areas, collective reparations, positive discrimination of budget allocation to ensure non-occurrence and institutional reform through the decentralisation of power and local participatory governance.[95] The first victim region claim was filed in June 2015 on behalf of Kasserine by the Forum Tunisien pour les Droits Économiques et Sociaux (Tunisian Forum for Economic and Social Rights), along with Avocats sans Frontières (Lawyers without Borders).[96]

The IVD report recommended reparations for victim regions that include the development of key sectors (agriculture, industry and tourism), as well as improving socio-economic indicators (education, health, water access, infrastructure, sanitation and access to cultural sites) and providing symbolic forms of reparation by publicly acknowledging the state's responsibility for the marginalisation of these regions. It also recommended adding the experience of victim regions into the national education curriculum and establishing a museum to commemorate those regions' struggles.

Specifically, the IVD recommends that the state create a new development programme focused on the agricultural sector that would cancel small farmers' debts, support young investors, subsidise seeds and fertilisers, develop efficient irrigation systems, support scientific research in the agricultural field and address issues related to collective and state-owned lands. For the industrial sector, the IVD programme proposes a development programme that would equally distribute industrial zones between regions, launch major development programmes in the victim regions and grant regions autonomy in how they decide to exploit their resources. The IVD also recommends that the government facilitate the creation of cooperatives, service companies and non-profit associations to promote social solidarity.

But while the recommendations may be a positive step towards rectifying some of the injustices committed against victim regions, the path forward is not clear. The IVD submitted its final report in March 2019, and according to the

Transitional Justice Law, the government must prepare a strategy and work plan to implement the IVD's recommendations within one year of the final report's publication. In July 2020, a parliamentary commission of eight representing members was set up to implement the IVD recommendations.[97] While the commission has begun the allocation of resources to some of the individual victims (33,000 victims have been provided with reparations either by financial compensation or rehabilitation services), the reparations for victim regions has not been addressed as of October 2021. And because of the July 2021 freezing of parliament, this process has not been able to continue. One concern regarding the victim regions process is that, by designating certain geographic areas as victims, the state is perpetuating long-standing divisions and pitting certain regions against each other – the very problem that the transitional justice process was meant to end. However, failing to acknowledge and address the systemic marginalisation of the prior regime could have the same effect.

Looking Ahead

During the Caid Essebsi government of 2014 to 2019, a common complaint was that there existed no political will to enforce decentralisation.[98] While President Saied, who came to office in October 2019, has advocated for direct democracy and more power for local officials, in his first three years in office, he has done little to advance decentralisation, instead further consolidating power in the central state and strengthening the presidency in the 2022 Constitution. Today, to avoid further destabilisation, the Tunisian government has no choice but to find a way to address the persistent socio-economic disparities between regions in the country and to raise the standard of living for the country's poorest residents. First, the Tunisian government should move forward with regional elections, which would remove the bureaucratic middleman between democratically elected municipal councillors and the central state. Authorities had planned to hold regional elections shortly after the 2019 presidential and parliamentary elections, but the challenges of forming a government in late 2019 and again in the summer of 2020, coupled with Saied's July 2021 coup, have stifled any progress. The current hybrid form of governance, with local authorities overseen by centrally appointed regional governors, undercuts the ability of local authorities to carry out their duties and prevents the implementation of decentralisation as envisaged by the constitution.

Second, local and international NGOs should continue to pressure the Tunisian government to implement the recommendations of the IVD, particularly in ways that would provide for a more level playing-field for Tunisians living in the interior and southern regions. This is an important substantive as well as symbolic measure. Implementing the IVD recommendations is a way to acknowledge the long-standing discrimination and intentional marginalisation of certain regions. President Saied, who has built a base of support amongst marginalised Tunisians, should be well poised to initiate this process.

Third, the international community should increase their investment outside the capital. The idea of a TGV line, which President Saied and President Macron discussed during Saied's June 2020 visit to Paris, would link Bizerte to the south, dramatically cutting down the travel time between south and north.[99] This would provide not only a physical link across the country, but also make the south a more attractive environment for private-sector investment. Another way to address the economic challenges in the interior would be to reform agricultural policy. The Tunisian government could shift away from an export-based agricultural framework towards one that prioritises food independence. Such an approach would reduce importation of labour-intensive products and increase their production in interior regions, thereby supporting job creation and agricultural development in the interior. The government should also promote appropriate agricultural technology such as prioritising domestic seed systems and end disadvantageous agriculture trade arrangements.

To help alleviate some of the economic pain brought about by the COVID-19 pandemic, the Tunisian government should focus on fighting tax fraud. An Oxfam report estimated the cost of tax fraud in Tunisia at 25 billion dinars, or 24 percent of GDP.[100] By recovering just 10 percent of this missing income, the government could have more than doubled its health budget. And recovering 25 percent of the fraud would have allowed for a 350 percent increase in spending on the COVID-19 response.[101]

Additionally, the government must acknowledge and address the impending damage brought on by climate change. According to the World Resources Institute, Tunisia will be among the most water-stressed countries in the world by 2040.[102] Water usage and distribution remain two of the clearest examples of marginalisation. As *Nawatt* reports, '[t]he highlands of Tunisia's north-west hold the national record for rainfall. And yet the region's scarcity of potable water is a nightmare for inhabitants'.[103] Sadiki also noted this phenomenon, specifying that the coastal and periphery stratification is evident here, where a larger share of Tunisia's water is allocated to Tunis, coastal areas and larger cities. Greater Tunis was cited to have almost universal access to water in 2010, but the same cannot be said about the Centre-West and North-West regions. The latter regions, despite possessing most of Tunisia's fresh water, consistently report water shortages during the summer, caused by deliberate government action that re-allocates fresh water to the centre and coastal cities, away from the interior and rural areas. In protest against the experienced injustice, civilians have obstructed the flow of pumps that transport water to Tunis.[104] At the time of this writing, Tunisia was in the midst of dramatic political, social and economic upheaval. As President Saied seeks to revise the entire Tunisian political system, while the pandemic appears to be receding, there are many opportunities for Tunisia to address the long-standing inequalities that have led to tremendous social pain and exacerbated the country's economic challenges.

Notes

1. Larbi Sadiki, 'Regional Development in Tunisia: The Consequences of Multiple Marginalization', *Brookings Doha Centre*, 2019, https://www.brookings.edu/research/regional-development-in-tunisia-the-consequences-of-multiple-marginalization/.
2. Sadiki, 'Regional Development in Tunisia'.
3. Finn Stepputat, 'Contemporary Governscapes: Sovereign Practice and Hybrid Orders Beyond the Centre', in *Local Politics and Contemporary Transformations in the Arab World*, ed. Cilja Harders, Anja Hoffmann, and Malika Bouziane (New York: Palgrave Macmillan, 2013), 25–43.

4. Daniela Huber and Lorenzo Kamel, 'Arab Spring: The Role of the Peripheries', *Mediterranean Politics* 20, no. 2 (4 May 2015): 127–41.
5. 'Decentralization: The Search for New Development Solutions in the Arab World's Peripheries', *Chatham House Middle East and North Africa Programme*, 27 May 2020, https://www.arab-reform.net/event/decentralization-the-search-for-new-development-solutions-in-the-arab-worlds-peripheries/.
6. 'Decentralization: The Search for New Development Solutions'.
7. Olfa Lamloum, 'Marginalisation, Insecurity and Uncertainty on the Tunisian-Libyan Border: Ben Guerdane and Dhehiba from the Perspective of Their Inhabitants', *International Alert*, 2016, https://www.international-alert.org/sites/default/files/Tunisia Libya_MarginalisationInsecurityUncertaintyBorder_EN_2016.pdf.
8. Neji Baccouche, 'Decentralization in Tunisia: Challenges and Prospects', in *Federalism: A Success Story?* ed. Hanns Bühler, Susanne Luther, and Volker L. Plän (Munich: Hanns-Seidel Stiftung, 2016): 29–33.
9. Sami Yassine Turki and Eric Verdeil, 'Tunisie: La constitution (du printemps) ouvre le débat sur la décentralisation', in *Local Governments and Public Goods: Assessing Decentralization in the Arab World*, ed. Mona Harb and Sami Atallah (Beirut: Lebanese Centre for Policy Studies, 2015): 11–45.
10. Turki and Verdeil, 'Tunisie'.
11. Rikke Hostrup Haugbølle, '"Together for Tunisia": Tribal Structures and Social and Political Mobilization', *Middle East Institute*, 19 October 2016, https://www.mei.edu/publications/together-tunisia-tribal-structures-and-social-and-political-mobilization.
12. Laryssa Chomiak, 'The Revolution in Tunisia Continues', *Middle East Institute*, 22 September 2016, https://www.mei.edu/publications/revolution-tunisia-continues.
13. Mona Harb and Sami Atallah, 'An Assessment of Decentralization and Service Delivery in the Arab World', in *Local Governments and Public Goods: Assessing Decentralization in the Arab World*, ed. Mona Harb and Sami Atallah (Beirut: Lebanese Centre for Policy Studies, 2015), 229–33.
14. Tamara Cofman Wittes, 'The States We Are In: Existing Models for Governance in the Middle East', in *Politics, Governance, and State-Society Relations*, convened by Tamara Cofman Wittes, *Brookings Institution*, 2016, https://www.brookings.edu/wp-content/uploads/2016/11/cmep_201611_mest_paper_final.pdf.
15. Hamza Meddeb, 'Tunisia's Geography of Anger: Regional Inequalities and the Rise of Populism', *Carnegie's Middle East*

Centre, 19 February 2020, https://carnegie-mec.org/2020/02/19/tunisia-s-geography-of-anger-regional-inequalities-and-rise-of-populism-pub-81086.
16. Meddeb, 'Tunisia's Geography of Anger'.
17. Francesco Cavatorta and Rikke Hostrup Haugbølle, 'The End of Authoritarian Rule and the Mythology of Tunisia under Ben Ali', *Mediterranean Politics* 17, no. 2 (1 July 2012): 179–95.
18. Haugbølle, 'Together for Tunisia'.
19. Ester Sigillò and Damiano De Facci, 'L'économie sociale et solidaire: Une nouvelle économie morale pour la Tunisie? La construction de l'« alternative » à Médenine', *L'Année du Maghreb*, no. 18 (18 June 2018): 51–68.
20. Sadiki, 'Regional Development in Tunisia'.
21. Sarah Yerkes and Marwan Muasher, 'Decentralization in Tunisia: Empowering Towns, Engaging People', *Carnegie Endowment for International Peace*, 17 May 2018, https://carnegieendowment.org/2018/05/17/decentralization-in-tunisia-empowering-towns-engaging-people-pub-76376.
22. Andrey Korotayev, Leonid Issaev, and Julia Zinkina, 'Centre-Periphery Dissonance as a Possible Factor of the Revolutionary Wave of 2013–2014: A Cross-National Analysis', *Cross-Cultural Research* 49, no. 5 (2015): 461–88.
23. Walid Namane, 'The Tataouine Protests and Political Stability in Tunisia', *Atlantic Council*, 6 July 2017, https://www.atlanticcouncil.org/blogs/menasource/the-tataouine-protests-and-political-stability-in-tunisia/.
24. Sadiki, 'Regional Development in Tunisia'.
25. Sadiki, 'Regional Development in Tunisia'.
26. Eric Gobe, *The Gafsa Mining Basin between Riots and a Social Movement: Meaning and Significance of a Protest Movement in Ben Ali's Tunisia* (Paris: Hal, 2010).
27. Gobe, *The Gafsa Mining Basin*.
28. Sam Kimball, 'Amazigh Languish in Underserved Pockets of Southeast Tunisia', *Al-Monitor*, 8 July 2020, https://www.al-monitor.com/originals/2020/07/tunisia-amazigh-politics-minorities-taoujout-marginalized.html.
29. Kimball, 'Amazigh Languish in Underserved Pockets of Southeast Tunisia'.
30. Kimball, 'Amazigh Languish in Underserved Pockets of Southeast Tunisia'.
31. 'Decentralization,' *Chatham House Middle East and North Africa Programme*.
32. Riadh Mouaker, discussion with the author, Tunis, February 2018.

33. Namane, 'The Tataouine Protests and Political Stability in Tunisia'.
34. 'Fiscal Justice in Tunisia, a Vaccine Against Austerity', *Oxfam*, 17 June 2020, https://oi-files-d8-prod.s3.eu-west-2.amazonaws.com/s3fs-public/2020-06/Fiscal%20justice%20Tunisia_vaccin_austerity_Summary_English.pdf).
35. 'Tunisia's Constitution of 2014', *Constitute Project*, n. d., https://www.constituteproject.org/constitution/Tunisia_2014.pdf.
36. Yassine Bellamine, 'A quand un projet de loi de décentralisation?' *Nawaat*, 2015, https://nawaat.org/portail/2015.
37. Lamine Ghanmi, 'Tunisia University Entrance Exams Highlight Regional Disparities', *Arab Weekly*, 6 July 2019, https://thearabweekly.com/tunisia-university-entrance-exams-highlight-regional-disparities. Ghanmi.
38. *La discrimination positive: Un principe constitutionnel à concrétiser pour la promotion de l'emploi décent dans les régions* (n. p.: République Tunisienne and Organisation Internationale du Travail, 2017).
39. *La discrimination positive*.
40. 'Annuaire statistique de la Tunisie: 2015–2019', *National Institute of Statistics*, 2021, http://ins.tn/sites/default/files/publication/pdf/annuaire-2019%20avec%20lien_1.pdf.
41. 'Tunisie en chiffres', *National Institute of Statistics*, 2021, http://ins.tn/sites/default/files/publication/pdf/tec-newform-2019-v7.pdf.
42. *La discrimination positive*.
43. 'Indicateurs de l'emploi et du chomage: Deuxieme trimestre 2019', *National Institute of Statistics*, August 2019, http://ins.tn/sites/default/files/publication/pdf/Note_ENPE_2T2019_F2.pdf.
44. 'Annual Report of Infrastructure Indicators: 2020', *National Institute of Statistics*, 2020, http://www.ins.tn/sites/default/files/publication/pdf/infrastructure%202020.pdf.
45. For a full table, see Yerkes and Muasher, 'Decentralization in Tunisia'.
46. 'Public Opinion Survey: Residents of Tunisia, December 3 – December 15, 2019', *Centre for Insights in Survey Research*, 2019, https://www.iri.org/wp-content/uploads/2020/11/tunisia_final_slides.pdf.
47. 'Public Opinion Survey: Residents of Tunisia, December 3 – December 15, 2019'.
48. 'Baromètre de popularité des 3 présidents – Vague 8: Mechichi dégringole', *Tunisie Numérique*, 2020, https://www.tunisienumerique.com/barometre-de-popularite-des-3-presidents-vague-8-mechichi-degringole/.

49. Civil society actor, interview with the author, Sidi Bouzid, February 2018.
50. Author's visit to Kesra, February 2018.
51. Youssef Cherif, 'The Kamour Movement and Civic Protests in Tunisia', *Carnegie Endowment for International Peace*, 2017, https://carnegieendowment.org/2017/08/08/kamour-movement-and-civic-protests-in-tunisia-pub-72774.
52. Achref Chibani, 'Demonstrations, Tear Gas, Arrests: Kamour Protests Return', *Meshkal*, 26 June 2020, https://meshkal.org/?p=1390.
53. Handa Chennaoui, 'Resistance in the South Radicalizes Despite Intimidation', *Nawaat*, 2017, https://nawaat.org/portail/2017/05/15/el-kamour-resistance-in-the-south-radicalizes-despite-intimidation/.
54. Chibani, 'Demonstrations, Tear Gas, Arrests'.
55. Chennaoui, 'Resistance in the South'.
56. Chennaoui, 'Resistance in the South'.
57. Chennaoui, 'Resistance in the South'.
58. Cherif, 'The Kamour Movement and Civic Protests in Tunisia'.
59. 'Tunisie : Nouveaux heurts à Tataouine où les manifestants réclament des emplois', *France24*, 2020, https://www.france24.com/fr/20200622-tunisie-nouveaux-heurts-%C3%A0-tataouine-o%C3%B9-les-manifestants-r%C3%A9clament-des-emplois.
60. 'Tunisia: Why the Tataouine Region Struggles with Unrest', *The North Africa Journal*, 29 June 2020.
61. 'Tunisia: Tataouine on Open Strike, Including Oil and Gas Fields', *Middle East Monitor*, 4 July 2020, https://www.middleeastmonitor.com/20200704-tunisia-tataouine-on-open-strike-including-oil-and-gas-fields/.
62. Frida Dahmani, 'Comment Hichem Mechichi a résolu le casse-tête d'El Kamour', *JeuneAfrique.com*, 10 November 2020, www.jeuneafrique.com/1072196/politique/tunisie-comment-hichem-mechichi-a-resolu-le-casse-tete-del-kamour/.
63. 'Government Unveils Decisions on Implementation of El Kamour Agreement,' *TAP*, 11 August 2020, www.tap.info.tn/en/Portal-Economy/13302076-government-unveils.
64. 'Fiscal Justice in Tunisia, a Vaccine Against Austerity'.
65. Emna Jobrane, 'Tunisian Doctors' Emigration Compounds Toll of Pandemic', *The Arab Weekly*, 23 September 2020, https://thearabweekly.com/tunisian-doctors-emigration-compounds-toll-pandemic.
66. Jobrane, 'Tunisian Doctors' Emigration'.
67. 'Tunisia's Economy Shrank 3% in the First Quarter of 2021', *Reuters*, 15 May 2021, sec. Africa, https://www.reuters.com/

world/africa/tunisias-economy-shrank-3-first-quarter-2021-2021-05-15/.
68. 'INS', http://www.ins.tn/en.
69. 'Overview', *World Bank*, https://www.worldbank.org/en/country/tunisia/overview.
70. 'Overview'.
71. Afef Hammami Marrakchi, 'Local Authorities in Tunisia Face Challenges of Post-COVID Economic Recovery', *Arab Reform Initiative*, 21 August 2020, https://www.arab-reform.net/publication/local-authorities-in-tunisia-face-challenges-of-post-covid-economic-recovery/.
72. Marrakchi, 'Local Authorities in Tunisia'.
73. 'Billions Committed, Millions Delivered', *Council on Foreign Relations*, 2 December 2021, https://www.thinkglobalhealth.org/article/billions-committed-millions-delivered.
74. Hafawa Rebhi, 'Tunisie: La démocratie à l'épreuve de la décentralisation', *Middle East Eye*, 31 January 2017, https://www.middleeasteye.net/fr/reportages/tunisie-la-democratie-lepreuve-de-la-decentralisation.
75. Decentralisation expert, interview with the author, Tunis, February 2018.
76. Sidi Bouzid Municipal Delegate, interview with the author, Sidi Bouzid, February 2018.
77. Mokhtar Hammami, interview with the author, Tunis, February 2018.
78. Civil Society Actors and Members of Parliament, interviews with the author, Tunis.
79. Eya Jrad, 'Tunisia Facing COVID-19: To Exceptional Circumstances, Exceptional Measures?' *Arab Reform Initiative*, 14 April 2020, https://www.arab-reform.net/publication/tunisia-facing-covid-19-to-exceptional-circumstances-exceptional-measures/.
80. Yerkes and Muasher, 'Decentralization in Tunisia'.
81. 'Decentralization', *Chatham House Middle East and North Africa Programme*.
82. Municipal councillor, interview with author, Tunis, December 2018.
83. 'Tunisia's Constitution of 2014'.
84. Deborah Kimble, Jamie Box, and Ginka Kapitanova, 'Making Decentralization Work in Developing Countries: Transforming Local Government Entities into High-Performing Local Government Organizations', *Urban Institute Centre on International Development and Governance*, 2012, https://www.urban.org/sites/default/files/publication/26271/412710-Making-Decentralization

-Work-in-Developing-Countries-Transforming-Local-Government-Entities-into-High-Performing-Organizations.PDF.
85. Kimble, Box, and Kapitanova, 'Making Decentralization Work in Developing Countries'.
86. Vito Tanzi, 'Pitfalls on the Road to Fiscal Decentralization', *Carnegie Endowment for International Peace*, 2001, https://carnegieendowment.org/2001/04/26/pitfalls-on-road-to-fiscal-decentralization-pub-688.
87. 'Decentralisation in Tunisia: Consolidating Democracy without Weakening the State', *International Crisis Group*, 26 March 2019, https://www.crisisgroup.org/middle-east-north-africa/north-africa/tunisia/198-decentralisation-en-tunisie-consolider-la-democratie-sans-affaiblir-letat.
88. 'Decentralization', *Chatham House Middle East and North Africa Programme*.
89. Article 12, 'Tunisia's Constitution of 2014'.
90. Ennahda Member of Parliament, interview with the author, Tunis, December 2018.
91. Bellamine, 'A quand un projet de loi de décentralisation?'
92. Rémy Prud'homme, 'The Dangers of Decentralization', *The World Bank Research Observer* 10, no. 2 (1995): 201–20.
93. Harb and Atallah, 'An Assessment of Decentralization and Service Delivery in the Arab World'.
94. Alia Gana, 'Usages sociaux de la justice transitionelle en Tunisie: À qui profite le statut de "région-victime"?' in *Justice et Réconciliation dans le Maghreb Post-Révoltes Arabes*, ed. Éric Gobe (Paris: Karthala, 2019), 121–37.
95. 'Addressing Inequality in Tunisia: Victim Regions and Transnational Justice', *IVD*, 2 February 2018, http://www.ivd.tn/addressing-inequality-in-tunisia-victim-regions-and-transitional-justice/?lang=en.
96. 'Demande relative à l'établissement du statut de "région-victime" de Kasserine', *Forum Tunisien pour les droits économiques et sociaux*, June 2015, https://www.asf.be/wp-content/uploads/2015/06/ASF_TUN_R--gionVictime_201506_FR.pdf.
97. Olfa Belhassine, 'Ayachi Hammami: "There's Been Mismanagement of Time" in Tunisia's Transnational Justice', *JusticeInfo.net*, 2020, https://www.justiceinfo.net/en/44954-ayachi-hammami-mismanagement-of-time-in-tunisia-transitional-justice.html.
98. Civil society activists' interviews with the author, Tunis, 2018 and 2019.
99. Maryline Baumard and Charlotte Bozonnet, 'Kaïs Saïed: "La Tunisie n'acceptera jamais la partition de la Libye"', *Le Monde*,

2020, https://www.lemonde.fr/afrique/article/2020/06/24/kais-saied-la-tunisie-n-acceptera-jamais-la-partition-de-la-libye_6044014_3212.html.
100. 'Fiscal Justice in Tunisia, a Vaccine Against Austerity'.
101. 'Fiscal Justice in Tunisia, a Vaccine Against Austerity'.
102. Cody Pope, 'Tunisian Thirst Uprising: A Nation on the Edge', *Circle of Blue*, 27 October 2016, https://www.circleofblue.org/2016/africa/a-nation-on-the-edge/; Andrew Maddocks, Robert Samuel Young, and Paul Reig, 'Ranking the World's Most Water-Stressed Countries in 2040', *World Resources Institute*, 25 August 2015, www.wri.org/blog/2015/08/ranking-world-s-most-water-stressed-countries-2040.
103. Venessa Szakal, 'Tunisia's Parched North', *Nawaat*, 2015, https://nawaat.org/portail/2015/12/29/tunisias-parched-north/.
104. Sadiki, 'Regional Development in Tunisia'.

5

Mauritania: The Multi-dimensionality of its Enduring Challenges

Fatima Hadji

Mauritania – a country located in a troubled region, is vast in geography, but less populated and less developed than its neighbours. Mauritania is also the bridge linking the North and the West of the African continent; rich in history and culture, it occupies a strategic location and has the potential to play a major role in Africa's economy and political development. However, Mauritania faces several challenges that harm its socio-economic growth, democratic development and long-term stability. The legacy of authoritarianism, instability, social complexities and the enduring economic and socio-political crisis have mired Mauritania's history for decades, as the country ranks thirty-three out of 176 states according to the 2021 Fragile States Index.[1]

Like many countries in the world, Mauritania is also dealing with environmental problems that are menacing its population, natural resources and stability. Water shortages, pollution and the encroachment of the Sahara on agricultural lands are the most pressing environmental issues. Moreover, fishing is an important part of the country's economy, but due to over-fishing Mauritania is faced with a potential biodiversity loss, surface water pollution and decreasing water quality.[2] Without reducing these problems and their impact, the political instability of the region remains a major issue that overshadows the efforts that Mauritania is making to overcome its economic, environmental and socio-political challenges.

Mauritania has been ruled by the military since 1978. Mauritania's political trajectory, military coups and ethno-cultural challenges are important components to consider when examining the country's democratic challenges.

Boubacar N'Daiye eloquently sums up the situation in Mauritania as follows:

> The country has recurring ethno-cultural tensions labelled as 'the national question' and symbolized by an unsettled 'human rights deficit'. The deferred military withdrawal from politics and genuine democratisation, which each colonel has promised, but none actually delivered, has yet to materialize.[3]

Without delving into the full history of Mauritania, as extensive literature and research have been conducted previously, this chapter will provide an overview of the country's enduring and inter-dependent political, economic, security and social challenges, as well as its prospects for democratisation.[4]

Mauritania's Defining Politics: Coups d'État

Mauritania has a complex regime that is characterised by political stagnation, resulting from decades of military rule and the lack of adequately addressing national unity or what some commentators call national reconciliation. It has been the scene of political instability since its independence in 1960, enduring nine coups or coup attempts since President Moktar Ould Daddah was overthrown in 1978, which has made it impossible for civilian rule to be established, since the coups d'état have not facilitated the necessary conditions for a peaceful and democratic alternation of power to take place. A chronological account of Mauritania's coups d'état is one way to demonstrate the dilemma and the complexity of the country's political struggle.

Mauritania's first coup d'état was organised in 1978 by Colonel Mustafa Ould Salek to overthrow President Daddah over an internal disagreement on the country's stance with respect to the Western Sahara conflict.[5] An economic crisis, heightened racial tensions between the Moors and the Blacks and additional disaccord on the Western Sahara propelled Lieutenant Colonel Mohamed Ould Louly to instigate another coup and take over the presidency in June 1979. However, his reign was short-lived. Ould Louly declared Mauritanian neutrality in the Western Sahara conflict and signed a peace agreement with the

Popular Front for the Liberation of Saguia el-Hamra and Rio de Oro (POLISARIO). Nevertheless, he was not able to restore national unity nor deal with the mounting economic crisis at the time. As a result, Colonel Mohamed Khouna Ould Haidalla overthrew him in 1980 and ruled Mauritania until 1984, when Ould Haidalla was ousted by Colonel Maaouya Ould Sidi Ahmed Taya.[6] Under his rule, Colonel Ould Taya promised to put the economy back on the right track, eliminate economic corruption and restore order in the public sector. However, as argues Anthony Pazzanita, the high level of corruption, combined with the 'persistent reshuffling of a narrow stratum of regime personnel to satisfy tribal and regional demands for influence', increased instability and economic stagnation and contributed to further politicisation of identities.[7]

Ould Taya remained in power far longer than his predecessors, surviving two attempted coups in 2003. However, in 2005, a coup carried out by the Military Council for Justice and Democracy (CMJD) headed by Colonel Vall Ould Mohamed ended President Taya's twenty-one-year reign.[8] Under Colonel Vall Ould Mohamed, Mauritania enacted several reforms, including a new constitution that was approved by popular referendum in 2007 and the election of new representatives. That same year, Mauritania held its first 'democratic' presidential elections, bringing to power President Sidi Ould Cheikh Abdallahi.[9] Some considered this transition a process-oriented model of democratisation in which citizens engaged in an electoral process to choose their civilian president.[10] However, despite the move towards a more democratic form of government, the military continued to exert a strong influence on Mauritanian politics. N'Diaye in his critical examination of the transition concluded that 'the transition process did not escape the well-known African military junta leader's proclivity to manipulate transitions to fulfil suddenly awakened self-seeking political ambitions, in violation of solemn promises'.[11] On this point, N'Diaye claims that the transition is a flawed democratic experiment that still provides the military junta with space for political involvement to preserve power. This is especially evident in the case of Abdallahi, who after coming to power dismissed several senior army commanders and after only seventeen months of his presidency was overthrown by the military.

Between August 2008 and July 2009, the military formed a state council to rule the country until General Mohamed Ould Abdel Aziz was elected in July 2009.[12] Abdel Aziz resigned in 2009 as a member of the military junta in order to run as a presidential candidate. Yasmine Akrimi and May Barth, citing Claude E. Welch Jr, note that the phenomenon of stepping out of uniform to run as a candidate for president has been predominant in African politics and is a model of 'personal transition' that serves as a stage for seemingly democratic elections.[13] Ould Abdel Aziz ruled Mauritania until August 2019, serving two presidential terms. He did not seek re-election in 2019. The military-backed candidate Ould El Ghazouani was then elected president in 2019, with 52.01 percent of the vote. Other candidates included anti-slavery activist Biram Ould Dah Abeid who won 18.58 percent and the Islamist-backed candidate Mohamed Ould Boubacar who received 17.87 percent of the vote.[14] The voter turnout was estimated at 63 percent according to the International Foundation for Electoral Systems (IFES).[15] In the 2014 presidential elections, the voter turnout was 56.46 percent, and in 2009 61.51 percent.[16] Similar to prior elections, Mauritania did not invite international observers for the pre-election assessment or the election day observation, with the exception of the African Union Election Observer Mission (AUEOM) that monitored the first round of presidential elections. AUEOM focused mostly on technical issues related to the political and security environment and on the methodology and Code of Conduct for AU election observation according to its press release dated 24 June 2019.[17] The specific AUEOM recommendations and observations have yet to be published in the Independent National Electoral Commission (CENI) website.

These elections did not reflect the aspirations of the Mauritanian people for a competitive electoral process that gives a non-military backed candidate a chance to win and for non-Arab communities to be represented. Even though the anti-slavery candidate Biram Ould Dah Abeid had a substantial following, Mohamed Ould El Ghazouani's win was definitive from the first round of elections, and the Military Council immediately validated the results.[18] The military regime, together with political stagnation, human rights violations and outstanding ethno-racial and cultural issues continue to hinder Mauritania's prospects for a democratic stable government and good governance. Yet, Mauritania's status in Freedom House's *Freedom in the World* report improved from 'not free' to 'partly free' following the presidential election of 2019, which marked the country's first democratic transition of power after decades of recurrent coups d'état and political deadlock.[19]

In general, the military's control and manipulation of elections, strengthened by their control of state resources, has led to coups that overthrew those presidents of whom the military did not approve. Yet, despite the military's control of major political, economic and security sectors and overall influence, the Mauritanian armed forces are perceived as being one of the least equipped and least advanced militaries in the world. The forces are poorly trained and lack advanced technology and weaponry to face the country's growing internal and external threats. Additionally, a long-standing trend is that the military penetrates the economy. The 2020 Bertelsmann Stiftung's Transformation Index (BTI) observes that the Mauritanian economy is 'heavily influenced by oligopolistic structures', which rely on political connections, interest group activity and tribal linkages and loyalties.[20] The 2020 BTI report, citing a World Bank 2017 systematic country diagnostic, notes that 'the participation of the private sector in the formal sector is confined to a discrete and concentrated set of interests'.[21] Combined, these factors have led to a weak state and the creation of an environment where terrorist groups such as al-Qa'ida in the Islamic Maghreb (AQIM) are able to take advantage of the country's vulnerabilities.[22] Entrenched ethnic-racial tensions and grievances, deprivation, economic inequality and the unstable political system make the marginalised and disaffected segments of society an attractive pool for AQIM recruitment.[23]

Other analysts also argued that, regardless of political reform efforts, Mauritania's de facto ruler has long been the military. While the 25 February movement, which emerged in the context of the 2011 Arab Spring uprisings, demanded constitutional reforms, separation of powers, an end to the military rule and transfer of power to civilians, the military remains the most powerful actor in the country. To underscore this, Yasmine Akrimi and May Barth examined Mauritania's political pathways by analysing the concept of 'personal transition' and asserted that 'the military maintains power through presenting or backing a candidate'.[24] Furthermore, engrained military political power is a recurring problem as decades of dictatorship have weakened civil institutions.[25]

In addition to the outsized power of the military, Mauritania's ethnic and racial divisions have led to political gridlock between the president and the opposition.[26] Within the country, there are minority non-Arab Black Africans – such as the Halpulaars (Fulanis), Soninkes, Bambaras and Wolofs – who are entirely outside Arabo-Berber society. These groups generally speak French or their own native languages, whereas the rest of the population speaks Hassaniyya Arabic. In addition, there are the Beidan ('whites') and Haratin ('freedmen') who constitute the Arabic-speaking Mauritanians. Haratin ('freedmen') are dark-skinned former slaves descended from Black Africans. Moors are made up of both Beidan and Haratin Arabs.[27] Social tensions between Arab-speaking descendants of slaves, white Moors and Afro-Mauritanians continue to exist in Mauritania's fractious society today.

The Economy: In Search of Equilibrium

Mauritania's economy is still largely based on agriculture, fisheries, livestock and extractive industries. According to the BTI 2020, mining, fisheries and oil resources represent 72 percent of Mauritania's revenues. The increase in production and revenue in the mining sector and the potential for gas production over the next few years provides a glimpse of hope for a steady economic recovery. Economist Samer Matta, however, elucidates that 'the macroeconomic outlook remains [. . .] subject to four main risks: prolonged impact of the pandemic, climatic hazards, possible delays in structural reforms and regional insecurity'.[28] With a Human Development Index score of 0.546, Mauritania ranks 157 out of 188 countries.[29] Mauritania also has an unequal resource distribution problem due to corruption and the ethnic-racial background favouritism, as described above. The Haratin and the Afro-Mauritanians occupy the bottom of the economic sphere. Their economic misfortunes, so argues Yahaya Ibrahim, are attributed to the 'after-effects of slavery'.[30]

World Bank reports have underscored the trends of Mauritania's rentier economy and a state-driven development model that 'facilitated pervasive rent-seeking by a concentrated set of political and economic elites'.[31] In addition, the centrality of public procurement and contracts in the hands of a select interest group underline the lack of a progressive approach to Mauritania's development model and public spending that continue to cripple the country's economic growth.[32] As part of its economic analysis, the Country Policy and Institutional Assessment (CPIA) shows that, in terms of policies for social inclusion and equity in public sector management and institutions, Mauritania has only increased its score by 0.1 percent from 2013 to 2019.[33] The CPIA measures indicators of gender equality, equity of public resource use, building human resources, social protection and labour, and policies and institutions for environmental sustainability.[34]

The COVID-19 pandemic negatively impacted Mauritania's already precarious economy and highlighted the socio-economic challenges in the country. In 2020, the pandemic largely affected domestic consumption, which has been disrupted since the downturn in global economic growth and the introduction of social distancing measures. As a result, GDP growth has plummeted from 5.9 percent in 2019 to between -2 percent and -6.8 percent in 2020.[35] The pandemic has also contributed to an increase in Mauritania's poverty rate from 5.4 to 6.3 percent between 2019 and 2020.[36] The COVID-19 pandemic has led to the fall of economic growth from 5.9 percent in 2019 to 1.5 percent in 2020. Specifically, the fishery and services sectors were severely affected due to the pandemic containment measures.[37] Nevertheless, international 'financial support and higher commodity prices for the exports of iron and gold led to an unexpected fiscal surplus in 2020'.[38] Oil, gas and mining continue to offer investment opportunities, as do tourism, agriculture, telecommunication and infrastructure projects, and electricity.

Mauritania is also an agricultural country and possesses natural resources such as gas, copper and iron. But environmental factors such as droughts are causing the desertification of agricultural soil, leading to internal displacement and decreasing water supplies. In addition, over-fishing and pollution continue to damage the coastal waters, resulting in the destruction of the ecosystem. The environmental degradation stimulated significant economic losses in livestock and agriculture, as Mauritania's rural populations risk the danger of limited access to water and food.

While Mauritania has many social, economic, security and political issues, the country seems to be progressing towards improving its economic situation. The government demonstrated political will and took significant steps to deal with droughts and desertification. For example, in the 1980s Mauritania joined the Club of Sahel and the Permanent Inter-State Committee to Fight Against Drought in the Sahel (CILSS) with the strategy of alleviating the impact of droughts and desertification in the Sahel, securing food self-sufficiency and better ecological balance.[39] In 2006, it created the National Office of Meteorology (ONM) to monitor the situation and assist with decision-making. In collaboration with other national and international organisations, the ONM provides detailed seasonal forecasts and monitors desertification, rainfall accumulation and the development of vegetation.[40] According to the Economic Freedom Index, Mauritania is rated at 56.1 and ranked at 128 out of 178 among the freest in 2021.[41] Mauritania has implemented a number of reforms, including the creation of a free trade zone in Nouadhibou,[42] in addition to conforming to the Extractive Industries Transparency Initiative (EITI) protocols, adopting an ethics code for civil servants and passing a declaration of assets bill for high-ranked personnel in the administration.[43] To improve governance and transparency, the International Monetary Fund, through its capacity development initiative, contributed to strengthening policy frameworks and advancing institutional reforms.[44]

Mauritania initiated the deregulation of the economy as part of its Strategy for Accelerated Growth and Shared Prosperity (SCAPP) for 2016–30, including improvement of public expenditures and the promotion of non-extractive industries.[45] Mauritania's SCAPP agenda for economic development encompasses a strategy based on three pillars, including the creation of a conducive, sustainable and inclusive environment for economic growth – developing human capital and guaranteeing access to basic services – and enhancing the rule of law and good governance. Each pillar consists of strategic focus areas such as increasing resilience of the vulnerable segments of society and promoting women's participation and efforts to combat gender-based discrimination in education, access to services and business.[46]

Corruption: A Persistent Issue

Like many poor and under-developed countries, Mauritania has a major corruption problem with a direct impact on the economy. The issue is rooted in many government sectors. There are several factors that hinder the country's development and prevent the full use of its natural resources, while government corruption remains at the top. Government officials and business elites revert to corrupt practices to benefit from tax exemption, as well as fishing and mining licenses. Corruption, ethnic favouritism and nepotism dominate the practices of issuing fishing and mining licenses as well as other official documents.[47] Furthermore, corruption has widened the inequality gap between rich and poor, exacerbated ethnic divides and permitted the rich to access opportunities at the expense of the poorer segments of society. Mauritania ranks 130 out of 180 countries with a score of twenty-nine out of 100 in Transparency International's 2020 Corruption Perception Index, falling three points from the previous year.[48] A global security report highlights that . . .

> . . . although progress has been made, laws and regulations are still not evenly and effectively enforced, largely because corruption is endemic in a society that is still largely based on familial and tribal relationships rather than strict adherence to the rule of law.[49]

In recent years, the government has made efforts to enforce the laws and punish the officials that violate them. For instance, the parliament opened an investigation into alleged high-level corruption and mismanagement of the country's resources during ex-president Mohamed Ould Abdel Aziz's time in power.[50] In March 2021, the conclusion of the investigation resulted in the detention of twenty-nine public officials, including Ould Abdel Aziz, and the 'state prosecutor formally charged 13 of these officials with bribery, money laundering, embezzlement and obstruction of justice charges'.[51] Ould Abdel Aziz was released and put under house arrest. Not everyone was happy with the treatment of Ould Abdel Aziz. His supporters reacted to the allegation and his arrest by claiming that this was an attempt at settling political scores. And while many view this as a positive step, Mauritania still has a long way ahead to diminish corruption and its remnants in the government, the judiciary and the economy.

Radicalism and Insecurity

Another issue that is preventing Mauritania from achieving its development goals is persistent insecurity. Many regional scholars and analysts have extensively surveyed issues and drivers of insecurity.[52] The consensus in the literature holds that Mauritania has a heightened risk of instability due to several factors: Mauritania's socio-economic infrastructure, tribal and ethnic divisions, and lack of political stability, which have undermined Mauritania's position in the Maghreb and the Sahel. Mauritania's security challenges are not new, as they date back to its independence, and terrorism is still a major threat to the country's stability and well-being.

Mauritania's political and socio-economic fragility and the insecurity of the region due to trans-border smuggling and trafficking makes it 'an easy target and haven for traffickers and armed groups, including transnational Islamist terrorist movements', according to Cédric Jourde.[53] Compared to other Sahel analysts, Jourde emphasises the notion of the 'economy of insecurity' – that is, the overlay of micro-politics and regional rivalries examining the influence of tribes over the cross-border trafficking and trade and the interests of both state and non-state actors. He adds that 'local politics can also seriously blur the difference between state and nonstate actors'.[54] Jourde stresses the complexity of the insecurity in the Sahel as well as the intersections of local, national and regional dynamics and the motives of political actors to engage with one another.[55]

Mauritania is a Muslim country with a moderate Malekite Islamic tradition that is socially conservative.[56] Sufi orders such as the Tijaniyya and Qadiriyya play a critical role as Sufism centres on the concept of spirituality. Sufism also emphasises traditional attitudes passed on by saints, shrines and sheikhs – that is, an Islam of Sufi orders – or what in Arabic is called *zawiya*. This has made Mauritania 'unreceptive to Ba'athist secular Arab nationalism'.[57] Yet, the *Tabligh* (missionary) movement and the exposure of young Mauritanian students to the interpretation of Islam during their tenure in the Gulf States have contributed to the spread of Salafism, a return to the origins of Islam, or a 'pristine Islam'.[58]

One source of insecurity is the rise of religious extremism since the early 2000s, which denotes a worrying setback to radical and traditional Islam known as Salafism. Many Mauritanian Muslims have expanded their understanding and practice of Islam beyond daily visible and spiritual practices such as fasting and practising, to encompass an ideological vehicle for governance, as an alternative to their current national government, due to its ineffectiveness and failures over time. However, there is a widespread appeal of the return to a fundamentalist and 'authentic' form of Islam, relying on perceptions of the Islamic 'golden age'.[59] The Islamist militancy has emerged as 'a cornerstone towards Islamic politics and against the expectations of so-called modern or westernized Muslim societies'.[60] Therefore, the Islamic movements have become the underlying power of social change. Unfortunately, the use of violence as a trademark of their global reach leads to an exaggerated belief that Islam is incompatible with liberty and democracy.[61]

Al-Qaeda in the Islamic Maghreb, or AQIM formed in 2005, when it changed its name from the Algerian Salafi Group for Call and Combat (GSPC) and announced its allegiance to Osama bin Laden. AQIM's prevalent identity is also its allegiance to Salafism. The word 'Salafi' comes from the Arabic phrase *as-salaf assaliheen*, which refers to the first three generations of Muslims (starting with the companions of the Prophet), otherwise known as the pious predecessors. Salafis are fundamentalists who believe in the original ways of Islam. Most, if not all, of the existing Salafist movements in the region emanated from Algerian Salafism, whose militant leaders were the first instructors of armed jihadist groups.[62] According to Malika Zeghal, Salafism is 'an orthodox reform movement that brought conservative Wahhabi doctrine'.[63] As such, local context and social dynamics coupled with the global narrative of jihadists have a contributing role in radicalisation and extremism. Since the early 2000s, AQIM has mainly operated in North and West Africa where its infamous track record has raised multiple questions about the structure of its different offshoots (such as Ansar Dine, Al-Mourabitoun, the Movement for Unity, the Islamic Movement of Azawad and Jihad in West Africa), their funding base and their ideology.

To strengthen the fight against terrorism, Mauritania has made considerable improvements to its armed forces since 2009. Mohamed Ould El Ghazouani, the former leader of the National Defence High Council who became Mauritania's president in 2019, created the eight Special Intervention Groups (GSI) to counter terrorist groups – which are described as 'small-unit teams that were designed to be versatile in both thinking and execution'.[64] In 2015, Mauritania established a strategic base in the region of Lemreya to restrict the movement of terrorists and traffickers. These were strategic steps that contributed to the transformation of the desert area of Mauritania, Mali and Alegria into a militarised zone. The government 'has also made serious efforts to strengthen' the oversight of preaching and re-affirming the teaching of moderate Malekite Islam.[65] Despite its security improvements, the country still has a long way to go to achieve security and stability.[66] Mauritania has not experienced any terrorist attacks in several years, but this does not mean that it is immune from future attacks. Being among the poorest in the world and with deeply divided societies, Sahelian countries' political rivalries also further complicate the drivers of insecurity in the region, and their democratic consolidation remains difficult and doubtful.

The Role of Regional Geopolitics

Mauritania lies in a strategic location in the African continent. The country shares its borders with the Western Sahara in the north, Algeria in the north-east, Mali in the east and south-east, and Senegal in the south-west. Further contributing to the country's security challenges, Mauritania is surrounded by countries that are marked by political turmoil and has been deeply impacted by conflicts with three areas in particular: the Western Sahara, Senegal and Mali. Mauritania is a member and host of the G5 Sahel, an alliance of five countries that cooperate on security matters and strengthen the capacity and resilience of governments and communities in the region to counter violent extremism. Since 1989, Mauritania has also been a member of the Arab Maghreb Union (AMU), with the objective of promoting cooperation and improved economic relations among the Maghreb countries. Real progress in 'the development of the AMU, however, remains limited and Mauritania – the weakest of the Maghreb economies – has benefited little'.[67]

The Western Sahara conflict is a predominant issue in North Africa, involving Morocco, the POLISARIO and Algeria, as Mohamed Daadaoui explains in Chapter Three. The territory in dispute includes the Western Sahara, Northern Mauritania and Southwest Algeria. The dispute over the Sahara has persisted for decades and over the years has forced Mauritania into delicate situations with its neighbours. The conflict remains an obstacle in the region's security, development and union, as it has caused a delay in the economy, foreign investment and overall growth of the region. While it extracted itself from the Western Sahara conflict in 1979, Mauritania lost a great deal and is still losing economically and politically. The disputed region became a zone of turmoil, illegal drugs and human trafficking, and it transformed Mauritania into a proxy battlefield. In the 1970s, Mauritania supported the Moroccan claim over the Western Sahara; however, then President Ould Daddah's stance on the conflict created internal tensions. Consequently, Mauritania underwent a regime change, renounced its claim on the Western Sahara and signed a peace treaty with the POLISARIO in 1979.

Many attribute the genesis of the 1989 Mauritania-Senegal conflict to the economic crisis in the Sahel, coupled with environmental challenges including drought, desertification and a dispute over grazing rights. The conflict rapidly transformed into an ethnic conflict and created high tensions between the two countries, resulting in broken diplomatic ties and thousands of refugees. This conflict has also created internal divisions between Mauritanians and weakened the country, as 'the Senegalese and other Black Africans view Mauritania as one of the desert buffer states between them and Arab North Africa. As a result, many see the recent events here in the context of an Arab push against Black Africa'.[68]

By most accounts, the conflict that has most affected Mauritania is the Northern Mali crisis of 2012, as the two countries share a border. There are many linkages between the two countries, since the populations share familial, cultural, economic and religious ties. Therefore, problems on one side of the Mauritania-Mali border also affect the other side of the border. The crisis in Mali impacted Mauritania's landscape politically, socially and economically.[69] Moreover, jihadist attacks in Mali, despite the presence of both substantial United Nations troops and French military operations, continue to impact Mauritania, as 'many Mauritanians particularly white Moors and Haratins have joined these groups'.[70]

Mauritania is faced with difficult choices. The Western Sahara conflict, the dispute between Mauritania and Senegal and, most recently, the Mali crisis have weakened Mauritania's economy and internal politics, further enfeebling its position in the region. For many years, Mauritania has been caught in the middle of cross-fires and faced threats from different fronts. Over time, these risks have drained the country's resources and debilitated its progress. These conflicts also continue to exacerbate the ethnic and racial tensions within Mauritanian society, at a time when the debate about national unity and reconciliation has been at the centre of Mauritanian politics and is a prerequisite for democratic reform.

Human Rights Deficits and Marginalisation: Lingering Threats to Social Cohesion

Historical and legal evidence confirms that Mauritania does not have a glorious past when it comes to respecting human rights, and its efforts at promoting social cohesion remain dismal. In this vein, Jourde views the ethnic tensions in Mauritania as two major political debates. The first concerns the change in the relationship between the political elite and the broader population, whereas the second pertains to the citizenship rights of the ethnic communities that were subjected to violence and abuse by the state.[71] Jourde also laments that, 'for many prodemocracy movements in Mauritania, the debates overlapped: democratising the regime and improving ethnic relations were mutually enforcing processes. Conversely, a deterioration of one would negatively affect the other'.[72]

Mauritania is a fragmented society with major political issues and civil rights violations that are deeply rooted and considered as somewhat acceptable or common practice.

Human rights violations in Mauritania include, inter alia, slavery, repression, police violence and government corruption. There are other human rights violations committed by the government against civilians. For instance, officials have engaged in alleged property restitution and forced Afro-Mauritanians out of their lands; in other instances, the government used its power to interfere and deny certain citizens the right to a fair public trial.[73] Despite the existence of laws that protect civil liberties, such as the Law on Associations recently approved by parliament, which alleviates restrictions on the registration of and funding for civil society organisations, numerous violations continue to be reported by international human rights groups and Mauritanian citizens.[74] These violations are mostly targeted at political opposition actors, rights organisations and any individuals who challenge government officials or the government in general.

The government employs violence and harassment to intimidate journalists, media outlets and bloggers.[75] For instance, the bloggers Cheikh Jiddou and Abderrahmane Weddady were detained for condemning corruption through a Facebook post.[76] This approach is used to prevent reporting on any issues that question the government's integrity, illegal practices or corruption. Repeatedly, journalists have been arrested without a legitimate reason and accused of defaming certain government officials.[77] The Mauritanian government also uses financial pressure as a form of censorship and content restriction. For example, several independent media outlets were threatened with insolvency when the government obliged them to pay back taxes which for years had not been paid and overlooked by government officials.[78] In 2020, there were reports of meetings held by government officials with the media 'to warn them regarding one-sided coverage of slavery or sensitive topics that could harm national unity or the country's reputation'.[79]

After the 2019 presidential elections, people took to the street to protest the victory by Ould El Ghazouani, claiming that the elections had been rigged. To disperse protesters, the police used violence and brutality.[80] Furthermore, human rights commentators make the argument that the insecurity in the Sahel is also used by regimes (including Mauritania) to impose restrictions and squander rights and freedoms, clamp down on and silence dissent under the pretext of countering extremism.[81] The insecurity in the region is usually used as a political resource to cover up the democracy deficit and to refocus the lens on the need for more security rather than democratisation and reform.

Slavery: A Lingering Issue that Cannot Be Ignored

Mauritania is a diverse and stratified state where ethnic groups, the Arab Moors and the Black Africans, are in a continual struggle for power. In 1961, Mauritania's new constitution deemed slavery illegal. However, the constitution was not enough to end this practice which is deeply rooted in society, as 'Black people have been enslaved on such a scale that the term Black has become synonymous with slave in Arabic. Systematic destruction of Black culture and civilisation became the order of the day wherever and whenever the Arabs gained a foothold in the country'.[82] It was not until the 1980s that slavery was officially abolished, making Mauritania the last country in the world to legally abolish the practice. Nearly four decades on, 'the legacy of slavery – or "vestiges" as the Mauritanian government terms it – still manifests across this vast, racially diverse, northwest African republic'.[83] According to the 2020 Global Slavery Index (GSI), there are 21.4 victims of modern slavery per 1,000 persons in Mauritania. Modern slavery is the exploitation of individuals through sexual exploitation, forced labour, forced marriage, domestic servitude and forced criminality. Mauritania ranks number four in the Africa region – after Eritrea, Burundi and the Central African Republic – in the estimated prevalence of modern slavery.[84]

To understand the context of slavery, a brief reminder of the ethnic composition of Mauritania is useful. In David Seddon's words, the . . .

> Mauritanian population consists of a majority (some two-thirds) of Arabic-speaking 'Moors' of mixed Arab, Berber and Black African descent, divided into tribal groupings and into major categories: the 'white' Moors (Beidan) and the 'Black' Moors (Haratin), the ex-slaves of the Beidan. The significant minority (at least one-third) of the population

consists of various Black African ethno-linguistic groups, including Peul (Pulaar), Toucouleur, Soninke and Wolof.[85]

The Moor class generally possesses wealth, economic and social power, while the freed slaves or former slaves still struggle to achieve economic independence and social integration.[86] The Black Afro-Mauritanians remain in the margins economically and politically.

Slavery was introduced to Mauritania by the Arab slave traders. Scholars argue that the Moor Arab elite intended to alter the Afro-Mauritanian historical past, by means of Arab ideology or Arabisation, which also deprived them of power, political voice and freedom for which the Afro-Mauritanians continue to fight today.[87] The Arabisation strategy of the Afro-Mauritanians was meant to create distance between the Afro-Mauritanians and the Black Moors known as Haratin. This strategy aimed to keep the Afro-Mauritanians under the control of the Arab Moors for political and economic dominance. Other observers note that Mauritania's slavery is based on a caste model where the Arabic-speaking Mauritanian Beidan possess political power and hold prestigious positions in society. The Beidan claim that they derive their power following the tradition of Ahl Sidi Mahmud (ASM) dating back to the eighteenth century, the great follower of the religious figure of Lemrabot Sidi Mahmud (LSM). LSM followers consolidated their political autonomy by military force in the nineteenth century. Beidan claim their religious and military tribal status irrespective of genealogy. Mariella Villasante-de Beauvais points out that 'their cohesion and social solidarity (*asabiyya*) are not based on genealogy (*nasab*) but rather on protection relationships (*jiwâr, hmâye*) and political alliances (*tahâluf*) which unite the descendants and followers of LSM'.[88]

Because slavery was first legally outlawed in 1981, the practice shifted its traditional practices from chains, punishment and captivity to mental, emotional and economic enslavement. As specified by Boubacar Messaoud, the leader of the organisation SOS-Slave, 'historically slaves in Mauritania did not need chains to be subdued because they are raised and taught to accept submission [. . .] they are chained in their heads'.[89] Furthermore, as Kevin Bales comments, 'the tribal and traditional ties between the families of slaves and their former masters remained as the entire social system maintains a culture of order and obedience'.[90]

The emotional link between master and slave is strong, as deep relationships are forged over time and loyalty is maintained given the fact that a slave's parents, grandparents and great-grandparents have worked and lived in the household of the same Moor family.[91] This is the paradox of Mauritanian slavery. Many slaves think of themselves as members of their master's family. Equally, as devout Muslims, '[m]any slaves believe that they are placed by God into their master's household, and that to leave it would be sinful'.[92] Historically, the slaves' owners relied on a false religious interpretation to convince the enslaved Africans of submission and servitude. Typically, access to heaven for them is linked to the satisfaction of their masters. If a slave wishes to enter heaven, he or she must serve and please the master.[93] The owners also limit their slaves' access to information and education to keep them under control and in bondage.

Another notable aspect of slavery is the distinction between male and female slaves. Bales comments that, 'in Moor society, wealth was traditionally measured in the number of female slaves a man owned. Though they are infrequently sold, a young male slave might go for $500 to $700, a mature female for $700 to $1,000, and a young healthy female for even more'.[94] Females were also under more control given that their children could be taken from them by their masters. Essentially, female slaves faced multi-faceted challenges in comparison to their male counterparts, as they were victimised twice based on their enslavement and their gender. Given this, a multi-level approach sensitive to gender dynamics is needed to understand Mauritania's deeply-rooted social issues and their impact on its human and economic development. Because Mauritania is divided along ethno-racial lines, analysing gender issues considering the social status and ethnicity is critical. This is because the poverty-afflicted population are women and particularly the Haratin and Afro-Mauritanians, as they face intersectional discrimination, including in employment.[95] The Social Institutions and Gender Index (SIGI) indicates that 'many Haratin women are subjected to domestic servitude or forced labour, lack social protection and are more vulnerable to physical and sexual abuse and mistreatment'.[96] Jourde adds that 'the treatment of women in Mauritania varies according to ethnicity, status group (or caste), geographical setting, and class'.[97]

The polarisation of identities between the Arab-speaking segment of society and the Afro-Mauritanians has shaped politics in the country for a long time. Demands for ethnic political representation, land tenure and inclusive socio-economic and national policies grew over time and created ongoing societal tensions. Civil society and international human rights organisations have pressured the government to take a radical approach to abolish slavery and give the Afro-Mauritanians their freedom and rights as full citizens. However, when slavery was outlawed in in 1981, there were no laws that criminalised or prosecuted slave-holders.[98] In 2007, a law was passed that criminalised slavery for the first time. A subsequent law replacing the 2007 law was passed in 2015. This time, the law categorises slavery as a crime against humanity and 'raises the act of slavery from an "offence" to a "crime", raising sentences of imprisonment to ten to twenty years'.[99]

Despite several attempts to eradicate slavery and achieve social cohesion and equality between Arab-speaking communities and Afro-Mauritanians, the government has failed to enforce the laws in practice, as not all forms of slavery have been eradicated.[100] Additionally, the 2019 election critics argue that the lack of addressing pervasive ethnic divisions suggests that President Mohamed Ould El Ghazouani's election 'signals the continuation of the systemic disenfranchisement of the country's Black communities'.[101]

The Marginalised

Mauritania has made relative progress and experienced a steady growth and improvement in the various sectors discussed in this chapter. Yet, the various dimensions of marginalisation – such as social, cultural, economic and political, particularly among the Afro-Mauritanian/Black communities – still exist. The study of marginalisation is, of course, nothing new. The concept of marginalisation and marginality have been studied extensively in the past.[102] To put the analysis in its proper context, social identity and deprivation cross paths, as they constitute an additional layer of marginalisation.

Celia Cook-Huffman defines identity as 'complex, historically bound, socially constructed, and thus ever moving'; through this unique lens, collective identity is referred to as 'social identity'.[103] For Henri Tajfel, social identities are constructed within specific relationships, time and space and become salient over time.[104] Tajfel's concept is focused on social categorisation based on the use of clan, language, race, ethnicity and other group characteristics and behaviours as identity markers. Additionally, the pursuit of distinctiveness allows inter-group stereotypes to play a critical role in social identity formation and evaluation.[105]

Usually, groups hold 'simplified beliefs or stereotypes of the other'.[106] This is applicable to the Beidan in Mauritania and their stereotypical image about the Afro-Mauritanians/ Black Mauritanians as descendent of slaves; therefore, their loyalty and servitude is to them, as the Beidan regard themselves as a distinguished social category. Social identities often build strong fences around their social and political spaces. From this perspective, Mauritania has implemented the Arabisation process since 1960s. The education system as well as the government administration system were Arabised. This engendered a reduction in the number of Afro-Mauritanians in the administration.[107] In this case, the ethno-racial identity and language are used as tokens of differentiation, since Black Mauritanians of African descent are non-Arabic speaking groups. This labelling, applying Janet Gross Stein's concept, is an effort to defend (Beidan) 'distinctive attributes as virtues and label the distinctiveness of others as vices'.[108] Because of this categorisation, Black Mauritanians live on the margins of society. Riccardo Ciavolella comments that 'large subaltern portions of Mauritanian society are struggling for better living conditions and political recognition'.[109]

Research also shows that the perception of deprivation is often linked to social comparison.[110] Disadvantaged or marginalised groups – that is, the Afro-Mauritanians in this case – feel an acute sense of relative deprivation which usually leads to an 'estimation of their economic and social position'.[111] The sentiments of deprivation are transformed to feelings of perceived grievances and inequality.[112] As a result, Black Mauritanians' sense of relative deprivation is manifested through under-development, lack of political voice and the centralisation of power that 'caused widespread discontent at the periphery and corruption and nepotism in the centre'.[113]

Black Mauritanians were excluded from access to political and economic power, as they endured the brunt of history or what some call '*les temps des blessures*'. The systematic processes of Arabisation and deprivation have largely contributed to the Afro-Mauritanians' struggle today. Garba Diallo writes: 'Arab Moors distorted and falsified Black history and achievements while glorifying their own. Blacks were pushed to the bottom of the social, economic and political ladder'.[114]

Mauritania is far from a functioning democracy. The country has taken measures towards reform at the political and economic level. Yet, Mauritania struggles to deal with the long-standing challenges of its fragmented social fabric. In addition to its history of slavery, social dynamics are still marked by a major factionalism between ethnic-racial groups that still proclaim their rights to inclusion and refute marginalisation. Pazzanita comments that 'a lack of national civic identity, then, appears to be a fixture of Mauritania's social and political scene'.[115]

Another marginalised group in Mauritania consists of women, who have always struggled for their rights and emancipation. Literature attests to women's suffering in an attempt to become citizens, active participants in decision-making processes and contributors to the socio-economic development of the country.[116] Mauritania is still on the verge of development and social change. In their attempt to advance democracy, women are still faced with the dilemma of having to grapple with reconciling between secular and Islamic forces, between the image of the harem and the 'new modern woman' and, importantly, between the local and global context of the modern era. Women are facing many challenges related to the 'the complexity and variability [. . .] of place and time'.[117]

As Sarah E. Yerkes discusses in Chapter Seven, women play an important role in development, including economic development; therefore, enhancing opportunities for women is critical. The World Bank concludes that 'gender inequalities in human capital cost Mauritania 19 percent of its national wealth'.[118] Furthermore, the *Women, Business and Law 2020* index ranks Mauritania at 177 among 190 economies globally when it comes to laws and regulations affecting women's economic opportunity.[119] This shows that Mauritania has significant legal and social barriers to women's empowerment and equal opportunities to contributing to and benefiting from the economy. Women's economic outcomes are linked to 'reforms and policies that aim at gender equality'.[120]

There will be no development and progress without women's contribution and gender equality and inclusiveness, and no democracy without equal rights and justice. Therefore, equity and justice towards women should be emphasised to enhance Mauritania's path towards progress and prosperity.

Looking Ahead: Pathways to Democracy

In recent years, Mauritania has been making progress to break with traditional social frameworks that resulted from the rigid hierarchical and communal structures based on ethnicity, tribe and caste. Abdel Wedoud Ould Cheikh called this the 'reinvention' of social structures since the formation of statehood following the colonial era.[121] Since the 1990s, the institutionalisation of political pluralism and elections, which hardly affected the authoritarian nature of the regime and the personalised forms of power, has created what Ould Cheikh referred to as 'competitive authoritarianism'.[122]

The democratic transition headed by the military did not seem to side-line them from the exercise of power, as the 'shadow of the most active officers [. . .] continues to hover over the decisions of the government at the ballot box, while the civilian component of power seems paralyzed by the multipolarity'.[123] Although democratisation has not radically changed the political structure of the country, it did slightly shift the balance of power towards reform through political parties and the development of civil society. On this point, Ismail Bouganour elaborates that the democratic transformation of Mauritania has been a result of the interaction of factors between the social and cultural spheres. The tribal nature of Mauritanian society underlies the perpetual identity of Mauritania's citizens.[124] Like most North African countries, Mauritania also witnessed protests during the Arab Spring; however, when compared to its neighbouring countries, change has been less consequential. The 2011 uprisings in the Middle East and

North Africa (MENA) provided the macro-political opportunity for organising in Mauritania. Modelled after the Tunisian and Egyptian Arab Spring protests, the 25 February movement in Mauritania has consciously avoided partisan political connections, in part because of the weakness of these traditional avenues of political action and the loss of their legitimacy over the last few decades, as well as in avoidance of any ethnic or socially divisive political demands. A clean start was declared, as the 25 February movement vowed that there would be 'no return to politics as usual'.[125] Unfortunately, the 25 February movement's intensity dwindled over time, along with its ability to demand real change.[126] However, as Ismail Bouganour clarifies, ...

> The country has undergone extensive transformation in the face of international pressure and influence that were brought to bear on it, and their effects have affected the process of transformation, especially those pertaining to the acknowledgement of human rights and freedoms of citizens.[127]

The most recent local and national legislative elections took place in 2018 and were more pluralistic with the participation of the opposition, which had boycotted previous elections. In 2019, the parliament approved a regional councils' law, taking an important step towards enhancing the decentralisation policy and local development declaration that Mauritania had adopted in 2010. On the economic front, Mauritania also developed a national strategy called Strategy for Accelerated Growth and Shared Prosperity (SCAPP 2016–30) to facilitate inclusive economic growth. While initiatives to evaluate these efforts remain in their infancy, the Mauritanian government received support from the African Development Fund (FAD) to recruit an expert evaluator to develop tools, instruments and analytical reports related to the progress of SCAPP.[128] Additionally, local civil society is steadily learning and engaging in monitoring and evaluation efforts, particularly now that the Association Law has been amended to allow civil society to engage with decision- and policy-makers. Yet, it is too early to conclude whether SCAPP has brought real change or not.

Conclusion

Mauritania's multi-layered and interconnected problems, accentuated by internal and regional dynamics, continue to define the Mauritanian political landscape today. Since independence, Mauritania has not engaged in substantial political change, nor initiated comprehensive reforms that can move the country towards a real democratic path. The 25 February movement and other grassroots organisations attempted to demand a political system that is based on the rule of law, human rights and the agency of the people, one that has the potential to transform politics in the country, without resorting to overthrowing the regime. However, its success has so far been limited. To respect its international commitments, polish its human rights record and maintain its position as a major regional player in the Sahel, Mauritania has taken significant strides towards change, but these have yet to yield any substantial results. The country continues to be challenged by recurrent political instability, lack of representation in its political system, severe socio-economic issues and deep-rooted ethnic cleavages. Therefore, the broader question remains: what model does Mauritania need to embark on to achieve a genuine democratic transition?

The answer rests on stimulating further debate about the progress as well as the pitfalls and setbacks of the country's movement towards greater openness and embarking on a democratic experiment that considers the complexities, social and cultural constructions of its society. Reconciling grievances and addressing the 'national question' calls for redefined political will that appreciates the centrality and the inseparability of the Afro-Mauritanian identity from that of the nation of Mauritania.

Notes

1. 'Fragile States Index', *The Fund for Peace*, n. d., https://fragilestatesindex.org.
2. Sidi Bobba and Sid El Kheir Ould Taleb EKhyar, 'Drought Conditions and Management Strategies in Mauritania', *Integrated Drought Management Programme*, n. d., https://www.droughtmanagement.info/literature/UNW-DPC_NDMP_Country_Report_Mauritania_2014.pdf.

3. Boubacar N'Diaye, 'The Legacy of Mauritania's Colonels: West Africa's Next Crisis?' *Centre for Democracy and Development*, 2016, https://www.academia.edu/29969715/The_Legacy_of_Mauritania_Colonels_West_Africas_Next_Crisis.
4. For further reading on the history of Mauritania, see the work of Mareilla Villassante Cervello, Abdel Wedoud Ould Cheikh, Boubacar N'Daiye, William Eagleton Jr, Clement Moore, Daniel Wisenwine and Anthony Pazzanita, to list just a few, in addition to what is written in Arabic and French on Mauritania's history.
5. The Western Sahara issue is an ongoing conflict between Morocco and the POLISARIO over the territory in the Western Sahara region. Mauritania was a party to the conflict; however, in 1979 Mauritania renounced its claim to the Western Sahara. For a chronology of the conflict, see 'TIMELINE: Western Sahara, a 50-Year-Old Dispute', *Reuters*, 4 January 2008, https://www.reuters.com/article/us-sahara-polisario/timeline-western-sahara-a-50-year-old-dispute-idUSL2163728820080104.
6. 'Mauritania Profile: Timeline', *BBC*, 19 February 2018, https://www.bbc.com/news/world-africa-13882166.
7. Anthony G. Pazzanita, 'Political Transition in Mauritania: Problems and Prospects', *Middle East Journal* 53, no. 1 (1999): 44–58.
8. The Military Council for Justice and Democracy (CMJD) is a political body that served as an interim government under Colonel Vall.
9. Dafna Hochman, 'Civil-Military Power Struggles: The Case of Mauritania', *Current History* 108, no. 718 (2009): 221–26.
10. Daniel Zisenwine, 'Mauritania's Democratic Transition: A Regional Model for Political Reform?' *The Journal of North African Studies* 12, no. 4 (1 December 2007): 481–99.
11. Boubacar N'Diaye, 'To "Midwife" – and Abort – a Democracy: Mauritania's Transition from Military Rule, 2005–2008', *The Journal of Modern African Studies* 47, no. 1 (2009): 129–52.
12. 'Mauritania Profile: Timeline'.
13. Yasmine Akrimi and May Barth, 'Mauritania: The Military's Presence in "Democracy"', *Brussels International Center: Democratic Development Series*, September 2019, https://www.bic-rhr.com/sites/default/files/inline-files/Mauritania%20Military%27s%20Presence%20in%20Democracy_0.pdf.
14. Kissima Diagana, 'Ruling Party Candidate Declared Winner of Mauritania Election', *Reuters*, 23 June 2019, https://www.reuters.com/article/us-mauritania-election/ruling-party-candidate-declared-winner-of-mauritania-election-idUSKCN1TO083.

15. 'Elections: Mauritania President (Round 1) 2019', *IFES Election Guide*, 2019, https://www.electionguide.org/elections/id/3220/.
16. 'Mauritania', *International IDEA*, n. d., https://www.idea.int/data-tools/country-view/214/40.
17. 'The Head of Mission to Mauritanian Elections of 24th June 2019 Briefs the Media on Mauritania Elections', *African Union*, 24 June 2019, https://au.int/sw/pressreleases/20190624/head-mission-mauritanian-elections-24th-june-2019-briefs-media-mauritania.
18. 'Elections: Mauritania President (Round 1) 2019'.
19. Sarah Repucci and Amy Slipowitz, 'Freedom in the World 2021: Democracy Under Siege', *Freedom House*, 2021, https://freedomhouse.org/report/freedom-world/2021/democracy-under-siege/acknowledgements.
20. 'Mauritania Country Report 2020', *BTI Transformation Index*, 2020, https://bti-project.org/fileadmin/api/content/en/downloads/reports/country_report_2020_MRT.pdf.
21. 'Mauritania Country Report 2020', *BTI Transformation Index*, 2020, https://bti-project.org/fileadmin/api/content/en/downloads/reports/country_report_2020_MRT.pdf.
22. Anouar Boukhars, 'Keeping Terrorism at Bay in Mauritania', *Africa Center for Strategic Studies*, 16 June 2020, https://africacenter.org/spotlight/keeping-terrorism-at-bay-in-mauritania/.
23. Anouar Boukhars, 'The Drivers of Insecurity in Mauritania', *Carnegie Endowment for International Peace*, April 2012, https://carnegieendowment.org/files/mauritania_insecurity.pdf.
24. Akrimi and Barth, 'Mauritania: The Military's Presence in "Democracy"'.
25. For more context, see the 2020 BTI Transformation Index and its 'definition of Mauritania's identity and the role of the military in political life. The politicisation of identities, between Arab-speaking groups (comprising of Bidha/While Moors and Haratin/freed slaves/Black Moors) and Black African communities (comprising Haalpulaaren, Wolof, Soonino and Bamana) has shaped the political scene since the colonial period'. 'Mauritania Country Report (2020)'.
26. Hochman, 'Civil-Military Power Struggles: The Case of Mauritania'.
27. Pazzanita, 'Political Transition in Mauritania: Problems and Prospects'.
28. Samer Matta, 'Mauritania Economic Update: Why It Is Essential to Enable Women to Participate Fully in Economic Activity?' *World Bank*, 2021, https://www.worldbank.org/en/country/mauritania/publication/mauritania-economic-update-

why-it-is-essential-to-enable-women-to-participate-fully-in-economic-activity.
29. 'Human Development Report 2020: The Next Frontier: Human Development and the Anthropocene', *United Nations Development Programme*, 2020, http://hdr.undp.org/sites/default/files/hdr2020.pdf.
30. Ibrahim Yahaya Ibrahim, 'Managing the Sahelo-Saharan Islamic Insurgency in Mauritania: The Local Stakes of the Sahelian Crisis', *Sahel Research Group at the University of Florida's Center for African Studies*, August 2014, https://sahelresearch.africa.ufl.edu/wp-content/uploads/sites/170/Yahaya_StakesMauritania_Final.pdf.
31. 'Islamic Republic of Mauritania: Turning Challenges into Opportunities for Ending Poverty and Promoting Shared Prosperity', *World Bank*, May 2017, https://documents1.worldbank.org/curated/en/311841500256927016/pdf/MAU-SCD-06292017.pdf.
32. 'Islamic Republic of Mauritania: Turning Challenges into Opportunities'.
33. 'Mauritania: Country Policy and Institutional Assessment', *World Bank*, 2019, https://documents1.worldbank.org/curated/en/668721595586560397/pdf/Country-Policy-and-Institutional-Assessment-CPIA-Africa-2019-Strengthening-Debt-Management-Capacity-Mauritania-Quick-Facts.pdf.
34. 'Mauritania: Country Policy and Institutional Assessment'.
35. 'Mauritania: Improving Education to Foster Social Cohesion and Support Economic Development', *ReliefWeb*, https://reliefweb.int/report/mauritania/mauritania-improving-education-foster-social-cohesion-and-support-economic.
36. 'Poverty and Equity Brief: Mauritania', *World Bank*, April 2021, https://databank.worldbank.org/data/download/poverty/987B9C90-CB9F-4D93-AE8C-750588BF00QA/AM2020/Global_POVEQ_MRT.pdf.
37. Matta, 'Mauritania Economic Update'.
38. '2021 Investment Climate Statements: Mauritania', *US Department of State*, https://www.state.gov/reports/2021-investment-climate-statements/mauritania/.
39. Bobba and El Kheir Ould Taleb EKhyar, 'Drought Conditions and Management Strategies in Mauritania'.
40. 'Coordinating the UN's Work on Water and Sanitation', *UN-Water*, https://www.unwater.org/.
41. 'Mauritania Economy: Population, GDP, Inflation, Business, Trade, FDI, Corruption', *The Heritage Foundation*, n. d., //www.heritage.org/index/country/mauritania.

42. 'Mauritania Country Report 2020'.
43. 'Mauritania: Anti-Corruption Study', *World Bank*, September 2008, https://openknowledge.worldbank.org/handle/10986/12731.
44. Some of these reforms/policy frameworks include public financial management (PFM), monetary and exchange rate policy, banking supervision and the expansion of social safety nets, in addition to supporting reforms to the business environment. For further details, see 'International Monetary Fund Country Report: The Sixth Review Under the Extended Credit Facility Arrangement and Request for Waiver of Nonobservance of a Performance Criterion', *International Monetary Fund*, March 2021, https://www.imf.org/en/Publications/CR/Issues/2021/03/11/Islamic-Republic-of-Mauritania-Sixth-Review-Under-the-Extended-Credit-Facility-Arrangement-50255.
45. 'Mauritania: Economic Reforms and Diversification Support Programme – Phase II (PAREDE II)', *African Development Bank Group*, n. d., https://projectsportal.afdb.org/dataportal/VProject/show/P-MR-K00-017.
46. For details on Accelerated Growth and Shared Prosperity (SCAPP) for 2016–2030, see 'Islamic Republic of Mauritania: Economic Development Documents', *International Monetary Fund*, 1 June 2018, https://www.imf.org/en/Publications/CR/Issues/2018/06/01/Islamic-Republic-of-Mauritania-Economic-Development-Documents-45918.
47. '2020 Country Reports on Human Rights Practices: Mauritania', *US Department of State*, 30 March 2021, https://www.state.gov/reports/2020-country-reports-on-human-rights-practices/mauritania/.
48. 'Corruption Perceptions Index 2020 – Mauritania', *Transparency International*, 2020, https://www.transparency.org/en/cpi/2020/index/mrt.
49. 'Mauritania: Corruption', *Global Security*, n. d., https://www.globalsecurity.org/military/world/africa/mr-corruption.htm.
50. Abdur Rahman Alfa Shaban, 'Mauritania Parliament Probing Ex-President over Corruption', *AfricaNews*, 16 February 2020, https://www.africanews.com/2020/02/16/mauritania-parliament-probing-ex-president-over-corruption/.
51. '2021 Investment Climate Statements: Mauritania'.
52. See the work of Stephanie Pezard and Anne-Kathrin Glatz, 'Arms in and around Mauritania: National and Regional Security Implications', *Small Arms Survey*, June 2010, https://www.smallarmssurvey.org/resource/arms-and-around-mauritania-national-and-regional-security-implications-occasional-paper-24;

Cedric Jourde, 'Sifting Through the Layers of Insecurity in the Sahel: The Case of Mauritania', *Africa Center for Strategic Studies*, September 2011, https://africacenter.org/wp-content/uploads/2016/06/ASB15EN-Sifting-Through-the-Layers-of-Insecurity-in-the-Sahel-The-Case-of-Mauritania.pdf; Boukhars, 'The Drivers of Insecurity in Mauritania'; Frederic Wehrey, 'Control and Contain: Mauritania's Clerics and the Strategy Against Violent Extremism', *Carnegie Endowment for International Peace*, March 2019, https://carnegieendowment.org/2019/03/29/control-and-contain-mauritania-s-clerics-and-strategy-against-violent-extremism-pub-78729; Ibrahim, 'Managing the Sahelo-Saharan Islamic Insurgency in Mauritania'; Paul Melly, 'Mauritania's Unfolding Landscape Elections, Hydrocarbons and Socio-Economic Change', *Chatham House*, April 2019, https://www.chathamhouse.org/sites/default/files/2019-04-11-Mauritania%27s%20Unfolding%20Landscape.pdf.

53. Jourde, 'Sifting Through the Layers of Insecurity in the Sahel'.
54. Jourde, 'Sifting Through the Layers of Insecurity in the Sahel'.
55. Jourde, 'Sifting Through the Layers of Insecurity in the Sahel'.
56. Melly, 'Mauritania's Unfolding Landscape Elections, Hydrocarbons and Socio-Economic Change'.
57. Melly, 'Mauritania's Unfolding Landscape Elections, Hydrocarbons and Socio-Economic Change'.
58. Melly, 'Mauritania's Unfolding Landscape Elections, Hydrocarbons and Socio-Economic Change'.
59. John L. Esposito, 'Political Islam and the West', *Defense Technical Information Center*, 1 January 2000, https://apps.dtic.mil/sti/pdfs/ADA426734.pdf.
60. Esposito, 'Political Islam and the West'.
61. Esposito, 'Political Islam and the West'.
62. Mohamed Salem Ould Mohamed, 'Purist Salafism in the Sahel and Its Jihadist Position', *Aljazeera Centre for Studies*, 17 July 2012, https://studies.aljazeera.net/en/reports/2012/07/201271777719710292.html.
63. Malika Zaghal, 'Religion et politique au Maroc aujourd'hui', *Institut Francais des Relations Internationales*, 2005, https://www.ifri.org/fr/publications/notes-de-lifri/religion-politique-maroc-aujourdhui.
64. Boukhars, 'Keeping Terrorism at Bay in Mauritania'. In his article, Boukhars comments that CSIs are combat groups that 'have been well-equipped with vehicles and supplies, especially fuel, water, and ammunition, for sustained independent counterterrorism operations lasting several days in the remote desert'.

65. Melly, 'Mauritania's Unfolding Landscape Elections, Hydrocarbons and Socio-Economic Change'.
66. Boukhars, 'Keeping Terrorism at Bay in Mauritania'.
67. David Seddon, 'The Political Economy of Mauritania: An Introduction', *Review of African Political Economy* 23, no. 68 (1996): 197–214.
68. Rone Tempest, 'In Senegal and Mauritania, Ethnic Conflict Rages Amid Talk of War', *Los Angeles Times*, 3 June 1989, https://www.latimes.com/archives/la-xpm-1989-06-03-mn-831-story.html.
69. Ibrahim, 'Managing the Sahelo-Saharan Islamic Insurgency in Mauritania'.
70. 'Mauritania Country Report 2020'.
71. Cédric Jourde, 'Ethnicity, Democratization, and Political Dramas: Insights into Ethnic Politics in Mauritania', *African Issues* 29, no. 1/2 (2001): 26–30.
72. Jourde, 'Ethnicity, Democratization, and Political Dramas'.
73. 'Mauritania 2019 Human Rights Report', *US Department of State*, 2019, https://mr.usembassy.gov/wp-content/uploads/sites/204/MAURITANIA-2019-HUMAN-RIGHTS-REPORT.pdf.
74. 'Mauritania 2019 Human Rights Report'.
75. 'Mauritania 2019 Human Rights Report'.
76. 'Islamic Republic of Mauritania Joint Submission to the UN Universal Periodic Review 37th Session of the UPR Working Group', *CIVICUS*, 9 July 2020, https://www.civicus.org/documents/MauritaniaUPRSubmission.EN.2020.pdf.
77. 'Islamic Republic of Mauritania Joint Submission'.
78. 'Mauritania 2019 Human Rights Report'.
79. 'Mauritania 2019 Human Rights Report'.
80. For further information and detailed accounts on various human rights violations against activists and opposition, see 'Islamic Republic of Mauritania Joint Submission'.
81. 'How the Islamic State Rose, Fell and Could Rise Again in the Maghrib', *Crisis Group*, 24 July 2017, https://www.crisisgroup.org/middle-east-north-africa/north-africa/178-how-islamic-state-rose-fell-and-could-rise-again-Maghrib.
82. Garba Diallo, *Mauritania: The Other Apartheid* (Uppsala: Nordiak Afrikainstitutet, 1993), 47.
83. Katherine Ann Wiley, *Work, Social Status, and Gender in Post-Slavery Mauritania* (Bloomington: Indiana University Press, 2018).
84. 'Africa', *Global Slavery Index*, 2018, https://www.globalslaveryindex.org/2018/findings/regional-analysis/africa/.
85. Seddon, 'The Political Economy of Mauritania'.

86. Bidhân/Beidan/Baydane/White Moors and Haratin/freed slaves/ Black Moors are Arabic-speaking groups. Black African communities or Afro-Mauritanians are comprised of Haalpulaaren, Wolof, Sooninko and Bamana.
87. Seddon, 'The Political Economy of Mauritania'.
88. Original quote in French: '... la cohésion ou solidarité sociale ('asabiyya) ne se fonde pas sur la généalogie (nasab), mais sur les relations de protection (jiwâr, hmâye) et d'alliance politique (tahâluf) unissant les descendants de l'ancêtre éponyme, Lemrâbot Sîdi Mahmûd'. Mariella Villasante-de Beauvais, 'Genèse de la hiérarchie sociale du pouvoir politique Beidan selon les traditions orales des Ahl Sidi Mahmud, Confédération de l'est Mauritanien', *Cahiers d'Études Africaines* 147, no. 3 (1997): 587–633.
89. 'Mauritania and Slavery: An Epidemic', *Priceonomics*, n. d., http://priceonomics.com/mauritania-and-slavery-an-epidemic/.
90. Kevin Bales, *Disposable People: New Slavery in the Global Economy*, 3rd edition (Berkeley: University of California Press, 2012).
91. Bales, *Disposable People*.
92. Bales, *Disposable People*.
93. 'Mauritania and Slavery'.
94. Bales, *Disposable People*.
95. 'Social Institutions and Gender Index 2019', *OECD Development Centre*, 2019, https://www.genderindex.org/wp-content/uploads/files/datasheets/2019/MR.pdf.
96. 'Social Institutions and Gender Index 2019'.
97. Cédric Jourde, 'Countries at the Crossroads 2011: Mauritania', *Freedom House*, n. d., https://www.europarl.europa.eu/meetdocs/2009_2014/documents/dmag/dv/dmag20120125_02_/dmag20120125_02_en.pdf.
98. John D. Sutter, 'Slavery's Last Stronghold', *CNN*, March 2012, http://www.cnn.com/interactive/2012/03/world/mauritania.slaverys.last.stronghold/index.html.
99. 'New Mauritanian Anti-Slavery Law Is Worthless If Not Implemented', *Anti-Slavery International*, 18 August 2015, https://www.antislavery.org/new-mauritanian-anti-slavery-law-worthless-not-implemented/.
100. 'World Report 2021: Mauritania', *Human Rights Watch*, 2021, https://www.hrw.org/world-report/2021/country-chapters/mauritania#.
101. Akrimi and Barth, 'Mauritania: The Military's Presence in "Democracy"'.

102. See Robert E. Park, 'Human Migration and the Marginal Man', *American Journal of Sociology* 33, no. 6 (1928): 881–93; E. V. Stonequist, *The Marginal Man: A Study in Personality and Culture Conflict* (New York: Scribner, 1937); R. De Koninck, 'Les pieds, la tête et la géographie: Notes sur la fonction organique d'une discipline académique', *Implications* 1 (1980): 33–46; Andre Vant, ed., *Marginalité Sociale, Marginalité Spatiale* (Paris: CNRS, 1986).
103. Celia Cook-Huffman, 'The Role of Identity in Conflict', in *Handbook of Conflict Analysis and Resolution*, ed. D. J. D. Sandole et al. (London: Routledge, 2009), 19–31. Note that the use of collective identity or social identity in this paper is to refer to Afro-Mauritanians/Black Africans as a collective group. The reference is to the collective identity, not the individual one.
104. Cook-Huffman, 'The Role of Identity in Conflict'.
105. Tajfel argues that social identity in inter-group conflict dynamics entails four key processes, including social categorisation, formation of social identity awareness, identification and psychological distinctiveness. T. McNamara, 'Theorizing Social Identity: What Do We Mean by Social Identity? Competing Frameworks, Competing Discourses', *TESOL Quarterly* 31, no. 3 (Autumn 1997): 561–67.
106. Marilynn B. Brewer, *Intergroup Relations*, 2nd edition (Buckingham: Open University Press, 2003).
107. Boukhars, 'The Drivers of Insecurity in Mauritania'.
108. Here, I am borrowing Stein's concept of social labelling. Janet Gross Stein, 'Image, Identity and the Resolution of Violent Conflict', in *Turbulent Peace: The Challenges of Managing International Conflict*, ed. Chester Crocker, Fen Hampson, and Pamela Aall (Washington, DC: USIP Press, 2001), 93.
109. Riccardo Ciavolella, 'Huunde Fof Ko Politik, Everything Is Politics: Gramsci, Fulani, and the Margins of the State in Mauritania', *Africa Today* 58, no. 3 (Spring 2012): 3–21.
110. Karina Korostelina, *Social Identity and Conflict: Structures, and Implications* (New York: Palgrave Macmillan, 2007).
111. Korostelina, *Social Identity and Conflict*.
112. Ted Robert Gurr, *Why Men Rebel* (Princeton: Princeton University Press, 1970). Gurr defines relative deprivation as 'a perceived discrepancy between men's value expectations and their value capabilities'. Specifically, for Gurr value expectations (VE) are constitutive of 'goods and conditions of life to which people believe they are rightfully entitled', while value capabilities (VC) entails 'the goods and conditions which they think they

are capable of attaining or maintaining, given the social means available to them'.
113. Diallo, *Mauritania: The Other Apartheid*.
114. Diallo, *Mauritania: The Other Apartheid*.
115. Pazzanita, 'Political Transition in Mauritania'.
116. For further reading on women in Mauritania, see the work of Valentine M. Moghadam, Urs Peter Ruf, Celine Lesourd and Heloise Finch-Boyer, George M. Voissett and Andrea Page, in addition to reports commissioned by the World Bank on gender equality and the UN Women Data Hub, to list just a few.
117. H. A. Seif, 'Contextualizing Gender and Labor: Class, Ethnicity, and Global Politics in the Yemeni Socio-Economy', in *Women's Rights, Human Rights: International Feminist Perspectives*, ed. Julie Stone Peters and Andrea Wolper (New York: Routledge, 1995), 289–300.
118. 'Mauritania Economic Update: Why It Is Essential to Enable Women to Participate Fully in Economic Activity', *World Bank*, https://www.worldbank.org/en/country/mauritania/publication/mauritania-economic-update-why-it-is-essential-to-enable-women-to-participate-fully-in-economic-activity.
119. World Bank, *Women, Business and the Law 2020* (n. p.: The World Bank, 2020).
120. World Bank, *Women, Business and the Law 2020*.
121. Abdel Wedoud Ould Cheikh, 'Autoritarisme compétitif, diversité ethnique et démocratie', 2008, https://www.academia.edu/6157344/Autoritarisme_comp%C3%A9titif_diversit%C3%A9_ethnique_et_d%C3%A9mocratie.
122. Cheikh, 'Autoritarisme compétitif, diversité ethnique et démocratie'.
123. Cheikh, 'Autoritarisme compétitif, diversité ethnique et démocratie'.
124. Ismail Bouganour, 'Civil Society and Democratic Transformation in Mauritania: The Paradigm of Transition and the Antecedents of Political Change', *Contemporary Arab Affairs* 10, no. 3 (2017): 372–91.
125. Harry Vanden, 'Social Movements, Hegemony, and New Forms of Resistance', *Latin American Perspectives* 34, no. 2 (March 2007): 17–30.
126. The 25 February movement's demands included limiting military involvement in politics and constitutional reforms.
127. Bouganour, 'Civil Society and Democratic Transformation in Mauritania'.
128. 'Monitoring Evaluation Expert', *Devex*, n. d., https://www.devex.com/jobs/monitoring-evaluation-expert-501084.

6

Plus ça change, plus c'est la même chose: The Herculean Task of Civilianising the Algerian State

Anouar Boukhars

The Algerian protest movement known as the Hirak that began in February 2019 as a mass demonstration against a nearly comatose President Abdelaziz Bouteflika's bid for a fifth term jolted the Algerian state out of its long years of stupor. Indeed, not since the massive protests and riots of October 1988, which up-ended the country's long-standing one-party rule was the Algerian state confronted with the untenability of a status quo marked by languid leadership, notorious political scandals and grand corruption. The Hirak punctured the singular narrative of regime stability that the country's ruling elite had consistently told about itself, particularly since the system successfully weathered the wave of pro-democracy revolts commonly known as the Arab Spring that shook North Africa and the Middle East beginning in 2010 and 2011. The millions of demonstrators who flooded Algeria's streets also exposed the vulnerabilities in the regime's grasp on power. The Algerian regime's stability has been based mostly on the informal power-sharing arrangement crafted in 1999 between a dominant military, influential security services and the president's civilian entourage, and it has derived its legitimacy claims from an authoritarian populist ideology and a mythical revolutionary past. The equilibrium of this formula of governing and domination of state and society routinised under the reign of Bouteflika was disrupted in April 2019, when the late Ahmed Gaïd Salah, then army chief of staff and deputy minister of defence, forced the president to resign and jailed several of his political and business allies.

The withering away of the Bouteflika power structure, however, did not mean the break-down of the Algerian political system or the decomposition of its central characteristic: the military as the key source of political power.[1] This primacy of the military establishment has defined post-colonial Algeria, even though it has taken different forms at different times.[2] To be sure, the military's preponderance of power and its control of all the main dimensions of the state have not gone unchallenged, as the Hirak had shown most vividly with its persistent and loud calls for 'a civilian state, not a military state'. The fate of earlier attempts to challenge the nature of the political system, however, offered a sobering preview of the enormity and ramifications of such a task in Algeria. From the Berber spring of 1980 to the Islamist electoral tsunami of 1990–91, the military establishment was willing to go to any length to maintain its status and grip on the main levers of power. Even milder attempts within the Algerian regime to rein in the military did not pan out. Indeed, neither inter-service rivalries nor competition between clans within the military have greatly disrupted the capability or resolve of this institution to neutralise any threat it perceives as detrimental to its interests and political agendas. This reality was exemplified most recently in the military's determination to weaken the Hirak, a heterogeneous movement that it views as too radical in its democratic demands.[3] As with previous revolutionary challenges, the military command structure orchestrated a controlled political transition that it has used to re-assert its grip over all factions within the military establishment and to re-affirm its preeminent position in the state.

But, as in the past, the consolidation of military primacy behind a façade of civilian governments has failed to resolve the multiple political, social and economic crises that Algeria faces. The generals hoped that the contested and controversial election of former Prime Minister Abdelmadjid Tebboune as president would help attenuate the regime's crisis of legitimacy through improvement in governance and management of the economy, in much the same way in which the anointment of Bouteflika in 1999 as head of state helped to restore legitimacy to the Algerian political system, even if temporarily. Tebboune's task, however, might be harder than Bouteflika's, as he lacks the stature that Bouteflika had back then, as well as the hydrocarbon bonanza, driven by years of high energy prices, that allowed the former president to swell the military budget to staggering heights, co-opt political opposition and buy social peace.

Thus, this is the dilemma that the Algerian regime faces today: for the military establishment to secure its prerequisites and privileges, it needs a stable form of competent civilian governance. The latter, however, is dependent on the military leadership's willingness to curtail its strangle-hold on governance structures. The proponents of civilianising the state face their own dilemmas. Their goals of democratic reforms will be hard to materialise without ironing out their divergences and changing the military's calculus of the risk of transitioning towards a more accountable political system. In other words, the challenge for democratic movements in Algeria is how to make democratisation a strategic choice for powerful military leaders.

The 'Guardians' of the Republic

Since Algeria's independence in 1962, the military establishment has loomed large over both state and society. Its far-reaching influence over domestic and foreign affairs has led a number of observers to summon the famous aphorism once applied to Prussia – that it was not a country with an army but an army with a country – to describe Algeria. As the main architect and guardian of the political system, the military has made and unmade all Algerian presidents. It has also set the rules and hierarchies that guarantee its autonomous existence while shaping competition over political participation and access to resources among the elites. The routinisation and internalisation of these structures and rules has de-personalised the ways in which the military as an institution runs its affairs and regulates the rules of the political game.[4] This de-personalisation began to take root after the death of Colonel Houari Boumédiène in 1978.

Boumédiène – who, as minister of defence and vice president, ousted President Ahmed Ben Bella in June 1965 – is credited with establishing the tutelary regime that has ever since placed the military establishment at the centre of the Algerian political system. The way in which the military as an institution exercised effective political power has taken different forms. In the first fluid post-coup years, Boumédiène, who anointed himself as president, undertook legislative and executive tasks through a twenty-six-member revolutionary council, comprised mainly of historical figures of the liberation war against France and army commanders of the military regions. During the war against France, Algerian insurgents divided the country into several military districts, with Boumédiène commanding the one around Oran. (After independence, Algeria became divided into several military regions, seven today, whose headquarters are located in strategic cities or towns.) After the foiled coup attempt by former Army Chief of Staff Colonel Tahar Zbiri in December 1967, Boumédiène began to assert his grip on the military and the whole state apparatus. Within a few years, he had managed to build a highly personalised system of rule that granted unparalleled powers of decision-making to himself and vast domains of influence to a military greatly purged of his rivals.

Two key entities – the military and the people – made up the ideological basis of Boumédiène's regime. Boumédiène was a charismatic and populist leader who vowed to fulfil the Algerians' aspirations for national dignity, economic development and social justice through state control of heavy industry, land redistribution and provision of modern public education and free healthcare.[5] The most recognisable character of this form of populist politics that Boumédiène championed and enforced was, however, its disdain for liberalism and utter hostility to political pluralism.[6] For him, the exercise of politics could only occur within the frameworks and regulations of the one-party political system under the National Liberation Front (FLN), founded in 1954 to wage war against French colonisation. Decision-making authority resided in the presidency and under the watchful eye of the military.

The death of Boumédiène in December 1978 disrupted this delicate balance between presidential power and that of the military. Boumédiène, a capable tactician, structured the political game in a way that ensured that no centre of power within the military or bureaucracy could emerge to challenge his control of the state apparatus. To rectify this imbalance vis-à-vis the presidency, the top military brass settled on the self-effacing Colonel Chadli Bendjedid as the new president of Algeria.[7] With this choice, the military institution signalled its determination to prevent the emergence of any towering presidential figure who could try to rule in his own right, even if his ultimate authority emanated from the military and its instruments of power.[8]

Bendjedid's reign consecrated a new power balance between the president as the formal head of the Algerian power structure and the senior army commanders as the actual power-holders. The uncharismatic Bendjedid lacked the unparalleled authority that Boumédiène had had over the armed forces. This handicap was aggravated in 1984 with the re-establishment of the General Staff of the People's National Army (ANP), which Boumédiène helped create in 1960 to unify the centrifugal tendencies of the National Liberation Army before abolishing it in December 1967 following Zbiri's aborted coup.[9] The rebirth of the General Staff weakened the authority that the president had hoped to exercise over the military. It also diluted the weight of the Ministry of Defence, which the president headed, in controlling the officer corps of the ANP.

The implications of this institutional change, which established 'an autonomous centre of political power and decision making within the army',[10] came to light after the 1988 bloody riots caused the president to initiate a short-lived democratic experiment.[11] Immediately after the Islamic Salvation Front (FIS) had scored its first victory in the municipal and regional elections in June 1990, the General Staff forced the president to cede his leadership of the Ministry of Defence to Chief of General Staff Khaled Nezzar. Twelve months later, Major General Nezzar and the General Staff stripped the president of more of his prerogatives, compelling him to fire his reformist Prime Minister Mouloud Hamrouche and cede the presidency of the FLN. The curtain finally fell on the president in December 1991 when the FIS won big in the first round of parliamentary elections. In January 1992, Nezzar and other senior commanders of the General Staff forced Bendjedid, who was reportedly willing to share power with an Islamist parliamentary majority and prime minister, to resign, and then they cancelled the country's first multi-party parliamentary elections.[12]

After the coup, the military leadership brought back from exile Mohamed Boudiaf, a founder of the revolutionary National Liberation Front and a hero of the Algerian war of independence against France, to serve as the head of a military-backed High Council of State. The top generals calculated that Boudiaf's historical stature could help outweigh the legitimacy that the deposed Islamists generated though the ballot box. Soon thereafter, however, buyer's remorse set in at the General Staff. Boudiaf, like Ben Bella before him, was a strong-willed political leader who resisted the primacy of the military over political leadership. His priorities in domestic politics – notably combatting corruption – and in foreign policy – resolving the political disagreements with Morocco, where he had lived for nearly three decades, over the Western Sahara dispute – were two issues that, as long-time Algeria expert John Entelis notes, 'struck at the heart of the army's self-interests'.[13] Five months after he had assumed the chairmanship of the military-backed collective presidency, Boudiaf was assassinated by one of his body-guards, Lieutenant Lambarek Boumaarafi.

The military leadership then selected the low-key Colonel Ali Kafi to lead the five-member collective presidency, known as the High Council of State, from 1992 to 1994. In 1994, the military high command scrapped the High Council of State and appointed General Liamine Zeroual, Algeria's defence minister since 1993, as interim head of state. Zeroual, who in November 1995 won the country's first multi-candidate presidential election since the 1992 coup, hoped to enhance the powers of the presidency, particularly since he retained the defence portfolio. But, as Bendjedid had discovered to his great chagrin, sitting at the top table of the Ministry of Defence is not tantamount to exercising authority and control over the army's General Staff or the intelligence services, which ascended in prominence and power as the Islamist insurgency that began in 1992 escalated in intensity and lethality. Zeroual's attempts to appoint his allies to lead the powerful General Staff and the formidable Department of Intelligence and Security (DRS), headed by General Mohamed 'Toufik' Mediène since September 1990, all came to naught. Hard-liners within the General Staff and the intelligence services also frustrated Zeroual's efforts to negotiate an end to a raging Islamist insurgency and civil war as well as his manoeuvres to take over the National Democratic Rally (RND), a state-sponsored party created in 1997.[14] With little room for manoeuvre and little hope to execute any of his priorities, Zeroual decided to throw in the towel in late 1998 and cut short his term in office by nearly two years.

Civil–Military Cohabitation

Zeroual's induced exit from the political stage closed a chapter on the broken balance between a shackled presidency and an all too powerful General Staff and Intelligence Services. The re-emergence of the Moroccan-born Abdelaziz Bouteflika, Boumédiène's long-time foreign minister and protégé, onto the national political scene ushered in a new phase in the tilted balance of power between the presidency and the main centres of power within the military. After Zeroual's resignation, Algerian generals needed a civilian president with an international reputation to help seal the deal on a settlement to the devastating decade-long civil-war that had ravaged Algeria, as well as to help restore the battered image of a military-dominated regime accused of gross human rights abuses. Bouteflika, who had turned down a similar offer in 1994, believed that the time was ripe to not only complete his climb to the political summit, a moment he had been imagining since he had been shoved out the door after the death of Boumédiène in 1978, but also to expand the scope of presidential authority.

Bouteflika's attempts to reconstruct the Algerian regime on the basis of strong presidential power saw a number of twists and turns along the way. From his first win of a one-man presidential race in 1999 to his 2013 stroke that left him wheelchair-bound and badly weakened, Bouteflika had shrewdly navigated the perilous waters of military politics and machinations.[15] In so doing, he capitalised on two remarkable features that had not been present during the time of his predecessors, but which came to define the better part of his reign: an oil bonanza that lasted until 2014 and a growing rift within the military between the General Staff and the Intelligence Services.

During his first term in office, Bouteflika skilfully built for himself the image of a unifier who, in his own words, helped 'to definitively turn the sombre pages of our history'.[16] Barely five months after taking office in mid-February 1999, he turned a peace deal that was already tentatively struck by the ANP and an appreciable number of armed groups into the Law on Civil Concord, and in September of that year he orchestrated a successful referendum on national reconciliation. The president also used his policies of reconciliation to position himself as the most credible civilian to divert accusations of war atrocities levelled against the military by some former Algerian army officers and international human rights organisations as well as to redeem the reputation of the military internationally.[17]

Bouteflika's resolve to 'bury the past' while milking the benefits of national reconciliation domestically and externally continued into the early years of his second term as president (2004–9).[18] In September 2005, Bouteflika secured popular approval through a referendum on the Draft Charter for Peace and National Reconciliation. In February 2006, the government issued the 'Decree Implementing the Charter for Peace and National Reconciliation', which offered amnesty to Islamist guerrillas willing to lay down their arms as well as shielded from prosecution security forces allegedly implicated in committing crimes during the Dirty War. Notably, the decree also made it a criminal offense 'to undermine the good reputation of [state] agents who honourably served the country or to tarnish the image of Algeria internationally'.[19]

Bouteflika's second term also witnessed the president's jockeying to restore the powers of the presidency that had prevailed when he had served as Boumediene's influential foreign minister. After he claimed the presidency in 1999, he famously vowed never to be 'three-quarters of a president'.[20] But during his first term, he confronted a challenge that most of his predecessors had had to reckon with: the inability to appoint his own military commanders and exert presidential authority over the defence establishment. Bouteflika's attempts to do so faced vociferous resistance from Mohamed Lamari, the army chief of staff since 1993. Lamari and his allies in the army command were happy with the president's successes in redeeming the reputation of the military establishment and removing Algeria from international isolation – both accomplishments were amplified after the terrorist attacks of 11 September 2001, which made Algeria an important state in the war against terrorism in the Sahel – but they had no intention of allowing Bouteflika to shift the balance of power that governed relations between the presidency and the military establishment since 1978. According to Algeria expert Hugh Roberts, Lamari and his supporters reportedly provoked 'lethal riots in Kabylia in the spring and summer of 2001' and then sought 'to channel the massive Kabyle protest movement that resulted into attacking the presidency, quietly encouraging extraordinarily vitriolic attacks on Bouteflika in the secularist press'.²¹ In the run-up to the presidential election of 2004, they opposed a second term for Bouteflika, encouraging his erstwhile Prime Minister Ali Benflis to run under the banner of the FLN.

Bouteflika's landslide victory in 2004 was a major reward by Algerian voters for his successful efforts in restoring relative peace to a country fatigued by years of brutal civil war. It was also a major upset for army commanders who failed to gain the support of the powerful DRS in their endeavours to get rid of Bouteflika. The latter skilfully used this divergence at the top echelon of the military establishment in his favour. Thus, emboldened by his big electoral win and the critical arbitration of the DRS in his favour against the commanders of the General Staff who opposed his re-election, Bouteflika decided to finally execute one of the primary goals of his presidency: restoring the authority of the Ministry of Defence, over which he presided, over the army. This necessitated restraining the powers of the General Staff, an objective that seemed tantalisingly within reach in the summer of 2004, when Bouteflika managed to finally force Lamari and his followers in the army command into retirement. This was the first time in over a decade that a president succeeded in exercising his constitutional authority to appoint and relieve senior officers of their command of the army.

This feat, however, did not signify the taming of the General Staff or the consecration of presidential authority over the whole defence establishment. The dismissal of the powerful Lamari and his replacement by the self-effacing Gaïd Salah may have curtailed the intrusion of the General Staff upon presidential authority, but such limits were always conditional on the preservation of the army's financial autonomy vis-à-vis political power, the vicissitudes of politics and the actual conditions of collaboration or discord between the army and the intelligence services.²² The provisional right-sizing of the powers of the ANP General Staff did not entail the extension of Bouteflika's authority over the intelligence services. The latter had grown in power and influence so that the DRS became the effective power-broker in Algeria. Its intelligence chief since 1990, General Mediène had by then outlasted several presidents, defence ministers and army commanders.

Duel with the DRS

A shadowy figure whose face had been kept out of the public view, Mediène, better known as Toufik, became the ultimate embodiment of mystery and intrigue. Algerians saw his Department of Intelligence and Security as a huge hydra with many tentacles that seemed to know no bounds, yet they knew little about the man who once reportedly referred to himself as the 'God of Algeria'.[23] This outsized reputation shrouded in secrecy had given Mediène an aura of mystique. It had also bred bitterness among several senior generals in the army who resented feeling subservient to an ascendant Mediène and his DRS officers who operated outside the normal military chain of command. Mediène's men not only infiltrated most organs of the state and society – including ministries, political parties, public corporations, unions, the press, universities and civil society organisations – but they also exercised surveillance of military officers, carried out judicial probes and arbitrarily arrested anyone whom they deemed a threat to the regime. Intelligence officers also had veto power on promotions of officers whom they vetted to ensure allegiance to the DRS. As Lahouari Addi put it, 'colonels and commanders of operational units were at the mercy of a report by a DRS lieutenant who was officially under their command'.[24] Mediène's men also bred indignation due to the material privileges that they reportedly enjoyed through their strategic position in the political economy of rents and redistribution.

Bouteflika's challenge in his second term was how to counter-balance the DRS's political influence. In his effort to get the edge in this duel, Bouteflika instrumentalised the internecine politics of competition and resentment within the military sector to his advantage. First, he tried to bind senior military officers to his regime. This was pursued, as noted above, by elevating to the rank of chief of staff a commander who had been forced into retirement by his superiors. Thus was born an alliance based on mutual interest and dependence between Bouteflika and Gaïd Saleh who had every interest in wedding the General Staff to the presidency in order to expand its share of material largesse and authority in the state. In this contest for power, Bouteflika also increased the influence of the Ministry of the Interior and boosted the role and size of the police. Equally significant in the president's efforts to balance the influence of the coercive sector, he built up a veritable clientelistic network in the high bureaucracy and among business oligarchs. Thus wrote Algerian scholar Rachid Ouaissa: 'a new power centre was born, this time around the president and the import barons'.[25] The latter profited from their proximity to the presidency to tap into the bonanza of foreign currency and drive an exponential growth in imports of consumer goods. The flooding of the Algerian market with imported goods sated the desires of an emerging middle class that Bouteflika showered with subsidies and loans, some of which were eventually written off.

The empowerment of new constituencies created a new social contract between the beneficiaries of economic rent and the presidency, which strove to control most public and private economic activity. This new coalition of business magnate profiteers, high functionaries in the public sector, public corporations and middle-/upper-class households replaced the old 'military-technocratic-administrative coalition'.[26] This alliance, however, did not share a common ideology. Hence, the presidential coalition was comprised of a cocktail of supporters and political parties that ranged from conservatives and secularists to nationalists and Berbers. All had a vested interest in sustaining a political system that combined crony capitalism and state control.

The astute Bouteflika also entangled military elites in this economic system that over the years had spawned rampant nepotism and corruption. Under the reign of Bouteflika, high-ranking military officers ventured into the booming real estate sector and established ties to influential businessmen. They also used their influence and political connections to help get state contracts for their family businesses as well as other tax privileges. At the regional level, military figures became entangled into networks of financial interests and nepotism with governors and political elites associated with the presidency.[27] This played out starkly in oil- and gas-producing areas such as the fourth military region of Ouargla, a sparsely populated but hydrocarbon-rich tract of desert in southeastern Algeria, where corruption became pervasive. In the 2000s, so writes Ali Bensaad, the Algerian army was 'no longer seen there as a shadow power, but as a trivialised actor in the race for profit'.²⁸ High-ranking officers and their children or their protégés, in association with multi-nationals, became the dominant actors in a wide range of different privatised activities linked to the oil sector. Such systemic corruption would reach a crescendo in 2018, when General Abderrazak Cherif, who by then had led the fourth military region of Ouargla for fifteen years, was arrested and later sentenced to fifteen years in prison for illicit enrichment and trading in influence.²⁹ At the local level, as writes Algerian researcher Belkacem Elguettaa, lower-echelon military officers also joined the scramble for illicit rent-seeking by erecting webs of corruption networks with mayors and heads of city government departments. 'Outside the official state bureaucracy', he added, military officers deepened their forays into the informal economy, most notably in peripheral areas. Smuggling operations covered 'a wide range of activities and commodities, from foodstuffs and gasoline to drugs and gold'.³⁰

During Bouteflika's second term, corruption became an essential component in the architecture of authoritarian rule which he was consolidating. As an instrument of state control, it was a tool of political negotiation to enable loyal rent-seekers or settle political scores. To Bouteflika's chagrin, however, the instrumentalisation of rent-seeking behaviour was not the exclusive prerogative of the presidential camp. In a context of intense inter-elite conflict, other actors, most notably the DRS, abetted corruption and used it as a cover to discredit its political opponents. Such instrumentalisation of corruption played out most vividly after Bouteflika changed the constitution to prolong his stay in office beyond 2009. Mediène, who was lukewarm towards Bouteflika's plans, saw his relationship with the president sour significantly after his election to a third term in April 2009. Bouteflika, at the time seventy-one, was already in poor health. He was suffering from stomach cancer and had 'been on dialysis since his election in 1999'.³¹ As a result, his brother, Said Bouteflika, was gradually becoming the president's 'gate-keeper'. Said also began building a political power base among the country's political and business elite, a signal of his political ambitions. Mediène 'watched Said's move towards centre stage with distaste'.³²

To check the presidential clan's ambitions, Mediène, likely fearing the possibility of suffering the same fate as General

Lamari who had been dismissed at the beginning of Bouteflika's second term, unleashed 'the age-old combination of "corruption" and "blackmail"'[33] on his real and potential enemies. This campaign targeted several political and business figures close to Bouteflika and his brother; foremost among them was Minister of Energy and Mines Chakib Khelil and Minister of the Department of Public Works Amar Ghoul. The exposure of massive corruption scandals in the state-owned energy giant Sonatrach and in the $12 billion East–West Highway Project developed by a Chinese–Japanese consortium was the opening salvo in a campaign to intimidate and discredit the president's allies. Bouteflika tried to retaliate by establishing an independent security commission to dig into the role that the DRS had played in the 1990s Dirty War, including the assassination of Mohamed Boudiaf, the first chairman of the HCE, and the mysterious death of General Saidi Fodil, whom then President Zeroual reportedly saw as a replacement of Mediène as head of the DRS.[34]

The flurry of corruption revelations and probes escalated in the run-up to legislative and local elections in 2012 and in anticipation of the 2014 presidential election. *Algerie News*, believed to be close to the DRS, accused several senior members of the presidential coalition, notably Minister of Industry Cherif Rahmani and the head of the ruling party, Abdelaziz Belkhadem, of taking bribes from companies to secure contracts. The daily *El Watan* published 'a four-page exposé over the misuse of public funds, including fancy cars and the construction of new seaside villas for ministers from public money'.[35] These revelations embarrassed and angered the presidential clan. They also seemed to unnerve other branches of the military who bitterly resented the authority and ability of the DRS's political and judicial police to investigate the country's bureaucracy, including the army. There were also grumblings about the DRS's failures to neutralise terrorist threats within Algeria. The kidnapping of three European NGO members in the highly militarised refugee camp of Tindouf in October 2011, the March 2012 suicide attack on a police base in Tamanrasset and the June 2012 attack in Ouargla were warning signs of significant gaps in intelligence. Yet, despite the simmering resentment and apprehensions about the DRS, by 2012 Mediène and his men seemed as strong as ever.

The Pendulum Swings

In early 2013, the pendulum began swinging away from Mediène and the DRS. The January 2013 terrorist siege of the Tigentourine gas plant at In Amenas in southeast Algeria for the first time struck at the hydrocarbon lifeline that underpins regime survival.[36] Even at the height of the civil war in the 1990s, the south and its oil installations were immune to attacks. In fact, it was in the deep south where the state interned thousands of Islamists and their sympathisers in concentration camps. The dramatic terrorist assault on the gas plant 'punctured the aura of invulnerability of Algeria's energy installations'.[37] It also embarrassed the military establishment which worried that the attack would dent their international reputation for fighting radical Islamist insurgents in a region increasingly destabilised by a brewing civil war in Libya and a raging insurgency in northern Mali.[38] That said, Gaïd Salah and his allies in the General Staff and the presidency saw an opportunity, as the saying goes, to never let a serious crisis go to waste. The attack weakened Mediène by exposing how incompetent the system over which he presided was, particularly at a sensitive time when the succession to Bouteflika was not yet resolved.[39] And the General Staff blamed Mediène for this severe intelligence failure and for the subsequent botched hostage rescue mission that was commanded by his deputy, General Bashir Tartag, also known as 'Le Bombardier' – the rescue mission left dozens of hostages dead.[40]

Thence began the offensive by Mediène's opponents to roll back the powers that the DRS had accumulated since the 1990s. The debilitating stroke that Bouteflika suffered in April 2013 increased both the stakes of guaranteeing a smooth presidential election in 2014 and the urgency to begin cutting off the tentacles of the DRS. After his return from the Val-de-Grace Hospital in Paris, Bouteflika 'launched his first strike, transferring the responsibilities of the DRS's media monitoring centre to the general staff of the army'.[41] Bouteflika's second strike targeted the judicial police, who were under the DRS, ordering an end to its authority to investigate corruption. In its stead, a new secret service, the Military Operational Central Department for Investigations (MOCDI), was established, and it became dependent on the army's chief of staff. Bouteflika also transferred to the General Staff other major responsibilities of the DRS – namely, the Central Directorate for Army Security (DCSA), which was also tasked with supervising the Counter-Terrorism Intelligence Department (OCCTID). Then came the turn of the 'the mythical DRS armed wing, the Special Task Force (STF)' to fall 'under the ground forces' command'.[42] After his re-election to a fourth term in April 2014, the ailing Bouteflika and his clan continued their offensive to further dismember DRS agencies. Bouteflika sacked several top intelligence generals and signed a decree 'to put an end to the DRS presence in public institutions, including ministries and state-owned firms'.[43] In September 2015, in a move that surprised and intrigued many Algerians, the ailing Bouteflika delivered the coup de grâce by firing Mediène. In January 2016, Bouteflika fired his last shot at the DRS by dissolving it and replacing it with the Directorate of Security Services.

The triumph of the Bouteflika regime over the DRS did not signify the consecration of civilian control over the military. Such a feat could not have happened without the support of the General Staff whose senior military officers had longed to restore their own authority and influence.[44] When the chapter of DRS ascendency came to a close, the Algerian political system returned to its primary characteristic where the General Staff and its chief acted as the system's backbone. With Bouteflika critically ill and the question of succession unsettled, some discord between the army and the president's civilian entourage seemed inevitable. Gaïd Salah might have owed Bouteflika his rise to prominence, but the military was not keen on seeing the president's younger brother take the reign of the presidency. But with the lack of consensus on succession, the military and the presidential clan 'continued to regard the automatic renewal of Bouteflika's presidency for an unprecedented fifth term as a magic formula for maintaining control of the country's politics while avoiding accountability'.[45] Meanwhile, the significant decline in the price of oil since mid-2014 strained the state's finances and jeopardised Bouteflika's social contract with a critical mass of the population. Rent from oil was 'no longer enough to co-opt the deadlocked middle classes', nor could 'it buy the loyalty of different segments of society'.[46] With hydrocarbon rents shrinking and socio-economic deficiencies deepening, something clearly had to give.

The Moment of Reckoning

That moment of reckoning finally arrived in the Spring of 2019. The announcement in February 2019 that Bouteflika, who was almost fully paralyzed, would again run for president, drove Algerians over the edge to revolt. For many people, the provocation of the regime was too great to tolerate, and the humiliation was just too much to bear. This outrage was first expressed in the streets of the Kabyle Berber town of Kerrata on 16 February 2019. There, an exasperated crowd ripped up and stomped on a portrait of Bouteflika. A week later, millions of demonstrators filled the streets of the capital and most Algerian cities. From then until the spread of the COVID-19 pandemic to Algeria in March 2020, thirteen months later, the country was swept up by unprecedented peaceful and festive protests on every Friday and most Tuesdays. Both the General Staff and the presidential clan were clearly caught off guard by the intensity and creativity of the street pressure.[47] At first, Gaïd Salah saw the hand of the old DRS behind the protests. Hence began another round of dismissals and reshuffles in the ranks of the security services. But the purge failed to subdue the protests. The Hirak was shaping up to be a formidable political opponent that cut across ideological lines. 'In reclaiming historical figures from the war of independence, in depoliticising religion, and in proclaiming the Amazigh identity of the Algerian people across the country', wrote Mohand Tilmatine, the movement stripped the regime 'of the narratives that once legitimised its authoritarian rule for a long time'.[48]

The General Staff tried to exhaust the energy of the Hirak by addressing the immediate causes that put Algeria in the crucible of stubborn protests. On 11 March 2019, President Bouteflika dropped his bid for a fifth term, and Prime Minister Ahmed Ouyahia announced his resignation. When this failed to placate the protesters, Gaïd Salah forced his erstwhile ally to resign on 2 April and called for early presidential elections to be held on 4 July 2019.[49] To keep the focus of Algerians' wrath on Bouteflika and his clan, and not the military-based system, Gaïd Salah and his supporters in the General Staff arrested several ministers and powerful businesspeople suspected of corruption. As the demonstrations continued, a far-reaching anti-corruption campaign cast an even wider net that snared even high-ranking military officers. 'The incredible speed and pace of such charges', wrote Entelis, 'is testimony to the precarious status of any individual, however closely tied he or she may have been to Bouteflika's architecture of control'.[50] By re-affirming 'the institutional primacy of state power', Gaïd Salah wanted to position the military as the ultimate saviour of the nation.

The arrests only galvanised the protesters to reject the military's proposed electoral time-table as it did not provide changes to the institutional order, mechanisms and rules, which in the past had produced rigged results. Thus, the protesters demanded the postponement of the elections and creation of a constituent assembly to replace the existing political order. Under intense street pressure, the military delayed the elections twice, even as it resumed the regime's old practices of selective repression and fomenting identity-based tensions in Algerian society through the banning and arrest of protestors in possession of Amazigh flags. The military's other decisions, procedures and appointments also followed the old playbook strategies of jettisoning some members of the old guard and recycling others into senior positions. But as the protesters' demands hardened and began targeting the generals themselves with slogans such as 'generals in the trash' and '*dawla madania machi' askaria*' ('civil not military state'), the military went ahead with their plan to define the political agenda and impose an electoral calendar that ensured the perpetuation of the military's behind-the-scenes dominance in society as well as polity.

However, the presidential election of December 2019 largely boycotted by Algerians, confirmed the protestors' distrust of the promises of a new political configuration. All five presidential candidates were members of the establishment, leaving protesters without a candidate behind whom they could get. The winner, Abdelmadjid Tebboune, was the ideal choice for the military leadership. He possessed neither the charisma nor the stature nor the ambition of some of his predecessors. As a faithful servant of the Algerian regime, he had acquired a reputation as technocrat. He was also not tainted by the massive corruption scandals of the Bouteflika era, during which he had served as cabinet minister – even if his own son had been arrested on graft charges after Bouteflika's fall (and later acquitted in February 2020). In fact, Tebboune used his brief stint as prime minister in 2017 – he had been relieved of his duties less than three months in office, 'when he fell out with influential business tycoons in the president's coterie' – to position himself as 'a man of integrity who stood up to Bouteflika'.[51]

Reconfiguring Authoritarianism

For many Algerians, however, Tebboune (aged seventy-four) and Major General Said Chengriha (also aged seventy-four), who succeeded Gaïd Salah (who had died just days after the presidential election), were the perfect embodiment of the famous epigram coined in 1849 by the French writer Jean-Baptiste Alphonse Karr: *'plus ça change, plus c'est la même chose'*, or 'the more things change, the more they remain the same'. It was no surprise that the Hirak continued protesting the regime's imposition of its transition as a fait accompli. The protesters' weight was particularly visible in the Berber region of Kabylia, where the rate of participation in the presidential election of December 2019 was almost zero. Through sustained peaceful street demonstrations and use of social media, the Hirak activists tried to discredit the actions of the authorities.

When the COVID-19 pandemic spread to Algeria at the beginning of the spring of 2020, it dealt these efforts a severe blow. The regime, which had already been deploying coercive techniques against activists, took full advantage of the pandemic lockdown to stifle the Hirak and force the culmination of its political roadmap. On 1 November 2020, a new constitution was approved in a referendum that saw historically low voter turnout at only 24 percent. Then came the turn for parliamentary and local elections, held in June and November 2021, respectively. Both elections had low participation rates that did not exceed 36 percent, according to official numbers. Unsurprisingly, the parliamentary and local elections also recycled the same political coalition that marked the Bouteflika era.[52]

The conclusion of the regime's political roadmap allowed the army to recede from the limelight while maintaining its political supremacy, albeit behind the scenes. The retreat had the advantage of refocusing 'public attention on Tebboune rather than on the military'.[53] The president had an uphill challenge to jumpstart an economy battered by the COVID-19 pandemic. The latter helped clear protesters out of the streets, but it exacerbated 'the woes of a state-dominated economy already scarred by years of falling oil prices and curbs on local and foreign investment'.[54] Indeed, protesters tried to revive weekly pro-democracy demonstrations on the second anniversary of the movement in February 2021, when thousands of Algerians marched in the capital and other cities, chanting the same slogans: 'A civilian state not a military state!', 'Enough is enough!' and 'The people want independence!'[55]

But in the absence of central leadership or a clear organiser at the helm, the Hirak faced a nearly impossible 'coordination game'.[56] Efforts to coalesce around a shared platform for demands also failed to materialise, despite notable attempts such as 'Nida 22', an online initiative that gathered a diverse coalition of activists with the aim of bridging emerging intra-Hirak divides. Tensions between Islamists and non-Islamists became more pronounced as time went by.[57] Secular activists of the Hirak suspected that members of the Europe-based Rachad Group, founded in 2007 by former members of the Islamic Salvation Front (FIS), were using the movement to advance an Islamist agenda. Others feared that their involvement could re-awaken the ghosts of Algeria's bloody civil war or be used by the enemies of the Hirak to discredit the pro-democracy movement.[58] Divisions also emerged within the Amazigh/Berber branch of the Hirak, with some groups demanding more political devolution, autonomy or outright independence for Kabylia from the Algerian state. The regime capitalised on these ideological and political differences to try and discredit the Hirak as a 'blessed movement', to use Tebboune's words, that had lost its way and was gradually being overtaken by radical Islamists (namely, Rachad) and separatists supported by Algeria's foreign enemies.[59] Following Tebboune's election, the regime escalated its campaign to portray Hirak activists as dupes of foreign conspiracies.

The Hirak also struggled to prove its staying power in the face of a cohesive military-led regime that has shown no inclination to negotiate a genuine overhaul of the power structures that could propel the country towards an inclusive and accountable democratic transition. Despite the internal rivalries that pitted the General Staff against the Intelligence Services in the

2000s and the factional divisions and purges that have persisted ever since, when push came to shove, the army stood uniformly behind Gaïd Salah, re-affirming once again the primacy of the military as an institution. The death of Gaïd Salah, who had been the face of the regime's manoeuvres to impose its political roadmap, could have created an opening for the Hirak to extract significant concessions from the regime. But, as in the past, the army demonstrated that it 'is a single block, not under the influence of one general but with consensus as its engine'.[60] The regime's escalation of selective repression also weakened the movement. Algerian authorities 'targeted dozens of protesters, journalists and activists with arbitrary arrests and prosecutions, for engaging in peaceful protests and expressing political opinions on social media', said Amnesty International.[61] Geopolitics played a role as well. Unlike the Sudan or Hong Kong protests, which garnered international attention and generated international pressure on the regimes, international coverage of the Hirak was awarded very limited space. The few powers with interest in Algeria were anxious to see a return to political stability in a country that is a major supplier of gas to Europe.

Conclusion

Algerians' hope for democracy has once again gone up in smoke. The impressive potency of months of peaceful protests and organising failed to dislodge the main pillars that have supported the post-independence Algerian political regime. The main holders of power are still concentrated in the military, the supreme arbiter and enforcer of political power. Despite Bouteflika's efforts at reshaping the balance of power, the power of the army leadership and its grip on political power is much more robust today than it was in the Bouteflika era, as the high army command does not have to reckon with counter-balancing powers in the intelligence services or the presidency. In other words, even if President Tebboune wanted to replicate Bouteflika's efforts to reduce his dependence on the army, he 'would not find an ally in the security forces'.[62]

In the short term, the military will likely support and pressure the presidency to enact a narrow programme of socio-economic reforms to prop up the political system and appease the Algerians' demands for democratic accountability. The military is hopeful that the significant spike in hydrocarbon prices, which reached their highest levels in the second half of 2021, will shore up the finances of the state and relieve the pressure on the country's military expenditure. The military and its political allies likely will also continue to whip up nationalist fervour in order to distract from the state's inability to stem inflation and address worsening food shortages, as well as to justify enforcement of national unity and high military expenses. Official rhetoric abounds with how Algeria is threatened by foreign conspiracies. The regime has, for example, intensified 'its strategic hostility against Morocco', whom it accuses of sponsoring Berber separatists and dissident Islamists.[63] The chief of the army and the president also accused Morocco of involvement in the devastating fires that ravaged Algeria in the summer of 2021. Most recently, the Algerian state agency accused the kingdom of writing the World Bank report that highlighted the vulnerabilities of the Algerian economy.[64]

For how long these strategies will delay Algerians' return to the streets is hard to tell. Most people are dissatisfied with their current situation. As for the Hirak, most activists have rejected the regime's reform road map, but their goals of democratic reforms will be hard to materialise without ironing out their divergences and changing the military's calculus of the risk of transitioning towards a more accountable political system. The challenge for democratic movements in Algeria remains how to make democratisation a strategic choice for powerful military leaders. For the military, their challenge is how to create a stable form of competent civilian governance that secures their prerequisites and privileges.

Notes

1. Flavien Bourrat, 'L'armée algérienne: Un état dans l'état?' *Les Champs de Mars* 23 (2012): 21–37.
2. Madjid Bencheikh, *Algérie, un système politique militarisé* (Paris: L'Harmattan, 2003).
3. Luis Martinez, 'L'armée Algérienne à l'épreuve du Mouvement Citoyen du Hirak', *The Conversation*, 18 February 2020, https://

theconversation.com/larmee-algerienne-a-lepreuve-du-mouvement-citoyen-du-hirak-131798.
4. Radidja Nemar, 'Au-delà des casernes: Le rôle de l'armée en Algérie', *Les Cahiers de l'Orient* 100 (2010): 19–32.
5. Benjamin Stora, *Histoire de l'Algérie de l'Indépendance à 1988* (Paris: Collections Repères, La Découverte, 2004).
6. Lahouari Addi, *L'impasse du populisme: L'Algérie, collectivité politique et état en construction* (Alger: Entreprise Nationale du Livre, 1990).
7. Lahouari Addi, 'Le système de pouvoir en Algérie, son origine et ses évolutions', *Confluences Méditerranée*, no. 115 (April 2020): 103–13.
8. Hugh Roberts, 'Demilitarizing Algeria', *Carnegie Endowment for International Peace*, May 2007, https://carnegieendowment.org/files/cp_86_final1.pdf.
9. Roberts, 'Demilitarizing Algeria'.
10. Roberts, 'Demilitarizing Algeria'.
11. In the late 1980s, the Algerian elite felt threatened by popular unrest over corruption and unemployment. Responding to the outbreak of riots in major Algerian cities, the government acted as authoritarian governments often do – with a massive show of force that claimed the lives of over 500 people. The brutality shocked Algerians and severely damaged the reputation of the army. Significantly weakened, the ruling National Liberation Front (FLN) calculated that the introduction of political reforms would restore stability and ease public bitterness. In February 1989, Algeria was, almost overnight, transformed from an authoritarian single-party state into a democratising one. Algerian authorities legalised opposition groups, including Islamist organisations, thus ending the dominance of the FLN and ushering in a new era that put Algeria on the brink of becoming, as William Quandt put it, 'the most free, most pluralistic, and most enthusiastic defender of democracy in the Arab world'. William B. Quandt, *Between Ballots and Bullets: Algeria's Transition from Authoritarianism* (Washington DC: Brookings Institution Press, 1998), 5. See also Anouar Boukhars, 'Political Violence in North Africa: The Perils of Incomplete Liberalization', *Brookings Doha Centre*, January 2011, https://www.brookings.edu/wp-content/uploads/2016/06/01_north_africa_boukhars.pdf.
12. Lahouari Addi, *L'Algérie et la démocratie* (Paris: La Découverte, 1994).
13. John P. Entelis, 'Algeria: Nation in Transition or Politics as Usual?' n. d.
14. Roberts, 'Demilitarizing Algeria'.

15. Farid Alilat, *Bouteflika: L'histoire secrète* (Paris: Éditions du Rocher, 2020).
16. 'Ex-Algerian President Abdelaziz Bouteflika, Ousted amid Protests, Dies', *The Associated Press*, 17 September 2021, https://apnews.com/article/africa-algiers-algeria-abdelaziz-bouteflika-carlos-the-jackal-38ec30f0f8812fbaf572058f3f88cd1c.
17. Habib Souaïdia, *La sale guerre* (Paris: La Découverte, 2001); Hichem Aboud, *La mafia des généraux* (Paris: Éditions J. C. Lattès, 2002); Mohammed Samraoui, *Chronique des années de sang* (Paris: Denoël, 2003).
18. Rachid Tlemçani, 'Algeria under Bouteflika: Civil Strife and National Reconciliation', *Carnegie Endowment for International Peace*, February 2008, https://carnegieendowment.org/files/cmec7_tlemcani_algeria_final.pdf.
19. 'Algeria: New Amnesty Law Will Ensure Atrocities Go Unpunished, Muzzles Discussion of Civil Conflict', *Human Rights Watch*, 1 March 2006, https://www.hrw.org/news/2006/02/28/algeria-new-amnesty-law-will-ensure-atrocities-go-unpunished.
20. 'Bouteflika: Algeria's Longest-Serving President', *France24*, 11 March 2019, https://www.france24.com/en/20190311-bouteflika-algerias-longest-serving-president.
21. Roberts, 'Demilitarizing Algeria'.
22. Rachid Ouaissa, 'Algérie: Quel rôle pour l'armée dans la transition démocratique?' *Telos*, 6 May 2019, https://www.telos-eu.com/fr/politique-francaise-et-internationale/algerie-quel-role-pour-larmee-dans-la-transition-d.html.
23. Jeremy Keenan, 'General Mohamed Toufik Mediene: "God of Algeria"', *Al Jazeera Online*, 29 September 2010, https://www.aljazeera.com/news/2010/9/29/general-mohamed-toufik-mediene-god-of-algeria.
24. Lahouari Addi, 'La chute de "Rab Dzaïr", le "Dieu d'Alger"', *Orient XXI*, 30 September 2015, https://orientxxi.info/magazine/la-chute-de-rab-dzair-le-dieu-d-alger,1036.
25. Rachid Ouaissa, 'Algeria: Between Transformation and Re-Configuration', in *Contextualising Transformation Processes and Lasting Crises in the Middle East and North Africa*, ed. Rachid Ouaissa, Friederike Pannewick, and Alena Strohmaier (Wiesbaden: Springer, 2021), 57.
26. Ouaissa, 'Algeria', 58.
27. Belkacem Elguettaa, 'The Military's Political Role in the New Algeria', in *Politics of Military Authoritarianism in North Africa*, ed. Yezid Sayigh and Nathan Toronto, *Carnegie Middle East Centre*, 17 March 2021, https://carnegie-mec.org/2021/03/17/military-s-political-role-in-new-algeria-pub-84076.

28. Ali Bensaad, 'Pourquoi l'Algérie est hors-jeu en Libye', *Orient XXI*, 7 July 2021, https://orientxxi.info/magazine/pourquoi-l-algerie-est-hors-jeu-en-libye,4896.
29. Salima Tlemcani, 'Le Général-major Abderrazak sherif condamné pour «enrichissement illicite»: 15 ans de réclusion criminelle et confiscation de tous les biens', *El Watan*, 30 May 2021, https://www.elwatan.com/edition/actualite/15-ans-de-reclusion-criminelle-et-confiscation-de-tous-les-biens-30-05-2021.
30. Elguettaa, 'The Military's Political Role in the New Algeria'.
31. Tahar Hani, 'Bouteflika to Seek Third Presidential Term', *France24*, 13 February 2009, https://www.france24.com/en/20090212-bouteflika-seek-third-presidential-term-.
32. Keenan, 'General Mohamed Toufik Mediene: "God of Algeria"'.
33. Keenan, 'General Mohamed Toufik Mediene: "God of Algeria"'.
34. Sadek Sellam, 'Algérie, des révélations sur le « coup d'Etat » de 1992', *Mondafrique*, 15 January 2016, https://mondafrique.com/algerie-des-revelations-sur-le-coup-detat-de-1992/.
35. Aomar Ouali and Paul Schemm, 'Algeria Scandals Mask High Level Power Struggle', *San Diego Union Tribune*, 24 November 2012, https://www.sandiegouniontribune.com/sdut-algeria-scandals-mask-high-level-power-struggle-2012nov24-story.html.
36. Habib Souaïdia, 'Révélations sur le drame d'In-Amenas: Trente otages étrangers tués par l'armée Algérienne, au moins neuf militaires tués', *Algeria Watch*, 11 February 2013, https://algeria-watch.org/?p=45434.
37. Anouar Boukhars, 'In the Eye of the Storm: Algeria's South and Its Sahelian Borders', in *Algeria Modern: From Opacity to Complexity*, ed. Luis Martinez and Rasmus Alenius Boserup (Oxford: Oxford University Press, 2016): 111–26.
38. Boukhars, 'In the Eye of the Storm'.
39. Ian Black, 'Algeria Hostage Crisis Could Weaken Veteran Spymaster', *The Guardian*, 25 January 2013, https://www.theguardian.com/world/2013/jan/25/algerian-hostage-crisis-tewfik-mediene.
40. Addi, 'Le système de pouvoir en Algérie, son origine et ses evolutions'.
41. Adlène Meddi, 'Algeria: The Secret Service Never Dies', *Middle East Eye*, 16 September 2015, https://www.middleeasteye.net/fr/news/algeria-secret-services-never-die-237305750.
42. Meddi, 'Algeria: The Secret Service Never Dies'.
43. Lamine Chikhi, 'Algeria's Bouteflika Consolidates Curbs on State Intelligence Agency', *Reuters*, 24 October 2014, https://www.reuters.com/article/us-algeria-politics/algerias-bouteflika-consolidates-curbs-on-state-intelligence-agency-idUSKCN0ID11120141024.

44. Addi, 'Le système de pouvoir en Algérie, son origine et ses evolutions'.
45. Entelis, 'Algeria: Nation in Transition or Politics as Usual?'
46. Ouaissa, 'Algeria: Between Transformation and Re-Configuration'.
47. Omar Benderra et al., eds., *Hirak en Algérie: Invention d'un Soulèvement* (Paris: La Frabrique, 2020); Aissa Kadri, *Algérie, décennie 2010–2020: Aux origines du mouvement populaire du 22 Février 2019* (Paris: Éditions du Croquant, 2020).
48. Mohand Tilmatine, 'La Kabylie dans le Hirak Algerien: Enjeux et perspectives', *Hérodote*, no. 180 (January 2021): 32–56.
49. Naouf Brahimi El Mili, *Histoire secrète de la chute de Bouteflika* (Paris: Éditions Archipel, 2020).
50. Entelis, 'Algeria: Nation in Transition or Politics as Usual?'
51. Lamine Chikhi, 'Algeria's New President Tebboune Faces Tough Challenge', *Reuters*, 13 December 2019, https://www.reuters.com/article/uk-algeria-tebboune-newsmaker-idUKKBN1YH1EF.
52. Zine Labidine Ghebouli, 'The Post-Hirak Presidency: Tebboune's Promises and Achievements Two Years On', *Middle East Institute*, 13 December 2021, https://www.mei.edu/publications/post-hirak-presidency-tebbounes-promises-and-achievements-two-years.
53. Sharan Grewal, 'Why Sudan Succeeded Where Algeria Failed', *Journal of Democracy* 32, no. 4 (October 2021): 102–14.
54. Heba Saleh, 'Algeria on the Brink as Pandemic and Low Oil Price Take Their Toll', *Financial Times*, 15 June 2021, https://www.ft.com/content/07691fbd-fa6c-414d-9299-ce848073a5d7.
55. 'Thousands of Algerians Defy Police to Mark Protest Anniversary', *France24*, 22 February 2021, https://www.france24.com/en/africa/20210222-thousands-of-algerians-defy-police-to-mark-protest-anniversary.
56. Grewal, 'Why Sudan Succeeded Where Algeria Failed'.
57. Ilhem Rachidi, 'Helpless Hirak? Democratic Disappointments in Algeria', *Carnegie Endowment for International Peace: Sada*, 10 June 2021, https://carnegieendowment.org/sada/84739.
58. 'Algeria Protesters at Crossroads as Islamists Take Spotlight', *Associated Press*, 15 April 2021, https://apnews.com/article/world-news-abdelaziz-bouteflika-algiers-algeria-c4471b25da99a9447e1324a75c1f3116.
59. 'Authentic Blessed Hirak Movement Saved Algerian State from Collapsing into Failed State', *Algeria Press Service*, 8 June 2021, https://www.aps.dz/en/algeria/39660-authentic-blessed-hirak-movement-saved-algerian-state-from-collapsing-into-failed-state.
60. Quoted in Grewal, 'Why Sudan Succeeded Where Algeria Failed'.

61. 'Algeria: Repressive tactics used to target Hirak activists two years on', *Amnesty International*, 22 February 2021, https://www.amnesty.org/en/latest/news/2021/02/algeria-repressive-tactics-used-to-target-hirak-activists-two-years-on/.
62. Elguettaa, 'The Military's Political Role in the New Algeria'.
63. Elguettaa, 'The Military's Political Role in the New Algeria'.
64. 'Algeria's Economic Update – Fall 2021', *World Bank*, 22 December 2021, https://www.worldbank.org/en/country/algeria/publication/algeria-economic-update-fall-2021.

7

Gender Imbalances across North Africa

Sarah E. Yerkes

Gender inequality remains a pervasive issue across the globe. In North Africa, while several states in the region have made broad public attempts at empowering women, gender gaps remain in everything from political participation over education to employment. These gaps have important local implications and have often been the focus of international attention. This chapter evaluates the status of gender equality in the region and examines efforts at addressing gender inequality – whether by national governments, local officials, local civil society actors or international donors. When discussing gender, I am not only describing the role of women. Rather, I use Valentine Moghadam's definition of 'a system of unequal social relations between men and women' in what Zakia Salime describes as 'a field of struggle and a marker for specific shifts in power arrangements'.[1]

Gender imbalances matter for a variety of ethical and practical reasons. On the most basic level, it is incumbent upon governments and societies to treat all their citizens equally, regardless of gender. Gender equality under the law, as well in practice, is a foundation for any just society. Furthermore, the lack of gender equality at the national level has trickle-down effects on the workplace and the home, and governments can use gender inequality as a tool to sow division within society. Additionally, several scholars have shown the connection between higher rates of women's employment and higher wages and a more equal position in the home, which can contribute to a more equal standing in marriage, family life and overall self-worth for women.[2]

On a state level, and specifically in North Africa, state

formation was crucial to developing and defining the role of women and their relationship with the post-colonial state. As Mounira Charrad argues, states address women's rights in different ways, 'depending on their own sources of support, their projects for the future society and the nature of other contenders to power within each historical context'.[3] She describes gender policies as 'pawns in broader conflicts and alliances. They become the outcome and sometimes a tool of struggles among social and political groups fighting over state power'.[4]

The way in which states address (or fail to address) gender inequality has several important implications for women more broadly and for society at large. First, on the political level, inequality in representation leads to less female-friendly policies across the board. When women are not present in positions of power or decision-making, their interests are less likely to be represented, and female-friendly policies are less likely to be proposed or adopted. This is a vicious cycle, in which the lack of visible females in positions of power leads to a lack of role models for young girls, making it harder for them to imagine themselves in positions of power or to strive for those positions. In fact, some scholars have shown that 'women workers, on average, appear to be less prone to corruption and nepotism than men workers'.[5] Broadly, many scholars find that economic growth and prosperity are significantly impacted by the degree of access that women attain to political participation.[6]

In the economic realm, there is a significant amount of literature drawing a connection between gender equality in education and economic growth.[7] This is due to a variety of factors including 'artificially restricting the pool of talent' and 'excluding highly qualified girls' by preventing girls and women from accessing the full spectrum of educational and employment opportunities.[8] In addition, higher levels of female education have been shown to reduce fertility levels as well as child mortality rates, both of which are correlated with higher economic growth rates.[9] This is especially important in the MENA region where, despite rising levels of literacy and education, equality has not translated into the workforce and where the share of women in the workforce is the lowest in the world.[10] Libya has the highest female labour force participation rate of any of the North African countries, at 34 percent, with Algeria the lowest at 17 percent, well below the global rate of 47.3 percent.[11] The

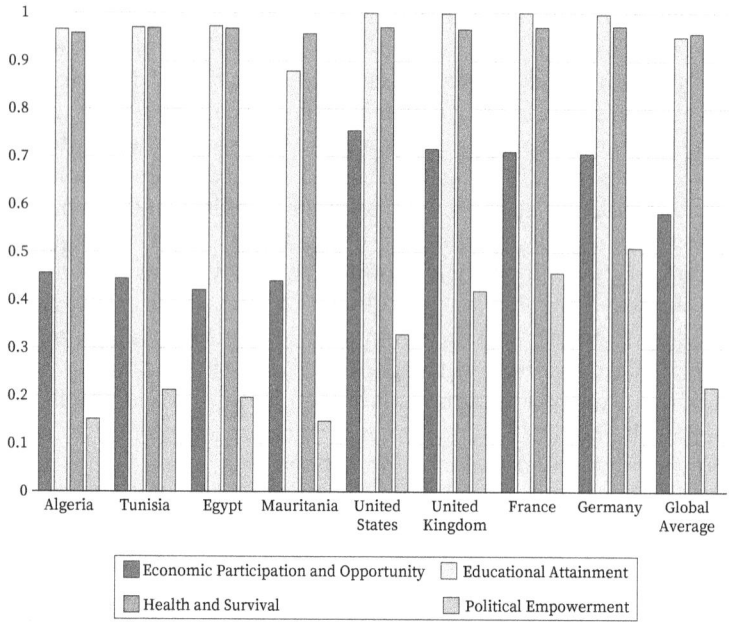

Figure 7.1 Global Gender Gap Index Scores, 2021
Robert Crotti et al., 'Global Gender Gap Report 2021' (Geneva: World Economic Forum, March 2021), https://www3.weforum.org/docs/WEF_GGGR_2021.pdf

MENA region has the largest gender gap of any region in the world, at 60.9 percent (compared to 77.6 and 76.4 for Western Europe and North America, respectively), according to the World Economic Forum's Global Gender Gap index, which measures the gap between men and women in four dimensions: economic participation and opportunity, educational attainment, health and survival, and political empowerment.[12] The same index estimates that it will take 142.4 years for the MENA region to close its gender gap at the current relative pace (compared to 52.1 years for Western Europe and 61.5 years for North America).[13]

Globally, women have just three-fourths of the legal rights afforded to men according to the World Bank's Women, Business and the Law Index.[14] The index, which measures indicators across eight areas (mobility, workplace, pay, marriage, parenthood, entrepreneurship, assets and pension) illustrates

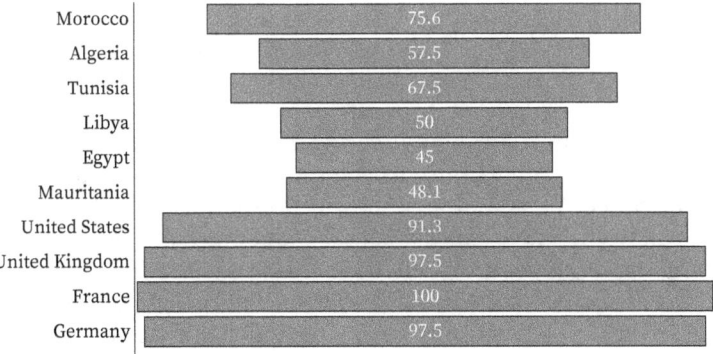

Figure 7.2 Women, Business and the Law Index Scores, 2021
'World Bank, Women, Business and the Law 2021' (The World Bank, 2021), https://doi.org/10.1596/978-1-4648-1652-9

that North Africa is a region that differs greatly in its legal protections for women. Morocco scores the highest, receiving 75.6 out of 100 (with 100 as the best possible score), with Mauritania and Egypt scoring only 48.1 and 45, respectively.[15] These legal rights matter because, as scholars have shown, 'having fewer discriminatory laws and policies in place results in larger investments in health and education (both for women themselves and for the next generation) and lower rates of sexually transmitted diseases'.[16]

State–Women Relations: A Historical Perspective

To understand the current politics and policies around gender in North Africa, it is necessary to examine the countries' long-term historical trajectories. These trajectories shaped contemporary shifts in gender policy in the MENA region. Fatima Mernissi's work has shown that the states simultaneously used a dual narrative of modernity and authenticity, describing women as 'agents of development' during the 1980s, which provided opportunities for both feminists and Islamists to challenge that narrative. As Salime notes, 'Mernissi points to the contradictions between rigidly patriarchal law regulating the domestic sphere and more sex-egalitarian legislation in the public sphere for Arab women – the constitution, public administration, regulations and so forth'.[17] Contrary to popular understandings, Islam and patriarchal norms did not primarily dictate gender outcomes during the colonial and post-independence eras. Rather, the process of state formation largely explains shifts in women's conditions. As Mounira Charrad argues, 'in theoretical terms [...] the integration of tribal kin groupings into the nation-state, as mediated by the political conflicts and alliances of the political leadership of the newly formed national state, shaped the development of family law policy' and gender policies in North Africa.[18]

In Tunisia and Morocco, gender reforms were enacted from above and took place very soon after independence with Codes of Personal Status. In Algeria, 'women were active in obstructing the most conservative plans to make the Algerian Family Code even more faithful to Maliki law'.[19] But they failed in creating an organised sustained movement. After Qadhafi's 1969 coup, Libyan women enjoyed higher standards of living and education, but they were uprooted from political and public life. Nasser's feminism from above established progressive rights for women without challenging the patriarchal structure in Egypt. In Mauritania, women's conditions depended on the leaders in power while greatly varying across ethnic and class lines. Thus, states regulated marriage, divorce, individual rights and responsibilities, contraception, the transmission of property through inheritance and other aspects of family law. They mediated – and sometimes instrumentalised – gender relations through the law, according to varying strategies of the political leadership.

Tunisia

During the colonial and post-independence periods, Tunisian women saw their rights manipulated by both nationalists and elites. From the 1930s to the 1950s, as the struggle for independence from France intensified, the nationalist movement – a diverse group including liberal Tunisian professionals and members of the religious establishment (such as Islamic scholars and judges) – took a conservative stance on women's rights. They wanted to keep the Islamic family law (shari'a) as it had historically existed in North Africa. The family law in the 1930s imposed several restrictions on women. For example, marriage was allowed as soon as a girl entered puberty; the bride's father or other male guardian was responsible for consent in the marriage contract (not the bride herself); a man could divorce a woman unilaterally; and men were allowed to marry up to four wives.[20] Treating women as a repository of national values, the nationalists sought to avoid ideological differences within the movement by taking the Islamic family law as a symbol of cultural identity, to be preserved at all costs in the fight against colonialism. Charrad argues that concepts such as Islam and the patriarchal state do not generally explain shifts in state policy on women's rights in Tunisia.[21] Instead, contests over state power dictate gender policy outcomes. The Neo-Destour – the leading nationalist party, which later became the Democratic Constitutional Rally (RCD) – and the state that it established sometimes opposed women's formal and legal civic rights, as had been the case before independence. It supported these rights at other times. This was the case immediately after independence and again in the 1990s, when the emergence of political Islam threatened the state by challenging the RCD's status as the sole legitimate party.

When Tunisia won independence from France in 1956, its first president, Habib Bourguiba, either delegitimised early independent feminist organisations or incorporated them into the state-funded National Union of the Tunisian Woman (UNFT). He then promoted the Code of Personal Status (CPS), a series of unprecedented progressive laws most notably abolishing polygamy, regulating divorce and requiring women's consent for marriage. However, the CPS was a reform from above, initiated by the political leadership without pressure from women groups or their participation in the drafting process. It maintained gender inequality in some areas, preserving the father's authority in the control of children and his prerogative in family affairs, as well as inequality in inheritance. Several modifications were introduced to the CPS, including a 1993 amendment, to move towards greater equality. But the code still has unequal aspects, especially in terms of inheritance.

By the early 1970s, Bourguiba's firm grip on feminist political action started to break down when Radhia Haddad, the Bourguiba-appointed UNFT president, criticised the lack of democracy in the country. In this period, the democratic women's agenda mostly centred on denouncing the one-party state ruled by the Neo-Destour. In 1978, some of these women founded the Tahar Haddad Club, which most scholars and activists call the first independent feminist group in Tunisia. Influenced by Betty Freidan, Simone de Beauvoir and Egyptian feminist Nawal Saadawi, the club denounced the social structures that perpetrated gender inequality and emphasised the role of women in Tunisia's socio-economic development. These earlier conditions led to the building of an autonomous, non-state-led, feminist movement in the country. Following the Tahar Haddad Club (1978–84), several stages anchored this movement. The most important of these were: the Tabarka Festival (1979); the women's committee within the Tunisian General Labour Union (UGTT); the national trade union centre in Tunisia (1981); the informal coalition of democratic women (1982); the *Nisaa* journal writers and editors (1984); the women's rights committee of the Tunisian League of Human Rights (LTDH) (1985); the Tunisian Association of Democratic Women (ATFD) (1989); and the Association of Tunisian Women for Development Research (AFTURD) (1989).[22]

Rich in their collective and individual experiences, Tunisian feminists decided that the autonomy of their movement was the very foundation of their fight. The principle of autonomy took on a double meaning – or, rather, a double break. Feminists broke organisationally with traditional political structures and epistemologically with conservative understandings of women's issues. They contested the father-figure that Bourguiba had embodied, criticised the domestic role to which women were confined and challenged the lack of full equality in the Code of Personal Status.[23] Today, the Tunisian Association of Democratic Women (ATFD) and the Association of Tunisian Women for Development Research (AFTURD) mainly represent the secular autonomous feminist movement in the country.

Egypt

Qasim Amin's 1899 book, *Tahrir al-Mar'a* (The Liberation of Woman) for decades was considered the first blueprint of a gender transformation in Egypt. Amin himself was thought of as one of the first feminists in the Arab world. However, he and several other nationalists of the period exemplified the penetrance of colonial ideology into mainstream Arabic discourse.[24] Much like other Orientalists, they singled out the veil (or hijab) as emblematic of women's oppression, thought of the treatment of women as a sign of Islam's inferiority and 'trapped the struggle for women's rights with struggles over culture'.[25] Leila Ahmed argues that, ultimately, Amin 'merely called for the substitution of Islamic-style male dominance by Western-style male dominance'.[26] This discourse framing Western values as antithetical and superior to Islamic values thus shaped women's conditions in Egypt during the country's British occupation.

In the late 1950s and the 1960s, Nasser's state feminism gave women access to more rights and social protections, without challenging the patriarchal structure of Egyptian society. Under Nasser, the 1956 Constitution and the new electoral law granted women the right to vote and the right to run for public office. The state extended legal labour protection for women – for instance, guaranteeing paid maternity leave and accessible childcare services. Middle-class women had access to greater educational opportunities and were strongly encouraged to work. The revised 1963 Constitution further affirmed Nasser's commitment to public equality.[27]

However, the foundations of the patriarchal state persisted. The personal status laws from the 1920s and 1930s remained in place. The regime dissolved feminist organisations and arrested activists such as Inji Aflatun and Zaynab al-Ghazali. The Ministry of Social Affairs then assumed the activities of dissolved charities and other independent organisations led by women.[28] Under Presidents Anwar Sadat and Hosni Mubarak, policies of economic and political liberalisation shrunk women's political and economic participation. The state also manipulated gender policies according to political calculations. At the beginning of his rule, Sadat attempted to consolidate his power and suppress Nasserists, so he cooperated with the Islamists. This led to major constitutional changes, including using Islamic law as the principal source of legislative rules in the 1971 Constitution and reversing women's statutory equality.[29] In the 1980s, the economic liberalisation under Mubarak led to a decreased state support for women's public equality and increased hostility towards state activism. Mervat Hatem argues that the 'social and economic retreat of the state and the consequent demise of state feminism in the 1980s undermined the prospects of lower-middle- class and working-class women'.[30] Instead, liberalisation benefited a small group of bourgeois and upper-middle-class women and led to creating further divisions among Egyptian women. Women's political and social organising became increasingly difficult. The state concurrently conducted what Lila Abu-Lughod calls the 'governmentalization of women's rights'.[31] Mubarak in 2000 established the National Council for Women (NCW), presided over by the first lady, Suzanne Mubarak. Although the NCW led to the attainment of increased rights for women, it was nonetheless a state tool that did not challenge the foundations of the patriarchal state.[32]

Libya

Libyan women's conditions prior to 2011 are the most under-studied among North African countries. The dearth of literature led to the prevalence of the narrative that the Qadhafi regime curtailed the rights of women under the monarchy. However, the situation is more complicated, and women's conditions were inextricably linked to the process of state-building. Following a struggle to end the Italian occupation, Libya gained independence in 1951 and became a constitutional monarchy in a federal system consisting of three states. Under King Idris, a new constitution granted equal citizenship rights to women and men.[33] The king sought to establish a participatory political system in which he would 'restore the position of societal forces historically crushed by the occupation' and ensure that all members of society enjoy the same rights and duties.[34] It is in this context that women translated a vision that rights and duties should be afforded to all members of society. Women then became more visible, formed unions and associations and 'participated in shaping public opinion through their writings and work in the media'.[35] As a result, and as a culmination of earlier feminist efforts, Hamida Tarkhan, known as 'Hamida Al-Enezi', in 1954 founded the Women's Renaissance Association, the first feminist organisation in the country. Based in Benghazi, Women's Renaissance demanded a woman's right to hold positions of leadership in politics and education, and it advanced women's entrepreneurship, especially through knitting and handicraft-making.[36] In 1963, women were granted the right to vote.

Qadhafi's 1969 coup changed the variables. The infamous slogan of the Qadhafi regime – 'whoever forms a party is a traitor' – encapsulates the level of political oppression that Libyans faced, including women. Qadhafi banned parties, unions and organisations not aligned with the government, severely shrinking the space for citizen engagement in public life. Although women continued to occupy some roles in leadership, their overall presence and participation was superficial and deliberately reduced.[37]

Qadhafi asserted that empowering women was central to the 1969 revolution. Libyan women thus had, at least on paper, an array of rights. For example, they had been appointed as judges since 1975; the Personal Status Law guaranteed their right to divorce; polygamy was restricted and illegal without the first wife's consent; and women married to non-Libyans could pass their Libyan citizenship to their children when they reached the age of eighteen.[38] In 1989, Libya acceded to the Convention on the Elimination of All Forms of Discrimination against Women (CEDAW) but maintained reservations to articles 2 and 16 (c) and (d).[39] Libya also made a general reservation that accession to the CEDAW 'cannot conflict with the laws on personal status derived from the Islamic Shariah'.[40] In 2004, Libya adopted an optional protocol that allowed women to petition a UN committee about violations of their rights, the first Arab country to adopt such a protocol. Despite these legal advancements, women's rights did not often translate into practice, and Libyan women suffered from the ruthless dictatorship under Qadhafi.

Algeria

A settlement colony of France since 1830, Algeria underwent a fierce war of independence between nationalist forces and French troops, which began in 1954 and ended with the overthrow of French rule and the establishment of a socialist independent government in 1962. As Marina Lazreg notes, 'most conspicuously, women were active participants in the war, foreshadowing a general change in relations between Algerian women and men'.[41] As she explains, '[y]et, throughout the war and after independence, the Algerian Nationalist leaders did not place the promotion of women's needs on its political agenda'.[42] The lack of women's organisation in a political faction or social formation meant that they did not have an organised way to pressure their leaders and 'could rely only on leaders' memories of their contribution to independence for the promotion of their rights and the recognition of their needs'.[43] In the end, and as is also the case in other countries in North Africa, the process of state formation heavily influenced women's conditions and gender policies.

This state formation adopted the sacrificial view of women formulated by the wartime National Liberation Front (FLN), while at the same time enabling women to benefit from some of its universalistic, gender-blind policies. Following independence, Bouthina Cheriet argues that the building of the Algerian nation state 'relied heavily on the eclectic and relatively mimetic adoption of universal and liberal criteria for citizenship'.[44] She notes that 'women's access to the public arena, and therefore to citizenship, is positively linked to a patronage dynamic: women remain dependent on the economic and social integration policies of the state, of which they become obedient "clients"'.[45] Women were still considered subservient to men, particularly in the family sphere, and the line between public and private was blurred. Thus, women lacked full independence at home as well as in society. Charrad further demonstrates that women's issues were 'held hostage' to political divisions and then subject to political expediency in Algeria. She argues that, 'using a carrot and stick strategy toward kin-based solidarities, the post-independence Algerian government shied away from either a conservative codification of family law or substantive reforms from independence in 1962 until 1984, as several plans for a national legislation were aborted'.[46] She notes that the 1984 Family Code was largely based on Islamic law, which many saw as 'a disappointment'.[47]

With the slow change to a capitalist economy, Algerian women again became 'the ideological pawns in the power politics that pit the FLN against its faith-based opposition', according to Lazreg.[48] The Family Code, she argues, 'illustrates the contradictions between the ideal of equality and the requirements of political expediency', and the subsequent 2005 amendment to the code 'fell short of the mark'.[49] However, further legal changes including laws criminalising violence against women and a change in the law on nationality that recognises children born to an Algerian mother as citizens made some headway in addressing the limitations of the Family Code.[50]

Morocco

Within a year of Morocco's independence in 1956, a family law was in place. Formulated by the government, this law was the result of the political choices by intellectuals and nationalist leaders in power, rather than a struggle from below. The Moroccan family law 'essentially reiterated Maliki family law in a more concise and codified manner'.[51] Brides did not agree to marriages; rather, their fathers or other male guardians did. Also, brides even did not need be present at the marriage ceremony for it to be considered valid. Polygyny remained legal. Divorce procedures stayed the same. However, repudiation had to be witnessed and recorded in writing by two witnesses.[52]

Charrad 'links the highly patriarchal family law to the importance of tribal and ethnic alliances at work during the formation of the nation state in Morocco'.[53] Salime further explains how the 'entrenched values of the agrarian patriarchal society' played a role in the new configuration of power within the state and in family law. The prevalence of these values led the king to assert his power after independence by 'inscribing national unity in the Islamic sharia at the expense of the *'urf* [. . .] customary law'.[54] As Salime argues, by institutionalising shari'a in the private sphere and specifically in the family law, the Moroccan family is the quintessential embodiment of Islamic identity. Therefore, the traditional family is instrumentalised as the core of the monarchy, and any call to reform the family law is a threat to the unity of the small family as well as the 'big one, the nation'.[55] As the only law claiming adherence to the shari'a, the *mudawwana* fell directly under the command of a king who used religious symbolism to legitimise his authority. On International Women's Day in 1999, the Moroccan government announced its 'National Plan of Action for Integrating Women into Development' (NPA). This tied feminism and gender to the state's economic and political liberalisation. Newly incumbent Prime Minister Abderrahmen al Yousouffi – a socialist and former political dissident – formulated a strategy for promoting women's rights in consultation with the feminist movement. The king undertook a new phase of liberalisation called political alternance. The feminist movement collaborated with the UN, the EU and the World Bank to come up with the NPA. The Islamists perceived these efforts as symptomatic of foreign intervention in the country, to push for a secular Westernised feminist agenda.[56]

The NPA ignored the Islamists' reservations, instead putting forth a 'liberal feminist rhetoric'.[57] This led to a major backlash from the Islamist movement, which eventually influenced the 2004 reform on the *mudawwana* to remain anchored in the shari'a law. What is crucial to understand here is that 'the debate was not limited to questions relating to reforming the family law but encompassed questions of "cultural imperialism", neo-colonialism and anti-globalisation claims'.[58]

Mauritania

During the pre-colonial period, Mauritanian women's status was mediated through Islamic jurisprudence (Maliki law) as well as customary law based on local cultural norms and mostly applied in criminal matters. Women turned to local Muslim scholars who exercised the function of a judge to rule on cases of divorce, inheritance and abuse. When the French colonised Mauritania in the late nineteenth century, they imposed a third system of jurisprudence. It mostly dealt with administrative and economic issues, whereas Islamic courts continued to manage questions of personal law. With its independence in 1960, the new Islamic Republic of Mauritania officially maintained the duality of jurisdictions, although it sought to have more control over family and marriage laws through the promulgation of the personal status code in 2001.[59]

Soon after independence, 'Mauritania slipped into a series of authoritarian regimes, both civilian and military'.[60] In 1984, Colonel Maaouya Ould Sidi Ahmed Taya seized power in a coup and eventually created a multi-party system in 1991. However, the system was far from democratic. Taya 'used state resources, repression and electoral manipulation to perpetuate his rule and that of his Republican, Democratic and Social Party (PROS)'.[61] These political developments largely affected women's ascension to positions of power and, although Mauritanian women had long been engaged in politics, they often occupied peripheral positions in formal political institutions. Women did not hold major positions in the government until 1986, when Khadijetou Mint Ahmed was made the Minister of Mines and Industry, a position she held until 1991.[62] Even though women's representation in the government slightly increased in subsequent years, it remained low. As Katherine Ann Wiley notes, '[b]y the mid 2000s only fourteen women had served at high levels of government. Most had held positions considered to be appropriate for women, such as those that dealt with women, health and youth. This phenomenon has largely continued into the 2010s; in 2014, 11 percent of ministers were women'.[63]

Women's positions also varied greatly across ethnic and class lines. Mauritania is composed of three major groups: the Bizan, the Haratin and Sub-Saharan African populations. The Bizan are one of Mauritania's major ethnic groups; its members have long dominated the country economically and politically and, thus, Bizan women are part of the economically privileged elite.[64] Haratin is the term used to refer to former slaves or descendants of slaves of the Bizan. As Mauritania was the last country in the world to abolish slavery in 1981, Haratin women had long been engaged in unfree labour. However, the Haratin population is far from homogeneous and includes a plurality of statuses.[65] Wiley argues that, despite the freedom now afforded to Haratin women, such as being able to own property and pass on possessions to their children, they maintain a lower social rank within society.[66] The third group is composed of Sub-Saharan African groups, including the Halpulaar, Wolof and Soninke, who populate the larger West Africa region. Wiley argues that, in the past two decades, 'educated women from all ethnic groups have found work as nurses, teachers, development workers and government employees. Women from all ethnic groups participate in agriculture or domestic work, although elite Bizan continue to avoid such pursuits unless absolutely necessary'.[67] However, the legacy of slavery and disproportionate access to wealth still affects women's opportunities today.

In the past few decades, economic and environmental challenges re-organised social and gender formations in Mauritania. Massive droughts in the 1970s led to large demographic shifts. Mauritanians with nomadic lifestyles or working in the countryside moved to cities, swelled the urban population and the labour force, yet still experienced great financial difficulty. Wiley argues that 'economic hardships were compounded by neo-liberal reforms in the 1980s and 1990s that aimed to promote economic growth' but led to increasing gaps between rich and poor, a declining GDP and growing unemployment. With the intensification of male migration, women of all classes and ethnicities assumed the bread-winner role, providing the sole or main income of their families. Since they could not depend on men's remittances, women were thus pressured to seek wage labour. For instance, in the town of Kankossa, in 2008, 44.2 percent of heads of household were women. Among these women, 31.1 percent were married, 29.7 percent were divorced and 39.1 percent were widowed.[68] These statistics reflect larger trends in Mauritania. Indeed, married women often found themselves the de facto heads of household when men travel to look for work elsewhere. Even when husbands are present, high poverty levels mean that few families can survive with one income only, forcing women into the labour force. Economic challenges have continued in recent decades, propelled by additional droughts and locust invasions, a series of military coups and the global economic crisis.

Women and the 2011 Uprisings

Women were at the forefront of the 2011 popular uprisings commonly known as the Arab Spring. They actively protested on the streets; mobilised networks; supplied food, shelter and medical aid; and organised through cyber-activism. Women were also active during the conflicts that came out of the uprisings. In Libya, for example, women participated in intelligence gathering, relief services and arms smuggling.[69] In Egypt, activist Asmaa Mahfouz, a founder of the 6 April Movement, was one of the first to urge Egyptians to protest President Mubarak's regime in Tahrir Square.[70] Following her viral Facebook video, tens of thousands participated in the nationwide 25 January demonstrations. In Tunisia, Lina Ben Mhenni covered first-hand the protests as they were happening in the interior regions of the country. She was one of the most active cyber-activists, and her blog, *A Tunisian Girl*, was censored during the Ben Ali era. Ben Mhenni was also nominated for the 2011 Nobel Peace Prize.

Some observers perceived women's broad social mobilisation as a novelty in the region. However, the 2011 uprisings were only the latest episode in the longer history of women's political participation. Dating back to the colonial period, women had played instrumental roles in the independence movements of their countries, most notably in Algeria and Egypt. North African women pursued their struggle and political participation in subsequent years in both feminist and non-feminist formations. This mobilisation came at a high cost. Protesting women in public squares were harassed, insulted, hit and, in some cases, even raped. Most of the gender violence was perpetrated by security forces, originally in a sporadic way, but later as part of a more systematic approach. In Tunisia, the Tunisian Association of Democratic Women (ATFD) documented several rape cases in the interior regions (Kasserine and Thela), and on 14 January several women protesters were raped while held in detention in the Interior Ministry.[71] Violence against Egyptian journalists and protesters was more widespread. Hundreds of women were beaten and sexually assaulted, by both counter-protesters and security forces.[72] Threatened with prosecution, some women in detention were forced to undergo 'virginity tests' by male army doctors.[73] Dina Tannir and Vivienne Badaan argue that these attacks were not only meant to 'suppress women's mobilization', but also to 'refocus the discourse' of their revolutionary involvement around 'issues of morality'.[74]

But women continued the struggle, and their broad participation had two central features. First, it feminised the revolution. Although women did not explicitly raise feminist slogans, their demands for freedom, social justice and democracy – echoed by their male counterparts – upheld the feminist principles of equality and justice. Second, this feminisation failed to significantly advance women's rights post-2011. Andrea Khalil argues that serious discussions about gender equality were side-lined by louder and ongoing complications of transnational democracy, constitution-drafting, elections and protracted questions of transitional justice. She states: 'All of these aspects of democratic transitions in North Africa have gender-related dimensions, yet these dimensions have been marginalized or recuperated by political agendas'.[75]

Current Efforts to Bring About Gender Equality, and Where they Fall Short

While each North African country has made some progress towards gender equality since independence, there remains a significant gap between men and women in the political and social spheres. In recent years, governments and civil society groups have undertaken a variety of measures to increase women's empowerment, with varying levels of success. Women's empowerment is challenging to quantify. Pippa Norris defines women's empowerment as encompassing four arenas: cultural empowerment, civic empowerment, decision-making empowerment and policy empowerment. Cultural empowerment consists of cultural values and social norms that promote gender equality and women's rights in both domestic and public spheres. Civic empowerment includes women's participation in civil society as well as collective action that allows women to influence the state, such as through voting, participating in political parties and through media. Decision-making empowerment refers to progress towards gender parity amongst those responsible for policy-making, including elected and appointed office-holders at the local and national levels, as well as senior civil service. And policy empowerment includes laws and regulations that promote gender equality, including protecting marital, sexual and reproductive rights, social welfare policies that protect women, preventing gender-based violence and promoting equal access to the workforce and equal pay.[76]

This chapter focuses on three of Norris' four areas of women's empowerment – civic empowerment, decision-making empowerment and policy empowerment – each of which is intertwined and helps contribute to a just and equitable state and society. Specifically, I discuss the role of constitutional reform to promote civic empowerment, gender quotas to promote decision-making empowerment and legal measures to promote policy empowerment. Full and equal political representation not only provides women with direct access to the levers of power to influence certain political interests that directly impact their lives – such as sexual health and reproductive rights, equal pay and inheritance rights and marriage laws – but also ensures that a state's decision-makers accurately reflect the make-up of society. Furthermore, research by the OECD has shown that greater participation of women in government can contribute to lowering inequality and improving public trust in government at the local and national levels.[77]

The 1995 Beijing UN Conference was a seminal moment for women's empowerment globally. The Platform of Action that emerged from the conference called on governments to move towards gender parity within public administration and legislatures and to encourage civil society organisations to promote gender equality across society.[78] In the Arab world, another defining moment was the 2010–11 Arab uprisings. Across the region, women were active in the uprisings but did not always reap the benefits of the openings that took place as institutions were either replaced or revised. As Hanane Darhour and Drude Dahlerup argue, '[h]istorical lessons from backlash in women's rights following revolutionary periods were intensively discussed within the women's movements, and there was a strong will to prevent history from repeating itself'.[79] Nevertheless, across the region, women were often side-lined once the social movements cleared the streets and returned home, and many faced serious challenges in trying to promote a women's rights agenda during the post-uprising negotiation process.

Norris argues that, although global support for gender equality has increased in the decades following the Beijing conference, this support has not translated into concomitant gains. She argues that a 'rising tide of socially liberal values has catalysed a cultural backlash among social conservatives feeling threatened by these profound shifts, heightening polarisation over cultural issues and mobilising moderate and extreme anti-gender and anti-feminist social movements actively seeking to undermine women's rights'.[80] Furthermore, the COVID-19 pandemic has led to negative consequences for women, including a rise in gender-based violence, lack of access to birth control and pushing some women out of the workforce. School closures and lack of access to childcare has forced many women to return to traditional gender roles and has made women less visible in the public sphere, with the potential to remove women's rights from the political agenda in the face of more urgent concerns.[81] Additionally, many women work in the informal sectors, such as food production, handicrafts and some tourism-related work, which were disproportionately affected by the COVID-19 pandemic. In the face of this backlash, enacting measures that empower women across the four arenas is more important than ever.

The growth in women's participation often begins at the local level. In the long-standing democracies of Britain and the United States, women's suffrage was first adopted at the local level and later spread to the national level.[82] There are fewer barriers to entry for women at the local level, including lower financial costs to run for office, as well as more opportunities to participate, given the larger number of local offices. Thus, when women enter politics locally, they can grow their political skills and networks, to assist in entering politics at the national level.[83]

Other factors contribute to the ability of women to access politics. Several scholars have found that women more easily achieve power in parliamentary systems rather than in presidential systems and that the ideology of the dominant party can have an impact on women's success.[84] Pressure is a powerful tool to encourage governments to increase the role of women. As Alice Kang and Aili Mari Tripp found, countries rarely adopt quota laws without internal pressure from coalitions.[85] Grassroots coalitions make the issue of women's representation a domestic concern, rather than the outcome of foreign interference.[86] Furthermore, local coalitions are most effective when they are broad and cross-cutting, bringing together actors from across religious and social divides.[87] Nadia Ait-Zai, the head of the Algerian Centre of Information for the Rights of Women and Children clearly stated that it had been the local organisations that were key to Algeria's adoption of quotas: 'We have been helped by the international communities. But the first work was done here in Algeria. When we wanted more representativeness of women in politics, the work was first made in Algeria, and it is we who did it'.[88]

In North Africa, home to some of the most progressive legal protections for women, it is imperative that governments and civil society both work to protect existing gains and prevent back-sliding. Additionally, much work remains in implementing the legal measures put in place to encourage gender parity. A major impediment to women's empowerment – inequitable gender norms and social pressures – renders moot many of the legislative measures at best and allows for violence against women at worst. As one report on the challenges to gender equality in Tunisia argues, . . .

> Political violence targeting women acts as a profound barrier to women's political participation. The traditional mentality that men are the decision-makers and violence against women is normal remains pervasive. As a result, men have the cultural coverage to act as gatekeepers for women's political activity using undue influence to outright violence.[89]

The Role of Gender Quotas

Governments and civil society actors have been working to increase both the number and influence of women in political structures for decades. One common tool to increase female representation in political structures is quotas. Quotas have steadily increased in use globally over the past few decades, at both the government-mandated and party levels.[90] More than three-quarters of all quota measures have been proposed since 1995.[91] Mona Lena Krook and Diana O'Brien found that there are no systematic explanations for quota adoption. Rather, quotas are present in a variety of different country contexts in places with different forms of government and different socio-economic characteristics.[92] Pressure, from foreign governments as well as local and international women's movements, has also been influential in convincing governments to enact measures increasing women's political representation. In Africa, women's participation in government increased significantly starting in 1975, the start of the UN Decade for Women. Many African governments added women's ministries to their cabinets at that time.[93] Quotas become popular in a variety of global contexts following the 1995 Platform of Action that came out of the UN Beijing Conference. The Platform called on governments to work towards gender parity within public institutions and to promote gender parity within non-governmental organisations, including labour unions, civil society organisations and the private sector. In part due to the pressure that came out of the Beijing Conference, the percentage of women in cabinets globally increased significantly, from just under 9 percent in 1999 to just under 17 percent in

2010.[94] And the percentage of women in legislatures in Africa nearly tripled, from 7.78 percent in 1990 to 22.2 percent in 2015.[95]

There are three types of quotas: reserved seats, party quotas and legislative quotas. Reserved seat quotas set aside a specific percentage of seats for women within a certain political structure.[96] Party quotas are voluntary measures chosen by parties whereby they promise to reserve a certain percentage of spots for women on an electoral slate. Legislative quotas are legal structures enacted by parliaments that require political parties to nominate a certain percentage of women on their slates.[97]

Within North Africa, quotas have taken on a variety of forms with varying levels of success. In Algeria, legislative quotas are in place for the lower house (National People's Assembly) as well as at the sub-national level. The Algerian government began adopting quotas following the civil war. The post-conflict environment and constitutional reform process allowed Algerian activists to advocate for more inclusion of women in the political sphere.[98] Quotas range from 20 percent for the smallest constituencies (those with four seats) to 50 percent for constituencies abroad.[99] Additionally, political parties are rewarded with state funding based on the number of women candidates elected at the national and sub-national levels.[100] Despite high numbers of reserved seats for women within party lists, quotas in Algeria have not translated into massive gains for women, as the law does not provide for ranking rules, meaning that few party lists are headed by women or alternate between male and female candidates.[101]

Egypt has a long history of quotas, beginning with Anwar Sadat who introduced reserved seats for women in 1979. Sadat's decision to add a gender quota was influenced by his wife's trip to Sudan at that time, where quotas had been in place for several years.[102] In Egypt today, quotas are in place for both houses of parliament as well as at the local level. The lower house (House of Representatives) adopted a new law in 2020, requiring 25 percent of seats to be reserved for women. This comes after an abysmal performance by women in the 2011–12 elections, when women represented only 2.2 percent of seats, with only eight women (1.8 percent) elected and two more appointed by the Supreme Council of the Armed Forces.

Today, the upper house (Senate) requires 10 percent of seats to be reserved for women. And 25 percent of elected local council seats are reserved for women.[103]

Libya has quotas in place at the national and local levels. In the country's 2012 elections that established the legislative body the General National Congress (GNC), women secured 16.5 percent of seats.[104] The quota system is Libya is complicated, as GNC seats are awarded in multiple ways. For the eighty seats elected by proportional representation from closed lists, parties must alternate between male and female candidates both vertically and horizontally. At the municipal level, candidates are divided into three categories: general candidates, women and former revolutionaries with special needs. But the law does not specify the number or percentage of women candidates within municipal councils.[105] There is a movement within Libya to move towards a minimum of 30 percent of women in all levels of government. The '30% Quota Campaign', an NGO coalition working on this goal, has so far succeeded in pushing the minister of culture to issue a decree to guarantee that at least 30 percent of leadership positions in the ministry will go to women.[106]

In Morocco, quotas exist in the lower house (House of Representatives) and at the local level. Morocco first introduced informal quotas for women in 2002, when political parties agreed to reserve thirty seats for women. In 2011, in the wake of the Arab Spring, the Moroccan government codified the quota system. Today, sixty seats are reserved for women in the 395-member House of Representatives, with an additional thirty seats reserved for people under the age of forty. At the local level, 30 percent of regional council seats are reserved for women.[107]

Mauritania has a complex electoral system but does reserve a portion of seats for women. Mauritania adopted a quota in 2012, and in the following election women's participation in parliament doubled to 25 percent.[108] In the parliament, forty seats are chosen through a closed-list proportional representation system, while an additional 106 seats are chosen to represent single and multi-member constituencies. Of the forty PR seats, half (twenty) are reserved for women.[109] Within the single and multi-member constituencies, there are additional quota rules. For constituencies with three seats, candidate lists are required to include a woman in the first or second position on the list. For larger constituencies, candidate lists must alternate between men and women. Additionally, parties that elect more women than required by law are eligible to receive a financial benefit. At the local level, women are guaranteed at least 20 percent of seats on municipal councils.[110]

Tunisia had some of the most advanced gender quotas globally, adopting both horizontal and vertical parity requirements for local elections. In the 2014 electoral law (Basic Law No. 16 of 2014), at the national level, parties were required to alternate between men and women on their candidate lists and to have gender parity on their lists, unless the list has an odd number of candidates. The 2022 electoral law (Decree No. 55 of 2022) removed gender quotas for the parliamentary elections. At the local level, parties must alternate between men and women on candidate lists but must also include women at the head of half of their lists.[111] In the 2018 municipal elections, the country's first-ever democratic local elections, quotas helped bring near gender parity, with women winning 47 percent of seats. Additionally, quotas for youth and persons with disabilities helped secure large gains for those groups – 37 percent and 25 percent of seats, respectively.[112]

The effectiveness of quotas varies. While quotas have been shown to increase the number of women in government, it is not clear whether they contribute to women's empowerment or to social change. As Norris argues, 'descriptive representation – measured by de jure gains in the proportion of women holding elected and appointed political offices – does not automatically translate into substantive representation, or the de facto empowerment for women'.[113] Some have argued that women are more likely to enact policies that improve health care and expand access to the labour market and education, which is linked to reducing gender inequality.[114] In studies of Nordic and other democracies, there is a clear link between higher numbers of women in parliament and women-friendly family policies.[115]

Others argue that quotas lead to tokenism, whereby women are elected not on their merits, but as 'tokens'. Quotas create a glass ceiling of sorts and can make women appear less credible to their male colleagues. Quotas, therefore, can backfire, decreasing the ability of women in government to carry out their agendas.[116] And some have found that there is no statistically significant impact of quotas on gender inequality.[117] Particularly in authoritarian settings, where women and men are prohibited from criticising the regime, quotas can 'take pressure off men elites to genuinely empower women'.[118] Even worse, an increasing visible presence of women in decision-making roles can ignite misogynistic and patriarchal forces to push back against the gains that women have made. This has borne out in Rwanda, the global leader in gender parity at the parliamentary level, where 'women politicians and activists who criticize the ruling government face harassment and repression'.[119] And in a survey by the Interparliamentary Union of Women Parliamentarians, 82 percent said that they had been subjected to psychological violence, 25 percent to physical violence and 20 percent to sexual violence.[120]

One of the major challenges to quota success is simply persuading women to participate in politics. Scholars have found that, even when they share similar qualifications, women are 'twice as likely than men to assert that they are "not at all qualified" to run for office and only half as likely to think that they would actually win. In other words: "women are more likely than men to dismiss their qualifications to run for office"'.[121]

These findings hold across cultural contexts. That is, even in places where women's cultural or socio-economic status trails that of men, women can become heads of state and prime ministers. In fact, Farida Jalalzai and Krook found a correlation between the presence of a female head of state or government with lower levels of gender parity in areas such as education, income and life expectancy.[122]

Another challenge is the party's willingness or ability to carry out quotas. As Jana Belschner argues, in the case of Tunisia's municipal elections, only Ennahda was able to tap into its vast membership networks to field enough lists that met the conditions for quotas. Other, smaller parties or lists simply lacked the human and financial resources to do so. She notes that 'smaller secular and left-leaning parties lost up to 15 percent of their submitted lists due to non-fulfilment of the "horizontal" gender parity quota and had to renounce around 50 percent of their campaign reimbursement for missing the PwD quota'.[123]

In the MENA region, quotas have had a strong symbolic effect, with some arguing that 'quotas, even in their most flawed form, in fact contribute to a transformation in attitudes toward women's role in the political sphere'.[124] As Lihi Ben Shitrit argues, in a region where between 70 and 80 percent of the pubic believes that men make better leaders than women, according to some survey data, quotas have a highly significant symbolic value in elevating women in the public eye.[125] Furthermore, there is a documented contagion effect of quotas. When women occupy an office, they can influence others to become engaged in politics or to encourage other institutions to adopt greater female representation.[126]

The Role of Legal Measures and Constitutions

Quotas are only one legislative tool used to promote gender equality within political institutions. A country's constitution sets the stage for how women are viewed by society at large. In North Africa, many countries had put relatively progressive provisions into their constitutions at independence and after. For example, Algeria, Morocco and Tunisia are some of the only countries globally who use both male and female pronouns in their constitutions.[127] The addition of progressive language did not necessarily correlate to gains for women and was not a sign of political liberalisation. Rather, authoritarian leaders often used the liberalisation of women's rights to counter Islamist groups and to promote themselves as modern leaders.[128] One current example is the appointment by Tunisian President Kais Saied of the Arab world's first female head of government – Najla Bouden. While Bouden's appointment is a landmark for Tunisia and the region, several Tunisian civil society activists have accused Saied of 'pink-washing', arguing that her appointment serves as a distraction from the authoritarian crackdown that he is undertaking.[129] Before Bouden's appointment, Saied issued an executive measure, Decree 117, which severely constricts the power of the head of government, making Bouden subservient to him and eliminating the separation of powers between the head of government and head of state. Nevertheless, Saied's moves did win him some measured praise from the international community and, for a short time, focused attention away from his harsh crackdowns on democracy in Tunisia. Additionally, measures that may appear to be aimed at promoting women's empowerment can backfire. Scholars note, for example, that the creation of a women's committee or a gender committee within decision-making bodies can end up harming women, as women are then less likely to serve on more powerful or influential committees, and are instead limited to only serve on women-related entities.[130]

The Arab uprisings provided an opportunity for activists to push for greater gender equality and to reform state institutions. The results have varied across North Africa, but in several places constitutional amendments brought de jure changes that on paper improved the rights for women, although those gains did not often translate into de facto improvements in the lives of women. One major impediment to the implementation of these laws is illiteracy. In many places, particularly in rural areas, women lack access to information about the laws that protect them. Legal costs are another impediment for women who seek to file a formal complaint or take part in the judicial process. In much of the region, government-funded legal aid services are not available, leaving victims without the means to seek justice.

The Libyan constitution underwent significant revision following the end of the Qadhafi regime. The constitutional declaration of 2011 did not directly address gender equality, but it did provide equal opportunities for all citizens and guarantee the respect of human rights and 'the freedom to adhere to international conventions that guarantee them'.[131] But as the Libyan civil war progressed, the situation for all activists, and particularly women, deteriorated. As Zahra Langhi, activist and co-founder and director of the Libyan Women's Platform for Peace, argued, '[a]ttacks on civil society had become more frequent and women activists were either killed or forced to flee the country. The Islamists hijacked the process. There were no guarantees for civil society, which has been shrinking. There are no women's rights now'.[132] Libya did put forth the Bill Concerning Care for Victims of Torture and Violence in 2011, which acknowledged the use of gender-based violence during the uprising, but the law was never passed. A 2014 decree also recognised the victims of gender-based violence during the uprising and allowed them access to reparations, but it is not clear if anyone has benefitted from this decree.

In Algeria, Tunisia and Morocco, legislatures have passed highly progressive laws combatting violence against women.

But as with many other issues, these laws have either not been implemented, or lack the education campaigns and societal awareness necessary to address the root causes of violence against women or to actualise the legislation.[133]

Personal Status Codes, or Family Laws are another vehicle for legislating women's rights. In Mauritania, women's civil society organisations helped push for the passage of a Personal Status Code in 2001, which raised the legal age of marriage to eighteen for both men and women and required the consent of women to marry. Following the Arab Spring, Morocco established a national programme to push for gender equality, known as ICRAM. The programme seeks to better integrate women into the country's social and economic development programmes and is focused on entrepreneurship.[134] One highly controversial law in Morocco was the provision in the Penal Code that allowed a rapist to escape prosecution by marrying his victim. This was finally overturned in Morocco in 2014, following the highly publicised case of the forced marriage of a sixteen-year-old rape victim in 2012. The victim committed suicide, and her case gained national attention, resulting in a national discussion around the law.[135]

Tunisia underwent a similar experience following a 2016 case in which the Tunisian court authorised a rapist to marry his thirteen-year-old victim, sparking outcry from civil society activists. In 2017, Tunisia passed a comprehensive law on the Elimination of Violence Against Women that included, amongst other provisions, the removal of the provision of the Penal Code that allowed rapists to marry their victims to escape prosecution.[136]

Algerian activists began mobilising for a new Family Code in 2003, under the slogan 'Twenty Years is Enough!' in reference to the 1984 Family Code, which was outdated. In 2005, the pressure campaign worked, and the Algerian government amended the Family Code, giving women substantially more rights to marriage, divorce and citizenship, including changing the legal age of marriage from twenty-one for men and eighteen for women to nineteen for both men and women. Women were no longer forced to marry against their will, and women were no longer prevented from marrying non-Algerians, while women married to foreigners were allowed to transmit their citizenship to their children. Women were also given broader rights in that the clause in the original code requiring the wife to obey her husband was removed.[137]

In Egypt, the 2014 Constitution provides a wide range of de jure rights for women, but few of these rights have been implemented. Additionally, the crackdown on civil society writ-large and political opposition has prevented women's rights activists from advocating for their cause. Egypt has long promoted gender equality amongst its official and quasi-official bodies to appeal to the West and to capture some of the more powerful sectors of civil society. During the revolution, men and women participated actively in the street protests, and women were able to enter the political sphere to a greater degree in the immediate aftermath of the revolution, during the brief period of democratic transition following the ouster of Hosni Mubarak. Women used their increased power to raise awareness of sexual harassment and assault, which proliferated during the mass protests of 2011. In 2017, President Sisi launched the National Strategy for the Empowerment of Egyptian Women 2030, which seeks to guide Egypt towards reaching the 2030 Sustainable Development Goals.[138] As a result, the 2014 Egyptian Constitution is quite progressive regarding gender equality. Article nine of the constitution states: 'The state ensures equal opportunity for all citizens without discrimination'. And Article 11 calls for equality in 'all civil, political, economic, social and cultural rights'. The constitution also affirms the commitment of the state to prevent gender-based violence.[139]

Sisi has used women's rights as one of the justifications for the coup that ousted democratically elected leader Mohamed Morsi and brought Sisi to power, arguing that the Muslim Brotherhood leadership sought to undermine women's rights. More recently, Sisi's government released the National Human Rights Strategy, which contains four focus areas including 'Human Rights of Women, Children, Persons with Disabilities, Youth and the Elderly'. The document addresses the political, social and economic empowerment of women as well as preventing violence against women. However, the overall strategy has been widely criticised by human rights activists.[140] Gamal Eid, director of the Arabic Network for Human Rights Information (ANHRI), said: 'The main goal is to produce a document to solely improve the image of the regime'.[141]

The Role of Civil Society

Civil society plays a crucial role in advocating for legislative changes and can be a necessary variable in determining whether quotas or other legislative measures are adopted. Scholars argue that grassroots coalitions of various civil society actors make it clear to policy-makers that the desire for change is home-grown, rather than an international import.[142] Kang and Tripp found that, 'without domestic coalitions, it is significantly less likely that quota laws are adopted to increase female legislative representation'.[143] Furthermore, effective coalitions are those that are 'expansive, cutting across ethnic, religious, party and other differences, particularly when it comes to issues that challenge societal beliefs and expectations because of the importance of showing widespread support of the reform from key sectors of society'.[144] Furthermore, coalitions have developed across North African countries, linking each country's individual demands to a broader push for societal change. The Collectif95 Maghreb Égalité, for example, is a network of more than eighty CSOs across North Africa.[145] And, as Tripp argues, despite international efforts to push for quotas by the UN and others, local actors and organisations are essential in translating policy to real-life impact.[146]

The Arab Spring undoubtedly provided women's rights groups with new opportunities for engagement and, in many countries, a more permissive environment, at least initially, to push for change. In Morocco, several new women's rights groups were created to address a wide spectrum of issues including identity, the role of Islam and control over one's body.[147] In Tunisia, hundreds of CSOs have been established since 2010, and the broader women's rights movement was very successful in both ensuring protections for gender equality within the 2014 Constitution and in pushing for further legislative protections. One issue that groups have been pushing for is allowing women equal inheritance to men. This was something promoted by former President Beji Caid Essebsi as well as a network of civil society groups, who succeeded in pressing for a change to the civil law, approved by parliament in 2018. However, President Saied has expressed opposition to changes in inheritance, and following his consolidation of power on 25 July 2021, advancements in this space are unlikely.

Egypt faced one of the most difficult battles in pressing for an end to sexual harassment, which has plagued the country for decades. In 2013, a UN study found that 99 percent of Egyptian women experienced sexual harassment, and 96.5 percent said they experienced sexual assault in the form of touching.[148] Egyptian activists were up against a pervasive problem as well as a cultural environment permissive to harassment and assault. A 2017 survey found that more than 75 percent of Egyptian men said that the way in which a woman dressed was 'a legitimate reason for harassment'.[149]

To address these issues, several initiatives were created, including 'We Will Not Keep Silent on Sexual Harassment', run by Hadia Abdel Fattah. She has described the many layers of work that need to be done to make progress on this issue: 'We need grassroots organizations along with art, culture, media and educational institutions to work together so that people on the streets know how to handle sexual harassment', she says. 'The person being harassed needs to know what to do and police officers need to know how to handle such cases. This also needs to translate to schools and workplaces across the country'.[150]

Some progress has been made, particularly in the immediate aftermath of the revolution, when some prominent cases of assault and abuse made it into the international media. Women's testimonials were collected, and maps made to show where harassment had occurred, all of which gained widespread public support and resulted in changes to the sexual harassment legislation, including providing for victims and witnesses in sexual assault cases to remain anonymous.[151]

Conclusion

Addressing the impediments to gender equality within North Africa will require a significant effort by North African governments, civil society groups and donors. At the political level, work must be done to attract both female candidates for office and women voters, such as through get-out-the-vote efforts targeting women, particularly rural women. Additionally, civil society groups and donors should encourage political parties to develop party platforms that address the concerns of female voters and have concrete plans to increase gender parity across society. Despite efforts at increasing the quantity of female members of parliament or members of cabinet, there has been little done to translate that quantitative increase into qualitative change for women in their daily lives. Thus, both male and female legislators should be encouraged to craft legislation that would have a tangible impact on the lives of women and help elevate their status within society. Given the connection between female employment/education and economic growth, governments and businesses should work to increase women's labour force participation by adopting family-friendly policies, such as parental leave and childcare subsidies as well as provisions for elder care, which would allow more women to enter and remain in the workforce.[152]

Along with promoting greater participation of women in public life, donors and local NGOs should provide resources to female candidates on protecting themselves from violence and harassment. Furthermore, in addressing the structural impediments to gender parity, efforts should be made at changing public attitudes, including not only discouraging violence against women, but also educating the public on the legal recourse to abuse and embedding women and allies within the police forces and other security services so that women feel safe reporting abuse. Some have recommended creating special police units aimed at dealing with cases of sexual assault and abuse, with specially trained officers, including women, to help victims feel at ease.[153] Efforts should also be made to document and address the impact of the COVID-19 pandemic on gender-based violence. While such a pandemic is unlikely to occur again soon, spikes in gender-based violence (GBV) tend to occur in conditions of temporary lockdowns or during holidays, and lessons from the pandemic can be used to devise legal and social mechanisms to prevent such spikes in the future. Recognising that a rise in GBV is one of the outcomes of the pandemic can also encourage donors to include efforts to combat GBV as part of their COVID-19 relief and recovery programmes in North Africa.

Finally, both the state and civil society have the tools to address gender norms within society that are impeding gender equality. All actors should work to normalise women's participation in public life and in positions of power. Local civil society groups should work with schools on education campaigns to highlight positive examples of female leaders and to teach both young women and men early on that women are just as capable as men of occupying positions of power. Local government can help by setting up leadership academies and student government associations for secondary school students to target young women and teach both men and women from an early age that women are capable leaders. For civil society organisations, there is an important role to play in working with journalists and the media establishment to remove gender bias and to make sure that men and women are covered equally in the press.[154]

Notes

1. Valentine Moghadam, 'Transnational Feminist Networks: Collective Action in an Era of Globalization', in *Globalization and Social Movements*, ed. Pierre Hamel, Henri Lustiger-Thaler, Jan Nederveen Pieterse, and Sasha Roseneil (New York: Palgrave, 2001), 129; Zakia Salime, *Between Feminism and Islam: Human Rights and Sharia Law in Morocco* (Minneapolis: University of Minnesota Press, 2011).
2. Stephan Klasen and Francesca Lamanna, 'The Impact of Gender Inequality in Education and Employment on Economic Growth: New Evidence for a Panel of Countries', *Feminist Economics* 15, no. 3 (1 July 2009): 91–132.
3. Mounira Charrad, *States and Women's Rights: The Making of Postcolonial Tunisia, Algeria, and Morocco* (Oakland: University of California Press, 2001), 241.
4. Charrad, *States and Women's Rights*, 241.
5. Klasen and Lamanna, 'The Impact of Gender Inequality'.
6. Laura Cabeza-García, Esther Del Brio, and Mery Oscanoa-Victorio, 'Gender Factors and Inclusive Economic Growth: The Silent Revolution', *Sustainability* 10, no. 2 (6 January 2018): e121.
7. Klasen and Lamanna, 'The Impact of Gender Inequality'.
8. Klasen and Lamanna, 'The Impact of Gender Inequality'; Stephan Klasen, 'Low Schooling for Girls, Slower Growth for All? Cross-Country Evidence on the Effect of Gender Inequality in Education on Economic Development', *The World Bank Economic Review* 16, no. 3 (1 December 2002): 345–73.
9. Klasen and Lamanna, 'The Impact of Gender Inequality'.
10. Katerina Dalacoura, 'Women and Gender in the Middle East and North Africa: Mapping the Field and Addressing Policy Dilemmas at the Post-2011 Juncture', *MENARA Final Reports*

3, March 2019. http://eprints.lse.ac.uk/100742/1/Dalacoura_Women_and_Gender.pdf, 35.
11. 'World Development Indicators', *World Bank*, n. d., https://databank.worldbank.org/reports.aspx?source=2&series=SL.TLF.CACT.FE.ZS&country=#.
12. Robert Crotti et al., 'Global Gender Gap Report 2021', *World Economic Forum*, March 2021, https://www3.weforum.org/docs/WEF_GGGR_2021.pdf.
13. Crotti et al, 'Global Gender Gap Report 2021'.
14. World Bank, *Women, Business and the Law 2021* (n. p.: The World Bank, 2021).
15. World Bank, *Women, Business and the Law 2021*.
16. World Bank, *Women, Business and the Law 2020* (n. p.: The World Bank, 2020).
17. Salime, *Between Feminism and Islam*.
18. Charrad, *States and Women's Rights*.
19. Mounira Charrad, 'State and Gender in the Maghrib', *MERIP*, 8 March 1990, https://merip.org/1990/03/state-and-gender-in-the-maghrib/.
20. Mounira Charrad, 'Policy Shifts: State, Islam and Gender in Tunisia, 1930s–1990s', *Social Politics: International Studies in Gender, State & Society* 4, no. 2 (1997): 284–319.
21. Charrad, 'Policy Shifts'.
22. Sana Ben Achour, *Féminisme d'état et féminisme autonome* (Tunis: Centre de Publication Universitaire, 2001), 413.
23. Several authors and Tunisian feminists have written about women challenging state power and the evolution of the feminist movement in Tunisia, including Ilham Marzouki, Azza Ghanmi, Dorra Mahfoudh and Amel Mahfoudh.
24. Leila Ahmed, *Women and Gender in Islam: Historical Roots of a Modern Debate* (New Haven: Yale, 1992).
25. Ahmed, *Women and Gender in Islam*; Nadia Guessous, 'Feminist Blind Spots and the Affect of Secularity: Disorienting the Discourse of the Veil in Contemporary Morocco', *Signs* 45, no. 3 (Spring 2020): 605–28.
26. Ahmed, *Women and Gender in Islam*.
27. Mervat F. Hatem, 'Economic and Political Liberation in Egypt and the Demise of State Feminism', *International Journal of Middle East Studies* 24, no. 2 (May 1992): 231–51.
28. Laura Bier, *Revolutionary Womanhood: Feminisms, Modernity, and the State in Nasser's Egypt* (Palo Alto: Stanford University Press, 2011).
29. Nahla Samaha, 'Women's Equality: No Longer a Part of Egypt's Constitution', *Atlantic Council*, 4 December 2012, https://www.at

lanticcouncil.org/blogs/menasource/women-s-equality-no-long
er-a-part-of-egypt-s-constitution/.
30. Hatem, 'Economic and Political Liberation in Egypt and the Demise of State Feminism'.
31. Lila Abu-Lughod and Rabab El-Mahdi, 'Beyond the "Woman Question" in the Egyptian Revolution', *Feminist Studies* 37, no. 3 (2011): 683–91.
32. Rana Magdy, 'Egyptian Feminist Movement: A Brief History', *openDemocracy*, n. d., https://www.opendemocracy.net/en/nor th-africa-west-asia/egyptian-feminist-movement-brief-history/.
33. '1951 دستور المملكة الليبية لسنة (Constitution of the Kingdom of Libya of 1951)', https://security-legislation.ly/ar/law/31474.
34. Zahra Langhi, 'Gender and State-Building in Libya: Towards a Politics of Inclusion', *The Journal of North African Studies* 19, no. 2 (15 March 2014): 200–10.
35. Langhi, 'Gender and State-Building in Libya'.
36. Ghady Kafala, 'الحركة النسوية في ليبيا ... نضال نسوي مستمر' (Women's Movement in Libya ... an Ongoing Feminist Struggle)', *Elbiro Media*, 30 December 2017, https://elbiro.net/feminism-move ment-in-libya/.
37. Langhi, 'Gender and State-Building in Libya'.
38. Langhi, 'Gender and State-Building in Libya'.
39. Article 2 states that '[s]tates Parties condemn discrimination against women in all its forms, agree to pursue by all appropriate means and without delay a policy of eliminating discrimination against women'. Article 16 states that '[s]tates Parties shall take all appropriate measures to eliminate discrimination against women in all matters relating to marriage and family relations and in particular shall ensure, on a basis of equality of men and women: (c) The same rights and responsibilities during marriage and at its dissolution; (d) The same rights and responsibilities as parents, irrespective of their marital status, in matters relating to their children; in all cases the interests of the children shall be paramount'. 'Convention on the Elimination of All Forms of Discrimination against Women', *United Nations Treaty Collection*, n. d., https://treaties.un.org/Pages/ViewDetails. aspx?src=IND&mtdsg_no=IV-8&chapter=4#34.
40. 'Convention on the Elimination of All Forms of Discrimination against Women'.
41. Marnia Lazreg, 'Gender and Politics in Algeria: Unraveling the Religious Paradigm', *Signs* 15, no. 4 (Summer 1990): 755–80.
42. Lazreg, 'Gender and Politics in Algeria'.
43. Marnia Lazreg, *The Eloquence of Silence: Algerian Women in Question*, 2nd ed. (New York: Routledge, 2019).

44. Boutheina Cheriet, 'Le genre et la citoyenneté comme « troc » dans l'Algérie postcoloniale', *Diogene* 225, no. 1 (2009): 89–100.
45. Cheriet, 'Le genre et la citoyenneté comme « troc » dans l'Algérie postcoloniale'. Author's translation.
46. Charrad, *States and Women's Rights*.
47. Charrad, *States and Women's Rights*.
48. Lazreg, *The Eloquence of Silence*.
49. Lazreg, *The Eloquence of Silence*.
50. Lazreg, *The Eloquence of Silence*.
51. Charrad, 'State and Gender in the Maghrib'.
52. Charrad, 'State and Gender in the Maghrib'.
53. Charrad, *States and Women's Rights*.
54. Salime, *Between Feminism and Islam*.
55. Salime, *Between Feminism and Islam*.
56. Salime, *Between Feminism and Islam*.
57. Salime, *Between Feminism and Islam*.
58. Salime, *Between Feminism and Islam*.
59. Camille Evrard and Erin Pettigrew, 'Encore une nouvelle victime . . . Le long chemin d'une législation à l'égard des femmes en Mauritanie', *L'Année du Maghrib*, no. 23 (20 December 2020): 271–302.
60. Cédric Jourde, 'Countries at the Crossroads 2011: Mauritania', *Freedom House*, n. d., https://www.europarl.europa.eu/meetdocs/2009_2014/documents/dmag/dv/dmag20120125_02_/dmag20120125_02_en.pdf.
61. Jake Dizard, Christopher Walker, and Vanessa Tucker, *Countries at the Crossroads 2011: An Analysis of Democratic Governance* (Lanham: Rowman & Littlefield, 2012).
62. Céline Lesourd, 'The Lipstick on the Edge of the Well: Mauritanian Women and Political Power (1960–2014)', in *Women's Movements in Post-'Arab Spring' North Africa*, ed. Fatima Sadiqi (New York: Palgrave Macmillan, 2016), 77; Fatima Sadiqi, ed., *Women's Movements in Post-'Arab Spring' North Africa* (New York: Palgrave Macmillan US, 2016).
63. Katherine Ann Wiley, 'Women in Mauritania', *Oxford Research Encyclopedia of African History*, 30 July 2020, https://doi.org/10.1093/acrefore/9780190277734.013.529.
64. Katherine Ann Wiley, *Work, Social Status, and Gender in Post-Slavery Mauritania* (Bloomington: Indiana University Press, 2018).
65. Corinne Fortier, 'Genre, statut et ethnicisation des Haratin de Mauritanie', *L'Ouest Saharien*, Devenir visibles dans le sillage de l'esclavage: La question ḥarāṭīn en Mauritanie et au Maroc, 10, no. 11 (2020): 171–86.

66. Wiley, *Work, Social Status, and Gender in Post-Slavery Mauritania*.
67. Wiley, 'Women in Mauritania'.
68. Meskerem Brhane, *Narratives of the Past, Politics of the Present Identity: Subordination and the Haratines of Mauritania* (unpubl. dissertation, University of Chicago, 1997).
69. 'Women and Participation in the Arab Uprisings A Struggle for Justice', *Economic and Social Commission for Western Asia*, August 2017, https://yptoolbox.unescapsdd.org/wp-content/uploads/2017/08/ESCWA_Women-and-Participation-in-the-Arab-Uprisings-A-struggle-for-Justice.pdf
70. 'Women and the Arab Spring: Taking Their Place?' *Fédération internationale des ligues des droits de l'Homme*, 8 March 2012, https://www.fidh.org/IMG/pdf/femmesarabangbassdef.pdf.
71. 'Women and the Arab Spring: Taking Their Place?'
72. 'Egypt: Epidemic of Sexual Violence', *Human Rights Watch*, 3 July 2013, https://www.hrw.org/news/2013/07/03/egypt-epidemic-sexual-violence.
73. 'Women and the Arab Spring: Taking Their Place?' Following Samira Ibrahim's case – who won a lawsuit against the military – the court declared 'virginity tests' illegal.
74. Dina Tannir and Vivienne Badaan, 'Women and Participation in the Arab Uprisings: A Struggle for Justice', *Economic and Social Commission for Western Asia*, 26 December 2013, https://yptoolbox.unescapsdd.org/wp-content/uploads/2017/08/ESCWA_Women-and-Participation-in-the-Arab-Uprisings-A-struggle-for-Justice.pdf.
75. Andrea Khalil, *Gender, Women and the Arab Spring* (London: Routledge, 2015).
76. Pippa Norris, 'The State of Women's Participation and Empowerment', *Sixty-Fifth Session of the Commission on the Status of Women*, 2020, https://www.unwomen.org/sites/default/files/Headquarters/Attachments/Sections/CSW/65/EGM/Norris_State%20of%20Womens%20Participation%20and%20Empowerment_BP1_CSW65EGM.pdf.
77. 'Women's Political Participation in Egypt: Barriers, Opportunities and Gender Sensitivity of Select Political Institutions', *OECD*, July 2018, https://www.oecd.org/mena/governance/womens-political-participation-in-egypt.pdf.
78. Aili Mari Tripp and Alice Kang, 'The Global Impact of Quotas: On the Fast Track to Increased Female Legislative Representation', *Comparative Political Studies* 41, no. 3 (March 2008): 338–61.
79. Hanane Darhour and Drude Dahlerup, *Double-Edged Politics on Women's Rights in the MENA Region* (London: Palgrave Macmillan, 2020).

80. Norris, 'The State of Women's Participation and Empowerment'.
81. Saskia Brechenmacher and Caroline Hubbard, 'How the Coronavirus Risks Exacerbating Women's Political Exclusion', *Carnegie Endowment for International Peace*, 17 November 2020, https://carnegieendowment.org/2020/11/17/how-coronavirus-risks-exacerbating-women-s-political-exclusion-pub-83213, 8.
82. Stefanie Nanes, '"The Quota Encouraged Me to Run": Evaluating Jordan's Municipal Quota for Women', *Journal of Middle East Women's Studies* 11, no. 3 (November 2015): 261–82.
83. Nanes, 'The Quota Encouraged Me to Run'.
84. Gretchen Bauer and Faith Okpotor, '"Her Excellency": An Exploratory Overview of Women Cabinet Ministers in Africa', *Africa Today* 60, no. 1 (Fall 2013): 77–97.
85. Alice J. Kang and Aili Mari Tripp, 'Coalitions Matter: Citizenship, Women, and Quota Adoption in Africa', *Perspectives on Politics* 16, no. 1 (March 2018): 73–91.
86. Kang and Tripp, 'Coalitions Matter'.
87. Kang and Tripp, 'Coalitions Matter'.
88. Kang and Tripp, 'Coalitions Matter'.
89. 'SheVotes Tunisia: Understanding Barriers to Women's Political Participation', *International Republican Institute*, 2020, https://www.iri.org/resources/shevotes-examines-barriers-to-womens-political-engagement-in-tunisia/.
90. Mona Lena Krook and Diana Z. O'Brien, 'The Politics of Group Representation: Quotas for Women and Minorities Worldwide', *Comparative Politics* 42, no. 3 (31 March 2010): 253–72.
91. Krook and O'Brien, 'The Politics of Group Representation'.
92. Krook and O'Brien, 'The Politics of Group Representation'.
93. Bauer and Okpotor, 'Her Excellency'.
94. Bauer and Okpotor, 'Her Excellency'.
95. Aili Mari Tripp, 'Women's Mobilisation for Legislative Political Representation in Africa', *Review of African Political Economy* 43, no. 149 (2 July 2016): 382–99.
96. Krook and O'Brien, 'The Politics of Group Representation'.
97. Tripp and Kang, 'The Global Impact of Quotas'.
98. Tripp, 'Women's Mobilisation for Legislative Political Representation in Africa'.
99. 'Gender Quotas Database', *International IDEA*, 29 April 2021, https://www.idea.int/data-tools/data/gender-quotas/country-view/200/35.
100. 'Gender Quotas Database'.
101. 'Gender Quotas Database'.
102. Krook and O'Brien, 'The Politics of Group Representation'.
103. 'Gender Quotas Database'.

104. 'Gender Quotas Database'.
105. 'Gender Quotas Database'.
106. Andrew Blunt, 'Libyan Ministry of Culture Approves Decree for 30% Gender Quota', 24 April 2020, https://www.ndi.org/our-stories/libyan-ministry-culture-approves-decree-30-gender-quota.
107. 'International IDEA', n. d., https://www.idea.int/data-tools/data/gender-quotas/country-view/200/35.
108. Tripp, 'Women's Mobilisation for Legislative Political Representation in Africa'.
109. 'Mauritania'. *International IDEA: Gender Quotas Database*, n. d. https://www.idea.int/data-tools/data/gender-quotas/country-view/214/35.
110. 'Mauritania'.
111. 'Tunisia'. *International IDEA: Gender Quotas Database*, n. d. https://www.idea.int/data-tools/data/gender-quotas/country-view/284/35.
112. Jana Belschner, 'Electoral Engineering in New Democracies: Strong Quotas and Weak Parties in Tunisia', *Government and Opposition* 57, no. 1 (2020): 1–18.
113. Norris, 'The State of Women's Participation and Empowerment'.
114. Valentina Dimitrova-Grajzl and Iyabo Obasanjo, 'Do Parliamentary Gender Quotas Decrease Gender Inequality? The Case of African Countries', *Constitutional Political Economy* 30, no. 2 (June 2019): 149–76.
115. Bauer and Okpotor, 'Her Excellency'.
116. Dimitrova-Grajzl and Obasanjo, 'Do Parliamentary Gender Quotas Decrease Gender Inequality?'
117. Dimitrova-Grajzl and Obasanjo, 'Do Parliamentary Gender Quotas Decrease Gender Inequality?'
118. Nanes, 'The Quota Encouraged Me to Run'.
119. 'The Number of Women in Elected Office Is Rising, But That Hasn't Meant More Power', *Foreign Policy*, 2 March 2021, https://foreignpolicy.com/2021/03/02/women-elected-office-representation-not-enough/.
120. Marie E. Berry, Yolande Bouka, and Marilyn Muthoni Kamuru, 'Implementing Inclusion: Gender Quotas, Inequality, and Backlash in Kenya', *Politics & Gender* (5 March 2020): 1–25.
121. Mona Lena Krook, 'Why Are Fewer Women than Men Elected? Gender and the Dynamics of Candidate Selection', *Political Studies Review* 8, no. 2 (May 2010): 155–68.
122. Farida Jalalzai and Mona Lena Krook, 'Beyond Hillary and Benazir: Women's Political Leadership Worldwide', *International Political Science Review* 31, no. 1 (January 2010): 5–21.

123. Belschner, 'Electoral Engineering in New Democracies'.
124. Lihi Ben Shitrit, 'Authenticating Representation: Women's Quotas and Islamist Parties', *Politics & Gender* 12, no. 4 (December 2016): 781–806.
125. Ben Shitrit, 'Authenticating Representation'.
126. Ben Shitrit, 'Authenticating Representation'.
127. Darhour and Dahlerup, *Double-Edged Politics on Women's Rights in the MENA Region*.
128. Darhour and Dahlerup, *Double-Edged Politics on Women's Rights in the MENA Region*.
129. Elizia Volkmann, 'Activists Call Tunisia's First Female Prime Minister Mere Distraction', *Al Monitor*, 10 November 2021, https://www.al-monitor.com/originals/2021/10/activists-call-tunisias-first-female-prime-minister-mere-distraction.
130. Christie Marie Arendt, 'From Critical Mass to Critical Leaders: Unpacking the Political Conditions behind Gender Quotas in Africa', *Politics & Gender* 14, no. 3 (September 2018): 295–322.
131. Souadou Lagdaf and Yahia H. Zoubir, 'The Struggle of the Women's Movements in Neo-Patriarchal Libya', *Oriente Moderno* 98, no. 2 (7 September 2018): 225–46.
132. Lagdaf and Zoubir, 'The Struggle of the Women's Movements in Neo-Patriarchal Libya'.
133. Darhour and Dahlerup, *Double-Edged Politics on Women's Rights in the MENA Region*.
134. Darhour and Dahlerup, *Double-Edged Politics on Women's Rights in the MENA Region*.
135. 'Gender Justice and Equality before the Law', *United Nations Development Programme*, 2019, https://www.undp.org/arab-states/publications/gender-justice-equality-law.
136. 'Gender Justice and Equality before the Law'.
137. Tripp, 'Women's Mobilisation for Legislative Political Representation in Africa'.
138. 'Women's Political Participation in Egypt'.
139. 'Egypt's Constitution of 2014', *Constitute Project*, n. d., https://www.constituteproject.org/constitution/Egypt_2014.pdf.
140. 'Egypt's Human Rights Strategy Is Finally out, But Will Bring Few "Major Developments" in Criminal Justice Reform, Says Source', *Mada Masr*, 12 September 2021, https://www.madamasr.com/en/2021/09/12/feature/politics/egypts-human-rights-strategy-is-finally-out-but-will-bring-few-major-developments-in-criminal-justice-reform-says-source/.
141. 'Egypt Announces Human Rights Strategy to Mixed Reviews', *Al-Monitor*, September 2021, https://www.al-monitor.com/origi

nals/2021/09/egypt-announces-human-rights-strategy-mixed-re
views.
142. Kang and Tripp, 'Coalitions Matter'.
143. Kang and Tripp, 'Coalitions Matter'.
144. Kang and Tripp, 'Coalitions Matter'.
145. Darhour and Dahlerup, *Double-Edged Politics on Women's Rights in the MENA Region*.
146. Tripp, 'Women's Mobilisation for Legislative Political Representation in Africa'.
147. Darhour and Dahlerup, *Double-Edged Politics on Women's Rights in the MENA Region*.
148. May El Habachi, 'Egypt's #MeToo Activists See Progress, But "the Road Ahead Is Long"', *World Politics Review*, 17 December 2020, https://www.worldpoliticsreview.com/in-egypt-women-s-rights-activists-see-progress-but-the-road-ahead-is-long/.
149. El Habachi, 'Egypt's #MeToo Activists See Progress'.
150. El Habachi, 'Egypt's #MeToo Activists See Progress'.
151. El Habachi, 'Egypt's #MeToo Activists See Progress'.
152. Maia Sieverding, 'The Role of the Care Economy in Promoting Gender Equality: Progress of Women in the Arab States 2020', *UN Women*, 2020, https://www2.unwomen.org/-/media/field%20office%20arab%20states/attachments/2021/01/unw_erf_report_final_8%20december.pdf?la=en&vs=1828.
153. El Habachi, 'Egypt's #MeToo Activists See Progress'.
154. 'SheVotes Tunisia: Understanding Barriers to Women's Political Participation'.

8

North Africa in the World

Sarah E. Yerkes and Maha Sohail AlHomoud

As the preceding chapters have shown, the way in which North Africa is addressing major global challenges such as economic stagnation, the decline of rentierism, climate change and socio-economic inequality has direct implications for North African citizens as well as those in surrounding states and regions. This chapter will examine the opposing directional effects – how external actors engage with North African states. It will look at five major actors – that is, the West (United States and Europe), the Gulf States, Sub-Saharan Africa, China and Russia – to understand both their interests in North Africa as well as the challenges and opportunities that those interests offer.

The West

The international community (in particular the United States, the European Union and the EU member states) have deep and important diplomatic and economic relationships with North Africa. Europe is inextricably tied to North Africa through geography as well as history. While the US has placed less emphasis on North Africa than on other parts of the MENA region (apart from Egypt), the country also maintains important security and economic ties with most North African states. As Richard Youngs notes, 'the EU's main focus has been on one part of the MENA region: the Mediterranean'.[1] Europe's contemporary approach towards North Africa began with the 1995 Barcelona Process (or the Euro Mediterranean Partnership Initiative), which developed a multi-lateral framework on security, political, social, cultural and economic relations between Europe and the countries of the southern Mediterranean. Through this process, North African states signed association agreements that opened the door to free trade agreements and allowed them access to aid from Europe; however, as Adel Abdel Ghafar and Anna Jacobs argue, '[t]hese free trade agreements suffered from blatant imbalances, and countries such as Algeria remained hesitant for several years to sign them because of the privileging of European industry over North African agriculture and the political conditions attached to the agreements'.[2] The Barcelona process evolved into the European Neighbourhood Policy (ENP) in 2004. The ENP was set up to 'create a ring of friendly, stable and prosperous countries around the European Union in order to guarantee stability along the outer borders of the EU'.[3]

Following the ENP, the 2008 Union for the Mediterranean was set up to facilitate exports from Mediterranean countries to Europe by offering technical and financial assistance. The programme asked southern Mediterranean countries to modernise their economic and social structures to increase their access to European markets, but most Mediterranean countries did not comply with the requests.[4] Tunisia and Morocco were two of the first countries to sign on to the Union for the Mediterranean. The events of the Arab Spring brought new opportunities for European engagement with North Africa and led the EU to revise the ENP, including adopting a 'more for more' principle that rewarded countries with additional support should they adopt additional reforms.[5] The newly created Support for Partnership Reform and Inclusive Growth (SPRING) fund allocated €350 million to be split amongst Arab states that demonstrated reforms. Of this amount, €100 million went to Tunisia. Two other smaller pots of money were also approved: an €80.5 million general aid package for the MENA region and a programme for strengthening civil society to the tune of €26.4 million. Additionally, shortly after the revolution in Tunisia, the EU was able to dramatically increase its bilateral aid for 2011 from a planned €240 million package to €390 million.[6]

A 2015 review further re-assessed the ENP in order to address the dramatic changes that had occurred within ENP member states in the previous four years, to devise a more differentiated approach towards the EU's Mediterranean neighbours and to allow greater flexibility for the EU to respond more rapidly to changes on the ground. In February 2021, the European Commission issued a 'new agenda for the Mediterranean', highlighting five key policy areas for cooperation: '1) human development, good governance and the rule of law; 2) strengthen resilience, build prosperity and seize the digital transition; 3) peace and security; 4) migration and mobility; and 5) green transition: climate resilience, energy and environment'.[7]

But despite the wide reach of the ENP, there is no singular European approach towards North Africa. Each of the member states has its own interests and objectives there, leaving the European Union itself as somewhat of a 'negligible political player in the MENA region, as it continuously looks to US leadership in a manner that precludes an independent policy on regional developments', according to a study by the European Council on Foreign Relations.[8] Individual European states vary dramatically in their engagement with North Africa. France is one of the most deeply entrenched countries in North Africa, but suffers from its dark colonial legacy in Algeria, Morocco and Tunisia. Germany has often positioned itself as the leader of Europe, playing a key role in the negotiations to end the Libyan civil war, for example, as Frederic Wehrey and Jacqueline Stomski describe in Chapter One. And both Italy and Spain, given their very close proximity to the African continent, have been intensely involved in the migration debate. The Nordic countries, particularly Sweden, have approached the region often through a rights lens, with a focus on a feminist foreign policy. As Charles Thepaut notes, North African economies are inextricably linked with Europe:

> Europe accounts for a third of Egypt's trade, and is the primary source of tourists to Tunisia, Morocco and Egypt. Spain has imported Libyan oil since the 1970s, and 46 percent of its gas comes from Algeria. Numerous European countries rely on energy supplies transiting the Mediterranean via ships and pipelines linking Europe with North African countries. The contest for prospective eastern Mediterranean gas is also a vital geopolitical issue for Greece and Cyprus.[9]

For the United States, North Africa has traditionally taken a backseat to other parts of the MENA region. Furthermore, both the Barack Obama and Donald Trump administrations shared the desire to disengage from the MENA region writ-large, and despite President Joe Biden's desire to re-engage with the world following Trump's 'America First' doctrine, the Biden administration also deprioritised the MENA region. While President George W. Bush took the opposite approach – heavily involving the United States in the region, initially through the Iraq war and then through the establishment of the Middle East Partnership Initiative aimed at promoting democracy in the region – President Obama came to office in 2008 with the desire to extricate the United States from the myriad conflicts and entanglements in the region. However, once the Arab Spring broke out in 2010–11, Obama was forced to re-engage – particularly in North Africa, the centre of the Arab Spring uprisings. But a US focus on the sub-region was short-lived. As the hope of the Arab Spring dissolved (with the exception of Tunisia at least initially), the United States largely sat on the side-lines, ceding most of the policy space to Europe.

The Trump administration simultaneously cozied up to the Sisi regime in Egypt, whom Trump referred to as 'my favourite dictator', and largely ignored an array of US interests in the region, from Tunisia's democratic transition over the growing migration crisis to overtures by China and Russia towards each North African state. The Biden administration has also stated a desire to extricate itself from the broader MENA region, but in its first year alone, was drawn into debates over human rights in Egypt, faced pressure to engage more forcefully in the Libyan peace process and was saddled with reviewing the abrupt shift in US policy regarding the Western Sahara which had been put in place in the waning days of the Trump administration. In a December 2021 press call, a senior Biden administration official acknowledged that, while the region is not always in the spotlight, 'the Middle East remains just a central focus of ours', due to its deep connections to US interests.[10] However, while the United States may not have been the driver for much of the Western approach to North Africa over the past decade, the United States has consistently shared Europe's concerns in the areas of security and migration and worked to deepen US economic ties in the region. And as Steven Cook argues, '[a] long look at the map will tell you almost everything one needs to know about North Africa and its importance to a core American interest – the stability and security of Europe'.[11]

Europe and the United States share several interests in North Africa, although individual countries prioritise these interests differently: maintaining stability, countering violent extremism, addressing the migration crisis, promoting economic prosperity and trade and limiting the reach of Russia and China. Each of these interests is inter-related, necessitating a highly nuanced foreign policy approach towards the region for both the United States and Europe.

Perhaps the most important interest of the West is maintaining stability in North Africa. Both the United States and Europe seek good governance and the rule of law as 'the basis for long-term stability and reduction of violent extremism in the region'.[12] Europe, which is just miles from North Africa's shores, is directly influenced by events in North Africa. The growing instability brought on by poor governance, repression and worsening socio-economic conditions bleeds across the Mediterranean through irregular migration, brain drain and violent extremism.

North Africa is home to groups and individuals representing both a direct and indirect threat to the West. The civil war in Libya, which was showing promising signs of ending at the time of this writing, has allowed violent extremism to flourish there, and violent extremists have trained in Libya to carry out attacks across North Africa, often targeting Western individuals or interests. Furthermore, the Western Sahara conflict and disputes over the Grand Ethiopian Renaissance Dam (GERD), which both are relatively quiet conflicts, have the potential to grow into violent confrontations, threatening stability in the region. As Michele Dunne describes in Chapter Two, the United States has been one of Egypt's key patrons on the GERD issue. The GERD, she argues, is 'at the top of the Egyptian agenda in bilateral relations with the United States'. As Frederic Wehrey and Jacqueline Stomski argue in Chapter One, the West has at times acted as a mediator (Germany) and a spoiler (France) in Libya and has often ceded the primary role to the United Nations and the African Union. Similarly, in the Western Sahara, which Mohammed Daadaoui describes in Chapter Three, France has split from the rest of Europe and continued to side with Morocco, while the rest of Europe and the United States have traditionally backed the UN-led process. Under the waning days of the Trump administration, however, the United States shifted its position regarding the Western Sahara, publicly expressing support for Moroccan sovereignty over the disputed region, as a quid pro quo for Morocco to deepen its relationship with Israel. And as Dunne notes in Chapter Two, the US has played a productive role in the negotiations between Ethiopia and Egypt over the GERD, most recently in February of 2020, when it led tripartite negotiations in Washington between Egypt, Sudan and Ethiopia, even suspending economic aid ($100 million) to Ethiopia after it had walked out of the negotiations.

Perhaps the most pressing issue for Europe is migration. Migration from North Africa to Europe as well as from Sub-Saharan Africa through North Africa to Europe has major humanitarian, economic, political and security implications for both sides. There have been several agreements between the European Union and North Africa regarding migration, including as part of the bilateral Association Agreements, as well as through the larger ENP. As Tasnim Abderrahim argues, . . .

> By developing cooperation with the EU within the ENP, partner countries are able to benefit from mobility packages in return for cooperation on readmission and the establishment of a governance system for border management. This includes, for instance, joint patrol missions between EU member states and the partner country.[13]

But as a report by the European Council on Foreign Relations argues, '[s]ome of these arrangements are not only highly questionable from the human rights and refugee law perspectives but are also unsustainable, given that they fail to address the core drivers of regional instability'.[14] The US does not have the same direct connection to migration as Europe; thus, instead it tends to follow Europe's lead and maintains consistent contact with Europe regarding its own policies.

Finally, both the United States and Europe seek to deter further Chinese and Russian influence in North Africa. Speaking of the broader MENA region, Youngs argues that 'in the last several years, other powers have pursued assertive diplomatic policies and the EU has lost much geostrategic weight in this region'.[15] Both China and Russia have increased their presence in the region over the past decade, and China, in particular, is seeking additional inroads through its Belt and Road Initiative (BRI), as will be discussed below. In the economic sphere, Europe remains the primary trading partner of regional states, but the United States has sought, through successive administrations, to increase trade and investment in the region. While efforts at regional integration – whether through the Maghreb Arab Union or through the Middle East Free Trade Area (MEFTA) – have made little progress, there is significant room for growth in trade, as Morocco remains the only African country to hold a US Free Trade Agreement.

The Gulf

Since the uprisings of the Arab Spring in 2010–11, the Gulf Cooperation Council (GCC) member states (primarily Saudi Arabia, the United Arab Emirates and Qatar) have sought to deploy aid, investment and financial transfers as tools towards achieving political interests, security objectives and shaping economic and political developments in the region, going as far as being involved in proxy battles in North Africa. Their strong involvement in the region, whether through employing soft or hard power tools, has also in part shaped the domestic political scenes of North African states. This is especially true given the fragile political imbalance that governments – such as that in Egypt, as Dunne describes in Chapter Two – are grappling with, making them more vulnerable and more dependent on external backing and the resulting influence that comes with such assistance. The Gulf States, on the other hand, financially and politically capable, exploit the region's 'disorder', vying for economic and political influence.[16] Like many leaders in the region, however, following the uprisings, the Gulf monarchs were also nervous that the protests which had unseated long-standing leaders – such as Tunisia's Zine el Abidine Ben Ali, Egypt's Hosni Mubarak, and eventually also Libya's Muammar al-Qadhafi – might come for them as well. Motivated by both internal and external security concerns, and the changing dynamics in religious discourse across the region, the GCC states have had to adopt flexible approaches to their support for religious groups and, subsequently, to adjust their economic policy in the region.

But there was not a single, unified Gulf approach to North Africa. Qatar, a long-time supporter of the Muslim Brotherhood (MB) and its offshoots, saw the potential for a rise of Islamist parties following the uprisings and was thus an 'unequivocal supporter of all protests from the very beginning', according to Florence Gaub, and a supporter of subsequent electoral victories of aligning parties in Egypt, Tunisia and Morocco.[17] This is exemplified through its employment of prominent figures from the Muslim Brotherhood in its state-run Al Jazeera network. The UAE, which vacillated between supporting regime change and preventing instability, took an opposing stance to Qatar, shown in the waves of arrests taking place in 2013 of any individuals perceived to be supportive of the MB's viewpoints, under the pretences of preventing 'Islamist coups'.[18] Saudi Arabia was more cautious than the other Gulf States in its approach towards the uprisings, given the regime's own challenges regarding internal religious dynamics, where the Saudi *Sahwa* (Islamic awakening) movement, at the time possessing influence in Saudi religious discourse, expressed strong support of Tunisia's Ennahda and Egypt's MB, amongst others. This is in addition to its status as the Custodian of the Two Holy Mosques.

The Gulf States have also increased their interest in North Africa as a form of economic diversification, especially when oil prices have declined. With high youth unemployment and widening budget deficits, GCC states are emphasising economic integration and openness in North Africa also as tools to pursue security interests. The absence of a unified approach, however, and differing ideological interests, in addition to power competition amongst the GCC states, as highlighted by the recently resolved rift between the bloc of Saudi Arabia, the UAE, and Bahrain, on one hand, and Qatar, on the other, have seeped their way into North African politics. This manifests itself in two main ways – financial support and diplomatic support, largely related to these diverging interests – and, despite the Gulf crisis officially ending on paper, it is unlikely to 'fundamentally reshape the geopolitical fault lines'.[19] The Saudi-UAE stance on Islamists has not changed, and Qatar has, since the boycott, developed closer relations with Turkey, carrying out joint military exercises, expanding the Turkish military base in Doha and entrenching their differences in North African states.

Gulf countries' financial support, to either political groups or specific interests in North Africa, motivated by their own interests, is one way the divide amongst the GCC states is apparent. Tunisia, whose democratic progress outpaced the rest of the region, became the subject of significant attention by both sides of the Gulf divide, due to early fears that the Tunisian revolution could spread to the Gulf and unseat some of the leadership there, and later due to the Gulf divide over the role of Islamist parties, where Tunisia has also been an outlier. The country's polarised domestic political scene translates to varying support for opposing parties by the Gulf States. Qatar (and Turkey) have had close ties to Ennahda, and when Ennahda has held power in the country, Tunisia has benefitted from Qatari and Turkish financial and political support. In 2012, the Qatari state financed a $1 billion loan to Tunis, promising employment for Tunisian youth, developing infrastructure and increasing the Tunisian central bank's holdings. Additionally, at the Tunisia 2020 conference in 2016, Qatar committed to a financial package of $1.25 billion, compared to the UAE, who only declared its intentions to sell its 35-percent share in Tunisie Telecom. Prior to 2011, Saudi Arabia and the UAE had heavily favoured the Tunisian regime under Ben Ali, and when Ennahda was more marginalised (such as under the Beji Caid Essebsi administration and following President Kais Saied's July 2021 coup), Tunisia saw more support from Saudi Arabia and the UAE, with less support from Qatar. Caid Essebsi heavily courted Saudi Arabia and the Saudi Crown Prince, Mohammed Bin Salman (MBS), ramping up military cooperation with Saudi Arabia, which included carrying out the first-ever military exercises with the Saudi Air Force just days after Jamal Khashoggi's murder.[20] MBS rewarded Caid Essebsi's loyalty while on a visit to Tunis in 2018, where he received the Grand Cordon of the Republic, the highest honour in Tunisia, with a promise to Tunisia of a large aid package including $800 million in loans.

The UAE, which had been Tunisia's second-largest Arab trading partner prior to the revolution 'saw its bilateral ties grow tense after 2011'.[21] Following the revolution, the UAE initially took a more cautious approach than Qatar or Saudi Arabia, halting its investments in Tunisia and distancing itself diplomatically, until the political alignment of the new democracy became clear. The relationship hit a low point when the UAE withdrew its ambassador to Tunis in September 2013 over a series of moves that were perceived to be against Emirati strategic interests, including the rise of Ennahda and Tunisia's neutrality in the Libyan conflict.[22]

But the influence of the Gulf in Tunisia should not be overestimated. Jonathan Fenton-Harvey argues that . . .

> . . . the potential for Saudi and UAE-backed counterrevolutionary activity in Tunisia is more limited than in Egypt or Sudan primarily because the military does not play a major role in dominating government affairs and there are fewer post-Arab-uprising reactionary forces to support [. . .] Despite efforts to hinder Tunisia's progress as an emerging independent democracy, the presidential elections of 2019 highlight that the country has largely withstood such counterrevolutionary activities. The victory of the populist independent former professor Kais Saied, not beholden to Gulf interests, illustrates the limits of their influence operations.[23]

Following the actions of President Saied on 25 July 2021, where he dismissed the government, froze parliament – in which Ennahda held a plurality of seats – and consolidated all authority in himself, citing rampant corruption and high unemployment as drivers to call for a state of emergency in the country, Emirati and Saudi news outlets celebrated the moment, marking the 'ousting' of the Brotherhood, referring to Ennahda.[24] Saudi Foreign Minister Prince Faisal bin Farhan and his Emirati counterpart Sheikh Abdullah bin Zayed both expressed support for Saied following the coup, while Qatar's Emir Sheikh Tamim al-Thani, in a phone call with Saied, 'appealed to all parties to adopt a path of dialogue', emphasising 'the importance of fixing foundations of the state of institutions and establishing the rule of law in Tunisia'.[25] Two months later, Saied reportedly sought Saudi and Emirati financial support to finance Tunisia's debts, but no agreement has been reached thus far.[26] Egypt has also been rumoured to have played an active role in the Tunisian crisis, with several sources reporting that not only did the Egyptian military's presence in Tunisia increase from April 2021 onward, building up to July, but also that the officials offered counsel to Saied in planning and executing the coup. More recently, Egyptian intelligence officer Colonel Ali Mohamed al-Faran was reported to be in cooperation with Khaled al-Yahyaoui, director-general of Tunisian presidential security and advisor to Saied, to execute further crackdowns on members of Ennahda.[27]

Prior to the GCC rift, Morocco and the Gulf States had developed close relations, converging on foreign policy files and benefitting economically through increased trade and investment. Leading up to the 2000s, Morocco shared close relations with Saudi Arabia; in the 1980s, Saudi Arabia had financed the Moroccan regime with $100 million a year for 'anti-POLISARIO' operations in the Western Sahara. A decade later, following the Iraqi invasion of Kuwait, King Hassan II reciprocated Saudi Arabia's generosity and provided the Saudi military forces with thousands of additional troops for protection.[28] In 2016, Saudi Arabia announced its military support to Morocco, in the form of a $22 billion military project, in addition to extending security intelligence assistance through the cooperation agreement signed between the two in 2015.[29] Similarly, Rabat's ties were present with Saudi's neighbours – the UAE, which retains a strong presence of Moroccan troops within the Emirati police force, and the Kingdom of Bahrain, where Rabat condemned 'Iranian interference' in response to the protests that erupted in Bahrain and across the region as part of the Arab Spring.[30]

Morocco and Jordan were both invited to join the Gulf Cooperation Council (GCC) after the Arab Spring, as a way to unite the Arab monarchies in the face of popular unrest in the region.[31] Morocco was presented with a five-year development plan, to precondition its joining of the bloc. Furthermore, the GCC's emphasis on strategic relations with the Mediterranean, exemplified by the UAE's recent recalibration of relations with Turkey, strengthens security and political interests. However, Morocco never joined the GCC, and after the split between Qatar and the UAE/Saudi Arabia, Morocco chose to maintain a position of 'benevolent neutrality vis-à-vis the GCC crisis', according to Antonio Occhiuto and Giorgio Cafiero.[32] Prior to the 2017 GCC rift, Morocco had benefitted from significant

Gulf support – particularly from Saudi Arabia, as evidenced by the 2016 $22 billion security deal.[33] But the decrease in oil prices saw a significant decline in Saudi support for Morocco, with Saudi investments dropping by 78 percent between 2015 and 2018. Morocco further angered Saudi Arabia when it suspended its participation in Saudi-led efforts in Yemen and recalled the Moroccan ambassador to Saudi Arabia in 2019 following a dispute over Morocco's claims in the Western Sahara.[34]

Morocco also saw a rift in its relationship with the UAE, recalling its ambassador to the UAE in March 2020, following the withdrawal of the Emirati ambassador to Rabat eleven months prior. The move is seen in part as retaliation for Morocco's tolerance for Islamist parties, which the UAE finds objectionable, and in part for what is perceived as Morocco cozying up to Qatar, including deepening military ties, as exemplified in Morocco's participation of the 'Impregnable Guard 2020' military exercise in Qatar, along with Jordan, Turkey, Oman and the US, amongst others, ahead of the 2022 World Cup in Doha.[35] Economic support has also grown between the two states, as in 2017 Morocco sent planes carrying food and other goods to Qatar immediately after the embargo had been imposed to prevent disruptions of food and supplies in Doha, and Qatar invested $150 million towards constructing water dams in southern Morocco.[36]

The Gulf rivalry is on display most clearly in Libya, as Frederic Wehrey and Jacqueline Stomski show in Chapter One. From the start of the Libyan uprising, Gulf States chose to back varying forces in Libya. Today, the UAE is one of the more prominent players in the geopolitical proxy battle, siding with Russia and Egypt to back Khalifa Haftar's Tobruk-based government by providing military technology. The UAE has also played a crucial financial role, providing Haftar around $10 billion worth of previously frozen assets.[37] Saudi Arabia has also provided financial backing to Haftar's camp.[38] On the other side of the conflict, Qatar, along with Turkey – which has given troops to the Government of National Accord (GNA) in exchange for drilling rights to oil exploration in the eastern Mediterranean, as part of the maritime and economic deal it signed with the GNA in 2019 – supports the Tripoli-based government.[39] Qatar's support has been both diplomatic and financial.⁴⁰ The end of the rift has brought to the forefront concerns about how the Gulf States are to mediate their opposing foreign policy strategies, especially in Libya. For the UAE, its significant stake in the Libyan conflict is interconnected with its desire to expand its influence and partnerships with Mediterranean partners, such as France, Greece and Egypt.

Like Libya, Egypt has been a key player in the Gulf rivalry, particularly in the battle over the role of the Muslim Brotherhood. The divide between Qatar and the UAE/Saudi Arabia was clear from the early days of the Egyptian revolution, when Saudi Arabia continued to support the Mubarak regime as Qatar hoped for Mubarak's fall. Under Muslim Brotherhood rule, Qatar increased its investment in Egypt by more than 1,000 percent.⁴¹ Qatar had also promised an additional $18 billion to Egypt, but once President Morsi was removed from power, that assistance package fell apart. Under President Sisi, Saudi Arabia and the UAE have become close partners with Egypt in a variety of domestic and geopolitical endeavours, such as dealing with Libya. Bolstering the Egyptian military's hold on power, Saudi Arabia has transferred substantial monetary aid to the Supreme Council of the Armed Forces (SCAF), even prior to Sisi's ascension to power. Saudi support to Egypt continued thereafter and since 2013 has totalled an estimated $10 to $12 billion.⁴² The total aid packages provided by Saudi Arabia, the UAE and Kuwait to the Egyptian Central Bank amounted to $30 billion from 2013 to 2016, shoring up Egyptian reserves and increasing its ability to purchase arms. Despite strengthening its position vis-à-vis the Gulf States following a $12 billion loan from the IMF in 2016, Egypt's economy remains vulnerable to developments in the Gulf, as many Egyptian workers reside in the Gulf and send remittances back home. COVID-19 has further exacerbated the exodus of migrant workers from the Gulf, including Egyptian workers, and lowered remittances as well as the activities of the Egyptian tourism sector, making it unlikely that Egypt will stop depending on its Gulf partners anytime soon.

Mauritania is not as much of a priority for the Gulf States as other North African countries, but the country has managed to maintain positive relations with most Gulf States, in part because of its traditions and history of Islamic scholarship.⁴³ Saudi support for Mauritania blossomed under former

President Abdel Aziz and King Salman. In 2015, Saudi Arabia deposited $300 million in the Mauritanian central bank reserves as a 'thank you' for Abdel Aziz's public offer to provide Mauritanian troops to support Saudi efforts in Yemen, although the troops were never dispatched.[44] Abdel Aziz was also a strong defender of MBS and supported the Saudi position as it faced international pressure regarding blogger Raif Badawi and Jamal Khashoggi.[45] MBS repaid Abdel Aziz with three development accords and a pledge to build the King Salman Hospital in Nouakchott during a December 2018 visit to Mauritania.[46]

Mauritania also won Saudi approval by breaking off relations with Qatar. Mauritania has long opposed Qatari behaviour, including what it perceives as a destabilising role in Mali and Qatar's continued support for political demonstrations in Mauritania.[47] Cafiero and al-Makahleh also argue that 'ultimately, Nouakchott's problems with Doha boil down to Al Jazeera's reporting on slavery and social issues in the African country'.[48] Under the new president, Mohamed Ould El Ghazouani, the UAE-Mauritania relationship has grown. In February 2020, former UAE President Sheikh Khalifa bin Zayed al-Nahyan allocated $2 billion for investment and development projects in Mauritania, as well as loans.[49]

Algeria's guarded sovereignty and wariness of foreign entanglements dating back to the French colonial experience has led to very little Gulf influence. It has maintained its own positions on several foreign policy files, including revoking Syria's membership from the Arab League, as promoted by Saudi Arabia and Qatar, and dissuation against the Saudi-led offensive in Yemen. It has also expressed support for Iran's right to develop nuclear capabilities.[50] Economically, Algeria is less dependent on the GCC than Tunisia or Morocco, with its top investors being China, Singapore, Spain and Turkey, but Gulf States continue to look for opportunities for influence. For instance, the UAE's DP World oversees Algerian ports, while Qatar's Ooredoo provides telecommunications. Algeria has closely relied on Russia for military support, as will be discussed later in this chapter, but it has been able to avoid some of the other traditional forms of Gulf interference due to its financial freedom as a hydrocarbons state. Additionally, Algeria's membership in the Organisation of Petroleum

Exporting Countries (OPEC), dominated by the Gulf nations, has brought Algeria closer to the Gulf than other North African states. As the Gulf International Forum argues, '[w]hile differences between Algeria and the Gulf as a bloc have always been stark, the Gulf's perception that Algeria was not actively pursuing a rival agenda prevented these divergences from escalating to outright confrontation'.[51]

In August 2021, Algeria broke off diplomatic relations with Morocco. Algerian Foreign Minister Ramtane Lamamra said that, while Algiers had 'been patient regarding Morocco's actions', it could not accept the kingdom's normalisation with Israel, following the Abraham Accords in 2020.[52] In the wake of deteriorating relations, Saudi Arabia, having maintained a neutral stance on the Western Sahara, as opposed to the UAE having a consulate in Laâyoune in overt support of Rabat, is uniquely positioned to mediate between the two and has extended the offer to lead talks, along with the EU.[53] This comes after the election of President Abdelmadjid Tebboune in 2019, which has brought with it increased diplomatic engagements with Saudi, the UAE and Qatar.[54]

Despite Algeria's status as an oil-rich state, the last few years of contracted economic growth, dwindling foreign reserves and widening fiscal deficits (16.4 percent of GDP in 2020), compounded by the impact of the COVID-19 pandemic on poverty and unemployment levels, have led Algeria to utilise diplomacy towards attracting foreign direct investment, to diversify its economy away from a hydrocarbons-based economic model.[55] However, current challenges in Algeria – such as corruption, heavy red tape and ease of doing business – limit Algiers' ability to attract and sustain long-term investments to finance projects.

On 5 January 2021, the ruler of Qatar, Emir Sheikh Tamim Al-Thani, landed in Al-Ula, Saudi Arabia, embracing the kingdom's Crown Prince, MBS, ahead of signing an agreement that would, at least on paper, end the rift between Qatar, the UAE, Bahrain and Saudi Arabia. The thirteen demands made by the blockading parties were not met by Qatar.[56] Relations between Qatar and Turkey continue to develop – with Qatar being Turkey's second-largest investor – while with Iran growing bilateral trade and cooperation continue to flourish.[57] As stated by the emir, the signing of the agreement will have no 'effect on our relationship with any other country'.⁵⁸ In November 2021, Sheikh Mohammed bin Zayed, Abu Dhabi's Crown Prince, visited Ankara for the first time in nearly ten years to meet with Turkish President Recep Tayyip Erdoğan; on the same day, the UAE committed to an investment spree in several sectors across Turkey, valued at $10 billion.⁵⁹ Although the Emiratis still oppose Islamist political orientations, a shift towards practical foreign policy to achieve security and economic cooperation through financial resources has driven the UAE's foreign policy calculus. In the same vein, Egyptian-Turkish relations are warming, and the Gulf States are pursuing talks with Iran, yet increased diplomacy has not produced substantive change at the political level, especially regarding the competing actions of the Gulf States across North Africa. Despite al-Ula, the drivers of the dispute remain salient, and like the Riyadh Agreement in 2014, the recent agreement's opaque nature and lack of enforcement measures to build back trust raises doubts that tensions caused by the GCC states' involvement in North Africa will be eased.

Sub-Saharan Africa

Like Europe, North Africa is inextricably linked to Sub-Saharan Africa through geography. North African states have taken different approaches both politically and economically towards their southern neighbours. One of the main areas of engagement has been through the African Union (AU). Egypt has strengthened its relationship with the African Union in recent years, following a bump on the road in 2013, when the AU revoked Egypt's membership due to President Sisi's coup. The AU suspension was annulled in 2014, and in 2019 Egypt took over the AU presidency. Although during its presidency Egypt 'attempted to raise its profile as an African nation', as Michele Dunne argues in Chapter Two, Sisi achieved very little in his time at the helm of the organisation.⁶⁰ During Egypt's presidency, the AU succeeded in advancing the African Continental Free Trade Area (AFCFTA), which came into force in May 2019. Economically, Sisi has tried to increase Egypt's ties with Sub-Saharan Africa, although trade between Egypt and the continent remains quite low.

Prior to 2011, Libya was the country best connected to Sub-Saharan Africa within the Maghreb. Libya's relationship with the African Union has been complicated in the wake of the 2011 uprisings. In 2011, the AU was accused of protecting Qadhafi – an accusation that then AU Chairperson Jean Ping dismissed, stating: 'Our ultimate objective was to avoid war. As a regional organisation, diplomacy is our main weapon, and the use of force is always a last resort when all other options have been exhausted'.[61] But when the UN Security Council adopted Resolution 1973 in March 2011, the AU was largely side-lined as the UN- and NATO-led coalition rejected AU efforts to mediate the crisis. Today, in post-Qadhafi Libya, there is a popular perception that the AU supported Qadhafi. As a cause or perhaps consequence of this perception, many black Libyans fighting in the army on behalf of Qadhafi were stigmatised as 'African mercenaries'.[62] The effect of these perceptions is that Libyans today are leaning away from Africa, although there are important exceptions which include African countries that actively supported the National Transitional Council. Further, the current unstable situation in Libya represents not only a security threat to its neighbours but would also entail significant economic losses for Sub-Saharan countries seeking further integration with the country.

The Western North African countries – Morocco, Algeria and Tunisia – have increasingly sought out opportunities for integration with Sub-Saharan Africa, both politically as well as economically. The Western Sahara conflict, which has been one of the primary impediments to either political or economic cooperation across North Africa, as Mohamed Daadaoui discusses in Chapter Three, has had the effect of creating competition between North African states for access to African markets as well as political dominance. The lack of regional economic integration across North Africa has encouraged North African countries to look south to further their economic reach. As Anthony Dworkin argues, . . .

> North African countries are searching for new markets and seeking to position themselves for the economic and demographic growth expected in sub-Saharan Africa in the coming years. This has been given new impetus by the continuing slow growth rates of North Africa's traditional European trading partners.[63]

Several North African states see themselves as regional economic (as well as religio-cultural) hubs and have steadily increased their trade with Sub-Saharan Africa.[64] And both Morocco and Tunisia have been able to take advantage of their Free Trade Agreements with Europe to position themselves better within the continent.

But attempts at further integration within the continent have not come without risk. When Morocco applied to join the Economic Community of West African States (ECOWAS) in February 2017, it faced significant pushback from Nigeria, the 'de facto regional hegemon'.[65]

Morocco re-joined the AU in January 2017, after a thirty-three-year absence over the membership of the Sahrawi Arab Democratic Republic (SADR) in the organisation. Morocco had left the AU's predecessor, the Organisation of African Unity (OAU), in 1984. The AU's support for Sahrawi independence was a red line for Morocco, leaving it as the only country on the continent to stay out of the body. But by sitting on the side-lines, Morocco found itself in a disadvantaged position and took a less defensive position that began by re-joining the AU, and it has so far succeeded in convincing nineteen African states to open diplomatic missions in the Western Sahara under their missions to Rabat.

Tunisia increased its interaction with Sub-Saharan Africa following the revolution. As Dworkin argues, . . .

> Tunisia is unique among North African countries in that its growing interest in sub-Saharan Africa has no obvious geopolitical motive. Tunisia is not seeking to deepen its engagement with the rest of the continent because of any strategic rivalry or security concerns, but essentially for economic reasons.[66]

Tunisia's first post-revolution president, Moncef Marzouki, visited Mali, Chad, Niger and Gabon in 2014, in an attempt to improve Tunisia's ties on the continent. Marzouki stressed that 'Africa is the future' and 'stated the need for Tunisia to invest more in its African identity, especially considering shared interests such as overcoming dependence on external actors and the fight against terrorism'.[67] In 2017, then Prime Minister Youssef Chahed undertook additional economic diplomacy, visiting several African countries including Niger, Burkina Faso and Mali, accompanied by a delegation of over a hundred business representatives. But not all of Tunisia's political class is on board with greater engagement with Africa. While Tunisia signed on to the AFCFTA, the Tunisian parliament failed to ratify the agreement when it was put to a vote in March 2020.[68]

In addition to economic cooperation, there is significant security cooperation, particularly between the Maghreb and Sahel countries. The main vehicle for intra-continental security coordination is the Trans-Sahara Counterterrorism Partnership (TSCTP), established in 2005 to address the security challenges facing West and North Africa. The programme seeks to improve the capacities of local law enforcement authorities as well as militaries to address the persistent terrorism threat in the region. Morocco, whose military capabilities have allowed it to play a leading role in the region, has also participated in the Global Counterterrorism Forum, and in 2016 Morocco provided Niger with military equipment to help in the fight against Boko Haram – the first time that Morocco had exported its equipment to a Sub-Saharan African nation.

Mauritania's interests in Sub-Saharan Africa are both economic and security-related. Mauritania has aimed at increasing trade flows in and through its capital, Nouakchott, to other West African States such as Mali and Burkina Faso, and especially through the Route de l'Espoir – the country's integral highway that runs from the west to the east of Mauritania. Mauritania is also an active member of the G5-Sahel. Linking security and development, Nouakchott became the host of a military staff college for the G5 and soon thereafter was able to attract €2.4 billion from donors towards financing over forty developmental projects across the Sahel.

While Algeria has closely guarded its sovereignty and while its legal framework discourages investment from abroad, a drop in oil prices over the past few years has pushed the country towards more economic cooperation with Algeria's southern neighbours. Under former President Abdelaziz Bouteflika, Algeria largely ignored Sub-Saharan Africa, turning its attention towards Europe and Asia instead.[69] President Tebboune, who was elected in December 2019, set out to re-build Algeria's relationship with its southern neighbours, attending the February 2020 AU summit where he announced Algeria's return to the continent. And in November 2020, Algerians approved a constitutional referendum that allows the armed forces to take part in multi-lateral peace-keeping operations abroad, in an effort to improve Algeria's standing as a security leader in Africa.[70] Algeria's primary approach to the African continent has long been in the security realm. Algeria played an instrumental role in designing the African Peace and Security Architecture that underpins the AU's security policy; occupied the key role of AU Commissioner for Peace and Security since 2002; and hosts the Africa Centre for Studies and Research on Terrorism.[71]

China

China has increased its overall investment in Africa in recent years, including in North Africa. China's primary vehicle for global investment is the Belt and Road Initiative (BRI). The BRI is made up of a land-based 'belt' and a maritime-based 'road', both of which seek to increase trade and expand the Chinese footprint in Central Asia, Europe and the MENA region. While much of the BRI is shrouded in secrecy, the Chinese government states that the BRI 'is designed to uphold the global free trade regime and the open world economy in the spirit of open regional cooperation'.[72] As China expert Doug Paal notes, the BRI was originally designed to 'deploy China's excess industrial capacity abroad'.[73] The initiative consists largely of infrastructure investment – including ports, bridges, railways, highways and upgraded power grids – although there is little public knowledge regarding the extent of the BRI to date, given that statistics and a budget and list of projects are not publicly available. Nevertheless, the BRI has the potential to both reward recipient countries with large amounts of funding, while simultaneously opening China to new markets for its goods. The icing on the cake is that the BRI also offers China a way to indirectly confront US and European supremacy in the region. However, China began its investment in infrastructure in Africa well before the advent of the BRI. China took on significant infrastructure investment in the region in the 1970s and 1980s, after Western donors and the World Bank stepped away from this sort of work.[74]

Morocco and China signed an implementation agreement for the BRI in January 2022. Trade between Morocco and

China has grown from \$4 billion in 2016 to \$6 billion in 2021, and Chinese companies have implemented eighty projects in Morocco.[75] Another Chinese investment vehicle is tourism. China overtook the United States as the largest source of outbound tourism globally (based on the number of trips and money spent abroad) in 2014.[76] China uses the Approved Destination Status programme as one way to control its tourism impact on other countries. Egypt joined the programme in 2002, Tunisia in 2004 and Morocco in 2007. The number of Chinese tourists in Morocco increased dramatically, from 10,000 in 2015 to 200,000 in 2018.[77] The programme determines whether countries can accept Chinese tour groups and whether they can promote their country as a tourist destination inside of China.[78] Given China's share of the tourism market, participating in this programme can be a major economic boon to countries. China has steadily increased its economic relationships across the Arab world, beginning with the establishment of the China–Arab States Cooperation Forum in 2004. Today, the China–Arab world relationship is largely focused on the Twenty-First Century Maritime Silk Road and China's '1+2+3 Cooperation Pattern', which includes (1) energy at the core; (2) infrastructure and trade and investment facilitation as the two wings, and (3) nuclear energy, space satellites and new sources of energy as the three final pillars.[79] China is also seeking to increase people-to-people engagement and cultural cooperation in the fields of science, education, health and media as part of its Arab world engagement strategy.

Another major Chinese interest in North Africa is North African access to the European market. Some North African states have preferential trade agreements with the European Union, which allow goods manufactured in those states to be exported to Europe with lower tariffs. After a change in the rules of origin for North African goods in Europe – meaning that North African countries can source products from China and still get the preferential treatment as if goods were fully sourced there – China has expressed interest in taking advantage of those relationships.[80] But, as Michael Singh notes, . . .

> Just as China is seeking to make its own difficult transition to a more market-oriented economy, many Middle Eastern

governments need to shrink their public sectors, reduce their spending, bolster their social safety nets, and encourage private sector-led growth. China is not the ideal partner for such a transition, given its own similar challenges.[81]

Education is another area in which China is expanding its outreach in North Africa, particularly through Confucius Institutes and Confucius Classrooms. Institutes are aimed at the university level, while classrooms are aimed at the secondary level. Both serve as hubs for Chinese language and culture, similar to the Alliance Française model or the German Goethe Institute model and provide Chinese-language classes as well as a variety of cultural classes such as 'Chinese medicine, history, culture, society, martial arts, theatre, flower arranging, paper cutting and occasionally contemporary topics'.[82] The first Confucius Institute was established in Seoul in 2004; as of 2021, there are more than 540 Confucius Institutes globally.[83] There exist seven Confucius Institutes in North Africa – two in Egypt (at Cairo University and Suez Canal University), one in Mauritania (at Nouakchott University), three in Morocco (at Mohammed V University, Hassan II University and Abdelmalek Essaadi University) and one in Tunisia (at the University of Carthage).[84] While officially Confucius Institutes serve as language hubs, Confucius Institutes have received pushback in the United States over fears of espionage.[85]

North Africa has also benefited from the way in which China approaches global power competition. As Sulmaan Khan notes, China and the West view global power competition differently. While the United States is focused on alliance-building and its relationship with its NATO allies, China seeks out friendships across the globe, meaning that, while great powers matter, 'smaller powers matter too'.[86] Jon Alterman similarly argues that China 'does not have a natural network of allies, instead it seeks out friendships wherever it can' – meaning that China's relationships with smaller countries such as those in North Africa are just as important as its relationships with larger ones.[87] China therefore recognises the importance of North Africa's geostrategic location and the economic and political access that North Africa can provide to the Sub-Saharan African market. China has been able to maintain relationships with a variety of Arab states over time, due to its 'Five Principles of Peaceful Coexistence', which prevent China from engaging in overtly political behaviour or encroaching on domestic affairs. The Five Principles include 'mutual respect for sovereignty and territorial integrity, mutual non-aggression, mutual non-interference in each other's internal affairs, equality and mutual benefit, and peaceful coexistence'.[88]

Russia

Russia's general approach to the region is both geopolitical (countering US influence and growing Russian clients) and economic.[89] Russia saw the Arab Spring as a threat to regional stability and experienced significant financial loss (around $10 billion) in lost military contracts.[90] Russia also sees many opportunities in the region – including expanded Mediterranean access, potential energy partnerships and arms sales, as well as proxy conflicts, such as in Libya.[91]

Algeria is Russia's closest partner in the region. In 2001, Russia and Algeria signed a Declaration on Strategic Partnership to strengthen economic and diplomatic ties.[92] In 2006, Russian President Vladimir Putin visited Algeria, resulting in major agreements on Russian arms sales to Algeria and cancelling $4.7 billion in Algeria's debt. The Algerian state gas company, Sonatrach, also signed an MOU with Russia's Gazprom in 2006, leaving Europe worried about potential price collusion between two of the three principal gas suppliers to the European Union. Algeria is also Russia's primary economic client in the region. In 2018, Russian exports to Algeria were 'more than 450 times greater than the imports of Algerian products by Russia'.[93] Russia supplied the Algerian military with around two-thirds of its weaponry between 2014 and 2018, and Algeria is Russia's third-largest customer after India and China. Despite the strong military and economic ties, Algeria maintains its neutral foreign policy position and has not allowed the relationship with Russia to have too much of an impact on Algeria's other relationships, such as with Europe, China or the United States. Russia has also largely stayed out of Algeria's political affairs. During the 2018–20 Hirak protests, for example, Russia did not endorse President Bouteflika's decision to run for another term as president, calling the Algerian uprisings an internal matter.

Next to Algeria, Russian involvement in North Africa is perhaps the most pronounced in Libya, as Frederic Wehrey and Jacqueline Stomski discuss in Chapter One. While Libya is not a vital interest for Russia, it has significant economic and geostrategic interests, including infrastructure projects, arms deals and trade in agricultural goods, all of which were threatened starting in 2011 during the UN campaign against Qadhafi. Like much of North Africa, Russia also sees Libya as a conduit into Sub-Saharan Africa.[94] One of the most direct lines between Russia and Libya is through Russia's support of Haftar. However, as Jalel Harchaoui argues, Moscow's relationship with Haftar is complicated.[95] As Harchaoui notes, Russia is using Haftar to ensure that its interests in Libya are protected, particularly securing 'more perennial access to key facilities there, such as, potentially, a naval base, more hydrocarbons concessions and the option to do business with Tripoli'.[96] Russian private military contractors have also made their way into Libya, in the service of Haftar and his forces. Additionally, Russia has played a key role in financing the Libyan National Army (LNA), printing more than $10 billion worth of Libyan dinar banknotes for the LNA without the consent of the central bank. However, starting in May 2020, Moscow cut back on the financial flows into Libya and has instead allowed the United Nations to move forward with banking-unification, which Moscow sees as a way forward for its own inroads into Libya. The Wagner group began its presence in Libya in 2018, providing training, hardware, non-kinetic security services and battlefield advice to Haftar. The Wagner Group has expanded its footprint in Libya, taking control of the Jufrah and Qardabiyah air bases.[97]

Russia and Egypt have strengthened their relationship over the past few years, mostly clearly through the Comprehensive Partnership and Strategic Cooperation agreement signed in January 2021.[98] The agreement covers trade, scientific and technical cooperation, education, tourism and cultural ties; it establishes a Russian-Egyptian Business Council and addresses military issues. Trade has been increasing between the two countries, and in February 2019 President Sisi ratified an Egypt-Russia economic agreement that allows Russia to operate an Industrial Zone in the Suez Canal Economic Zone.[99] Sisi also agreed to the construction of the Dabaa nuclear power plant, led by the Russian company Rosatom State Nuclear Energy Corporation, which upon completion will have the capacity to generate up to half of Egypt's power needs. In the military sphere, Russia agreed to sell twenty Su-35 fighter jets to Egypt in March 2019, in a $1.5 billion deal.[100] This is part of Russia's wider effort to bring more of the world into its military operating systems. However, this is not easy to do, given Egypt's reliance on US equipment and training for the past four decades.[101]

Each of the remaining three North African countries – Morocco, Tunisia and Mauritania – has a far more limited relationship with Russia than the rest of the region. Like much of North Africa, Russia views Tunisia as a potential gateway to the African market.[102] The relationship between the two countries since the revolution has primarily focused on energy, tourism and counter-terrorism. Russia has supplied military equipment to the Tunisian government since 2014.[103] Russian tourist numbers have increased dramatically over the past few years (with the exception of 2020, due to COVID-19 restrictions). While most of Europe discouraged travel to Tunisia following the attacks on the Bardo Museum and Sousse hotel in 2015, Russia encouraged travel to Tunisia, and Russians continue to visit Tunisia's tourist sites in large numbers.[104]

Russia and Morocco have been strengthening diplomatic and economic ties since 2014, when King Mohammed VI announced his intention to deepen Morocco's ties with Moscow. In 2016, King Mohammed travelled to Moscow and signed a series of agreements with Putin, including an extradition treaty, a fisheries agreement, a joint declaration on fighting terrorism, as well as cooperation agreements on a variety of issues including energy, tourism and religious affairs. Since 2019, scholars have noted a deepening of the relationship beyond trade and economic ties towards more cooperation on regional issues and what Tamba Koundouno expects could turn into a strategic partnership.[105]

The Mauritania-Russia relationship is quite limited. There have been a few minor hiccups in the relationship in recent years, such as a dispute regarding fishing subsidies following Russia's accession to the World Trade Organization in 2012.[106] Russia has also assisted Mauritania as part of the G5 to help combat terrorism in the Sahel.[107]

Conclusion

While North Africa is a region that often takes a backseat to other issues in the Middle East, the challenges facing the region and the ways in which North African governments have addressed those challenges have direct implications for Europe, Sub-Saharan Africa and the Middle East. Each of the major global challenges discussed throughout this volume – from climate change over the decline of rentierism and socio-economic inequality to the COVID-19 pandemic – not only has consequences for the people of North Africa, but also the potential to reach far beyond the borders of North Africa. The region, which sits between the Middle East, Africa and Europe, is highly consequential for each of the actors discussed here – the West, the Gulf, Sub-Saharan Africa, China and Russia. And as this chapter has shown, for each of these global players, North Africa offers significant challenges as well as opportunities.

For the West, North Africa is not only an important economic partner, but also an increasingly reliable security partner. Southern Europe relies on North Africa to keep the migration crisis at bay and is heavily invested in security and stability along the Southern Mediterranean. The North African diasporas in Europe provide another important link between the two continents. For the United States, the region is home to several important and long-standing partnerships, from Egypt – one of the top recipients of US foreign assistance globally – to Morocco and Tunisia, both major non-NATO Allies. The US-European alliance also informs the US approach to North Africa, and while the two have not always taken the same approach towards the countries of the region, they each have invested significantly both financially and diplomatically in the stability of North Africa.

As is the case with the United States and Europe, strategic interests, power competition and economic cooperation drive the Gulf's engagement in North Africa, although subject to political and ideological fault lines. China's investment flows to Africa also enable the Gulf States to access expanding economic flows given its strategic location, where the Emirates have employed its ports and shipping borders to facilitate imports to Africa. Furthermore, the Gulf itself is an important financial investor in North Africa, across a wide range of sectors, including physical and digital infrastructure, agriculture, manufacturing, pharmaceuticals and oil and gas, constituting as much as 20 percent of foreign direct investment, such as that in Egypt since 2010.[108] In a reciprocal manner, the Gulf states also rely on North African migrants to work, often relegated to the private sector and low-paid or informal work, with the GCC being a host to an estimated 4,500,00 million Egyptians in 2017.[109] Gulf economic transfers to North Africa serve to achieve several objectives: first, they further economic diversification and boost overall trade and FDI flows across the two regions, and second, they bolster the states' own political stability and security, and influence North African domestic politics. The Gulf States view North Africa as ground to contest power, amongst themselves and with other states such as Iran and Turkey, clearly evident in Libya, which has become highly securitised and involves Gulf States supporting opposing factions.

Sub-Saharan Africa is inextricably linked to North Africa through geography. Home to some of the largest land masses on the continent as well as important economic and political players, it is impossible to separate North Africa from its southern neighbours. The African Union has played an important role in mediating the conflicts in the region, most recently playing a key role in the GERD negotiations between Egypt and Ethiopia, as well as the Western Sahara conflict, which has been an influential aspect of cross-continental diplomacy. As North African countries continue to push for greater integration within the African continent both politically and economically, the ties between the two sub-regions will likely grow.

For China and Russia, North Africa presents an opportunity for greater economic reach (in the case of China) and military influence (in the case of Russia). Both global powers recognise the geostrategic importance of the region and seek to grow their global reach by expanding their influence within and across North Africa. While, with few exceptions, the countries of North Africa have managed to largely avoid Chinese and Russian overreach thus far, deteriorating economic conditions and potential for US retreat from the region open the possibility of growing Chinese and Russian influence at the expense of Western (particularly US) interests.

Opportunities for Engagement

Recognising North Africa's importance to the various actors discussed above, there are a variety of opportunities for engagement by external actors in North Africa. For the United States, the Biden administration must balance its security interests with a desire to promote good governance and democracy. For the US partners in the region – specifically Morocco, Tunisia and Egypt – there are inherent risks in pushing too hard on American security partners. As Thomas Carothers and Benjamin Press argue, ...

> ... confronting partner governments over their political shortcomings risks triggering hostility that would jeopardise the security benefits that such governments provide to Washington. Yet giving them a free pass on democracy and rights issues undercuts the credibility of US appeals to values, bolstering the damaging perception that America only pushes for democracy against its adversaries or in strategically irrelevant countries.[110]

Furthermore, they note that 'soft-pedalling democracy' might actually undercut US interests, as pushing for good governance and democracy could help strengthen partner countries and build more robust long-term relationships.[111]

The Biden administration's re-affirmation of its commitment towards America's European friends and allies offers another opportunity. As the Biden administration seeks to re-establish its ties with Europe and re-affirm its relationship with its European allies, North Africa offers a way forward. Jeremy Shapiro, an expert with the European Council on Foreign Relations, notes that Europe is at times limited in its ability to strike out on its own due to 'Europe's dependence on the US for its own security'.[112] As one EU member state diplomat said: 'When there is a crisis, we tend to ask first, "What does Washington think?" and second, "What do we think ourselves?"'[113]

Nevertheless, for Europe, North Africa offers a particularly robust foreign policy arena to step out of the American shadow. As Thepaut argues, the United States and Europe have traditionally been at odds over their differing approaches towards the MENA region due to 'geography, distinct histories, a military power gap, divergences in foreign policy culture and domestic items'.[114] Specifically, he notes that 'the Mediterranean is understood in the United States as NATO's southern flank, strategically less important than the eastern one. But for Southern European states, the Mediterranean defines their strategic depth, and is an immediate area for power projection'.[115]

As the Biden administration seeks to re-evaluate its own immigration policies, it should work with Europe to 'protect the human rights of asylum seekers and refugees and to ensure that North African and European governments have the resources they need to support refugees and asylum seekers and provide adequate border security to decrease irregular migration'.[116] The commitment of the Biden administration and the EU towards addressing climate change offers an opportunity for cooperation within North Africa. As the preceding chapters have shown, climate change offers real and serious consequences across North Africa. Thus, even in places where US and European influence may be in decline, addressing issues such as water and food scarcity, over-population and desertification is a goal that North Africa and the West share and an area where Western support is welcome.

For North African governments, particularly those most resistant to political reform, recognising the connection between good governance and stability can help both alleviate some of the short-term socio-economic disparities and build trust with increasingly angry and frustrated publics. The dominance of militaries in North African regimes – to varying degrees – points to the need for security sector reform, which involves political and civil rights, institutional capability, judicial independence and the economy. Institutional reform, especially in the business environments of the region – through combatting corruption, increasing transparency, streamlining laws and civil procedures and reducing red tape – will also boost both the flows of foreign direct investment into North African states and can assist in providing jobs and welfare for growing populations. Diversifying away from a public-sector-dominated economy into private-sector-led growth will require promoting the development of small to medium enterprises (SMEs) and providing opportunities for youth and women, as well as traditionally and socially marginalised communities.

Additionally, North African states and civil society actors should take advantage of the renewed transatlantic relationship to build a case for greater US attention to the region. One area where each North African country could get traction is in combatting climate change. Each North African country is facing growing challenges related to climate change, including water scarcity, food insecurity, desertification and greater migration to and through the region. With both Washington and Brussels committed to addressing climate change in real and sustainable ways, North African states should seek to tap into resources available to help address climate change.

Finally, with increasing interest in the region from both Russia and China, North African states will need to evaluate the risks versus the rewards that could come from cozying up to the various global powers. Each of the major global actors – Russia, China, the United States and Europe – has certain comparative advantages in North Africa, and it will be up to the North African governments and people to determine where they want to spend their political capital. While Russia and China may be tempting – particularly to those actors that are not eager to embrace democratic values – any perceived shift towards Russia and China is likely to endanger relations with the United States and Europe.

Notes

1. Richard Youngs, *The European Union and Global Politics* (London: Red Globe Press, 2021).
2. Adel Abdel Ghafar, ed., *The European Union and North Africa: Prospects and Challenges* (Washington DC: Brookings Institution Press, 2019), 3.
3. Edzard Wesselink and Ron Boschma, 'European Neighbourhood Policy: Its History, Structure, and Implemented Policy Measures', *Journal of Economic and Human Geography* 108, no. 1 (February 2017): 4–20.
4. 'IEMed Mediterranean Yearbook 2020', *IEMed*, 2020, https://www.iemed.org/med-yearbook/iemed-mediterranean-yearbook-2020/.
5. 'European Neighbourhood Policy (ENP)', *European Commission:*

European External Action Service, 29 July 2021, https://www.eeas.europa.eu/eeas/european-neighbourhood-policy_en.
6. Charles Thepaut, 'A Vanishing West in the Middle East', *Washington Institute for Near East Policy*, 2022, https://www.washingtoninstitute.org/policy-analysis/vanishing-west-middle-east-recent-history-us-europe-cooperation-region.
7. 'European Neighbourhood Policy (ENP)'.
8. 'Mapping European Leverage in the MENA Region', *European Council on Foreign Relations*, December 2019, https://ecfr.eu/special/mapping_eu_leverage_mena.
9. Thepaut, 'A Vanishing West in the Middle East'.
10. 'Background Press Call on Broad Middle East Regional Year-End Discussion', *The White House*, 17 December 2021, https://www.whitehouse.gov/briefing-room/press-briefings/2021/12/17/background-press-call-on-broad-middle-east-regional-year-end-discussion/.
11. Steven A. Cook, 'Europe's Future Will Be Decided in North Africa', *Foreign Policy*, 18 July 2019, https://foreignpolicy.com/2019/07/18/europes-future-will-be-decided-in-north-africa/.
12. Thomas Hill and Sarah Yerkes, 'A New Strategy for U.S. Engagement in North Africa', *United States Institute of Peace* and *Carnegie Endowment for International Peace*, February 2021, http://carnegieendowment.org/files/HillYerkes-ANewStrategyforUSEngagementinNorthAfrica-Feb2021.pdf.
13. Tasnim Abderrahim, 'Pushing the Boundaries: How to Create More Effective Migration Cooperation across the Mediterranean – European Council on Foreign Relations', *European Council on Foreign Relations*, 15 January 2019, https://ecfr.eu/publication/pushing_the_boundaries_effective_migration_cooperation_across_mediterranean/.
14. 'Mapping European Leverage in the MENA Region'.
15. Youngs, *The European Union and Global Politics*.
16. Marc Lynch, 'The New Arab Order', *Foreign Affairs*, 14 August 2018, https://www.foreignaffairs.com/articles/middle-east/2018-08-14/new-arab-order.
17. Florence Gaub, *The Gulf Moment: Arab Relations Since 2011* (n. p.: Strategic Studies Institute and US Army War College Press, 2015).
18. 'UAE Sentences "Coup Plotters" to Jail', *The Guardian*, 2 July 2013, https://www.theguardian.com/world/2013/jul/02/uae-sentences-coup-plotters-jail.
19. Anna L. Jacobs, 'Resolution of Gulf Rift Not Likely to Mend Fault Lines in North Africa', *The Arab Gulf States Institute in Washington*, 21 January 2021, https://agsiw.org/resolution-of-gulf-rift-not-likely-to-mend-fault-lines-in-north-africa/.

20. Asma Ajroudi, 'Saudi Arabia's Uncertain Investment in Tunisia', *Carnegie Endowment for International Peace: Sada*, 13 October 2020, https://carnegieendowment.org/sada/78003.
21. Youssef Cherif, 'Tunisia's Fledgling Gulf Relations', *Carnegie Endowment for International Peace: Sada*, 19 October 2020, https://carnegieendowment.org/sada/67703.
22. Cherif, 'Tunisia's Fledgling Gulf Relations'.
23. Jonathan Fenton-Harvey, 'Regional Uprisings Confront Gulf-Backed Counterrevolution', *MERIP*, 17 December 2019, https://merip.org/2019/12/regional-uprisings-confront-gulf-backed-counterrevolution/.
24. Claire Parker, 'Influential Voices in Egypt, Saudi Arabia and UAE Celebrate Tunisia Turmoil as Blow to Political Islam', *The Washington Post*, 27 July 2021, https://www.washingtonpost.com/world/2021/07/27/tunisia-gulf-information-campaign/.
25. 'Prince Faisal Reiterates Saudi Support for Tunisia's Stability in Meeting with President Saied', *Saudi Gazette*, 30 July 2021, https://saudigazette.com.sa/article/609308/SAUDI-ARABIA/Prince-Faisal-reiterates-Saudi-support-for-Tunisias-stability-in-meeting-with-President-Saied; 'UAE Expresses Full Confidence and Support for Tunisia-Statement', *Reuters*, 28 July 2021, https://www.reuters.com/world/middle-east/uae-expresses-full-confidence-support-tunisia-statement-2021-07-28/; 'Qatar Emir Appeals to All Parties in Tunisia Political Crisis to Pursue Dialogue', *Reuters*, 28 July 2021, https://www.reuters.com/world/middle-east/qatar-emir-expressed-necessity-overcome-current-political-crisis-tunisia-emir-2021-07-28/.
26. Jihen Laghmari, 'Tunisia Reaches Out to Gulf Nations as Economic Woes Deepen', *Bloomberg*, 16 October 2021, https://www.bloomberg.com/news/articles/2021-10-16/tunisia-in-talks-with-uae-saudi-arabia-for-funds-official-says.
27. David Hearst, 'Tunisia: Egyptian Intelligence Officer Plotting Crackdown on Ennahda Party', *Middle East Eye*, 12 January 2022, https://www.middleeasteye.net/news/tunisia-egypt-intelligence-officer-plotting-ennahda-crackdown.
28. Samia Errazzouki, 'A Monarchical Affair: From Morocco to the Arabian Peninsula', *Jadaliyya*, 10 April 2012, https://www.jadaliyya.com/Details/25580/A-Monarchical-Affair-From-Morocco-to-the-Arabian-Peninsula.
29. Adel Abdel Ghafar and Anna L. Jacobs, 'Morocco-Saudi Relations: Trouble amongst Royals?' *Brookings Institution: Order from Chaos*, 1 March 2019, https://www.brookings.edu/blog/order-from-chaos/2019/03/01/morocco-saudi-relations-trouble-amongst-royals/.

30. Elena Maestri, 'The Role of the GCC in North Africa in Light of the "Arab Spring"', in *North African Politics: Change and Continuity*, ed. Yahia H. Zoubir and Gregory White (New York: Routledge, 2016), 350–70.
31. Jacobs, 'Morocco-Saudi Relations'.
32. Antonio Occhiuto and Giorgio Cafiero, 'Why the Downward Spiral in Morocco-UAE Relations?' *Responsible Statecraft*, 31 March 2020, https://responsiblestatecraft.org/2020/03/31/why-the-downward-spiral-in-morocco-uae-relations/.
33. 'Saudi Arabia to Provide $22 Billion to Morocco's Military Industry', *Morocco World News*, 7 January 2016, https://www.moroccoworldnews.com/2016/01/176944/saudi-arabia-to-provide-22-billion-to-moroccos-military-industry/.
34. Imru Al-Qays and Talha Jebril, 'The Moroccan-Saudi Rift: The Shattering of a Privileged Political Alliance', *Al Jazeera Centre for Studies*, 3 April 2019, http://studies.aljazeera.net/en/reports/2019/04/190403105317297.html.
35. 'Morocco Takes Part in "Impregnable Guard" Drill in Qatar', *The North Africa Post*, 23 March 2021, https://northafricapost.com/48452-morocco-takes-part-in-impregnable-guard-drill-in-qatar.html.
36. 'On Orders of King Mohammed VI, Morocco Sends Food Supply to Qatar', *Morocco World News*, 12 June 2017, https://www.moroccoworldnews.com/2017/06/219564/morocco-send-planes-loaded-food-supply-qatar; Jacobs, 'Resolution of Gulf Rift Not Likely to Mend Fault Lines in North Africa'.
37. Fenton-Harvey, 'Regional Uprisings Confront Gulf-Backed Counterrevolution'.
38. Fenton-Harvey, 'Regional Uprisings Confront Gulf-Backed Counterrevolution'.
39. Patrick Wintour, 'Turkish Troops Deploy to Libya to Prop up Embattled Government', *The Guardian*, 5 January 2020, https://www.theguardian.com/world/2020/jan/05/turkish-troops-deploy-to-libya-to-prop-up-embattled-government; 'Turkey Says May Begin Oil Exploration under Libya Deal in Three-Four Months', *Reuters*, 29 May 2020, https://www.reuters.com/article/us-turkey-libya-drilling/turkey-says-may-begin-oil-exploration-under-libya-deal-in-three-four-months-idUSKBN2352EL.
40. Guma El-Gamaty, 'Qatar, the UAE and the Libya Connection', *Al Jazeera Online*, 12 June 2017, https://www.aljazeera.com/opinions/2017/6/12/qatar-the-uae-and-the-libya-connection/.
41. Eduard Soler i Lecha, 'Gulf Rivalries Reach North Africa', in *IEMed Mediterranean Yearbook 2018* (Barcelona: IEMed, 2018).

42. Inken Wiese and Sebastian Sons, 'Engagement of Arab Gulf States in Egypt and Tunisia: Rationale and Implications', *DGAP*, 13 October 2020, https://dgap.org/en/events/engagement-arab-gulf-states-egypt-and-tunisia-rationale-and-implications.
43. Melly, 'Mauritania's Unfolding Landscape: Elections, Hydrocarbons and Socio-Economic Change'.
44. Daniela Gressani, Kevin Fletcher, and Paloma Anós Casero, 'Islamic Republic of Mauritania: Request for a Three-Year Arrangement Under the Extended Credit Facility – Debt Sustainability Analysis', *International Monetary Fund*, November 2017, https://www.imf.org/en/Publications/CR/Issues/2017/12/13/Islamic-Republic-of-Mauritania-Three-Year-Arrangement-under-the-Extended-Credit-Facility-45465, 17.
45. 'Mauritania Breaks Diplomatic Ties with Qatar, Gabon Voices Condemnation', *Reuters*, 7 June 2017, https://www.reuters.com/article/us-gulf-qatar-mauritania/mauritania-breaks-diplomatic-ties-with-qatar-gabon-voices-condemnation-idUSKBN18X2ZH.
46. 'Mohammed Bin Salman Arrives in Mauritania amid Protests', *Morocco World News*, 2 December 2018, https://www.moroccoworldnews.com/2018/12/259323/mbs-mohammed-bin-salman-mauritania-protests/.
47. Giorgio Cafiero and Shehab al-Makahleh, 'Mauritania's Anti-Qatar Animus', *Middle East Policy* 26, no. 2 (2019): 121–28.
48. Cafiero and al-Makahleh, 'Mauritania's Anti-Qatar Animus'.
49. Alain Faujas, 'Finances publiques: Les Émirats à la rescousse de la Mauritanie', *JeuneAfrique.com*, 3 February 2020, https://www.jeuneafrique.com/890560/economie/finances-publiques-les-emirats-a-la-rescousse-de-la-mauritanie/.
50. 'We Can Expect Stronger Algeria-Iran Ties as Israel Plans to Establish a Base in Morocco', *Middle East Monitor*, 23 November 2021, https://www.middleeastmonitor.com/20211123-we-can-expect-stronger-algeria-iran-ties-as-israel-plans-to-establish-a-base-in-morocco/.
51. 'Algeria's Changing Status: A Complicated State for Gulf Influence', *Gulf International Forum*, 8 April 2019, https://gulfif.org/algerias-changing-status-a-complicated-state-for-gulf-influence/.
52. 'Algeria Breaks off Relations with Morocco, Citing Fires and Israel', *The Africa Report*, 25 August 2021, https://www.theafricareport.com/121545/algeria-breaks-off-relations-with-morocco-citing-fires-and-israel/.
53. 'Mohammed VI Ropes in Mohamed Bin Salman to Mend Algiers Rift', *Africa Intelligence*, 1 September 2021, https://www.africaintelligence.com/north-africa/2021/09/01/mohammed-

vi-ropes-in-mohamed-bin-salman-to-mend-algiers-rift, 109688354-art.
54. Anna L. Jacobs, 'Another Morocco-Algeria Rupture Jeopardizes Gulf Outreach, Regional Connectivity', *The Arab Gulf States Institute in Washington*, 14 September 2021, https://agsiw.org/another-morocco-algeria-rupture-jeopardizes-gulf-outreach-regional-connectivity/.
55. 'The World Bank in Algeria', *World Bank*, n. d., https://www.worldbank.org/en/country/algeria/overview#1.
56. 'What Are the 13 Demands given to Qatar?', *Gulf News*, 23 June 2017, https://gulfnews.com/world/gulf/qatar/what-are-the-13-demands-given-to-qatar-1.2048118.
57. Umar Farooq, 'Turkish Firms Eye Boon in Deepening Bilateral Ties with Qatar', *Al Jazeera Online*, 10 December 2021, https://www.aljazeera.com/news/2021/12/10/hlturkish-firms-eye-boon-in-deepening-bilateral-ties-with-qatar.
58. Andrew England, 'Qatar Says Deal to End Gulf Crisis Will Not Change Its Ties with Iran', *Financial Times*, 7 January 2021, https://www.ft.com/content/ea1e7058-960d-416c-93dc-f4f8c7945c12#.
59. Tamara Qiblawi, 'What a Crown Prince's Trip to Turkey Tells Us about the Post-American Middle East', *CNN*, 24 November 2021, https://www.cnn.com/2021/11/24/middleeast/uae-turkey-detente-middle-east-cmd-intl/index.html.
60. 'Egypt and the African Union', *Middle East Institute*, 10 February 2020, https://www.mei.edu/blog/egypt-and-african-union.
61. Jean Ping, 'African Union Role in the Libyan Crisis', *Pambazuka News*, 15 December 2011, https://www.pambazuka.org/governance/african-union-role-libyan-crisis.
62. Dawit Toga, 'The African Union and the Libyan Revolution: The Efficacy of the African Peace and Security Architecture'. *World Peace Foundation: African Politics, African Peace*, June 2016, https://sites.tufts.edu/wpf/files/2017/07/12.-AU-and-Libyan-Revolution-D.-Toga.pdf, 3.
63. Anthony Dworkin, 'A Return to Africa: Why North African States Are Looking South', *European Council on Foreign Relations*, July 2020, https://ecfr.eu/publication/a_return_to_africa_why_north_african_states_are_looking_south/.
64. Faten Aggad and Tasnim Abderrahim, 'How North Africa's Look towards the South Can Shake up AU-EU Relations', *European Centre for Development Policy Management*, November 2017, https://ecdpm.org/talking-points/north-africa-south-shake-up-au-eu-relations/.

65. Imru Al-Qays and Talha Jebril, 'Morocco-ECOWAS: Good Intentions Are Not Enough', *MIPA*, 13 February 2020, https://mipa.institute/7323.
66. Dworkin, 'A Return to Africa'.
67. Aggad and Abderrahim, 'How North Africa's Look towards the South Can Shake up AU-EU Relations'.
68. Sana Adouni, 'Tunisian Parliament Urged to Pass Africa Free Trade Bill', *Middle East Online*, 3 October 2020, https://middle-east-online.com/en/tunisian-parliament-urged-pass-africa-free-trade-bill.
69. Saber Blidi, 'Algeria Is Seeking to Recapture Lost Influence in Africa', *The Arab Weekly*, 25 April 2020, https://thearabweekly.com/algeria-seeking-recapture-lost-influence-africa.
70. Dworkin, 'A Return to Africa'; Jacob Lees Weiss, 'Algerian Constitutional Amendments Create Conditions for Military Intervention in Libya', *Terrorism Monitor* 18, no. 22 (3 December 2020), https://jamestown.org/program/algerian-constitutional-amendments-create-conditions-for-military-intervention-in-libya/.
71. Benjamin Nickels, 'Algeria's Role in African Security', *Carnegie Endowment for International Peace: Sada*, 2014, https://carnegieendowment.org/sada/55239.
72. 'Vision and Proposed Actions Outlined on Jointly Building Silk Road Economic Belt and 21st-Century Maritime Silk Road', *China Daily*, 30 March 2015, http://language.chinadaily.com.cn/2015-03/30/content_19950951.htm.
73. Jon Alterman et al., 'China in the Middle East: Part Two', *Center for Strategic and International Studies*, 27 January, 2020, https://www.csis.org/node/55328.
74. Deborah Brautigam, *The Dragon's Gift: The Real Story of China in Africa* (Oxford: Oxford University Press, 2009).
75. 'Morocco, China Sign Belt Road Initiative Implementation Agreement', *The North Africa Post*, https://northafricapost.com/54725-morocco-china-sign-belt-road-initiative-implementation-agreement.html.
76. Mordechai Chaziza, 'China in the Middle East: Tourism as a Stealth Weapon,' *Middle East Quarterly* 26, no. 4 (Fall 2019), https://www.meforum.org/59293/mordechai-chaziza-china-in-the-middle-east.
77. "Morocco, China Sign Belt Road Initiative Implementation Agreement'.
78. Shawn Arita, Sumner La Croix, and James Mak, 'How China's Approved Destination Status Policy Spurs and Hinders Chinese

Travel Abroad', *UHERO: The Economic Research Organization at the University of Hawai'i*, 19 October 2012. https://uhero.hawaii.edu/wp-content/uploads/2019/08/WP_2012-6R.pdf, 20.

79. 'China's Arab Policy Paper', *Embassy of the People's Republic of China in the Kingdom of Saudi Arabia*, January 2016.
80. Chris Alden and Faten Aggad-Clerx, 'Chinese Investments and Employment Creation in Algeria and Egypt', *African Development Bank*, 2012, https://www.afdb.org/fileadmin/uploads/afdb/Documents/Publications/Brochure%20China%20Anglais.pdf.
81. Michael Singh, 'Chinese Policy in the Middle East in the Wake of the Arab Uprisings', in *Toward Well-Oiled Relations? China's Presence in the Middle East Following the Arab Spring*, ed. Niv Horesh (New York: Palgrave Macmillan, 2016), 162–79.
82. David Shambaugh, *China Goes Global: The Partial Power*, 1st edition (Oxford and New York: Oxford University Press, 2013).
83. 'Confucius Institutes Around the World: 2021', 26 May 2015, https://www.digmandarin.com/confucius-institutes-around-the-world.html.
84. 'Confucius Institutes Around the World: 2021'.
85. 'As Scrutiny of China Grows, Some U.S. Schools Drop a Language Program', *NPR.org*, https://www.npr.org/2019/07/17/741239298/as-scrutiny-of-china-grows-some-u-s-schools-drop-a-language-program.
86. Jon Alterman et al., 'China in the Middle East: Part One', *Center for Strategic and International Studies*, 21 January 2020, https://www.csis.org/podcasts/babel-translating-middle-east/china-middle-east-part-one.
87. Alterman et al., 'China in the Middle East: Part One'.
88. 'China's Arab Policy Paper'.
89. 'Exploiting Chaos: Russia in Libya', *Center for Strategic and International Studies*, 8 February 2021, https://www.csis.org/blogs/post-soviet-post/exploiting-chaos-russia-libya.
90. Tobias Schumacher and Cristian Nitoiu, 'Russia's Foreign Policy towards North Africa in the Wake of the Arab Spring', *Mediterranean Politics* 20, no. 1 (2015): 97–104.
91. Sarah Feuer and Anna Borshchevskaya, 'Russia Makes Inroads in North Africa', *Washington Institute for Near East Policy*, 2 November 2017, https://www.washingtoninstitute.org/policy-analysis/russia-makes-inroads-north-africa.
92. Malek Mousli, 'Algerian-Russian Cooperation: True Strategic Partnership?', *Vestnik RUDN: International Relations* 19 (15 December 2019): 284–92.
93. Adlene Mohammedi, 'Russia-Algeria: A Flexible and Pragmatic Partnership', *FMES*, 8 February 2021, https://fmes-france.org/

russia-algeria-a-flexible-and-pragmatic-partnership-by-adlene-mohammedi/.

94. Jideofor Adibe, 'What Does Russia Really Want from Africa?', *Brookings Institution: Africa in Focus*, 14 November 2019, https://www.brookings.edu/blog/africa-in-focus/2019/11/14/what-does-russia-really-want-from-africa/.

95. 'The Pendulum: How Russia Sways Its Way to More Influence in Libya', *War on the Rocks*, 7 January 2021, https://warontherocks.com/2021/01/the-pendulum-how-russia-sways-its-way-to-more-influence-in-libya/.

96. 'ВЗГЛЯД / «Татнефть» Решила Возобновить Геологоразведку в Ливии и Сирии: Новости Дня', https://vz.ru/news/2020/12/18/1076381.html.

97. 'Les Émirats et le bouclier noir: Quand des centaines de Soudanais sont envoyés sur le front libyen', *Le Vif*, 7 July 2020, https://www.levif.be/actualite/international/les-emirats-et-le-bouclier-noir-quand-des-centaines-de-soudanais-sont-envoyes-sur-le-front-libyen/article-normal-1283237.html; '«Проект»: В Ливии служит группировка российских военных во главе с, замкомандующего ВДВ', *БИЗНЕС Online*, https://www.business-gazeta.ru/news/438497.

98. 'Strategic Cooperation Agreement between Russia and Egypt Comes into Force', *Egypt Independent*, 12 January 2021, sec. Egypt, https://egyptindependent.com/strategic-cooperation-agreement-between-russia-and-egypt-comes-into-force/.

99. 'Establishing Russian Industrial Zone in Egypt Comes into Force', *EgyptToday*, 1 February 2019, https://www.egypttoday.com/Article/3/64142/Establishing-Russian-Industrial-Zone-in-Egypt-comes-into-force.

100. 'Russia Seals $1.5bn Military Jet Deal with Egypt', *The Times*, 5 February 2021, https://www.thetimes.co.uk/article/2bn-su-35-fighter-jet-order-strengthens-russia-egypt-military-ties-3vt99kprx.

101. Andrew Miller and Michele Dunne, 'Losing Egypt to Russia Isn't the Real Problem – But Collapse Is', *Carnegie Endowment for International Peace*, 5 February 2021, https://carnegieendowment.org/2018/07/20/losing-egypt-to-russia-isn-t-real-problem-but-collapse-is-pub-76918.

102. 'Russia Makes Inroads in North Africa', *The Washington Institute*, 3 February 2021, https://www.washingtoninstitute.org/policy-analysis/russia-makes-inroads-north-africa.

103. 'Russia to Supply Military Equipment to Tunisia', *TASS*, 3 February 2021, https://tass.com/russia/748207.

104. 'Russia on Tunisia's Borders', *Middle East Monitor*, 14 March

2017, https://www.middleeastmonitor.com/20170314-russia-on-tunisias-borders/.
105. Tamba François Koundouno, 'Morocco-Russia Intensify Relations as Strategic Interests Converge', *Morocco World News*, 31 December 2019, https://www.moroccoworldnews.com/2019/12/290187/morocco-russia-relations-strategic-interests/.
106. 'Russia Threatens to Call on WTO after Mauritania Says It Should Respect Same Conditions as Subsidised EU Fleets', *Agritrade*, 3 February 2021, https://agritrade.cta.int/Fisheries/Topics/ACP-EU-relations-FPAs/Russia-threatens-to-call-on-WTO-after-Mauritania-says-it-should-respect-same-conditions-as-subsidised-EU-fleets.html.
107. 'Press Release on Deputy Foreign Minister Mikhail Bogdanov's Consultations with Permanent Secretary of the Group of Five for the Sahel Maman Sambo Sidikou', *Ministry of Foreign Affairs of the Russian Federation*, 3 February 2021, https://www.mid.ru/foreign_policy/news/-/asset_publisher/cKNonkJE02Bw/content/id/3164378.
108. Michele Dunne, 'Egypt: Looking Elsewhere to Meet Bottomless Needs – As Gulf Donors Shift Priorities, Arab States Search for Aid', *Carnegie Endowment for International Peace*, 9 June 2020, https://carnegieendowment.org/2020/06/09/egypt-looking-elsewhere-to-meet-bottomless-needs-pub-82010.
109. David Butter, 'Egypt and the Gulf: Allies and Rivals', *Chatham House*, 20 April 2020, https://www.chathamhouse.org/2020/04/egypt-and-gulf.
110. Thomas Carothers and Benjamin Press, 'Navigating the Democracy-Security Dilemma in U.S. Foreign Policy: Lessons from Egypt, India, and Turkey', *Carnegie Endowment for International Peace*, 2021, https://carnegieendowment.org/files/Carothers_Press_DemSecDilemma.pdf.
111. Carothers and Press, 'Navigating the Democracy-Security Dilemma in U.S. Foreign Policy'.
112. Thepaut, 'A Vanishing West in the Middle East'.
113. Thepaut, 'A Vanishing West in the Middle East'.
114. Thepaut, 'A Vanishing West in the Middle East'.
115. Thepaut, 'A Vanishing West in the Middle East'.
116. Hill and Yerkes, 'A New Strategy for US Engagement in North Africa'.

Bibliography

'دستور المملكة الليبية لسنة 1951' (Constitution of the Kingdom of Libya of 1951)'. https://security-legislation.ly/ar/law/31474.

'2 Million Egyptian Women Have No Access to Contraceptives: Officials'. *Egypt Today*, 11 July 2018. https://www.egypttoday.com/Article/1/53760/2-million-Egyptian-women-have-no-access-to-contraceptives-officials.

'2020 Country Reports on Human Rights Practices: Mauritania'. *US Department of State*, 30 March 2021. https://www.state.gov/reports/2020-country-reports-on-human-rights-practices/mauritania/.

'2021 Investment Climate Statements: Mauritania'. *US Department of State*. https://www.state.gov/reports/2021-investment-climate-statements/mauritania/.

'32.5% of Egyptians Live in Extreme Poverty: CAPMAS'. *Egypt Today*, 1 August 2019. https://www.egypttoday.com/Article/1/73437/32-5-of-Egyptians-live-in-extreme-poverty-CAPMAS.

'5 Months of Government "Blockage" – What Was It All for?' *Moroccan World News*, 31 March 2017. https://www.moroccoworldnews.com/2017/03/212561/5-months-government-blockage.

Abdel Tawab, Nahla, Nesrine Salama, Sally Radwan, and Mohamed Ramy. 'Effects of COVID-19 Pandemic on Fertility in Egypt'. *USAID* and *Evidence*, 2021. https://www.un.org/development/desa/pd/sites/www.un.org.development.desa.pd/files/undesa_pd_2021_egm_session_v_nahla_abdel-tawab.pdf.

Abderrahim, Tasnim. 'Pushing the Boundaries: How to Create More Effective Migration Cooperation across the

Mediterranean'. *European Council on Foreign Relations*, 15 January 2019. https://ecfr.eu/publication/pushing_the_boundaries_effective_migration_cooperation_across_mediterranean/.

Abdrbba, Mohamed Omar M. 'Water Supply Systems in Cyrenaica during the Greek and Roman Periods: Cyrene in Context'. *Libyan Studies* 50 (2019): 99–105.

Aboud, Hichem. *La mafia des généraux*. Paris: Éditions J. C. Lattès, 2002.

Abouzzohour, Yasmina. 'Progress and Missed Opportunities: Morocco Enters Its Third Decade Under King Mohammed VI'. *Brookings Institution*, 29 July 2020. https://www.brookings.edu/research/progress-and-missed-opportunities-morocco-enters-its-third-decade-under-king-mohammed-vi.

'Abraham Accords Peace Agreement: Treaty of Peace, Diplomatic Relations and Full Normalization Between the United Arab Emirates and the State of Israel'. *United States Department of State*, 15 September 2020. https://www.state.gov/wp-content/uploads/2020/09/UAE_Israel-treaty-signed-FINAL-15-Sept-2020-508.pdf.

Abu-Lughod, Lila, and Rabab El-Mahdi. 'Beyond the "Woman Question" in the Egyptian Revolution'. *Feminist Studies* 37, no. 3 (2011): 683–91.

Addi, Lahouari. 'Le système de pouvoir en Algérie, son origine et ses evolutions'. *Confluences Méditerranée*, no. 115 (April 2020): 103–13.

Addi, Lahouari. *L'Algérie et la démocratie*. Paris: La Découverte, 1994.

Addi, Lahouari. *L'impasse du populisme: L'Algérie, collectivité politique et état en construction*. Alger: Entreprise Nationale du Livre, 1990.

Addi, Lahouari. 'La chute de "Rab Dzaïr", le "Dieu d'Alger"'. *Orient XXI*, 30 September 2015. https://orientxxi.info/magazine/la-chute-de-rab-dzair-le-dieu-d-alger, 1036.

'Addressing Inequality in Tunisia: Victim Regions and Transnational Justice'. *IVD*, 2 February 2018. http://www.ivd.tn/addressing-inequality-in-tunisia-victim-regions-and-transitional-justice/?lang=en.

Adibe, Jideofor. 'What Does Russia Really Want from Africa?' *Brookings Institution: Africa in Focus*, 14 November 2019. https://

www.brookings.edu/blog/africa-in-focus/2019/11/14/what-does-russia-really-want-from-africa/.

Adouni, Sana. 'Tunisian Parliament Urged to Pass Africa Free Trade Bill'. *Middle East Online*, 3 October 2020. https://middle-east-online.com/en/tunisian-parliament-urged-pass-africa-free-trade-bill.

'Advisory Opinion of the International Court of Justice'. *International Court of Justice*, 16 October 1975. https://www.icj-cij.org/public/files/case-related/61/061-19751016-ADV-01-00-EN.pdf.

'Affaire Mouhcine Fikri: Le roi intervient'. *L'Economiste*, 30 October 2016. https://www.leconomiste.com/flash-infos/affaire-mouhcine-fikri-le-roi-intervient.

'Africa'. *Global Slavery Index*, 2018. https://www.globalslaveryindex.org/2018/findings/regional-analysis/africa/.

Aggad, Faten, and Tasnim Abderrahim. 'How North Africa's Look towards the South Can Shake up AU-EU Relations'. *European Centre for Development Policy Management*, 27 November 2017. https://ecdpm.org/talking-points/north-africa-south-shake-up-au-eu-relations/.

'Agreement between the Republic of Sudan and the United Arab Republic for the Full Utilization of the Nile Waters'. *Food and Agriculture Organization of the United Nations*, 8 November 1959. https://www.fao.org/3/w7414b/w7414b13.htm.

'Agreement on Declaration of Principles between The Arab Republic of Egypt, The Federal Democratic Republic of Ethiopia and The Republic of the Sudan on The Grand Ethiopian Renaissance Dam Project (GERDP)'. *Food and Agriculture Organization of the United Nations*, 23 March 2015. https://leap.unep.org/content/treaty/agreement-declaration-principles-between-arab-republic-egypt-federal-democratic.

Ahmed, Leila. *Women and Gender in Islam: Historical Roots of a Modern Debate*. New Haven: Yale University Press, 1992.

Ahmida, Ali Abdullatif. *Forgotten Voices: Power and Agency in Colonial and Post-Colonial Libya*. Abingdon: Taylor & Francis, 2013.

Ajroudi, Asma. 'Saudi Arabia's Uncertain Investment in Tunisia'. *Carnegie Endowment for International Peace: Sada*, 13 October 2020. https://carnegieendowment.org/sada/78003.

Akrimi, Yasmine, and May Barth. 'Mauritania: The Military's

Presence in "Democracy"'. *Brussels International Center: Democratic Development Series*, September 2019. https://www.bic-rhr.com/sites/default/files/inline-files/Mauritania%20Military%27s%20Presence%20in%20Democracy_0.pdf.

Al-Anani, Khalil. 'Egypt's Changing Policy in Libya: Opportunities and Challenges'. *Arab Center Washington DC*, 21 January 2021. https://arabcenterdc.org/resource/egypts-changing-policy-in-libya-opportunities-and-challenges/.

Al-Atrush, Samer, Jennifer Jacobs, and Margaret Talev. 'Trump Backed Libyan Strongman's Attack on Tripoli, U.S. Officials Say'. *Bloomberg News*, 24 April 2019. https://www.bloomberg.com/news/articles/2019-04-24/trump-libya-haftar-tripoli?sref=QmOxnLFz.

Al-Qays, Imru, and Talha Jebril. 'Morocco-ECOWAS: Good Intentions Are Not Enough'. *MIPA*, 13 February 2020. https://mipa.institute/7323.

Al-Qays, Imru, and Talha Jebril. 'The Moroccan-Saudi Rift: The Shattering of a Privileged Political Alliance'. *Al Jazeera Centre for Studies*, 3 April 2019. http://studies.aljazeera.net/en/reports/2019/04/190403105317297.html.

Al-Sherbini, Ramadan. 'Mursi Warns Ethiopia over Nile Dam'. *Gulf News*, 11 June 2013. https://gulfnews.com/world/mena/mursi-warns-ethiopia-over-nile-dam-1.1195550.

Al-Talbi, Ilhalm. 'Water Shortage in the Maghreb: Morocco's Thirst Revolution'. *Goethe Institut: Perspectives*, March 2021. https://www.goethe.de/prj/ruy/en/watlife/21718884.html.

Alami, Aida. 'Protests Erupt in Morocco over Fish Vendor's Death in Garbage Compactor'. *The New York Times*, 30 October 2016, sec. World. https://www.nytimes.com/2016/10/31/world/middleeast/protests-erupt-in-morocco-over-fish-vendors-death-in-garbage-compactor.html.

Alden, Chris and Faten Aggad-Clerx. 'Chinese Investments and Employment Creation in Algeria and Egypt'. *African Development Bank*, 2012. https://www.afdb.org/fileadmin/uploads/afdb/Documents/Publications/Brochure%20China%20Anglais.pdf.

Alfa Shaban, Abdur Rahman. 'Mauritania Parliament Probing Ex-President over Corruption'. *AfricaNews*, 16 February 2020. https://www.africanews.com/2020/02/16/mauritania-parliament-probing-ex-president-over-corruption/.

'Algeria Breaks off Relations with Morocco, Citing Fires and

Israel'. *The Africa Report*, 25 August 2021. https://www.theafr icareport.com/121545/algeria-breaks-off-relations-with-mo rocco-citing-fires-and-israel/.

'Algeria: New Amnesty Law Will Ensure Atrocities Go Unpunished, Muzzles Discussion of Civil Conflict'. *Human Rights Watch*, 1 March 2006. https://www.hrw.org/ news/2006/02/28/algeria-new-amnesty-law-will-ensure-atrocities-go-unpunished.

'Algeria Protesters at Crossroads as Islamists Take Spotlight'. *Associated Press*, 15 April 2021. https://apnews.com/article/ world-news-abdelaziz-bouteflika-algiers-algeria-c4471b25d a99a9447e1324a75c1f3116.

'Algeria: Repressive tactics used to target Hirak activists two years on'. *Amnesty International*, 22 February 2021. https://www.amnesty.org/en/latest/news/2021/02/algeria-repressive-tactics-used-to-target-hirak-activists-two-years-on/.

'Algeria's Changing Status: A Complicated State for Gulf Influence'. *Gulf International Forum*, 8 April 2019. https://gu lfif.org/algerias-changing-status-a-complicated-state-for-gu lf-influence/.

'Algeria's Economic Update – Fall 2021'. *World Bank*, 22 December 2021. https://www.worldbank.org/en/country/ algeria/publication/algeria-economic-update-fall-2021.

Alilat, Farid. *Bouteflika: L'histoire Secrète*. Paris: Éditions du Rocher, 2020.

'All According to Plan: The Rab'a Massacre and Mass Killings of Protestors in Egypt'. *Human Rights Watch*, 2014. https://www. hrw.org/sites/default/files/reports/egypt0814web_0.pdf.

Allan, Tony. 'The Concept of Virtual Water'. *World Energy 46: Water Stories. Eni S.p.A.*, 20 March 2020. https://www.eni. com/static/en-IT/world-energy-magazine/water-stories. html#slide11.

Altaeb, Malak. 'Water Politics in Libya: A Crisis of Management Not Scarcity'. *Arab Reform*, 29 June 2021. https://www.arab-reform.net/publication/water-politics-in-libya-a-crisis-of-management-not-scarcity/.

Alterman, Jon, et al., 'China in the Middle East: Part One', *Center for Strategic and International Studies*, January 21, 2020, https://www.csis.org/node/55328.

Alterman, Jon, et al. 'China in the Middle East: Part Two', *Center for Strategic and International Studies*, January 27, 2020, https:// www.csis.org/podcasts/babel-translating-middle-east.

Anderson, Lisa. '"They Defeated Us All": International Interests, Local Politics and Contested Sovereignty'. *The Middle East Journal* 71, no. 2 (2017): 229–47.

'Annuaire statistique de la Tunisie: 2015–2019'. *National Institute of Statistics*, 2021. http://ins.tn/sites/default/files/publication/pdf/annuaire-2019%20avec%20lien_1.pdf.

'Annual Report of Infrastructure Indicators: 2020'. *National Institute of Statistics*, 2020. http://www.ins.tn/sites/default/files/publication/pdf/infrastructure%202020.pdf.

Ansar, Asmaa. 'الرى: وضع استراتيجية قومية حتى ٢٠٥٠ لحل كافة المشكلات والأزمات' [Ministry of Water Resources and Irrigation: National Strategy in Place until 2050 to Solve All Problems and Crises]'. *Youm7*, 26 July 2021. https://www.youm7.com/story/2021/7/26/الرى-تم-وضع-استراتيجية-قومية-حتى-2050-لحل-كافة-المشكلات/5399182.

Aqeil, Hussein, James Tindall, and Edward Moran. 'Water Security and Interconnected Challenges in Libya'. *TinMore Institute Centre for Water Security*, November 2012. http://www.tinmore.com/pdf/WS121027_WaterSecurityLibya.pdf.

Archick, Kristin, and Derek E. Mix. 'The United States and Europe: Responding to Change in the Middle East and North Africa'. *Congressional Research Service Report for Congress*, 12 June 2013, 36. https://www.files.ethz.ch/isn/165485/210923.pdf.

Arendt, Christie Marie. 'From Critical Mass to Critical Leaders: Unpacking the Political Conditions behind Gender Quotas in Africa'. *Politics & Gender* 14, no. 3 (September 2018): 295–322.

Arita, Shawn, Sumner La Croix, and James Mak. 'How China's Approved Destination Status Policy Spurs and Hinders Chinese Travel Abroad'. *UHERO: The Economic Research Organization at the University of Hawai'i*, 19 October 2012. https://uhero.hawaii.edu/wp-content/uploads/2019/08/WP_2012-6R.pdf.

'As Scrutiny of China Grows, Some U.S. Schools Drop a Language Program'. *NPR*, 17 July 2019. https://www.npr.org/2019/07/17/741239298/as-scrutiny-of-china-grows-some-u-s-schools-drop-a-language-program.

Assaad, Ragui, Caroline Krafft, and Shaimaa Yassin. 'Job

Creation or Labor Absorption? An Analysis of Private Sector Job Growth in Egypt'. *Middle East Development Journal* 12, no. 2 (2 July 2020): 177–207.

'Authentic Blessed Hirak Movement Saved Algerian State from Collapsing into Failed State'. *Algeria Press Service*, 8 June 2021. https://www.aps.dz/en/algeria/39660-authentic-blessed-hirak-movement-saved-algerian-state-from-collapsing-into-failed-state.

Ayyad, Ibrahim. 'Egypt Warns Europe against Illegal Immigration amid Nile Dam Impasse'. *Al-Monitor*, 9 July 2021. https://www.al-monitor.com/originals/2021/07/egypt-warns-europe-against-illegal-immigration-amid-nile-dam-impasse.

Azer, Sherif. '"Behind the Sun": How Egypt Denies Forced Disappearances'. *The Tahrir Institute for Middle East Policy*, 30 April 2018. https://timep.org/commentary/analysis/behind-the-sun-how-egypt-denies-forced-disappearances/.

Baccouche, Neji. 'Decentralization in Tunisia: Challenges and Prospects'. In *Federalism: A Success Story?* Ed. Hanns Bühler, Susanne Luther, and Volker L. Plän, 29–33. Munich: Hanns-Seidel Stiftung, 2016.

'Background Press Call on Broad Middle East Regional Year-End Discussion'. *The White House*, 17 December 2021. https://www.whitehouse.gov/briefing-room/press-briefings/2021/12/17/background-press-call-on-broad-middle-east-regional-year-end-discussion/.

Badi, Emadeddin. 'Exploring Armed Groups in Libya: Perspectives on SSR in a Hybrid Environment'. *Geneva Center for Security Sector Reform*, 23 November 2020. https://www.dcaf.ch/exploring-armed-groups-libya-perspectives-ssr-hybrid-environment.

Bales, Kevin. *Disposable People: New Slavery in the Global Economy*, 3rd edition. (Berkeley: University of California Press, 2012).

Barbash, Fred. 'Navy SEALs Board Mystery Tanker Morning Glory Near Cyprus. No One Hurt, Pentagon Says'. *The Washington Post*, 17 March 2014. https://www.washingtonpost.com/news/morning-mix/wp/2014/03/17/navy-seals-board-tanker-morning-glory-near-cyprus-no-one-hurt-pentagon-says/.

'Baromètre de popularité des 3 présidents – Vague 8: Mechichi dégringole'. *Tunisie Numérique*, 2020. https://www.tunisienu merique.com/barometre-de-popularite-des-3-presidents-va gue-8-mechichi-degringole/.

Bauer, Gretchen, and Faith Okpotor. '"Her Excellency": An Exploratory Overview of Women Cabinet Ministers in Africa'. *Africa Today* 60, no. 1 (Fall 2013): 77–97.

Baumard, Maryline, and Charlotte Bozonnet. 'Kaïs Saïed: "La Tunisie n'acceptera jamais la partition de la Libye"'. *Le Monde*, 24 June 2020. https://www.lemonde.fr/afrique/artic le/2020/06/24/kais-saied-la-tunisie-n-acceptera-jamais-la-pa rtition-de-la-libye_6044014_3212.html.

Bayat, Asef. *Life as Politics: How Ordinary People Change the Middle East*. Amsterdam: Amsterdam University Press, 2013.

Becker, Jo, and Eric Schmitt. 'As Trump Wavers on Libya, an ISIS Haven, Russia Presses On'. *The New York Times*, 17 February 2018. https://www.nytimes.com/2018/02/07/wo rld/africa/trump-libya-policy-russia.html.

Beehler, William Henry. *The History of the Italian-Turkish War: September 29, 1911, to October 18, 1912*. Annapolis: Advertiser-Republican, 1913.

Belhassine, Olfa. 'Ayachi Hammami: "There's Been Mismanagement of Time" in Tunisia's Transnational Justice'. *JusticeInfo.net*, 2020. https://www.justiceinfo.net/en/ 44954-ayachi-hammami-mismanagement-of-time-in-tunis ia-transitional-justice.html.

Bellamine, Yassine. 'A quand un projet de loi de décentralisation?' *Nawaat*, 2015. https://nawaat.org/portail/ 2015.

Belschner, Jana. 'Electoral Engineering in New Democracies: Strong Quotas and Weak Parties in Tunisia'. *Government and Opposition* 57, no. 1 (2022): 108–25.

Ben Achour, Sana. *Féminisme d'état et féminisme autonome*. Tunis: Centre de Publication Universitaire, 2001.

Ben Shitrit, Lihi. 'Authenticating Representation: Women's Quotas and Islamist Parties'. *Politics & Gender* 12, no. 4 (December 2016): 781–806.

Bencheikh, Madjid. *Algérie, un système politique militarisé*. Paris: L'Harmattan, 2003.

Benderra, Omar, François Gèze, Salima Mellah, and Rafik Labjaoui, eds. *Hirak en Algérie: Invention d'un soulèvement*. Paris: La Frabrique, 2020.

Bensaad, Ali. 'Pourquoi l'Algérie est hors-jeu en Libye'. *Orient XXI*, 7 July 2021. https://orientxxi.info/magazine/pourquoi-l-algerie-est-hors-jeu-en-libye,4896.
Berry, Marie E., Yolande Bouka, and Marilyn Muthoni Kamuru. 'Implementing Inclusion: Gender Quotas, Inequality, and Backlash in Kenya'. *Politics & Gender* 16, no. 1 (2020): 1–25.
Bier, Laura. *Revolutionary Womanhood: Feminisms, Modernity, and the State in Nasser's Egypt*. Palo Alto: Stanford University Press, 2011.
'Billions Committed, Millions Delivered'. *Think Global Health*, 2 December 2021. https://www.thinkglobalhealth.org/article/billions-committed-millions-delivered.
Black, Ian. 'Algeria Hostage Crisis Could Weaken Veteran Spymaster'. *The Guardian*, 25 January 2013. https://www.theguardian.com/world/2013/jan/25/algerian-hostage-crisis-tewfik-mediene.
Blidi, Saber. 'Algeria Is Seeking to Recapture Lost Influence in Africa'. *The Arab Weekly*, 25 April 2020. https://thearabweekly.com/algeria-seeking-recapture-lost-influence-africa.
Blunt, Andrew. 'Libyan Ministry of Culture Approves Decree for 30% Gender Quota'. *NDI*, 24 April 2020. https://www.ndi.org/our-stories/libyan-ministry-culture-approves-decree-30-gender-quota.
Bobba, Sidi, and Sid El Kheir Ould Taleb EKhyar. 'Drought Conditions and Management Strategies in Mauritania'. *Integrated Drought Management Programme*, n. d. https://www.droughtmanagement.info/literature/UNW-DPC_NDMP_Country_Report_Mauritania_2014.pdf.
Bouganour, Ismail. 'Civil Society and Democratic Transformation in Mauritania: The Paradigm of Transition and the Antecedents of Political Change'. *Contemporary Arab Affairs* 10, no. 3 (2017): 372–91.
Boukhars, Anouar. 'Political Violence in North Africa: The Perils of Incomplete Liberalization'. *Brookings Doha Center Analysis Paper*, no. 3 (January 2011). https://www.brookings.edu/wp-content/uploads/2016/06/01_north_africa_boukhars.pdf.
Boukhars, Anouar. 'In the Eye of the Storm: Algeria's South and Its Sahelian Borders'. In *Algeria Modern: From Opacity to Complexity*, ed. Luis Martinez and Rasmus Alenius Boserup, 111–26. Oxford: Oxford University Press, 2016.

Boukhars, Anouar. 'Keeping Terrorism at Bay in Mauritania'. *Africa Center for Strategic Studies*, 16 June 2020. https://africacenter.org/spotlight/keeping-terrorism-at-bay-in-mauritania/.

Boukhars, Anouar. 'The Drivers of Insecurity in Mauritania'. *Carnegie Endowment for International Peace*, April 2012. https://carnegieendowment.org/files/mauritania_insecurity.pdf.

Bourrat, Flavien. 'L'armée algérienne: Un état dans l'état ?' *Les Champs de Mars* 23 (2012): 21–37.

'Bouteflika: Algeria's Longest-Serving President'. *France24*, 11 March 2019. https://www.france24.com/en/20190311-bouteflika-algerias-longest-serving-president.

Bowsher, Gemma, P. Bogue, and P. Patel. 'Small and Light Arms Violence Reduction as a Public Health Measure: The Case of Libya'. *Conflict and Health* 12, no. 29 (2018): 1–9.

Brachet, Julien. 'Policing the Desert: The IOM in Libya Beyond War and Peace'. *Antipode* 48, no. 2 (2016): 272–92.

Braut-Hegghammer, Målfred. *To Join or Not to Join the Nuclear Club: How Nations Think about Nuclear Weapons: Lessons from the Middle East*. N. p.: Middle East Studies at the Marine Corps University, 2013.

Brautigam, Deborah. *The Dragon's Gift: The Real Story of China in Africa*. Oxford: Oxford University Press, 2009.

Brechenmacher, Saskia, and Caroline Hubbard. 'How the Coronavirus Risks Exacerbating Women's Political Exclusion'. *Carnegie Endowment for International Peace*, 17 November 2020. https://carnegieendowment.org/2020/11/17/how-coronavirus-risks-exacerbating-women-s-political-exclusion-pub-83213.

Brewer, Marilynn B. *Intergroup Relations*, 2nd edition. Buckingham: Open University Press, 2003.

Brhane, Meskerem. 'Narratives of the Past, Politics of the Present Identity: Subordination and the Haratines of Mauritania'. Unpubl. Diss. University of Chicago, 1997.

Brzoska, Michael. 'Weather Extremes, Disasters, and Collective Violence: Conditions, Mechanisms, and Disaster-Related Policies in Recent Research'. *Current Climate Change Reports* 4 (2018): 320–29.

Butter, David. 'Egypt and the Gulf: Allies and Rivals'. *Chatham House*, 20 April 2020. https://www.chathamhouse.org/2020/04/egypt-and-gulf.

Cabeza-García, Laura, Esther Del Brio, and Mery Oscanoa-Victorio. 'Gender Factors and Inclusive Economic Growth: The Silent Revolution'. *Sustainability* 10, no. 2 (6 January 2018): e121 [14 pages].

Cafiero, Giorgio, and Shehab al-Makahleh. 'Mauritania's Anti-Qatar Animus'. *Middle East Policy* 26, no. 2 (2019): 121–28.

Camale, Claude. *Myth and History in Ancient Greece: The Symbolic Creation of a Colony*. Princeton: Princeton University Press, 2003.

Carothers, Thomas, and Benjamin Press. 'Navigating the Democracy-Security Dilemma in U.S. Foreign Policy: Lessons from Egypt, India, and Turkey'. *Carnegie Endowment for International Peace*, 2021. https://carnegieendowment.org/files/Carothers_Press_DemSecDilemma.pdf.

Cavatorta, Francesco, and Rikke Hostrup Haugbølle. 'The End of Authoritarian Rule and the Mythology of Tunisia under Ben Ali'. *Mediterranean Politics* 17, no. 2 (1 July 2012): 179–95.

Charrad, Mounira. 'Policy Shifts: State, Islam and Gender in Tunisia, 1930s–1990s'. *Social Politics: International Studies in Gender, State & Society* 4, no. 2 (1997): 284–319.

Charrad, Mounira. 'State and Gender in the Maghrib'. *MERIP*, 8 March 1990. https://merip.org/1990/03/state-and-gender-in-the-maghrib/.

Charrad, Mounira. *States and Women's Rights: The Making of Postcolonial Tunisia, Algeria, and Morocco*. Oakland: University of California Press, 2001.

Chayes, Sarah, and Sarah Peck. 'The Oil Curse: A Remedial Role for the Oil Industry'. *Carnegie Endowment for International Peace*, 30 September 2015. https://carnegieendowment.org/2015/09/30/oil-curse-remedial-role-for-oil-industry-pub-61445.

Chaziza, Mordechai. 'China in the Middle East: Tourism as a Stealth Weapon,' *Middle East Quarterly* 26, no. 4 (Fall 2019), https://www.meforum.org/59293/mordechai-chaziza-china-in-the-middle-east.

Cheikh, Abdel Wedoud Ould. 'Autoritarisme compétitif, diversité éthnique et démocratie'. 2008. https://www.academia.edu/6157344/Autoritarisme_comp%C3%A9titif_diversit%C3%A9_ethnique_et_d%C3%A9mocratie.

Chellel, Kit, Matthew Campbell, and K. Oanh Ha. 'Six Days in Suez: The Inside Story of the Ship That Broke Global Trade'.

Bloomberg, 24 June 2021. https://www.bloomberg.com/news/features/2021-06-24/how-the-billion-dollar-ever-given-cargo-ship-got-stuck-in-the-suez-canal.

Chennaoui, Handa. 'Resistance in the South Radicalizes Despite Intimidation'. *Nawaat*, 15 May 2017. https://nawaat.org/portail/2017/05/15/el-kamour-resistance-in-the-south-radicalizes-despite-intimidation/.

Cheriet, Boutheina. 'Le genre et la citoyenneté comme « troc » dans l'Algérie postcoloniale'. *Diogene* 225, no. 1 (2009): 89–100.

Cherif, Youssef. 'Tunisia's Fledgling Gulf Relations'. *Carnegie Endowment for International Peace: Sada*, 19 October 2020. https://carnegieendowment.org/sada/67703.

Cherif, Youssef. 'The Kamour Movement and Civic Protests in Tunisia'. *Carnegie Endowment for International Peace*, 8 August 2017. https://carnegieendowment.org/2017/08/08/kamour-movement-and-civic-protests-in-tunisia-pub-72774.

Chibani, Achref. 'Demonstrations, Tear Gas, Arrests: Kamour Protests Return'. *Meshkal*, 26 June 2020. https://meshkal.org/?p=1390.

Chikhi, Lamine. 'Algeria's New President Tebboune Faces Tough Challenge'. *Reuters*, 13 December 2019. https://www.reuters.com/article/uk-algeria-tebboune-newsmaker-idUKKBN1YH1EF.

Chikhi, Lamine. 'Algeria's Bouteflika Consolidates Curbs on State Intelligence Agency'. *Reuters*, 24 October 2014. https://www.reuters.com/article/us-algeria-politics/algerias-bouteflika-consolidates-curbs-on-state-intelligence-agency-idUSKCN0ID11120141024.

'China's Arab Policy Paper'. *Embassy of the People's Republic of China in the Kingdom of Saudi Arabia*, January 2016.

Chomiak, Laryssa. 'The Revolution in Tunisia Continues'. *Middle East Institute*, 22 September 2016. https://www.mei.edu/publications/revolution-tunisia-continues.

Ciavolella, Riccardo. 'Huunde Fof Ko Politik: Everything Is Politics: Gramsci, Fulani, and the Margins of the State in Mauritania.' *Africa Today* 58, no. 3 (Spring 2012): 3–21.

Cincotta, Richard, and Karim Sadjadpour. 'Iran in Transition: The Implications of the Islamic Republic's Changing Demographics'. *Carnegie Endowment for International Peace*,

December 2017. https://carnegieendowment.org/files/CP3 24_Iran_in_Transition_Final.pdf.

Cole, Peter. 'Borderline Chaos? Stabilizing Libya's Periphery'. *The Carnegie Endowment for International Peace*, 2012. https://carnegieendowment.org/files/stablizing_libya_periphery.pdf.

'Confucius Institutes Around the World: 2021', 26 May 2015. https://www.digmandarin.com/confucius-institutes-around-the-world.html.

Constant, Louay, Ifeanyi Edochie, Peter Glick, Jeffrey Martini, and Chandra Garber. *Barriers to Employment That Women Face in Egypt: Policy Challenges and Considerations*. Santa Monica: RAND Corporation, 2020. https://doi.org/10.7249/RR2868.

'Convention on the Elimination of All Forms of Discrimination against Women'. *United Nations Treaty Collection*, n. d. https://treaties.un.org/Pages/ViewDetails.aspx?src=IND&mtdsg_no=IV-8&chapter=4#34.

Cook-Huffman, Celia. 'The Role of Identity in Conflict'. In *Handbook of Conflict Analysis and Resolution*, ed. D. J. D. Sandole, S. Byrne, I. Sandole-Staroste, and J. Senehi, 19–31. London: Routledge, 2009.

Cook, Steven A. 'Europe's Future Will Be Decided in North Africa'. *Foreign Policy*, 18 July 2019. https://foreignpolicy.com/2019/07/18/europes-future-will-be-decided-in-north-africa/.

'Coordinating the UN's Work on Water and Sanitation'. *UN Water*, n. d. https://www.unwater.org/.

'Corruption Perceptions Index 2020 – Mauritania'. *Transparency International*, 2020. https://www.transparency.org/en/cpi/2020/index/mrt.

'Country Profile: Egypt'. *FAO AQUASTAT Reports, Food and Agriculture Organization of the United Nations*, 2016. https://www.fao.org/3/i9729en/I9729EN.pdf.

Crotti, Robert, Kusum Kali Pal, Vesselina Ratcheva, and Saadia Zahidi. 'Global Gender Gap Report 2021'. *World Economic Forum*, March 2021. https://www3.weforum.org/docs/WEF_GGGR_2021.pdf.

Daadaoui, Mohamed. 'Of Monarchs and Islamists: The "Refo-Lutionary" Promise of the PJD Islamists and Regime Control in Morocco'. *Middle East Critique* 26, no. 4 (2 October 2017): 355–71.

Daadaoui, Mohamed. *Maintaining the Makhzen: Rituals of Power and the Islamist Challenge*. New York: Palgrave, 2011.

Daadaoui, Mohamed. 'A Moroccan Monarchical Exception?' *Foreign Policy*, 14 December 2012. https://foreignpolicy.com/2012/12/14/a-moroccan-monarchical-exce ption/.

Daadaoui, Mohamed. 'Islamism and the State in Morocco'. *Hudson Institute*, 29 April 2016. http://www.hudson.org/rese arch/12286-islamism-and-the-state-in-morocco.

Daadaoui, Mohamed. 'Maghreb Blog'. http://www.maghreblog.com/.

Daadaoui, Mohamed. 'Morocco's "Spring" and the Failure of the Protest Movement'. *HuffPost*, 24 February 2016. https://www.huffpost.com/entry/moroccos-spring-and-the-failure-of-the-protest-movement_b_9287158.

Daadaoui, Mohamed. 'Morocco's King Just Named a New Prime Minister, in Case You Forgot Who's in Charge'. *Washington Post*, 20 March 2017. https://www.washingtonpost.com/ne ws/monkey-cage/wp/2017/03/20/moroccos-king-just-named-a-new-prime-minister-in-case-you-forgot-whos-in-charge/.

Daadaoui, Mohamed. 'Morocco's Unmissed Opportunity in the Western Sahara'. *Arab Center Washington DC*, 21 December 2020. https://arabcenterdc.org/resource/moroccos-unmiss ed-opportunity-in-the-western-sahara/.

Daadaoui, Mohamed. 'On Stephen Zunes' Statement about Morocco, Israel, and the Western Sahara'. *Maghreb Blog*, 11 September 2012.

Daadaoui, Mohamed. 'The King's Dilemma in Morocco'. *Al Jazeera Online*, 6 November 2017. https://www.aljazeera.com/opinions/2017/11/6/the-kings-dilemma-in-morocco.

Daadaoui, Mohamed. 'The Western Sahara Conflict: On Authoritarianism and Self-Determination'. *Muftah*, 25 June 2013. https://muftah.org/the-western-sahara-conflict-on-aut horitarianism-self-determination/#.Yyjps3bMK38.

Daadaoui, Mohamed. 'The Western Sahara Conflict: Towards a Constructivist Approach to Self-Determination'. *The Journal of North African Studies* 13, no. 2 (1 June 2008): 143–56.

Daadaoui, Mohamed. 'Whither the Arab Spring in Morocco'. *Muftah*, 19 August 2011. https://muftah.org/whither-the-ar ab-spring-in-morocco/#.Yyjk8nbMK38.

Dahmani, Frida. 'Tunisie: Comment Hichem Mechichi a résolu le casse-tête d'El Kamour'. *JeuneAfrique.com*, 10 November 2020. https://www.jeuneafrique.com/1072196/politique/tunisie-comment-hichem-mechichi-a-resolu-le-casse-tete-del-kamour/.

Dalacoura, Katerina. 'Women and Gender in the Middle East and North Africa: Mapping the Field and Addressing Policy Dilemmas at the Post-2011 Juncture'. *MENARA Final Reports* 3, March 2019. http://eprints.lse.ac.uk/100742/1/Dalacoura_Women_and_Gender.pdf.

Darhour, Hanane, and Drude Dahlerup. *Double-Edged Politics on Women's Rights in the MENA Region*. London: Palgrave Macmillan, 2020.

De Haas, Hein. 'The Myth of Invasion: The Inconvenient Realities of African Migration to Europe'. *Third World Quarterly* 29, no. 7 (2008): 1305–22.

De Koninck, R. 'Les pieds, la tête et la géographie: Notes sur la fonction organique d'une discipline académique'. *Implications* 1 (1980): 33–46.

De Waal, Alex. 'The African Union and the Libya Conflict of 2011'. *Reinventing Peace*, 19 December 2012. https://sites.tufts.edu/reinventingpeace/2012/12/19/the-african-union-and-the-libya-conflict-of-2011/.

Dearden, Ann. 'Independence for Libya: The Political Problems'. *The Middle East Journal* 4, no. 4 (October 1950): 395–409.

'Decentralisation in Tunisia: Consolidating Democracy without Weakening the State'. *International Crisis Group*, 26 March 2019. https://www.crisisgroup.org/middle-east-north-africa/north-africa/tunisia/198-decentralisation-en-tunisie-consolider-la-democratie-sans-affaiblir-letat.

'Decentralization: The Search for New Development Solutions in the Arab World's Peripheries'. *Chatham House Middle East and North Africa Programme*, 27 May 2020. https://www.arab-reform.net/event/decentralization-the-search-for-new-development-solutions-in-the-arab-worlds-peripheries/.

'Demande relative à l'établissement du statut de "région-victime" de Kasserine'. *Forum Tunisien pour les droits économiques et sociaux*, June 2015. https://www.asf.be/wp-content/uploads/2015/06/ASF_TUN_R--gionVictime_201506_FR.pdf.

Diagana, Kissima. 'Ruling Party Candidate Declared Winner

of Mauritania Election'. *Reuters*, 23 June 2019. https://www.reuters.com/article/us-mauritania-election/ruling-party-candidate-declared-winner-of-mauritania-election-idUSKCN1TO083.

Diallo, Garba. *Mauritania: The Other Apartheid*. Uppsala: Nordiak Afrikainstitutet, 1993.

Dimitrova-Grajzl, Valentina, and Iyabo Obasanjo. 'Do Parliamentary Gender Quotas Decrease Gender Inequality? The Case of African Countries'. *Constitutional Political Economy* 30, no. 2 (June 2019): 149–76.

'Displacement Tracking Matrix'. *International Organization for Migration*, n. d. https://migration.iom.int/europe/arrivals?type=arrivals.

Dizard, Jake, Christopher Walker, and Vanessa Tucker. *Countries at the Crossroads 2011: An Analysis of Democratic Governance*. Lanham: Rowman & Littlefield, 2012.

Dizboni, Ali, and Karim El-Baz. 'Understanding the Egyptian Military's Perspective on Su-35 Deal'. *Washington Institute for Near East Policy: Fikra Forum*, 15 July 2021. https://www.washingtoninstitute.org/policy-analysis/understanding-egyptian-militarys-perspective-su-35-deal.

Dunne, Charles W. 'The Grand Ethiopian Renaissance Dam and Egypt's Military Options'. *Arab Center Washington DC*, 30 July 2020. https://arabcenterdc.org/resource/the-grand-ethiopian-renaissance-dam-and-egypts-military-options/.

Dunne, Michele. 'Egypt: Looking Elsewhere to Meet Bottomless Needs – As Gulf Donors Shift Priorities, Arab States Search for Aid'. *Carnegie Endowment for International Peace*, 9 June 2020. https://carnegieendowment.org/2020/06/09/egypt-looking-elsewhere-to-meet-bottomless-needs-pub-82010.

Dunne, Michele. 'Fear and Learning in the Arab Uprisings'. *Journal of Democracy* 31, no. 1 (January 2020): 189–92.

Dunne, Michele. 'Sisi Builds a Green Zone for Egypt'. *Current History* 117, no. 803 (1 December 2018): 355–58.

Dworkin, Anthony. 'A Return to Africa: Why North African States Are Looking South'. *European Council on Foreign Relations*, 3 July 2020. https://ecfr.eu/publication/a_return_to_africa_why_north_african_states_are_looking_south/.

'Egypt 2021'. *Amnesty International*, 2020. https://www.amnesty.org/en/location/middle-east-and-north-africa/egypt/report-egypt/.

'Egypt and the African Union'. *Middle East Institute*, 10 February 2020. https://www.mei.edu/blog/egypt-and-african-union.

'Egypt Announces Human Rights Strategy to Mixed Reviews'. *Al-Monitor*, September 2021. https://www.al-monitor.com/originals/2021/09/egypt-announces-human-rights-strategy-mixed-reviews.

'Egypt: Current Climate: Climatology'. *World Bank*, 2020. https://climateknowledgeportal.worldbank.org/country/egypt/climate-data-historical.

'Egypt: Epidemic of Sexual Violence', *Human Rights Watch*, 3 July 2013, https://www.hrw.org/news/2013/07/03/egypt-epidemic-sexual-violence.

'Egypt Fertility Rate 1950–2021'. *Macrotrends*, 2021. https://www.macrotrends.net/countries/EGY/egypt/fertility-rate.

'Egypt Investigates Evidence of Extrajudicial Executions by Egyptian Army in North Sinai'. *Amnesty International*, 5 August 2021. https://www.amnesty.org/en/latest/news/2021/08/egypt-investigate-evidence-of-extrajudicial-executions-by-egyptian-army-in-north-sinai/.

'Egypt Population 2021'. *World Population Review*, 2021. https://worldpopulationreview.com/countries/egypt-population.

'Egypt's Constitution of 2014'. *Constitute Project*, n. d. https://www.constituteproject.org/constitution/Egypt_2014.pdf.

'Egypt's Debt Sustainability'. *Economic Intelligence Unit*, 27 July 2020. http://country.eiu.com/article.aspx?articleid=669932250.

'Egypt's FM Receives DRC Counterpart in Cairo to Discuss Resumption of GERD Talks'. *Egypt Today*, 16 September 2021. https://www.egypttoday.com/Article/1/107883/Egypt's-FM-receives-DRC-counterpart-in-Cairo-to-discuss-resumption.

'Egypt's Hope for a Military Base in the Horn of Africa Is Waning'. *Egypt Watch*, 24 August 2020. https://egyptwatch.net/2020/08/24/egypts-hope-for-a-military-base-in-the-horn-of-africa-is-waning/.

'Egypt's Human Rights Strategy Is Finally out, But Will Bring Few "Major Developments" in Criminal Justice Reform, Says Source'. *Mada Masr*, 12 September 2021. https://www.madamasr.com/en/2021/09/12/feature/politics/egypts-human-rights-strategy-is-finally-out-but-will-bring-few-major-developments-in-criminal-justice-reform-says-source/.

'Egypt's Population Officially Hits the 100 Million Milestone'.

Ahram Online, 11 February 2020. https://english.ahram.org.eg/NewsContent/1/64/363276/Egypt/Politics-/Egypts-population-officially-hits-the--million-mil.aspx.

'Egypt's Suez Canal Revenues up 4.7% in Last 5 Years – Chairman'. *Reuters*, 6 August 2020. https://www.reuters.com/article/egypt-economy-suezcanal-idUSL8N2F84GW.

El Habachi, May. 'Egypt's #MeToo Activists See Progress, but "the Road ahead Is Long"'. *World Politics Review*, 17 December 2020. https://www.worldpoliticsreview.com/in-egypt-women-s-rights-activists-see-progress-but-the-road-ahead-is-long/.

El Markaby, Alya. 'Q&A: Unpacking the Environmental and Economic Impacts of the GERD with Engineer Mohammed Basheer'. *Mada Masr*, 25 August 2021. https://www.madamasr.com/en/2021/08/25/feature/politics/qa-unpacking-the-environmental-and-economic-impacts-of-the-gerd-with-engineer-mohammed-basheer/.

El Mili, Naouf Brahimi. *Histoire secrète de la chute de Bouteflika*. Paris: Éditions Archipel, 2020.

El-Gamaty, Guma. 'Qatar, the UAE and the Libya Connection'. *Al Jazeera Online*, 12 June 2017. https://www.aljazeera.com/opinions/2017/6/12/qatar-the-uae-and-the-libya-connection/.

Elguettaa, Belkacem. 'The Military's Political Role in the New Algeria'. In *Politics of Military Authoritarianism in North Africa*, ed. Yezid Sayigh and Nathan Toronto. *Carnegie Middle East Center*, 2021. https://carnegie-mec.org/2021/03/17/military-s-political-role-in-new-algeria-pub-84076.

Elmaslouhi, Mariam. 'Protests Erupt in Morocco Following Fish Vendor's Brutal Death in Garbage Compactor'. *Global Voices*, 31 October 2016. https://globalvoices.org/2016/10/31/morocco-protests-fish-vendors-death/.

England, Andrew. 'Qatar Says Deal to End Gulf Crisis Will Not Change Its Ties with Iran'. *Financial Times*, 7 January 2021. https://www.ft.com/content/ea1e7058-960d-416c-93dc-f4f8c7945c12#.

Entelis, John P. 'Algeria: Nation in Transition or Politics as Usual?' n. d.

Errazzouki, Samia, and Allison L. McManus. 'Roundtable Introduction: Beyond Dominant Narratives on the Western Sahara'. *Jadaliyya*, 3 June 2013. https://www.jadaliyya.com/

Details/28716/Roundtable-Introduction-Beyond-Dominant-Narratives-on-the-Western-Sahara.

Errazzouki, Samia. 'A Monarchical Affair: From Morocco to the Arabian Peninsula'. *Jadaliyya*, 10 April 2012. https://www.jadaliyya.com/Details/25580/A-Monarchical-Affair-From-Morocco-to-the-Arabian-Peninsula.

Errazzouki, Samia. 'Morocco's King Replaces PM Benkirane amidst Post-Election Deadlock'. *Reuters*, 15 March 2017. https://www.reuters.com/article/us-morocco-politics-idUSKBN16M3A9.

Esposito, John L. 'Political Islam and the West'. *Defense Technical Information Center*, 1 January 2000. https://apps.dtic.mil/sti/pdfs/ADA426734.pdf.

'Establishing Russian Industrial Zone in Egypt Comes into Force'. *Egypt Today*, 1 February 2019. https://www.egypttoday.com/Article/3/64142/Establishing-Russian-Industrial-Zone-in-Egypt-comes-into-force.

'EU Court Annuls EU-Morocco Trade Deals over Western Sahara Consent'. *Reuters*, 29 September 2021. https://www.reuters.com/world/europe/eu-court-annuls-eu-morocco-trade-deals-over-western-sahara-consent-2021-09-29/.

'European Neighbourhood Policy (ENP)'. *European Commission: European External Action Service*, 29 July 2021. https://www.eeas.europa.eu/eeas/european-neighbourhood-policy_en.

Evrard, Camille, and Erin Pettigrew. 'Encore une nouvelle victime ... Le long chemin d'une législation à l'égard des femmes en Mauritanie'. *L'Année du Maghreb*, no. 23 (20 December 2020): 271–302.

'Ex-Algerian president Abdelaziz Bouteflika, Ousted amid Protests, Dies'. *Associated Press*, 17 September 2021. https://apnews.com/article/africa-algiers-algeria-abdelaziz-bouteflika-carlos-the-jackal-38ec30f0f8812fbaf572058f3f88cd1c.

'Exchange of Notes Between Her Majesty's Government in the United Kingdom and the Egyptian Government on the Use of Waters of the Nile for Irrigation'. *International Water Law Project*, 7 May 1929. https://www.internationalwaterlaw.org/documents/regionaldocs/Egypt_UK_Nile_Agreement-1929.html.

'Exploiting Chaos: Russia in Libya'. *Center for Strategic and*

International Studies, 8 February 2021. https://www.csis.org/blogs/post-soviet-post/exploiting-chaos-russia-libya.

'FACTBOX: Nile River Agreements and Issues'. *Reuters*, 27 July 2009, sec. Environment. https://www.reuters.com/article/us-egypt-nile-factbox-sb/factbox-nile-river-agreements-and-issues-idUSTRE56Q3MD20090727.

Fahmy, Nabil. 'The Renaissance Dam after the Security Council'. *The Cairo Review of Global Affairs*, Summer 2021. https://www.thecairoreview.com/essays/the-renaissance-dam-after-the-security-council/.

Farooq, Umar. 'Turkish Firms Eye Boon in Deepening Bilateral Ties with Qatar'. *Al Jazeera Online*, 10 December 2021. https://www.aljazeera.com/news/2021/12/10/hlturkish-firms-eye-boon-in-deepening-bilateral-ties-with-qatar.

Farouk, Yasmine. 'The Middle East Strategic Alliance Has a Long Way to Go'. *Carnegie Endowment for International Peace*, 8 February 2019. https://carnegieendowment.org/2019/02/08/middle-east-strategic-alliance-has-long-way-to-go-pub-78317.

Faujas, Alain. 'Finances publiques: Les Émirats à la rescousse de la Mauritanie'. *JeuneAfrique.com*, 3 February 2020. https://www.jeuneafrique.com/890560/economie/finances-publiques-les-emirats-a-la-rescousse-de-la-mauritanie/.

Fedi, L., M. Amer, and A. Rashad. 'Growth and Precariousness in Egypt'. *International Labour Organization*, 2019. https://www.ilo.org/wcmsp5/groups/public/---ed_emp/documents/publication/wcms_735169.pdf.

Fenton-Harvey, Jonathan. 'Regional Uprisings Confront Gulf-Backed Counterrevolution'. *MERIP*, 17 December 2019. https://merip.org/2019/12/regional-uprisings-confront-gulf-backed-counterrevolution/.

Ferguson, James, and Akhil Gupta. 'Spatializing States: Toward an Ethnography of Neoliberal Governmentality'. *American Ethnologist* 29, no. 4 (2002): 981–1002.

Feuer, Sarah, and Anna Borshchevskaya. 'Russia Makes Inroads in North Africa'. *Washington Institute for Near East Policy*, 2 November 2017. https://www.washingtoninstitute.org/policy-analysis/russia-makes-inroads-north-africa.

'Final Report of the Panel of Experts on Libya Established Pursuant to Resolution 1973 (2011)'. *United Nations Security Council*, 8 March 2021. https://reliefweb.int/report/libya/

final-report-panel-experts-libya-established-pursuant-resolution-1973-2011-s2017466.

'Fiscal Justice in Tunisia: A Vaccine against Austerity'. *Oxfam*, 17 June 2020. https://oi-files-d8-prod.s3.eu-west-2.amazonaws.com/s3fs-public/2020-06/Fiscal%20justice%20Tunisia_vaccin_austerity_Summary_English.pdf.

Fordham, Alice. 'Mohammed Bin Zayed Visits Cairo to "Stand by Our Brothers in Egypt"'. *The National News*, 1 September 2013. https://www.thenationalnews.com/world/mena/mohammed-bin-zayed-visits-cairo-to-stand-by-our-brothers-in-egypt-1.477295.

'Foreign Relations of the United States, 1949, Western Europe, Volume IV'. *Office of the Historian*. https://history.state.gov/historicaldocuments/frus1949v04/d317.

Fortier, Corinne. 'Genre, statut et éthnicisation des Haratin de Mauritanie'. *L'Ouest Saharien: Devenir visibles dans le sillage de l'esclavage: La question h.arāt.īn en Mauritanie et au Maroc* 10, no. 11 (2020): 171–86.

'Fragile States Index'. *The Fund for Peace*, n. d. https://fragilestatesindex.org.

'Fuel Exports (% of Merchandise Exports): Libya'. *World Bank*, 2018. https://data.worldbank.org/indicator/TX.VAL.FUEL.ZS.UN?locations=LY.

'Full Text of King Mohammed VI Speech on the Throne Day'. *Morocco World News*, July 2017. https://www.moroccoworldnews.com/2017/07/224848/full-text-king-mohammed-vi-speech-throne-day.

'Full Text of King Mohammed VI's Address to the Nation Marking Morocco's Throne Day'. *Morocco on the Move*, 31 July 2017. https://moroccoonthemove.com/2017/07/31/full-text-king-mohammed-vis-address-nation-marking-moroccos-throne-day/.

Gana, Alia. 'Usages sociaux de la justice transitionelle en Tunisie: À qui profite le statut de "région-victime"?' In *Justice et réconciliation dans le Maghreb post-révoltes Arabes*, ed. Éric Gobe, 121–37. Paris: Karthala, 2019.

Gaub, Florence. *The Gulf Moment: Arab Relations Since 2011*. N. p.: Strategic Studies Institute and U.S. Army War College Press, 2015.

Gaucan, Violetta. 'Japan and Libya: Different Impacts on World

Markets'. *Journal of Knowledge Management, Economics and Information Technology* 1, no. 2 (2011): 1–10.

Gejam, A. M. S. 'Climate Change and Sea Level Rise Impacts on Seawater Intrusion at Jefara Plain, Libya'. *Nature and Science* 14, no. 3 (2016): 75–81.

'Gender Justice and Equality before the Law'. *United Nations Development Programme*, 2019. https://www.undp.org/arab-states/publications/gender-justice-equality-law.

'Gender Quotas Database'. *International IDEA*, 29 April 2021. https://www.idea.int/data-tools/data/gender-quotas/country-view/200/35.

Ghafar, Adel Abdel, ed. *The European Union and North Africa: Prospects and Challenges*. Washington DC: Brookings Institution Press, 2019.

Ghanmi, Lamine. 'Tunisia University Entrance Exams Highlight Regional Disparities'. *The Arab Weekly*, 6 July 2019. https://thearabweekly.com/tunisia-university-entrance-exams-highlight-regional-disparities.

Ghebouli, Zine Labidine. 'The Post-Hirak Presidency: Tebboune's Promises and Achievements Two Years On'. *Middle East Institute*, 13 December 2021. https://www.mei.edu/publications/post-hirak-presidency-tebbounes-promises-and-achievements-two-years.

Gobe, Eric. *The Gafsa Mining Basin between Riots and a Social Movement: Meaning and Significance of a Protest Movement in Ben Ali's Tunisia*. Paris: Hal, 2010.

Goldberg, Jeffrey. 'The Obama Doctrine'. *The Atlantic*, 10 March 2016. https://www.theatlantic.com/magazine/archive/2016/04/the-obama-doctrine/471525/.

'Government Unveils Decisions on Implementation of El Kamour Agreement'. *TAP*, 8 November 2020. http://www.tap.info.tn/en/Portal-Economy/13302076-government-unveils.

Gressani, Daniela, Kevin Fletcher, and Paloma Anós Casero. 'Islamic Republic of Mauritania: Request for a Three-Year Arrangement Under the Extended Credit Facility – Debt Sustainability Analysis'. *International Monetary Fund*, 13 December 2017. https://www.imf.org/en/Publications/CR/Issues/2017/12/13/Islamic-Republic-of-Mauritania-Three-Year-Arrangement-under-the-Extended-Credit-Facility-45465.

Grewal, Sharan. 'Why Sudan Succeeded Where Algeria Failed'. *Journal of Democracy* 32, no. 4 (October 2021): 102–14.

Guerraoui, Saad. 'Jerada, the Graveyard of Clandestine Miners in Eastern Morocco'. *The Arab Weekly*, 15 February 2018. https://thearabweekly.com/jerada-graveyard-clandestine-miners-eastern-morocco.

Guessous, Nadia. 'Feminist Blind Spots and the Affect of Secularity: Disorienting the Discourse of the Veil in Contemporary Morocco'. *Signs* 45, no. 3 (Spring 2020): 605–28.

'Gulf Aid to Egypt since 30 June More Than $20 Billion: El-Sisi'. *Ahram Online*, 6 May 2014. https://english.ahram.org.eg/NewsContent/1/64/100653/Egypt/Politics-/Gulf-aid-to-Egypt-since--June-more-than--billion-E.aspx.

Gurr, Ted Robert. *Why Men Rebel*. Princeton: Princeton University Press, 1970.

Habib, Heba, and Erin Cunningham. 'Egypt's "Gift to the World" Cost $8 Billion and Probably Wasn't Necessary'. *The Washington Post*, 6 August 2015. https://www.washingtonpost.com/news/worldviews/wp/2015/08/06/egypts-gift-to-the-world-cost-8-billion-and-probably-wasnt-necessary/.

Hani, Tahar. 'Bouteflika to Seek Third Presidential Term'. *France24*, 13 February 2009. https://www.france24.com/en/20090212-bouteflika-seek-third-presidential-term-.

Harb, Mona, and Sami Atallah. 'An Assessment of Decentralization and Service Delivery in the Arab World'. In *Local Governments and Public Goods: Assessing Decentralization in the Arab World*, ed. Mona Harb and Sami Atallah, 229–33. Beirut: The Lebanese Center for Policy Studies, 2015.

Harchaoui, Jalel. 'Libya's Looming Crisis for the Central Bank'. *War on the Rocks*, 1 April 2019. https://warontherocks.com/2019/04/libyas-looming-contest-for-the-central-bank/.

Harvey, Katherine, and Bruce Riedel. 'Egypt, Iraq, and Jordan: A New Partnership 30 Years in the Making?' *Brookings Institution: Order from Chaos*, 2 July 2021. https://www.brookings.edu/blog/order-from-chaos/2021/07/02/egypt-iraq-and-jordan-a-new-partnership-30-years-in-the-making/.

Hassanein, Haisam. 'Normalization Is Making Cairo Uncomfortable'. *The Washington Institute for Near East Policy*, 19 August 2020. https://www.washingtoninstitute.org/policy-analysis/normalization-making-cairo-uncomfortable.

Hatem, Mervat F. 'Economic and Political Liberation in Egypt and the Demise of State Feminism'. *International Journal of Middle East Studies* 24, no. 2 (May 1992): 231–51.

Haugbølle, Rikke Hostrup. '"Together for Tunisia": Tribal Structures and Social and Political Mobilization'. *Middle East Institute*, 19 October 2016. https://www.mei.edu/publicatio ns/together-tunisia-tribal-structures-and-social-and-politic al-mobilization.

Hearst, David. 'Tunisia: Egyptian Intelligence Officer Plotting Crackdown on Ennahda Party'. *Middle East Eye*, 12 January 2022. https://www.middleeasteye.net/news/tunisia-egypt-in telligence-officer-plotting-ennahda-crackdown.

Heggy, Essam, Zane Sharkawy, and Abotalib Zaki Abotalib. 'Egypt's Water Budget Deficit and Suggested Mitigation Policies for the Grand Ethiopian Renaissance Dam Filling Scenarios'. *Environmental Research Letters*, 11 June 2021. https://doi.org/10.1088/1748-9326/ac0ac9.

Hill, Thomas, and Sarah Yerkes. 'A New Strategy for US Engagement in North Africa'. *United States Institute of Peace* and *Carnegie Endowment for International Peace*, February 2021. http://carnegieendowment.org/files/HillYerkes-ANew StrategyforUSEngagementinNorthAfrica-Feb2021.pdf.

Hochman, Dafna. 'Civil-Military Power Struggles: The Case of Mauritania'. *Current History* 108, no. 718 (2009): 221–26.

'How the Islamic State Rose, Fell and Could Rise Again in the Maghreb'. *Crisis Group*, 24 July 2017. https://www.crisisgro up.org/middle-east-north-africa/north-africa/178-how-isla mic-state-rose-fell-and-could-rise-again-maghreb.

Huber, Daniela, and Lorenzo Kamel. 'Arab Spring: The Role of the Peripheries'. *Mediterranean Politics* 20, no. 2 (4 May 2015): 127–41.

'Human Development Report 2020: The Next Frontier: Human Development and the Anthropocene'. *United Nations Development Programme*, 2020.

Ibrahim, Ibrahim Yahaya. 'Managing the Sahelo-Saharan Islamic Insurgency in Mauritania: The Local Stakes of the Sahelian Crisis'. *Sahel Research Group at the University of Florida's Center for African Studies*, August 2014. https:// sahelresearch.africa.ufl.edu/wp-content/uploads/sites/170/ Yahaya_StakesMauritania_Final.pdf

'IEMed Mediterranean Yearbook 2020'. *IEMed*, 2020. https:// www.iemed.org/med-yearbook/iemed-mediterranean-yearbook-2020/.

'Elections: Mauritania President (Round 1) 2019'. *IFES Election Guide*, 2019. https://www.electionguide.org/elections/id/3220/

'Immigrazione, Italia e libia insieme per pattugliare le coste Libiche'. *La Repubblica*, 27 December 2007.

'Indicateurs de l'emploi et du chomage: Deuxieme trimestre 2019'. *National Institute of Statistics*, August 2019. http://ins.tn/sites/default/files/publication/pdf/Note_ENPE_2T2019_F2.pdf.

'INS'. http://www.ins.tn/en.

'International IDEA'. *International IDEA*, n. d. https://www.idea.int/data-tools/data/gender-quotas/country-view/200/35.

'International Monetary Fund Country Report: The Sixth Review Under the Extended Credit Facility Arrangement and Request for Waiver of Non Observance of a Performance Criterion'. *International Monetary Fund*, March 2021. https://www.imf.org/en/Publications/CR/Issues/2021/03/11/Islamic-Republic-of-Mauritania-Sixth-Review-Under-the-Extended-Credit-Facility-Arrangement-50255

Irwin-Hunt, Alex. 'A Signal for Morocco's Development'. *FDI Intelligence*, 23 December 2020 https://www.fdiintelligence.com/article/79117.

'Islamic Republic of Mauritania: Economic Development Documents'. *International Monetary Fund*, 1 June 2018. https://www.imf.org/en/Publications/CR/Issues/2018/06/01/Islamic-Republic-of-Mauritania-Economic-Development-Documents-45918.

'Islamic Republic of Mauritania Joint Submission to the UN Universal Periodic Review 37th Session of the UPR Working Group'. *CIVICUS*, 9 July 2020. https://www.civicus.org/documents/MauritaniaUPRSubmission.EN.2020.pdf.

'Islamic Republic of Mauritania: Turning Challenges into Opportunities for Ending Poverty and Promoting Shared Prosperity'. *World Bank*, May 2017. https://documents1.worldbank.org/curated/en/311841500256927016/pdf/MAU-SCD-06292017.pdf.

'Italy'. *Observatory of Economic Complexity*, 2010. https://oec.world/en/profile/country/ita?yearSelector2=importGrowthYear16.

'Italy Warns of a New Wave of Immigrants to Europe'. *Spiegel International*, 24 February 2011. https://www.spiegel.de/in

ternational/europe/libyan-crisis-italy-warns-of-a-new-wave-of-immigrants-to-europe-a-747459.html.

Jacobs, Adel Abdel Ghafar and Anna L. 'Morocco-Saudi Relations: Trouble amongst Royals?' *Brookings Institution: Order from Chaos*, 1 March 2019. https://www.brookings.edu/blog/order-from-chaos/2019/03/01/morocco-saudi-relations-trouble-amongst-royals/.

Jacobs, Anna L. 'Another Morocco-Algeria Rupture Jeopardizes Gulf Outreach, Regional Connectivity'. *The Arab Gulf States Institute in Washington*, 14 September 2021. https://agsiw.org/another-morocco-algeria-rupture-jeopardizes-gulf-outreach-regional-connectivity/.

Jacobs, Anna L. 'Resolution of Gulf Rift Not Likely to Mend Fault Lines in North Africa'. *The Arab Gulf States Institute in Washington*, 21 January 2021. https://agsiw.org/resolution-of-gulf-rift-not-likely-to-mend-fault-lines-in-north-africa/.

Jalalzai, Farida, and Mona Lena Krook. 'Beyond Hillary and Benazir: Women's Political Leadership Worldwide'. *International Political Science Review* 31, no. 1 (January 2010): 5–21.

Jobrane, Emna. 'Tunisian Doctors' Emigration Compounds Toll of Pandemic'. *The Arab Weekly*, 23 September 2020. https://thearabweekly.com/tunisian-doctors-emigration-compounds-toll-pandemic.

Jourde, Cédric. 'Countries at the Crossroads 2011: Mauritania'. *Freedom House*, n. d. https://www.europarl.europa.eu/meetdocs/2009_2014/documents/dmag/dv/dmag20120125_02_/dmag20120125_02_en.pdf.

Jourde, Cédric. 'Ethnicity, Democratization, and Political Dramas: Insights into Ethnic Politics in Mauritania'. *African Issues* 29, no. 1/2 (2001): 26–30.

Jourde, Cedric. 'Sifting Through the Layers of Insecurity in the Sahel: The Case of Mauritania'. *Africa Center for Strategic Studies*, September 2011. https://africacenter.org/wp-content/uploads/2016/06/ASB15EN-Sifting-Through-the-Layers-of-Insecurity-in-the-Sahel-The-Case-of-Mauritania.pdf.

Jrad, Eya. 'Tunisia Facing COVID-19: To Exceptional Circumstances, Exceptional Measures?' *Arab Reform Initiative*, 14 April 2020. https://www.arab-reform.net/publication/tunisia-facing-covid-19-to-exceptional-circumstances-exceptional-measures/.

Kadri, Aissa. *Algérie, décennie 2010–2020: Aux origines du mouvement populaire du 22 Février 2019*. Paris: Éditions du Croquant, 2020.

Kafala, Ghady. 'Women's Movement in Libya ... an Ongoing Feminist Struggle نضال نسوي مستمر ... الحركة النسوية في ليبيا'. *Elbiro Media*, 30 December 2017. https://elbiro.net/feminism-movement-in-libya/.

Kang, Alice J., and Aili Mari Tripp. 'Coalitions Matter: Citizenship, Women, and Quota Adoption in Africa'. *Perspectives on Politics* 16, no. 1 (March 2018): 73–91.

Keenan, Jeremy. 'General Mohamed Toufik Mediene: "God of Algeria"'. *Al Jazeera Online*, 29 September 2010. https://www.aljazeera.com/news/2010/9/29/general-mohamed-toufik-mediene-god-of-algeria.

'Kenya, Egypt Sign Defence Deal as Cairo Moves to Consolidate Its Position on Ethiopia Dam'. *Middle East Monitor*, 27 May 2021. https://www.middleeastmonitor.com/20210527-kenya-egypt-sign-defence-deal-as-cairo-moves-to-consolidate-its-position-on-ethiopia-dam/.

Khalil, Andrea. *Gender, Women and the Arab Spring*. London: Routledge, 2015.

Khorrami, Nima. 'Deadlock on the Nile'. *Carnegie Endowment for International Peace: Sada*, 22 July 2020. https://carnegieendowment.org/sada/82344.

Kimball, Sam. 'Amazigh Languish in Underserved Pockets of Southeast Tunisia'. *Al-Monitor*, 8 July 2020. https://www.al-monitor.com/originals/2020/07/tunisia-amazigh-politics-minorities-taoujout-marginalized.html.

Kimble, Deborah, Jamie Box, and Ginka Kapitanova. 'Making Decentralization Work in Developing Countries: Transforming Local Government Entities into High-Performing Local Government Organizations'. *Urban Institute Center on International Development and Governance*, November 2012. https://www.urban.org/sites/default/files/publication/26271/412710-Making-Decentralization-Work-in-Developing-Countries-Transforming-Local-Government-Entities-into-High-Performing-Organizations.PDF.

Kimenyi, Mwangi S., and John Mukum Mbaku. 'The Limits of the New "Nile Agreement"'. *Brookings Institution: Africa in Focus*, 28 April 2015. https://www.brookings.edu/blog/africa-in-focus/2015/04/28/the-limits-of-the-new-nile-agreement/.

Klasen, S. 'Low Schooling for Girls, Slower Growth for All? Cross-Country Evidence on the Effect of Gender Inequality in Education on Economic Development'. *The World Bank Economic Review* 16, no. 3 (1 December 2002): 345–73.

Klasen, Stephan, and Francesca Lamanna. 'The Impact of Gender Inequality in Education and Employment on Economic Growth: New Evidence for a Panel of Countries'. *Feminist Economics* 15, no. 3 (1 July 2009): 91–132.

Korostelina, Karina. *Social Identity and Conflict: Structures and Implications*. New York: Palgrave Macmillan, 2007.

Korotayev, Andrey, Leonid Issaev, and Julia Zinkina. 'Center-Periphery Dissonance as a Possible Factor of the Revolutionary Wave of 2013–2014: A Cross-National Analysis'. *Cross-Cultural Research* 49, no. 5 (2015): 461–88.

Koundouno, Tamba François. 'Morocco-Russia Intensify Relations as Strategic Interests Converge'. *Morocco World News*, 31 December 2019. https://www.moroccoworldnews.com/2019/12/290187/morocco-russia-relations-strategic-interests/.

Krafft, Caroline, and Ragui Assaad. 'Why the Unemployment Rate Is a Misleading Indicator of Labor Market Health in Egypt'. *Economic Research Forum*, 1 January 2014. https://erf.org.eg/publications/why-the-unemployment-rate-is-a-misleading-indicator-of-labor-market-health-in-egypt/.

Krook, Mona Lena, and Diana Z. O'Brien. 'The Politics of Group Representation: Quotas for Women and Minorities Worldwide'. *Comparative Politics* 42, no. 3 (31 March 2010): 253–72.

Krook, Mona Lena. 'Why Are Fewer Women than Men Elected? Gender and the Dynamics of Candidate Selection'. *Political Studies Review* 8, no. 2 (May 2010): 155–68.

La discrimination positive: Un principe constitutionnel à concrétiser pour la promotion de l'emploi décent dans les régions. N. p.: République Tunisienne and Organisation Internationale du Travail, 2017.

Lacher, Wolfram. *Libya's Fragmentation: Structure and Process in Violent Conflict*. London: Bloomsbury, 2020.

Lacher, Wolfram. 'Magnates, Media, and Mercenaries: How Libya's Conflicts Produce Transnational Networks Straddling North Africa and the Middle East'. *Project on Middle East Political Science*, June 2020. https://pomeps.org/

magnates-media-and-mercenaries-how-libyas-conflicts-pr
oduce-transnational-networks-straddling-africa-and-the-mi
ddle-east.

Laessing, Ulf, and Ahmed Elumami. 'In Battle for Libya's Oil, Water Becomes a Casualty'. *Reuters*, 2 July 2019. https://www.reuters.com/article/us-libya-security-water-insight/in-battle-for-libyas-oil-water-becomes-a-casualty-idUSKCN1T X0KQ.

Lagdaf, Souadou, and Yahia H. Zoubir. 'The Struggle of the Women's Movements in Neo-Patriarchal Libya'. *Oriente Moderno* 98, no. 2 (7 September 2018): 225–46.

Laghmari, Jihen. 'Tunisia Reaches out to Gulf Nations as Economic Woes Deepen'. *Bloomberg*, 16 October 2021. https://www.bloomberg.com/news/articles/2021-10-16/tuni sia-in-talks-with-uae-saudi-arabia-for-funds-official-says.

Lamloum, Olfa. 'Marginalisation, Insecurity and Uncertainty on the Tunisian-Libyan Border Ben Guerdane and Dhehiba from the Perspective of Their Inhabitants'. *International Alert*, 2016. https://www.international-alert.org/sites/defau lt/files/TunisiaLibya_MarginalisationInsecurityUncertainty Border_EN_2016.pdf.

Langhi, Zahra. 'Gender and State-Building in Libya: Towards a Politics of Inclusion'. *The Journal of North African Studies* 19, no. 2 (15 March 2014): 200–10.

Lazreg, Marnia. *The Eloquence of Silence: Algerian Women in Question*, 2nd edition. New York: Routledge, 2019.

Lazreg, Marnia. 'Gender and Politics in Algeria: Unraveling the Religious Paradigm'. *Signs* 15, no. 4 (Summer 1990): 755–80.

Leigh, Matthew. 'Lucan and the Libyan Tale'. *The Journal of Roman Studies* 90 (2000): 95–109.

'Les Émirats et le bouclier noir: Quand des centaines de Soudanais sont envoyés sur le front Libyen'. *Le Vif*, 7 July 2020. https://www.levif.be/actualite/international/les-emira ts-et-le-bouclier-noir-quand-des-centaines-de-soudanais-so nt-envoyes-sur-le-front-libyen/article-normal-1283237.html.

Lesourd, Céline. 'The Lipstick on the Edge of the Well: Mauritanian Women and Political Power (1960–2014)'. In *Women's Movements in Post-'Arab Spring' North Africa*, ed. Fatima Sadiqi, 77–93. New York: Palgrave MacMillan, 2016.

'Letter Dated 15 February 2013 from the Panel of Experts

on Libya Established Pursuant to Resolution 1973 (2011) Addressed to the Security Council'. *United Nations Security Council*, 9 March 2013. https://www.securitycouncilreport.org/atf/cf/%7B65BFCF9B-6D27-4E9C-8CD3-CF6E4FF96FF9%7D/s_2013_99.pdf.

Lewis, Aidan, and Ulf Laessing. 'Libyans Dig for Water in Latest Test for Capital's Residents'. *Reuters*, 2 July 2019. https://www.reuters.com/article/us-libya-security-tripoli/libyans-dig-for-water-in-latest-test-for-capitals-residents-idUSKBN1CW2SH.

'Libya', *Observatory of Economic Complexity*, 2010, https://oec.world/en/profile/country/lby?yearSelector1=exportGrowthYear16.

'Libya Is a Major Energy Exporter, Especially to Europe'. *US Energy Information Administration*, 12 March 2011. https://www.eia.gov/todayinenergy/detail.php?id=590.

Lindsey, Ursula. 'The Anti-Cairo'. *Places Journal*, March 2017. https://placesjournal.org/article/the-anti-cairo/?cn-reloaded=1.

'List of Products Exported by Libya, State Of'. *Trade Map*, n. d. https://www.trademap.org/Product_SelCountry_TS.aspx?nvpm=1%7c434%7c%7c%7c%7c2709%7c%7c%7c4%7c1%7c1%7c2%7c2%7c1%7c1%7c1%7c1%7c1.

Lust-Okar, Ellen. *Structuring Conflict in the Arab World: Incumbents, Opponents, and Institutions*. Cambridge: Cambridge University Press, 2007.

Lutterbeck, Derek. 'Migrants Weapons and Oil: Europe and Libya After the Sanctions'. *Journal of North African Studies* 14, no. 2 (2009): 169–84.

Lynch, Marc. 'The New Arab Order'. *Foreign Affairs*, October 2018. https://www.foreignaffairs.com/articles/middle-east/2018-08-14/new-arab-order.

Maddocks, Andrew, Robert Samuel Young, and Paul Reig. 'Ranking the World's Most Water-Stressed Countries in 2040'. *World Resources Institute*, 25 August 2015. www.wri.org/blog/2015/08/ranking-world-s-most-water-stressed-countries-2040.

Maestri, Elena. 'The Role of the GCC in North Africa in Light of the "Arab Spring"'. In *North African Politics: Change and Continuity*, ed. Yahia H. Zoubir and Gregory White, 350–70. New York: Routledge, 2016.

Magdy, Rana. 'Egyptian Feminist Movement: A Brief History'. *openDemocracy*, n. d. https://www.opendemocracy.net/en/north-africa-west-asia/egyptian-feminist-movement-brief-history/.

Majdi, Yassine. 'Qu'est-ce que le "tahakoum"?' *TelQuel*, 7 July 2016. https://telquel.ma/2016/07/07/quest-ce-tahakoum_150 4927.

Malka, Haim. 'Turbulence Ahead: The North African Maghreb in 2019'. *Center for Strategic and International Studies*, 11 January 2019. https://www.csis.org/analysis/turbulence-ahead-north-african-maghreb-2019.

Mandour, Maged. 'Dollars to Despots: Sisi's International Patrons'. *Carnegie Endowment for International Peace: Sada*, 19 November 2020. https://carnegieendowment.org/sada/83277.

Mandour, Maged. 'The Sinister Side of Sisi's Urban Development'. *Carnegie Endowment for International Peace: Sada*, 10 May 2021. https://carnegieendowment.org/sada/84504.

'Mapping European Leverage in the MENA Region'. *European Council on Foreign Relations*, December 2019. https://ecfr.eu/special/mapping_eu_leverage_mena.

Marrakchi, Afef Hammami. 'Local Authorities in Tunisia Face Challenges of Post-COVID Economic Recovery'. *Arab Reform Initiative*, 21 August 2020. https://www.arab-reform.net/publication/local-authorities-in-tunisia-face-challenges-of-post-covid-economic-recovery/.

Marsh, Nicholas. 'Brothers Came Back with Weapons: The Effects of Arms Proliferation from Libya'. *PRISM* 6, no. 4 (2017): 78–97.

Martinez, Luis. 'L'armée Algérienne à l'épreuve du mouvement citoyen du Hirak'. *The Conversation*, 18 February 2020. https://theconversation.com/larmee-algerienne-a-lepreuve-du-mouvement-citoyen-du-hirak-131798

Masbah, Mohammed. '"Let It Spoil!" Morocco's Boycott and the Empowerment of "Regular" Citizen'. *Al Jazeera Centre for Studies*, 14 November 2018. https://studies.aljazeera.net/en/reports/2018/11/181114115931285.html.

Masri, Lena. '"Two Is Enough," Egypt Tells Poor Families as Population Booms'. *Reuters*, 20 February 2019. https://www.reuters.com/article/us-egypt-population/two-is-enough-egypt-tells-poor-families-as-population-booms-idUSKCN1Q91RJ.

Matta, Samer. 'Mauritania Economic Update: Why It Is Essential to Enable Women to Participate Fully in Economic Activity'. *World Bank*, 2021. https://www.worldbank.org/en/country/mauritania/publication/mauritania-economic-update-why-it-is-essential-to-enable-women-to-participate-fully-in-economic-activity.

'Mauritania'. *International IDEA: Gender Quotas Database*, n. d. https://www.idea.int/data-tools/data/gender-quotas/country-view/214/35.

'Mauritania'. *International IDEA*, n. d. https://www.idea.int/data-tools/country-view/214/40.

'Mauritania 2019 Human Rights Report'. *US Department of State*, 2019. https://mr.usembassy.gov/wp-content/uploads/sites/204/MAURITANIA-2019-HUMAN-RIGHTS-REPORT.pdf.

'Mauritania and Slavery: An Epidemic'. *Priceonomics*, n. d. http://priceonomics.com/mauritania-and-slavery-an-epidemic/.

'Mauritania: Anti-Corruption Study'. *World Bank*, September 2008. https://openknowledge.worldbank.org/handle/10986/12731.

'Mauritania Breaks Diplomatic Ties with Qatar, Gabon Voices Condemnation'. *Reuters*, 7 June 2017. https://www.reuters.com/article/us-gulf-qatar-mauritania/mauritania-breaks-diplomatic-ties-with-qatar-gabon-voices-condemnation-idUSKBN18X2ZH.

'Mauritania: Corruption'. *Global Security*, n. d. https://www.globalsecurity.org/military/world/africa/mr-corruption.htm.

'Mauritania: Country Policy and Institutional Assessment'. *World Bank*, 2019. https://documents1.worldbank.org/curated/en/668721595586560397/pdf/Country-Policy-and-Institutional-Assessment-CPIA-Africa-2019-Strengthening-Debt-Management-Capacity-Mauritania-Quick-Facts.pdf.

'Mauritania Country Report 2020'. *BTI Transformation Index*, 2020. https://bti-project.org/fileadmin/api/content/en/downloads/reports/country_report_2020_MRT.pdf.

'Mauritania: Economic Reforms and Diversification Support Programme – Phase II (PAREDE II)'. *African Development Bank Group*, n. d. https://projectsportal.afdb.org/dataportal/VProject/show/P-MR-K00-017.

'Mauritania Economic Update: Why It Is Essential to Enable Women to Participate Fully in Economic Activity'. *World*

Bank, 1 June 2021. https://www.worldbank.org/en/country/ mauritania/publication/mauritania-economic-update-why-it-is-essential-to-enable-women-to-participate-fully-in-economic-activity.

'Mauritania Economy: Population, GDP, Inflation, Business, Trade, FDI, Corruption'. *The Heritage Foundation*, n. d. www.heritage.org/index/country/Mauritania.

'Mauritania: Improving Education to Foster Social Cohesion and Support Economic Development – Mauritania'. *ReliefWeb*, n. d. https://reliefweb.int/report/mauritania/mauritania-improving-education-foster-social-cohesion-and-support-economic.

'Mauritania Profile: Timeline'. *BBC*, 19 February 2018. https://www.bbc.com/news/world-africa-13882166.

Mbaku, John Mukum. 'The Controversy over the Grand Ethiopian Renaissance Dam'. *Brookings Institution: Africa in Focus*, 5 August 2020. https://www.brookings.edu/blog/africa-in-focus/2020/08/05/the-controversy-over-the-grand-ethiopian-renaissance-dam/.

McCollum, Jonathan. 'Reimagining Mediterranean Spaces: Libya and the Italo-Turkish War, 1911–1912'. *Diacrone* 23, no. 3 (2015). https://journals.openedition.org/diacronie/2356#quotation.

McNamara, T. 'Theorizing Social Identity: What Do We Mean by Social Identity? Competing Frameworks, Competing Discourses'. *TESOL Quarterly* 31, no. 3 (Autumn 1997): 561–67.

Meddeb, Hamza. 'Tunisia's Geography of Anger: Regional Inequalities and the Rise of Populism'. *Carnegie's Middle East Center*, 19 February 2020. https://carnegie-mec.org/2020/02/19/tunisia-s-geography-of-anger-regional-inequalities-and-rise-of-populism-pub-81086.

Meddi, Adlène. 'Algeria: The Secret Service Never Dies'. *Middle East Eye*, 16 September 2015. https://www.middleeasteye.net/fr/news/algeria-secret-services-never-die-237305750.

Melly, Paul. 'Mauritania's Unfolding Landscape Elections, Hydrocarbons and Socio-Economic Change'. *Chatham House*, April 2019. https://www.chathamhouse.org/sites/default/files/2019-04-11-Mauritania%27s%20Unfolding%20Landscape.pdf.

Miller, Andrew, and Michele Dunne. 'Losing Egypt to Russia Isn't the Real Problem – But Collapse Is'. *Carnegie Endowment for International Peace*, 20 July 2018. https://carnegieendow ment.org/2018/07/20/losing-egypt-to-russia-isn-t-real-probl em-but-collapse-is-pub-76918.

Moghadam, Valentine. 'Transnational Feminist Networks: Collective Action in an Era of Globalization.' In *Globalization and Social Movements*, ed. Pierre Hamel, Henri Lustiger-Thaler, Jan Nederveen Pieterse, and Sasha Roseneil, 111–39. New York: Palgrave, 2001.

'Mohammed VI Ropes in Mohamed Bin Salman to Mend Algiers Rift'. *Africa Intelligence*, 1 September 2021. https:// www.africaintelligence.com/north-africa/2021/09/01/ mohammed-vi-ropes-in-mohamed-bin-salman-to-mend-algiers-rift,109688354-art.

'Mohammed Bin Salman Arrives in Mauritania amid Protests'. *Morocco World News*, 2 December 2018. https://www.moroc coworldnews.com/2018/12/259323/mbs-mohammed-bin-sal man-mauritania-protests/.

Mohammedi, Adlene. 'Russia-Algeria: A Flexible and Pragmatic Partnership'. *FMES*, 8 February 2021. https://fmes-france. org/russia-algeria-a-flexible-and-pragmatic-partnership-by-adlene-mohammedi/.

Molina, Irene Fernandez. 'The Monarchy vs. the 20 February Movement: Who Holds the Reins of Political Change in Morocco?' *Mediterranean Politics* 16, no. 3 (2011): 435–41.

Molina, I. Fernandez, and M. H. de Larramendi, eds. *Foreign Policy in North Africa: Navigating Global, Regional and Domestic Transformations*. New York: Routledge, 2020.

Moneim, Doaa A. 'Egypt's External Debt up to $134.8 Bln in Q3 FY2020/21: CBE'. *Ahram Online*, 11 July 2021. https:// english.ahram.org.eg/NewsContent/3/12/416983/Business/ Economy/Egypt%E2%80%99s-external-debt-up-to--bln-in-Q-FY-CBE.aspx.

'Monitoring Evaluation Expert'. *Devex*, n. d. https://www.devex. com/jobs/monitoring-evaluation-expert-501084.

'More Jobs, Better Jobs: A Priority for Egypt'. *World Bank*, June 2014. https://documents1.worldbank.org/curated/en/92683 1468247461895/pdf/884470EG0repla00Box385343B00PUBLI C0.pdf.

'Morocco Approves King Mohammed's Constitutional Reforms'. *BBC*, 2 July 2011. https://www.bbc.com/news/wo rld-africa-13976480.

'Morocco, China Sign Belt Road Initiative Implementation Agreement'. *The North Africa Post*, 5 January 2022. https://northafricapost.com/54725-morocco-china-sign-belt-road-initiative-implementation-agreement.html.

'Morocco Country Report'. *Arab Barometer* V, 2019. https://www.arabbarometer.org/wp-content/uploads/ABV_Morocco_Report_Public-Opinion_Arab-Barometer_2019.pdf.

'Morocco: Imider Amazigh Movement Decides to Dismantle Protest Camp after 8 Years'. *Nationalia*, 9 September 2019. https://www.nationalia.info/brief/11245/morocco-imider-amazigh-movement-decides-to-dismantle-protest-camp-after-8-years.

'Morocco Press Agency (MAP) Press Release'. *Morocco Press Agency*, n. d. http://www.mapexpress.ma/ar/actualite/.

'Morocco Stops Cooperation with German Embassy'. *Middle East Monitor*, 3 March 2021. https://www.middleeastmonitor.com/20210303-morocco-stops-cooperation-with-german-embassy/.

'Morocco Takes Part in "Impregnable Guard" Drill in Qatar'. *The North Africa Post*, 23 March 2021. https://northafricapost.com/48452-morocco-takes-part-in-impregnable-guard-drill-in-qatar.html.

'Morocco Trade Picture'. *European Commission*, n. d. https://ec.europa.eu/trade/policy/countries-and-regions/countries/morocco/index_en.htm.

'Morocco Vows to Punish Culprits as Protests Rage over Fishmonger's Death'. *Middle East Eye*, 1 November 2016. https://www.middleeasteye.net/news/morocco-vows-punish-culprits-protests-rage-over-fishmongers-death.

Mousli, Malek. 'Algerian-Russian Cooperation: True Strategic Partnership?' *Vestnik RUDN: International Relations* 19 (15 December 2019): 284–92.

N'Diaye, Boubacar. 'To "Midwife" – and Abort – a Democracy: Mauritania's Transition from Military Rule, 2005–2008'. *The Journal of Modern African Studies* 47, no. 1 (2009): 129–52.

N'Diaye, Boubacar. 'The Legacy of Mauritania's Colonels: West Africa's Next Crisis?' *Centre for Democracy and Development*, 2016. https://www.academia.edu/29969715/The_Legacy_of_Mauritania_Colonels_West_Africas_Next_Crisis.

Namane, Walid. 'The Tataouine Protests and Political Stability in Tunisia'. *Atlantic Council*, 6 July 2017. https://www.atlant iccouncil.org/blogs/menasource/the-tataouine-protests-and-political-stability-in-tunisia/.

Nanes, Stefanie. '"The Quota Encouraged Me to Run": Evaluating Jordan's Municipal Quota for Women'. *Journal of Middle East Women's Studies* 11, no. 3 (November 2015): 261–82.

Nemar, Radidja. 'Au-delà des casernes: Le rôle de l'armée en Algérie'. *Les Cahiers de l'Orient* 100 (2010): 19–32.

'New Mauritanian Anti-Slavery Law Is Worthless If Not Implemented'. *Anti-Slavery International*, 18 August 2015. https://www.antislavery.org/new-mauritanian-anti-slavery-law-worthless-not-implemented/.

Nickels, Benjamin. 'Algeria's Role in African Security'. *Carnegie Endowment for International Peace: Sada*, 2014. https://carneg ieendowment.org/sada/55239.

Nikiel, Catherine A., and Elfatih A. B. Eltahir. 'Past and Future Trends of Egypt's Water Consumption and Its Sources'. *Nature Communications* 12 (2021): art. No. 4508.

Norris, Pippa. 'The State of Women's Participation and Empowerment'. In *Sixty-Fifth Session of the Commission on the Status of Women*, 2020. https://www.unwomen.org/sites/default/files/Headquarters/Attachments/Sections/CSW/65/EGM/Norris_State%20of%20Womens%20Participation%20and%20Empowerment_BP1_CSW65EGM.pdf.

Occhiuto, Antonio, and Giorgio Cafiero. 'Why the Downward Spiral in Morocco-UAE Relations?' *Responsible Statecraft*, 31 March 2020. https://responsiblestatecraft.org/2020/03/31/why-the-downward-spiral-in-morocco-uae-relations/.

'OECD-FAO Agricultural Outlook 2018–2027'. *OECD/FAO*, 3 July 2018. https://www.oecd-ilibrary.org/agriculture-and-food/oecd-fao-agricultural-outlook-2018-2027_agr_outlook-2018-en.

'Off the Radar: Human Rights in the Tindouf Refugee Camps'. *Human Rights Watch*, 18 October 2014. https://www.hrw.org/report/2014/10/18/radar/human-rights-tindouf-refugee-ca mps#.

'On Orders of King Mohammed VI, Morocco Sends Food Supply to Qatar'. *Morocco World News*, 12 June 2017. https://www.moroccoworldnews.com/2017/06/219564/morocco-se nd-planes-loaded-food-supply-qatar.

Ottaway, Marina. 'Morocco: Can the Third Way Succeed?' *Carnegie Endowment for International Peace*, 31 July 2012. https://carnegieendowment.org/2012/07/31/morocco-can-third-way-succeed-pub-48968.

Ottaway, Marina. 'The New Moroccan Constitution: Real Change or More of the Same?' *Carnegie Endowment for International Peace*, 2011. https://carnegieendowment.org/2011/06/20/new-moroccan-constitution-real-change-or-more-of-same-pub-44731.

Ouaissa, Rachid. 'Algeria: Between Transformation and Re-Configuration'. In *Contextualising Transformation Processes and Lasting Crises in the Middle East and North Africa*, ed. Rachid Ouaissa, Friederike Pannewick, and Alena Strohmaier. Wiesbaden: Springer, 2021.

Ouaissa, Rachid. 'Algérie: Quel rôle pour l'armée dans la transition démocratique?' *Telos*, 6 May 2019. https://www.telos-eu.com/fr/politique-francaise-et-internationale/algerie-quel-role-pour-larmee-dans-la-transition-d.html.

Ouali, Aomar, and Paul Schemm. 'Algeria Scandals Mask High Level Power Struggle'. *The San Diego Union-Tribune*, 24 November 2012. https://www.sandiegouniontribune.com/sdut-algeria-scandals-mask-high-level-power-struggle-2012nov24-story.html.

Ould Mohamed, Mohamed Salem. 'Purist Salafism in the Sahel and Its Jihadist Position'. *Al Jazeera Centre for Studies*, 17 July 2012. https://studies.aljazeera.net/en/reports/2012/07/20127177719710292.html.

'Overview'. *World Bank*, 21 June 2021 https://www.worldbank.org/en/country/tunisia/overview.

Palacio, Anna. 'Spain-Morocco Tensions: How the EU Can Make Progress on Western Sahara'. *European Council of Foreign Relations*, 17 June 2021. https://ecfr.eu/article/spain-morocco-tensions-how-the-eu-can-make-progress-on-western-sahara/.

Paoletti, Emanuela. 'Power Relations and International Migration: The Case of Italy and Libya'. *Political Studies* 59, no. 2 (2011): 269–89.

Park, Robert E. 'Human Migration and the Marginal Man'. *American Journal of Sociology* 33, no. 6 (1928): 881–93.

Parker, Claire. 'Influential Voices in Egypt, Saudi Arabia and UAE Celebrate Tunisia Turmoil as Blow to Political Islam'.

The Washington Post, 27 July 2021. https://www.washingtonpost.com/world/2021/07/27/tunisia-gulf-information-campaign/.

Parker, Richard Bordeaux. *Uncle Sam in Barbary: A Diplomatic History*. Gainesville: University Press of Florida, 2004.

Pazzanita, Anthony G. 'Political Transition in Mauritania: Problems and Prospects'. *Middle East Journal* 53, no. 1 (1999): 44–58.

Pezard, Stephanie, and Anne-Kathrin Glatz. 'Arms in and around Mauritania: National and Regional Security Implications'. *Small Arms Survey*, June 2010. https://www.smallarmssurvey.org/resource/arms-and-around-mauritania-national-and-regional-security-implications-occasional-paper-24.

Ping, Jean. 'African Union Role in the Libyan Crisis'. *Pambazuka News*, 15 December 2011. https://www.pambazuka.org/governance/african-union-role-libyan-crisis.

Pope, Cody. 'Tunisian Thirst Uprising: A Nation on the Edge'. *Circle of Blue*, 27 October 2016. https://www.circleofblue.org/2016/africa/a-nation-on-the-edge/.

'Poverty and Equity Brief: Mauritania'. *World Bank*, April 2021. https://databank.worldbank.org/data/download/poverty/987B9C90-CB9F-4D93-AE8C-750588BF00QA/AM2020/Global_POVEQ_MRT.pdf.

'Press Release on Deputy Foreign Minister Mikhail Bogdanov's Consultations with Permanent Secretary of the Group of Five for the Sahel Maman Sambo Sidikou', *Ministry of Foreign Affairs of the Russian Federation*, 3 February 2021, https://www.mid.ru/foreign_policy/news/-/asset_publisher/cKNonkJE02Bw/content/id/3164378.

'Prince Faisal Reiterates Saudi Support for Tunisia's Stability in Meeting with President Saied'. *Saudi Gazette*, 30 July 2021. https://saudigazette.com.sa/article/609308/SAUDI-ARABIA/Prince-Faisal-reiterates-Saudi-support-for-Tunisias-stability-in-meeting-with-President-Saied.

Prud'homme, Rémy. 'The Dangers of Decentralization'. *The World Bank Research Observer* 10, no. 2 (1995): 201–20.

'Public Opinion Survey: Residents of Tunisia, December 3 – December 15, 2019'. *Center for Insights in Survey Research*, 2019. https://www.iri.org/wp-content/uploads/2020/11/tunisia_final_slides.pdf.

'Qatar Emir Appeals to All Parties in Tunisia Political Crisis to Pursue Dialogue'. *Reuters*, 28 July 2021. https://www.reuters.com/world/middle-east/qatar-emir-expressed-necessity-overcome-current-political-crisis-tunisia-emir-2021-07-28/.

Qiblawi, Tamara. 'What a Crown Prince's Trip to Turkey Tells Us about the Post-American Middle East'. *CNN*, 24 November 2021. https://www.cnn.com/2021/11/24/middleeast/uae-turkey-detente-middle-east-cmd-intl/index.html.

Quandt, William B. *Between Ballots and Bullets: Algeria's Transition from Authoritarianism*. Washington DC: Brookings Institution Press, 1998.

Rachidi, Ilhem. 'Helpless Hirak? Democratic Disappointments in Algeria'. *Carnegie Endowment for International Peace: Sada*, 10 June 2021. https://carnegieendowment.org/sada/84739.

Raineri, Luca. 'Robot Fighting: Libya and the Wars of the Future'. *Security Praxis*, 13 December 2019. https://securitypraxis.eu/robot-fighting-libya/.

Ramali, Khadeja. 'A Light in Libya's Fog of Disinformation'. *Africa Center for Strategic Studies*, 9 October 2020. https://africacenter.org/spotlight/light-libya-fog-disinformation/.

Rebhi, Hafawa. 'Tunisie: La démocratie à l'épreuve de la décentralisation'. *Middle East Eye*, 31 January 2017. https://www.middleeasteye.net/fr/reportages/tunisie-la-democratie-lepreuve-de-la-decentralisation.

Repucci, Sarah, and Amy Slipowitz. 'Freedom in the World 2021: Democracy Under Siege'. *Freedom House*, 2021. https://freedomhouse.org/report/freedom-world/2021/democracy-under-siege/acknowledgements.

Rettman, Andrew. 'Libya Is Test of EU Geopolitics, Ex-UN Inspector Says'. *EUobserver*, 25 February 2020. https://euobserver.com/foreign/147536.

Riggs-Perla, Joy, Carol Carpenter-Yaman, Leslie B. Curtain, Andrew Kantner, Pinar Senlet, Mona El Shafei, and Mellen Duffy Tanamly. 'Egypt Health and Population Legacy Review'. *USAID*, March 2011. https://pdf.usaid.gov/pdf_docs/PDACR591.pdf.

Roberts, Hugh. 'Demilitarizing Algeria'. *Carnegie Endowment for International Peace*, May 2007. https://carnegieendowment.org/files/cp_86_final1.pdf.

Ronen, Yehudit. 'Libya: Teetering Between War and Diplomacy the Islamic State's Role in Libya's Disintegration'. *Diplomacy and Statecraft* 28, no. 1 (2017): 118–23.
Roser, Max. 'Fertility Rate'. *Our World in Data*, 2014. https://ourworldindata.org/fertility-rate.
'Russia Makes Inroads in North Africa'. *The Washington Institute*, 3 February 2021. https://www.washingtoninstitute.org/policy-analysis/russia-makes-inroads-north-africa.
'Russia on Tunisia's Borders'. *Middle East Monitor*, 14 March 2017. https://www.middleeastmonitor.com/20170314-russia-on-tunisias-borders/.
'Russia Seals $1.5bn Military Jet Deal with Egypt'. *The Times*, 5 February 2021. https://www.thetimes.co.uk/article/2bn-su-35-fighter-jet-order-strengthens-russia-egypt-military-ties-3vt99kprx.
'Russia Threatens to Call on WTO after Mauritania Says It Should Respect Same Conditions as Subsidised EU Fleets'. *Agritrade*, 3 February 2021. https://agritrade.cta.int/Fisheries/Topics/ACP-EU-relations-FPAs/Russia-threatens-to-call-on-WTO-after-Mauritania-says-it-should-respect-same-conditions-as-subsidised-EU-fleets.html.
'Russia to Supply Military Equipment to Tunisia'. *TASS*, 3 February 2021. https://tass.com/russia/748207.
Ryan, Missy, and Gillian Brockell. 'A War Fought, a War Avoided: Libya and Syria Tested Obama's Core Values'. *Washington Post*, 3 June 2016. https://www.washingtonpost.com/graphics/national/obama-legacy/intervention-libya-and-syrian-crisis.html.
Sabry, Mohamed. 'Egypt Thaws Relations with Qatar after Long-Running Feud.' *Al-Monitor*, 8 January 2021. https://www.al-monitor.com/originals/2021/01/egypt-qatar-gulf-rift-reconciliation-muslim-brotherhood.html.
Sadiki, Larbi. 'Regional Development in Tunisia: The Consequences of Multiple Marginalization'. *Brookings Doha Center*, 2019. https://www.brookings.edu/research/regional-development-in-tunisia-the-consequences-of-multiple-marginalization/.
Sadiqi, Fatima, ed. *Women's Movements in Post-'Arab Spring' North Africa*. New York: Palgrave Macmillan, 2016.
Saied, Mohamed. 'Could Israel Help Egypt Break Nile Dam

Deadlock?' *Al-Monitor*, 20 July 2021. https://www.al-monit or.com/originals/2021/07/could-israel-help-egypt-break-ni le-dam-deadlock.

Saleh, Heba. 'Algeria on the Brink as Pandemic and Low Oil Price Take Their Toll'. *Financial Times*, 15 June 2021. https:// www.ft.com/content/07691fbd-fa6c-414d-9299-ce848073 a5d7.

Salime, Zakia. *Between Feminism and Islam: Human Rights and Sharia Law in Morocco*. Minneapolis: University of Minnesota Press, 2011.

Samaha, Nahla. 'Women's Equality: No Longer a Part of Egypt's Constitution'. *Atlantic Council*, 4 December 2012. https:// www.atlanticcouncil.org/blogs/menasource/women-s-equa lity-no-longer-a-part-of-egypt-s-constitution/.

Samraoui, Mohammed. *Chronique des années de sang*. Paris: Denoël, 2003.

'Saudi Arabia to Provide $22 Billion to Morocco's Military Industry'. *Morocco World News*, 7 January 2016. https://www. moroccoworldnews.com/2016/01/176944/saudi-arabia-to- provide-22-billion-to-moroccos-military-industry/.

Sayigh, Yezid. 'Praetorian Spearhead: The Role of the Military in the Evolution of Egypt's State Capitalism 3.0'. *London School of Economics Middle East Centre*, January 2021. http:// eprints.lse.ac.uk/108516/2/PraetorianSpearhead.pdf.

Schilling, Janpeter, and Lisa Krause. 'Climate Change and Conflict in Northern Africa'. *Oxford Bibliographies*, 20 November 2019. https://www.oxfordbibliographies.com/ view/document/obo-9780199363445/obo-9780199363445-00 90.xml.

Schilling, Janpeter, and Lisa Krause. 'Climate Change Vulnerability, Water Resources, and Social Implications in North Africa'. *Regional Environmental Change* 20, no. 15 (2020): 1–12.

Schumacher, Tobias, and Cristian Nitoiu. 'Russia's Foreign Policy towards North Africa in the Wake of the Arab Spring'. *Mediterranean Politics* 20, no. 1 (2015): 97–104.

Scott, James. *Weapons of the Weak: Everyday Forms of Peasant Resistance*. New Haven: Yale University Press, 1985.

Scott, James. *Domination and the Art of Resistance*. New Haven: Yale University Press, 1992.

Seddon, David. 'The Political Economy of Mauritania: An

Introduction'. *Review of African Political Economy* 23, no. 68 (1996): 197–214.

Seif, H. A. 'Contextualizing Gender and Labor: Class, Ethnicity, and Global Politics in the Yemeni Socio-Economy'. In *Women's Rights, Human Rights: International Feminist Perspectives*, ed. Julie Stone Peters and Andrea Wolper, 289–300. New York: Routledge, 1995.

Sellam, Sadek. 'Algérie, des révélations sur le « coup d'état » de 1992'. *Mondafrique*, 15 January 2016. https://mondafrique.com/algerie-des-revelations-sur-le-coup-detat-de-1992/.

Shambaugh, David. *China Goes Global: The Partial Power*, 1st edition. Oxford and New York: Oxford University Press, 2013.

'SheVotes Tunisia: Understanding Barriers to Women's Political Participation'. *International Republican Institute*, 2020. https://www.iri.org/resources/shevotes-examines-barriers-to-womens-political-engagement-in-tunisia/.

Shiferaw, Lidet Tadesse. 'Peace and Security in Africa: Drivers and Implications of North Africa's Southern Gaze'. *European Center for Development Policy Management*, October 2019. https://ecdpm.org/publications/peace-security-africa-drivers-implications-north-africas-southern-gaze/.

Sieverding, Maia. 'The Role of the Care Economy in Promoting Gender Equality: Progress of Women in the Arab States 2020'. *UN Women*, 2020. https://www2.unwomen.org/-/media/field%20office%20arab%20states/attachments/2021/01/unw_erf_report_final_8%20december.pdf?la=en&vs=1828.

Sigillò, Ester, and Damiano De Facci. 'L'économie sociale et solidaire: Une nouvelle économie morale pour la Tunisie? La construction de l'« alternative » à Médenine'. *L'Année du Maghreb* 18, no. 18 (18 June 2018): 51–68.

Singh, Michael. 'Chinese Policy in the Middle East in the Wake of the Arab Uprisings'. In *Toward Well-Oiled Relations? China's Presence in the Middle East Following the Arab Spring*, ed. Niv Horesh, 162–79. New York: Palgrave Macmillan, 2016.

'Sisi Links Political Unrest to Population Growth in Public Address Calling for Birth Control'. *Mada Masr*, 17 February 2021. https://www.madamasr.com/en/2021/02/17/news/politics/sisi-links-political-unrest-to-population-growth-in-public-address-calling-for-birth-control/.

'Sisi Says Egypt's Population Growth Needs to Fall to 400K Annually for 10 Years'. *Egypt Independent*, 10 March 2021. https://egyptindependent.com/sisi-says-egypts-population-growth-needs-to-fall-to-400k-annually-for-10-years/.

'Skills Mismatch and Underemployment: How to Boost Employment of Young Women and Men in Egypt'. *International Labour Organization*, 2015. https://www.ilo.org/wcmsp5/groups/public/---africa/---ro-abidjan/---sro-cairo/documents/publication/wcms_499397.pdf.

Slaughter, Anne-Marie. 'Why Libya Sceptics Were Proved Badly Wrong'. *The Financial Times*, 24 August 2011. https://www.ft.com/content/18cb7f14-ce3c-11e0-99ec-00144feabdc0#axzz1W1l269ak.

'Social Institutions and Gender Index 2019'. *OECD Development Centre*, 2019. https://www.genderindex.org/wp-content/uploads/files/datasheets/2019/MR.pdf.

Sojka, R. E., D. L. Bjorneberg, and J. A. Entry. 'Irrigation: An Historical Perspective'. In *Enyclopedia of Soil Science*, 1st edition, by Rattan Lal, 745–49. New York: Marcel Dekker, 2002.

Soler i Lecha, Eduard. 'Gulf Rivalries Reach North Africa'. In *IEMed Mediterranean Yearbook 2018* (Barcelona: IEMed, 2018).

Souaïdia, Habib. 'Révélations sur le drame d'In-Amenas: Trente otages étrangers tués par l'armée Algérienne, au moins neuf militaires tués'. *Algeria Watch*, 11 February 2013. https://algeria-watch.org/?p=45434.

Souaïdia, Habib. *La sale guerre*. Paris: La Découverte, 2001.

Specia, Megan, and David E. Sanger. 'How the "Libya Model" Became a Sticking Point in North Korea Nuclear Talks'. *The New York Times*, 16 May 2018, sec. World. https://www.nytimes.com/2018/05/16/world/asia/north-korea-libya-model.html.

Springborg, Robert. *Egypt*, 1st edition. Cambridge and Medford: Polity Press, 2017.

Stein, Janet Gross. 'Image, Identity and the Resolution of Violent Conflict'. In *Turbulent Peace: The Challenges of Managing International Conflict*, ed. Chester Crocker, Fen Hampson, and Pamela Aall, 93–111. Washington DC: USIP Press, 2001.

Stepputat, Finn. 'Contemporary Governscapes: Sovereign Practice and Hybrid Orders Beyond the Center'. In *Local Politics and Contemporary Transformations in the Arab World*, ed. Cilja Harders, Anja Hoffmann, and Malika Bouziane, 25–42. New York: Palgrave Macmillan, 2013.

Stonequist, E. V. *The Marginal Man: A Study in Personality and Culture Conflict*. New York: Scribner, 1937.

Stora, Benjamin. *Histoire de l'Algérie de l'indépendance à 1988*. Paris: Collections Repères, La Découverte, 2004.

'Strategic Analysis: Repercussions of Chinese Investments in the Nile River Basin'. *MAX Security Solutions*, n. d. https://www.max-security.com/reports/strategic-analysis-reprecussions-of-chinese-investments-in-the-nile-river-basin/.

'Strategic Cooperation Agreement between Russia and Egypt Comes into Force'. *Egypt Independent*, 12 January 2021, sec. Egypt. https://egyptindependent.com/strategic-cooperation-agreement-between-russia-and-egypt-comes-into-force/.

'Suspension of US Aid to Ethiopia Is Yet Another Example of Trump's Disregard for Africa'. *The Conversation*, 27 September 2020. https://theconversation.com/suspension-of-us-aid-to-ethiopia-is-yet-another-example-of-trumps-disregard-for-africa-146460.

Sutter, John D. 'Slavery's Last Stronghold'. *CNN*, March 2012. http://www.cnn.com/interactive/2012/03/world/mauritania.slaverys.last.stronghold/index.html.

Szakal, Venessa. 'Tunisia's Parched North'. *Nawaat*, 2015. https://nawaat.org/portail/2015/12/29/tunisias-parched-north/.

Takelou, Jean Marie. 'Libya: Vandalism Threatens Large Man-Made River that Supplies the Country'. *Afrik21*, 4 August 2021. https://www.afrik21.africa/en/libya-vandalism-threatens-large-man-made-river-that-supplies-the-country/.

Tannir, Dina, and Vivienne Badaan. 'Women and Participation in the Arab Uprisings: A Struggle for Justice'. *Economic and Social Commission for Western Asia*, 26 December 2013. https://yptoolbox.unescapsdd.org/wp-content/uploads/2017/08/ESCWA_Women-and-Participation-in-the-Arab-Uprisings-A-struggle-for-Justice.pdf.

Tanzi, Vito. 'Pitfalls on the Road to Fiscal Decentralization'. *Carnegie Endowment for International Peace*, 2001. https://carnegieendowment.org/2001/04/26/pitfalls-on-road-to-fiscal-decentralization-pub-688.

Tempest, Rone. 'In Senegal and Mauritania, Ethnic Conflict Rages amid Talk of War'. *Los Angeles Times*, 3 June 1989.

https://www.latimes.com/archives/la-xpm-1989-06-03-mn-831-story.html.

Thames, Frank C., and Margaret S. Williams. *Contagious Representation: Women's Political Representation in Democracies around the World*. New York: New York University Press, 2013.

'The Head of Mission to Mauritanian Elections of 24th June 2019 Briefs the Media on Mauritania Elections'. *African Union*, 24 June 2019. https://au.int/sw/pressreleases/201906 24/head-mission-mauritanian-elections-24th-june-2019-brie fs-media-mauritania.

'The Islamic Republic of Iran's Flavored Condoms, Free Vasectomies, and Gender Reassignment Surgery'. *HuffPost*, 18 June 2014. https://www.huffpost.com/entry/the-islamic-republic-of-i_2_b_5481323.

'The Number of Women in Elected Office Is Rising, but That Hasn't Meant More Power'. *Foreign Policy*, 2 March 2021. https://foreignpolicy.com/2021/03/02/women-elected-office-representation-not-enough/.

'The Pendulum: How Russia Sways Its Way to More Influence in Libya'. *War on the Rocks*, 7 January 2021. https://waron therocks.com/2021/01/the-pendulum-how-russia-sways-its-way-to-more-influence-in-libya/.

'The World Bank in Algeria'. *World Bank*, n. d. https://www.wo rldbank.org/en/country/algeria/overview#1.

Thepaut, Charles. 'A Vanishing West in the Middle East'. *Washington Institute for Near East Policy*, 2022. https://www. washingtoninstitute.org/policy-analysis/vanishing-west-mi ddle-east-recent-history-us-europe-cooperation-region.

'Thousands of Algerians Defy Police to Mark Protest Anniversary'. *France24*, 22 February 2021. https://www.fra nce24.com/en/africa/20210222-thousands-of-algerians-defy-police-to-mark-protest-anniversary.

Tilmatine, Mohand. 'La Kabylie dans le Hirak Algerien: Enjeux et perspectives'. *Hérodote*, no. 180 (January 2021): 32–56.

'TIMELINE: Western Sahara, a 50-Year-Old Dispute'. *Reuters*, 4 January 2008. https://www.reuters.com/article/us-sahara-polisario/timeline-western-sahara-a-50-year-old-dispute-id USL2163728820080104.

'Tiran and Sanafir: Developments, Dynamics and Implications'. *The Tahrir Institute for Middle East Policy*, 9 August 2017.

https://timep.org/wp-content/uploads/2017/08/Tiran-and-Sanafir-Developments-Dynamics-and-Implications-web.pdf.

Tlemçani, Rachid. 'Algeria under Bouteflika: Civil Strife and National Reconciliation'. *Carnegie Endowment for International Peace*, February 2008. https://carnegieendowment.org/files/cmec7_tlemcani_algeria_final.pdf.

Tlemcani, Salima. 'Le Général-major Abderrazak Cherif condamné pour «enrichissement illicite»: 15 ans de réclusion criminelle et confiscation de tous les biens'. *El Watan*, 30 May 2021. https://www.elwatan.com/edition/actualite/15-ans-de-reclusion-criminelle-et-confiscation-de-tous-les-biens-30-05-2021.

Toga, Dawit. 'The African Union and the Libyan Revolution: The Efficacy of the African Peace and Security Architecture'. *World Peace Foundation: African Politics, African Peace*, June 2016. https://sites.tufts.edu/wpf/files/2017/07/12.-AU-and-Libyan-Revolution-D.-Toga.pdf.

Tripp, Aili Mari. 'Women's Mobilisation for Legislative Political Representation in Africa'. *Review of African Political Economy* 43, no. 149 (2 July 2016): 382–99.

Tripp, Aili Mari, and Alice Kang. 'The Global Impact of Quotas: On the Fast Track to Increased Female Legislative Representation'. *Comparative Political Studies* 41, no. 3 (March 2008): 338–61.

'Trump Warns Ethiopia of Egyptian Attack on Dam'. *The Independent*, 24 October 2020. https://www.independent.co.ug/trump-warns-ethiopia-of-egyptian-attack-on-dam/.

'Tunisia'. *International IDEA: Gender Quotas Database*, n. d. https://www.idea.int/data-tools/data/gender-quotas/country-view/284/35.

'Tunisia's Constitution of 2014'. *Constitute Project*, n. d. https://www.constituteproject.org/constitution/Tunisia_2014.pdf.

'Tunisia's Economy Shrank 3% in the First Quarter of 2021'. *Reuters*, 15 May 2021, sec. Africa. https://www.reuters.com/world/africa/tunisias-economy-shrank-3-first-quarter-2021-2021-05-15/.

'Tunisia: Tataouine on Open Strike, Including Oil and Gas Fields'. *Middle East Monitor*, 4 July 2020. https://www.middleeastmonitor.com/20200704-tunisia-tataouine-on-open-strike-including-oil-and-gas-fields/.

'Tunisia: Why the Mataouine Region Struggles with Unrest'. *The North Africa Journal*, 29 June 2020.

'Tunisie en chiffres'. *National Institute of Statistics*, 2021. http://ins.tn/sites/default/files/publication/pdf/tec-newform-2019-v7.pdf.

'Tunisie: Nouveaux heurts à Tataouine où les manifestants réclament des emplois'. *France24*, 2020. https://www.france24.com/fr/20200622-tunisie-nouveaux-heurts-%C3%A0-tataouine-o%C3%B9-les-manifestants-r%C3%A9clament-des-emplois.

'Turkey Says May Begin Oil Exploration under Libya Deal in Three-Four Months'. *Reuters*, 29 May 2020. https://www.reuters.com/article/us-turkey-libya-drilling/turkey-says-may-begin-oil-exploration-under-libya-deal-in-three-four-months-idUSKBN2352EL.

Turki, Sami Yassine, and Eric Verdeil. 'Tunisie; La constitution (du printemps) ouvre le débat sur la décentralisation'. In *Local Governments and Public Goods: Assessing Decentralization in the Arab World*, ed. Mona Harb and Sami Atallah, 11–45. Beirut: Lebanese Center for Policy Studies, 2015.

'UAE Expresses Full Confidence and Support for Tunisia-Statement'. *Reuters*, 28 July 2021. https://www.reuters.com/world/middle-east/uae-expresses-full-confidence-support-tunisia-statement-2021-07-28/.

'UAE Sentences "Coup Plotters" to Jail'. *The Guardian*, 2 July 2013. https://www.theguardian.com/world/2013/jul/02/uae-sentences-coup-plotters-jail.

Vanden, Harry. 'Social Movements, Hegemony, and New Forms of Resistance'. *Latin American Perspectives* 34, no. 2 (March 2007): 17–30.

Vant, Andre, ed. *Marginalité Sociale, Marginalité Spatiale*. Paris: CNRS, 1986.

Villasante-de Beauvais, Mariella. 'Genèse de la hiérarchie sociale du pouvoir politique Bidan selon les traditions orales des Ahl Sidi Mahmud, confédération de l'est Mauritanien'. *Cahiers d'Études Africaines* 147, no. 3 (1997): 587–633.

'Vision and Proposed Actions Outlined on Jointly Building Silk Road Economic Belt and 21st-Century Maritime Silk Road'. *China Daily*, 30 March 2015. http://language.chinadaily.com.cn/2015-03/30/content_19950951.htm.

Vittori, Jodi. 'Mitigating Patronage and Personal Enrichment in U.S. Arms Sales'. In *From Hardware to Holism: Rebalancing America's Security Engagement with the Arab States*, ed. Michele Dunne and Frederic Wehrey. *Carnegie Endowment for International Peace*, 18 May 2021. https://carnegieendowment.org/2021/05/18/from-hardware-to-holism-rebalancing-america-s-security-engagement-with-arab-states-pub-84520.

Volkmann, Elizia. 'Activists Call Tunisia's First Female Prime Minister Mere Distraction'. *Al-Monitor*, October 2021. https://www.al-monitor.com/originals/2021/10/activists-call-tunisias-first-female-prime-minister-mere-distraction.

Walsh, Declan. 'Where Did Chad Rebels Prepare for Their Own War? In Libya'. *The New York Times*, 22 April 2021. https://www.nytimes.com/2021/04/22/world/africa/chad-rebels.html.

'Water Accounting in the Nile River Basin: Remote Sensing for Water Productivity'. *Food and Agriculture Organization of the United Nations* and *IHE Delft Institute for Water Education: WaPOR Water Accounting Series*, 2020. https://www.fao.org/3/ca9895en/ca9895en.pdf.

'We Can Expect Stronger Algeria-Iran Ties as Israel Plans to Establish a Base in Morocco'. *Middle East Monitor*, 23 November 2021. https://www.middleeastmonitor.com/20211123-we-can-expect-stronger-algeria-iran-ties-as-israel-plans-to-establish-a-base-in-morocco/.

'"We Do Unreasonable Things Here": Torture and National Security in al-Sisi's Egypt'. *Human Rights Watch*, 5 September 2017. https://www.hrw.org/report/2017/09/05/we-do-unreasonable-things-here/torture-and-national-security-al-sisis-egypt.

Wehrey, Frederic, and Peter Cole. 'Building Libya's Security Sector'. *Carnegie Endowment for International Peace*, 6 August 2013. https://carnegieendowment.org/2013/08/06/building-libya-s-security-sector-pub-52603.

Wehrey, Frederic. 'This War Is Out of Our Hands: The Internationalization of Libya's Post-2011 Conflicts from Proxies to Boots on the Ground'. *Center for New America Studies*, September 2020. https://www.newamerica.org/international-security/reports/this-war-is-out-of-our-hands/

Wehrey, Frederic. *The Burning Shores: Inside the Battle for the New Libya*. New York: Farrar, Straus, & Giroux, 2018.

Wehrey, Frederic. 'Bleeding Fuel'. *Carnegie Endowment for International Peace: Diwan*, 14 June 2017. https://carnegie-mec.org/diwan/71223.
Wehrey, Frederic. 'Control and Contain: Mauritania's Clerics and the Strategy Against Violent Extremism'. *Carnegie Endowment for International Peace*, 29 March 2019. https://carnegieendowment.org/2019/03/29/control-and-contain-mauritania-s-clerics-and-strategy-against-violent-extremism-pub-78729.
Wehrey, Frederic. 'Libyans Are Winning the Battle Against the Islamic State'. *Foreign Policy*, 30 June 2016. https://foreignpolicy.com/2016/06/30/libyans-are-winning-the-battle-against-the-islamic-state/.
Wehrey, Frederic. 'Testimony in "The Crisis in Libya": Next Steps and U.S'. In *Foreign Policy Options: Hearing before the Committee on Foreign Relations of the United States Senate, 115th Congress*, 2017. https://www.govinfo.gov/content/pkg/CHRG-115shrg40164/html/CHRG-115shrg40164.htm.
Wehrey, Frederic. 'When the Islamic State Came to Libya'. *The Atlantic*, 10 February 2018. https://www.theatlantic.com/international/archive/2018/02/isis-libya-hiftar-al-qaeda-syria/552419/.
Wehrey, Frederic. 'Winning the Peace: Armed Groups and Security Sector Challenges'. *Brookings Institution* and *Crisis Response Council*, 3 July 2021. https://www.youtube.com/watch?v=JenfLeN-Mv4&feature=emb_title.
Weiss, Jacob Lees. 'Algerian Constitutional Amendments Create Conditions for Military Intervention in Libya'. *Terrorism Monitor* 18, no. 22 (3 December 2020). https://jamestown.org/program/algerian-constitutional-amendments-create-conditions-for-military-intervention-in-libya/.
Wesselink, Edzard, and Ron Boschma. 'European Neighbourhood Policy: Its History, Structure, and Implemented Policy Measures'. *Journal of Economic and Human Geography* 108, no. 1 (February 2017): 4–20.
Wezeman, Pieter D., Dr Aude Fleurant, Alexandra Kuimova, Dr Diego Lopes da Silva, Dr Nan Tian, and Siemon T. Wezeman. 'Trends in International Arms Transfers, 2019'. *SIPRI Arms Transfers Database*, March 2020. https://sipri.org/sites/default/files/2020-03/fs_2003_at_2019.pdf.

'What Are the 13 Demands Given to Qatar?' *Gulf News*, 23 June 2017. https://gulfnews.com/world/gulf/qatar/what-are-the-13-demands-given-to-qatar-1.2048118.

'"What Do I Care If You Die?" Negligence and Denial of Health Care in Egyptian Prisons'. *Amnesty International*, 25 January 2021. https://www.amnesty.org/en/documents/mde12/3538/2021/en/.

'What Does Italy Import?' *Observatory of Economic Complexity*, 2010. https://oec.world/en/visualize/tree_map/hs92/import/ita/all/show/2018/.

Wiese, Inken, and Sebastian Sons. 'Engagement of Arab Gulf States in Egypt and Tunisia: Rationale and Implications'. *DGAP*, 13 October 2020. https://dgap.org/en/events/engagement-arab-gulf-states-egypt-and-tunisia-rationale-and-implications.

Wiley, Katherine Ann. 'Women in Mauritania'. *Oxford Research Encyclopedia of African History*, 30 July 2020. https://doi.org/10.1093/acrefore/9780190277734.013.529.

Wiley, Katherine Ann. *Work, Social Status, and Gender in Post-Slavery Mauritania*. Bloomington: Indiana University Press, 2018.

Wilson, Andrew. 'Foggara Irrigation and Early State Formation in the Libyan Sahara: The Garamantes of Fazzan'. *Schriftenreihe der Frontinus-Gesellschaft* 26 (2005): 223–34.

Wintour, Patrick. 'Turkish Troops Deploy to Libya to Prop up Embattled Government'. *The Guardian*, 5 January 2020. https://www.theguardian.com/world/2020/jan/05/turkish-troops-deploy-to-libya-to-prop-up-embattled-government.

Wittes, Tamara Cofman. 'The States We Are in: Existing Models for Governance in the Middle East'. In *Politics, Governance, and State-Society Relations*, convened by Tamara Cofman Wittes. *Brookings Institution*, 2016. https://www.brookings.edu/wp-content/uploads/2016/11/cmep_201611_mest_paper_final.pdf.

'Women and Participation in the Arab Uprisings A Struggle for Justice'. *Economic and Social Commission for Western Asia*, August 2017. https://yptoolbox.unescapsdd.org/wp-content/uploads/2017/08/ESCWA_Women-and-Participation-in-the-Arab-Uprisings-A-struggle-for-Justice.pdf.

'Women and the Arab Spring: Taking Their Place?' *Fédération internationale des ligues des droits de l'homme*, 8 March 2012. https://www.fidh.org/IMG/pdf/femmesarabangbassdef.pdf.

'Women's Political Participation in Egypt: Barriers, Opportunities and Gender Sensitivity of Select Political Institutions'. *OECD*, July 2018. https://www.oecd.org/mena/governance/womens-political-participation-in-egypt.pdf.

World Bank. *Women, Business and the Law 2020*. N. p.: The World Bank, 2020.

World Bank. *Women, Business and the Law 2021*. N. p.: The World Bank, 2021.

'World Development Indicators'. *DataBank*, n. d. https://databank.worldbank.org/reports.aspx?source=2&series=SL.TLF.CACT.FE.ZS&country=#.

'World Report 2021: Mauritania'. *Human Rights Watch*, 2021. https://www.hrw.org/world-report/2021/country-chapters/mauritania#.

Yerkes, Sarah, and Marwan Muasher. 'Decentralization in Tunisia: Empowering Towns, Engaging People'. *Carnegie Endowment for International Peace*, 2018. https://carnegieendowment.org/2018/05/17/decentralization-in-tunisia-empowering-towns-engaging-people-pub-76376.

Youngs, Richard. *The European Union and Global Politics*. London: Red Globe Press, 2021.

Youssef, Adhan. 'Egypt's Pledge to Send Troops Was Not in Context of Yemen War: Saudi General'. *Daily News Egypt*, 18 April 2017. https://dailynewsegypt.com/2017/04/18/egypts-pledge-send-troops-not-context-yemen-war-saudi-general/.

Zaghal, Malika. 'Religion et politique au Maroc aujourd'hui'. *Institut Francais des Relations Internationales*, 2005. https://www.ifri.org/fr/publications/notes-de-lifri/religion-politique-maroc-aujourdhui.

Zelin, Aaron Y. 'When Jihadists Learn How to Help'. *The Washington Post*, 7 May 2014. https://www.washingtonpost.com/news/monkey-cage/wp/2014/05/07/when-jihadists-learn-how-to-help/.

Zisenwine, Daniel. 'Mauritania's Democratic Transition: A Regional Model for Political Reform?' *The Journal of North African Studies* 12, no. 4 (1 December 2007): 481–99.

'ВЗГЛЯД / «Татнефть» Решила Возобновить Геологоразведку в Ливии и Сирии: Новости Дня'. https://vz.ru/news/2020/12/18/1076381.html.

'«Проект»: В Ливии служит группировка российских военных во главе с замкомандующего ВДВ'. *БИЗНЕС Online*, 2019. https://www.business-gazeta.ru/news/438497.

Index

Note: f indicates a figure, n indicates a note

AQIM *see* al-Qa'ida in the Islamic Maghreb
Abdel Fattah, Hadia, 223
Abderrahim, Tasnim, 239
Abu-Lughod, Lila, 202
Addi, Lahouari, 177
African Commission on Human and People's Rights, 63
African Continental Free Trade Area (AFCFTA), 249
African Union (AU), 5, 63, 64, 94, 238, 249, 260; *see also* Organisation of African Unity
African Union Election Observer Mission (AUEOM), 138
Ahmed, Abiy, 63
Ahmed, Leila, 201
Ahmida, Ali Abdullatif, 35n4
Ait-Zai, Nadia, 212
Akrimi, Yasmine, 138, 139–40
Algeria
  and African Union, 5, 253
  Algerie News, 180
  corruption, 178, 179, 180, 181, 183–4
  counterterrorism, 5, 182
  coup (1992), 172
  COVID-19 pandemic, 185, 186
  democracy, 170, 172, 187, 188
  East–West Highway Project, 180
  economy, 178, 186, 188, 248
  elections, 172, 173, 176, 180, 183, 184, 185
  elites, 179
  and European Union, 235
  Family Code, 204, 220
  foreign policy, 173, 247–8
  gas, 5, 178, 256
  gender equality, 198, 203–4, 212, 214, 218–21
  High Council of State, 173
  human rights, 174–5
  hydrocarbons, 169, 178, 181, 182, 188
  intelligence services, 173, 176, 177–80, 181, 182
  Islamists, 173, 175, 181, 186; Islamic Salvation Front (FIS), 172, 186
  labour force, 195–6
  military establishment, 168, 169–74, 176, 178, 184, 185–8
  and Morocco, 188, 248
  National Democratic Rally (RND), 173

Algeria (*cont.*)
  National Liberation Front (FLN), 171, 176, 204
  national reconciliation, 174–5
  'Nida 22' initiative, 186
  oil, 178, 182, 247–8
  People's National Army: General Staff (ANP), 172, 173, 174, 176, 177, 181, 182, 183
  protests, 183, 184; Hirak protest movement, 168, 169, 183, 185, 186, 187, 188, 286; Kabylia, 175
  as a republic, 76
  and Russia, 256
  and security, 253
  and Sub-Saharan Africa, 250, 252–3
  and terrorism, 175, 180, 181
  Tindouf, 92
  wars against France, 171
  El Watan (newspaper), 180
  and Western Sahara, 90, 93
Alterman, Jon, 255
Amazigh (Berbers), 32, 79, 81, 83, 107–8, 183, 184
Amin, Qasim, 200, 201
Anderson, Lisa, 16
Ansar al-Sharia, 23
Arab Maghreb Union (AMU), 147
Arab Spring/Arab Uprisings, 1, 2, 5–6, 74, 75, 102, 168
  Gulf States and, 241
  Russia and, 256
  United States and, 237
  women and, 208–9, 211, 222
  Arabic Network for Human Rights Information (ANHRI), 221
Assad, Ragui, 46
Attalah, Sami, 104
Aty, Mohamed Abdel, 65

Baccouche, Neji, 103
Badaan, Vivienne, 209
Bahrain
  and Israel, 59
  monarchy, 75–6
  and United Arab Emirates, 244
  see also Gulf States
Bales, Kevin, 151–2
Barth, May, 138, 139–40
al-Bashir, Omar, 63
Bayat, Asef, 78
Belschner, Jana, 217
Ben Ali, Zine el Abidine, 105, 106, 108
Ben Bella, President Ahmed, 170
Ben Mhenni, Lina, 208
Ben Shitrit, Lihi, 217–18
Ben Youssef, Salah, 103
Bendjedid, President Chadli, 171–2
Benflis, Ali, 176
Benkirane, Abdelilah, 84, 85, 87–8
Bensaad, Ali, 178–9
Berbers *see* Amazigh
Biden, President Joseph, 59, 64, 95, 237, 261, 262
bin Zayed, Sheikh Abdullah, 243
bin Zayed, Mohammed, 58
Bouazizi, Mohamed, 83, 108
Boudiaf, Mohamed, 172–3, 180
Bouganour, Ismail, 156, 157
Boumédiène, Houari, 170–1
Bourguiba, President Habib, 103, 104, 199
Bouteflika, President Abdelaziz, 168, 169–70, 174–6, 177–8, 179, 180, 181–2, 183, 252
Bouteflika, Said, 179
Britain
  Egypt: occupation of, 201
  and Libya, 15, 16, 22
  women's suffrage, 212
Bush, President George W., 237

INDEX 327

Cafiero, Giorgio, 244, 247
Carothers, Thomas, 261
Ceuta, 94
Chad
  Chadian Front for Change and Concord in Chad (FACT), 20
  and Libya, 19
Chahed, Youssef, 251-2
Charrad, Mounira, 195, 198, 199, 204, 205
Chayes, Sarah, 2
Chengriha, Major General Said, 185
Cheriet, Bouthina, 204
Cherif, General Abderrazak, 179
China
  Belt and Road Initiative (BRI), 240, 253
  China-Arab States Cooperation Forum, 254
  Confucius Institutes, 255
  economic relationships, 254-5
  and Ethiopia, 51
  and global power competition, 255-6
  influence of, 2, 5, 239-40, 259, 260, 263
  and Morocco, 94, 253-4
  and tourism, 254
Chomiak, Laryssa, 104
Ciavolella, Riccardo, 154
civil society organisations (CSOs), 119, 222
climate change, 31-3, 127, 262, 263
colonialism, 76
  Egypt, 200
  Morocco, 92, 206
  Tunisia, 103, 198-9
Cook, Steven, 237-8
Cook-Huffman, Celia, 154
corruption, 122
  Algeria, 178, 179, 180, 181, 183-4
  and gender, 195
  Mauritania, 140, 143-4
COVID-19 pandemic, 1
  Algeria, 185, 186
  Egypt, 48, 246
  and gender equality, 211-12, 224
  Libya, 34
  Mauritania, 141
  Tunisia, 2, 101, 115, 116-18, 120

Dahlerup, Drude, 211
Darhour, Hanane, 211
Deby, President Idris, 20
democracy, 168, 209, 237, 243, 261
  Algeria, 170, 172, 186, 187, 188
  Mauritania, 137, 139, 156-7, 158
  Tunisia, 2, 118, 121, 123, 137, 199, 200, 218
Democratic Republic of Congo, 64
Diallo, Garba, 155
drones, 14, 20, 59
Dworkin, Anthony, 250, 251

Economic Community of West African States (ECOWAS), 251
education
  Algeria, 171
  and economic growth, 194, 195
  Egypt, 44, 46, 49, 53, 58, 66, 201, 223, 257
  and gender, 3, 194, 195, 196, 197, 216, 217
  Libya, 198, 202
  Mauritania, 143, 152, 154
  Tunisia, 109, 110, 111, 112f, 124
Egypt
  and African states, 62

Egypt (*cont.*)
  and African Union, 5
  agriculture, 50
  air power, 59
  Arab Spring, 208
  brain drain, 54
  colonialism, 200
  contraception, 47
  COVID-19 pandemic, 49, 246
  Dabaa nuclear power plant, 257–8
  demography, 44–8
  economy, 48–9, 54–7
  education, 44, 46, 49, 53, 58, 66, 201, 223, 257
  elites, 53, 54
  employment, 44, 46, 48–9, 51
  and European Union, 236
  external patrons, 43
  foreign debt, 57
  gender equality, 44, 197, 198, 200–2, 223
  gender quotas, 214–15
  gendered violence, 209
  global challenges to, 3
  global role, 57–65
  governance challenges, 52–7
  government, 43
  and Gulf States, 58–61, 246, 260
  human rights, 53, 63, 221
  internal challenges, 43–57, 66
  and Iraq, 61
  Islamists, 42–3, 75; *see also* Muslim Brotherhood
  and Jordan, 61
  and Libya, 19, 22, 60–1
  migration from, 260
  military, 43, 258
  Muslim Brotherhood, 18, 45, 221
  pan-Arabism, 16
  and peace negotiations, 5
  population, 42, 44–5, 52, 66
  and Qatar, 246
  regional role, 42–3, 57, 61
  as a republic, 76
  and Russia, 257–8
  Suez Canal, 42, 54–5, 257
  and Tunisia, 244
  and Turkey, 60–1, 249
  United States and, 5–6, 45–6, 237, 238, 239
  war with Yemen, 60
  water supply, 43, 44, 49–52, 66; Aswan Dam, 50, 52; Grand Ethiopian Renaissance Dam (GERD), 51, 52, 61–2, 63, 64–5, 238, 239
  weapons purchases, 56
Elguettaa, Belkacem, 179
Eltahir, Elfatih, 52
energy, 5, 28, 29, 30, 49, 54, 169, 180, 181, 236, 256, 258; *see also* gas; hydrocarbons; oil
Entelis, John, 173, 184
Erdoğan, President Recep Yayyip, 61, 249
Essebsi, President Beji Caid, 125, 222, 242
Ethiopia: Grand Ethiopian Renaissance Dam (GERD), 43, 51, 52, 61–2, 64–5, 238, 239, 260
Europe
  influence of, 263
  migration to, 2–3, 4–5, 6, 14, 25–8, 239, 259, 262
  and United States, 261–2
European Union, 234, 235, 236, 238, 239, 254, 259
  and Algeria, 235
  Barcelona Process, 234–5
  and Egypt, 47, 236
  European Neighbourhood Policy (ENP), 235–6
  and Morocco, 93, 93–4, 95

and Tunisia, 117
see also France; Germany; Italy; Spain

Fahmy, Nabil, 65
Faisal bin Farhan, Prince, of Saudi Arabia, 243
Fakhfakh, Elyes, 116, 120
al-Faran, Colonel Ali Mohamed, 244
feminism
  and Arab Spring, 208–9
  Egypt, 200, 201
  Libya, 202
  Morocco, 205–6
  state, 201–2
  Tunisia, 200
  see also gender equality
Fenton-Harvey, Jonathan, 243
Ferguson, James, 28
Fernandez-Molina, Irene, 4
Fikri, Mohsin, 81–2
Fodil, General Saidi, 180
France, 235, 236
  and Algeria, 171, 172, 203
  colonial legacy, 236
  and Egypt, 43, 56
  and gender, 196f, 197f
  and Libya, 15, 19, 20, 24, 60, 238, 246
  and Mauritania, 206
  and Morocco, 76
  and Tunisia, 103, 117, 118, 198, 199
  and Western Sahara, 238

G5 Sahel, 146, 252
Gadaffi, Muammar *see* Qadhafi, Muammar
Gaïd Salah, Ahmed, 168, 176, 177, 181, 182, 183, 184, 185, 186, 187
gas
  Algeria, 178, 256

European trade, 236
  Mauritania, 141
  Russia, 256
  Tunisia, 113, 114, 115, 116
Gaub, Florence, 241
gender equality, 3–4
  Algeria, 198, 203–4, 212, 214, 218, 219–20, 220–1
  and Arab Spring, 208–9, 211, 222
  civil society and, 222–3, 224–5
  COVID-19 pandemic effects, 211–12, 224
  and economic growth, 195
  Egypt, 44, 197, 198, 200–2, 214–15, 221, 223
  gender quotas, 213–18, 222
  Global Gender Gap index, 196
  Libya, 198, 202–3, 215, 219
  Mauritania, 152–3, 155–6, 197, 198, 206–8, 215–16, 220
  Morocco, 197, 198, 205–6, 215, 219–20, 222
  Rwanda, 217
  and slavery, 152–3
  Tunisia, 198–200, 213, 216, 217, 218–19, 220, 222
Germany, 236
  and Libya, 238
  and Morocco, 94
Ghafar, Adel Abdel, 235
El-Ghoul, Dhaou, 116
Gulf Cooperation Council (GCC), 240–1, 242, 244
Gulf States, 240–9, 259–60
  and Egypt, 65–6, 260
  and Libya, 260
  and Mauritania, 246–7
  migration to, 260
  monarchies, 76
  see also Bahrain; Iraq; Kuwait; Qatar; Saudi Arabia; United Arab Emirates
Gupta, Akhil, 28

Gurr, Ted Robert, 166n112
Gwirah, President Ahmed, 108

Haddad, Radhia, 199
Haftar, Khalifa, 19, 20, 24, 25, 30, 32, 60, 245–6, 257
Hamad bin 'Issa al-Khalifa, King of Bahrain, 76
Hammami, Mokhtar, 118–19
Harb, Mona, 104
Harchaoui, Jalel, 257
Hassan II, King of Morocco, 244
Hatem, Mervat, 201
Hill, Thomas, 6
Huber, Daniela, 102
human rights
 African Commission on Human and People's Rights, 63
 Algeria, 174–5
 Arabic Network for Human Rights Information (ANHRI), 221
 Egypt, 53, 221
 Libya, 20, 22
 Mauritania, 136
 and migration, 27, 262
 Tunisia, 200
 Western Sahara, 91

Ibrahim, Yahaya, 140
identity, 154
Idris Al-Senussi, King of Libya, 16, 29, 202
immigration *see* migration
International Monetary Fund, 65, 109, 117, 142, 246
Iran
 contraception, 47–8
 Gulf States and, 248, 249
 and Iraq, 61
Iraq, 61, 76; *see also* Gulf States
Islam
 and gender equality, 197; Algeria, 204; Egypt, 201; Libya, 203; Morocco, 205, 206; Tunisia, 198–9
 Mauritania, 144–5, 146, 152, 206
 see also Salafism; Sufism
Islamic Salvation Front (FIS), 172, 186
Islamic State, 3, 6, 14, 22, 23–5
Islamists
 Algeria, 173, 175, 181, 186
 Gulf States, 242
 Libya, 19, 23, 219
 Mauritania, 145
 Morocco, 74
 Qatar, 241
 Saudi Arabia, 241
 see also Islamic State; Muslim Brotherhood
Israel, 5, 57, 58, 59, 63, 64, 95, 239, 248
Italo-Turkish War, 12
Italy, 236
 and Libya, 15
 and migration, 26–7
 and oil, 30

Jacobs, Anna, 235
Jalalzai, Farida, 217
Jathran, Ibrahim, 30
Al Jazeera network, 241
Jiddou, Cheikh, 149
Jordan
 and Egypt, 61
 and Gulf Cooperation Council, 244
 monarchy, 75, 76
Jourde, Cédric, 144, 148, 152–3
journalists: harassment of, 149

Kafi, Colonel Ali, 173
Kang, Alice, 212, 222
Kemal, Lorenzo, 102
Khalil, Andrea, 209

Khan, Sulmaan, 255
al-Khattabi, Abdelkrim, 82
Kherigi, Intissar, 103, 108, 120, 122
Koundouno, Tamba François, 258
Krafft, Caroline, 46
Krook, Mona Lena, 213, 217
Kuwait: and Egypt, 58, 246; *see also* Gulf States

Lamari, Mohamed, 175, 176, 180
Langhi, Zahra, 219
Lazreg, Marina, 203
Lemrabot Sidi Mahmud (LSM), 151
liberal interventionism, 13
Libya
   and African Union, 250
   agriculture, 32, 33
   Arab Spring, 208
   arms, 21–2, 27
   Benghazi, 19, 22, 23, 24, 27
   civil war, 19–20, 22, 23, 75, 238
   and climate change, 31–3
   and counterterrorism, 23, 24–5
   COVID-19 pandemic, 34
   Cyrenaica, 12, 31, 36n12
   Derna, 22, 23
   divisions, 17
   and Egypt, 19, 22, 60
   elections, 17–18
   elites, 12, 16–17, 20, 25–6, 34
   external powers, 14–20, 34
   extremism, 22; *see also* Islamists
   female labour force, 195
   Fezzan, 23, 25, 31, 36n14
   gender equality, 198, 202–3, 215, 219
   global challenges to, 3, 34
   global significance of, 13
   Government of National Accord (GNA), 25, 245
   Gulf States and, 260
   human rights, 20, 22
   Islamists, 23–4, 25; Islamic State, 14, 23–4, 24–5
   media, 18
   and migration, 14, 25–8, 106
   monarchy, 202
   Muntaisr clan, 36n12
   name origins, 12
   and North Korea, 13
   oil, 16, 28–31, 33, 236, 245
   and Russia, 19, 20, 257
   Sanussis, 36n12, 36n14
   and Saudi Arabia, 245
   Second World War, 12, 15
   security, 18
   Sirte, 24, 25, 30
   strategic significance of, 12
   Tripoli, 30, 60, 245, 257; Haftar's attack on (2019), 19; Islamic State, 23; liberation (2011), 17; unity government, 19; water supplies, 32
   Tripolitania, 15
   Tuareg separatists, 21
   and United Arab Emirates, 245
   and water, 31–3
Lindsey, Ursula, 56

Macron, President Emmanuel, 126
Mahfouz, Asmaa, 208
al-Makahleh, Shehab, 247
Mali, 21, 147–8
Malka, Haim, 4–5
Mandour, Maged, 56
Marrakchi, Afef Hammami, 117
Marzouki, President Moncef, 251
Matta, Samer, 140
Mauritania
   25 February movement, 139, 157, 158
   Arabisation process, 154

Mauritania (*cont.*)
  censorship, 149
  corruption, 140, 143–4
  coups d'état, 136–40
  COVID-19 pandemic, 141
  democracy, 139, 156–7, 158
  demography, 207–8
  economy, 137, 139, 140–4, 208
  education, 154
  elections, 137, 138, 149, 157
  elites, 141
  environmental issues, 135, 141–2
  ethnic and racial divisions, 140, 149–50, 207
  fishing, 135
  gender equality, 152–4, 155–6, 197, 198, 206–8, 220
  gender quotas, 215–16
  and Gulf States, 246–7
  human rights, 136, 148–56
  insecurity, 144–8
  Islam, 144–5, 146
  and Mali, 147–8
  marginalised groups, 153–6
  military rule, 135, 136, 138–40
  natural resources, 141
  oil, 141
  and Qatar, 247
  reforms, 137, 142, 158
  regional geopolitics, 146–8
  religious extremism, 145
  and Russia, 258
  and Saudi Arabia, 246–7
  and Senegal, 147
  slavery, 149, 150–3, 207
  and Sub-Saharan Africa, 252
  terrorism, 139
  transition, 2–3
  and Western Sahara, 90
Mechichi, Hichem, 116
Mediène, General Mohamed 'Toufik', 173, 176, 177, 179–80, 181, 182

Mediterranean, 238
  gas, 236
  and migration, 14, 26
  oil rights, 245
  strategic significance, 42, 262
  Union for the Mediterranean, 235
Mernissi, Fatima, 197
Messaoud, Boubacar, 151
migration
  to Ceuta, 94
  from Egypt, 260
  to Europe, 4–5, 26, 27, 239
  to Gulf States, 260
  and human rights, 27, 262
  International Organization for Migration (IOM), 39n57
  Libya and, 14, 25–8, 106
  from Tunisia, 106, 116–17
  United States and, 239
Mint Ahmed, Khadijetou, 206–7
Moghadam, Valentine, 194
Mohammed VI, King of Morocco, 78, 79, 80, 81, 82, 83, 85, 86, 87, 94–5, 205, 258
Mohammed Bin Salman, Crown Prince of Saudi Arabia, 242, 247, 248
Mohammed Bin Zayed, Crown Prince of Abu Dhabi, 249
monarchies, 75–6; *see also under* Morocco
Moors, 136, 140, 148, 149, 150, 151, 155, 160n25, 164n86
Morocco
  20 February movement, 77, 78–80, 81, 83, 84
  Africa strategy, 94–5
  and Algeria, 188, 248
  and China, 94, 253–4
  civil liberties, 82–3
  colonialism, 92, 206
  elections, 80, 87, 88
  elites, 85

and European Union, 93–4, 235
family law, 205
foreign policy, 5, 74–5, 90
gender equality, 197, 198, 205–6, 219–20, 222
gender quotas, 215
and Global Counterterrorism Forum, 252
and Gulf Cooperation Council, 244
al-Hoceima, 81–2, 83, 84
and Israel, 58, 95
Makhzen, 77, 81, 82, 83, 87, 88
monarchy, 74, 75, 76–8, 79, 80, 81, 82, 83–4, 85–7, 89, 90, 96; *see also* Hassan II, King of Morocco; Mohammed VI, King of Morocco,
Party of Justice and Development (PJD), 74, 84, 85, 87–90
political contestation, 90
political participation, 84
protests, 81, 95–6; Hirak, 74, 81–5, 86
and Qatar, 245
Rabat, 82
Rally of National Independents (RNI), 89
reforms, 74, 79–80, 83
Rif, 82, 83
and Russia, 258
and Saudi Arabia, 244, 245
social activism, 84–5
Social Union of Popular Forces (USFP), 89
and Sub-Saharan Africa, 250, 251
Tanger Med Port, 94
and United Arab Emirates, 244, 245
wealth gap, 83

and Western Sahara conflict, 90–5
Morsi, President Mohamed, 57, 58, 61, 62, 64, 221, 248
Mouaker, Riadh, 109
Mubarak, President Hosni, 6, 42, 43, 48, 53, 54, 57, 64, 201, 202, 221, 240, 246
Mubarak, Suzanne, 202
Muslim Brotherhood, 18, 45, 221, 241, 246

al-Nahyan, Sheikh Khalifa bin Zayed, 247
Nasser, President Gamal Abdel, 57, 62, 198, 201
NATO, 13, 17, 20, 27, 60, 250, 255, 259, 262
N'Daiye, Boubacar, 136, 137
Nezzar, Major General Khaled, 172
Nikiel, Catherine, 52
Nile river 42, 50, 51, 52, 63, 64, 65, 66
  Nile Basin Initiative, 62
  see also Ethiopia: Grand Ethiopian Renaissance Dam
Norris, Pippa, 210, 211, 216
North Korea, 13

Obama, President Barack, 5–6, 13, 24, 237
O'Brien, Diana, 213
Occhiuto, Antonio, 244
oil, 2, 65, 66, 76, 241, 245, 260
  Algeria, 9, 174, 178, 179, 181, 182, 186, 247–8, 252
  Libya, 6, 7, 12, 16, 28–31, 33, 34, 236, 245
  Mauritania, 2, 140, 141
  Mediterranean, 245
  Russia and, 30
  Tunisia, 113, 114, 115, 116
  United Arab Emirates and, 30

Organisation of African Unity (OAU), 251; *see also* African Union
Organisation of Petroleum Exporting Countries (OPEC), 247–8
Othmani, Saadeddine, 87
Ottoman Empire, 12, 15; *see also* Turkey
Ouaissa, Rachid, 178
Ould Abdel Aziz, President Mohamed, 138, 143–4
Ould Boubacar, Mohamed, 138
Ould Cheikh, President Abdallahi, Sidi, 137
Ould Cheikh, Abdel Wedoud, 156
Ould Daddah, President Moktar, 136, 147
Ould Dah Abeid, Biram, 138
Ould Ghazouani, President Mohamed, 138, 146, 149, 153, 247
Ould Haidalla, Colonel Mohamed Khouna, 137
Ould Louly, Lieutenant Colonel Mohamed, 136–7
Ould Salek, Colonel Mustafa, 136
Ould Sid Ahmed Taya, President Maaouya, 137, 206
Ouyahia, Ahmed, 183

Paal, Doug, 253
pan-Arabism, 16
Paoletti, Emanuela, 26
Pazzanita, Anthony, 137, 155
Peck, Sarah, 2
Ping, Jean, 250
POLISARIO Front, 90, 91, 92, 93, 94, 137, 147, 244
Press, Benjamin, 261
Prud'homme, Rémy, 123
Putin, President Vladimir, 256

Qadhafi, Muammar, 8, 12–13, 14, 16, 17, 23, 29, 30, 219, 240, 257
  African Union's support for, 250
  and dissent, 22, 202–3
  and gender equality, 203
  and migration, 25, 26–7
  and terrorism, 16, 21, 22
  and water supply, 31–2
al-Qa'ida in the Islamic Maghreb (AQIM), 139, 145–6
Qatar
  and Algeria, 247, 248
  and Arab Spring, 241, 243
  boycott of, 59–60
  and Egypt, 58, 246
  influence of, 3
  and Islamism, 241
  and Libya, 18, 19, 245–6
  and Mauritania, 247
  and Morocco, 245
  and protest, 241
  and Tunisia, 242
  and Turkey, 241–2, 248–9
  and United Arab Emirates, 59, 244, 246
  see also Gulf Cooperation Council; Gulf States

Roberts, Hugh, 175
Russia
  and Algeria, 247, 256
  and Egypt, 257–8
  influence of, 2, 3, 5, 239–40, 256–8, 260, 263
  and Libya, 19, 20, 257
  and Mauritania, 258
  and Morocco, 258
  and oil, 30
  and Tunisia, 258
  see also Soviet Union
Rwanda, 217

Sadat, President Anwar, 57, 201, 214
Sadiki, Larbi, 101, 106, 127
Sahel, 5, 28, 106, 147, 149, 158, 252
  drought, 142
  terrorism, 20, 93, 144, 175, 228
Sahrawi Arab Democratic Republic (SADR), 90, 251
Sahrawi people, 5, 90, 91, 92, 251
Saied, President Kais, 113, 115, 125, 126, 127, 218, 222, 243, 244
Salafism, 145
Salime, Zakia, 194, 197, 205
Salman, King of Saudi Arabia, 58
Sanafir (Red Sea island), 58–9
Saudi Arabia, 2, 4
  and Arab Spring, 241
  and Egypt, 18, 58–9, 64, 246
  and Ethiopia, 64
  and Libya, 16, 19, 245
  and Mauritania, 246–7
  and Morocco, 244, 245, 248
  and Qatar, 59
  Sahwa movement, 241
  and Sudan, 63, 64
  and Tunisia, 2, 242, 243
  see also Gulf States
Seddon, David, 149–51
Shapiro, Jeremy, 261
Shiferaw, Lidet Tadesse, 5
Singh, Michael, 254–5
al-Sisi, President Abdel Fattah
  and African diplomacy and security, 62, 63
  and African Union (AU), 249
  and finance, 54, 55, 56–7, 58
  foreign policy, 57
  and Grand Ethiopian Renaissance Dam, 62, 64, 65
  and Gulf States, 246
  and human rights, 53, 75
  and Libya, 61
  and 'Middle East Security Alliance' (proposed), 60
  and military rule, 43
  and population control, 3, 47
  and Russia, 257
  and Sudan, 63
  and Trump, President Donald, 237
  and women's rights, 221
social media, 79
social movements: 'non-movements', 78, 81, 84–5
Soviet Union, 16, 90
Spain, 5, 92, 94, 236, 247; *see also* Ceuta
Springborg, Robert, 53
Stein, Janet Gross, 154
Sub-Saharan Africa, 249–53, 260
Sudan, 7, 23, 59, 187, 214, 239, 243
  agriculture, 64
  and human rights, 63
  and Israel, 59
  and Libya, 19
  and Nile Basin Initiative, 62–3
  water supply, 51, 52
Sufism, 144–5
Syria
  civil war, 75
  and Libya, 22
  reconstruction of, 61
  United States and, 13

Tajfel, Henri, 154
Tannir, Dina, 209
Tarkhan, Hamida, 202
Tartag, General Bashir, 181
Tebboune, President Abdelmadjid, 169, 184–5, 186, 187, 248, 252

terrorism
  counterterrorism, 5, 20, 22, 23, 24–5; Global Counterterrorism Forum, 252; Trans-Sahara Counterterrorism Partnership (TSCTP), 252
  Mauritania, 139, 146
  Qadhafi, Muammar and, 16, 22
  Sahel, 93
al-Thani, Sheikh Tamim, 243, 248
Thepaut, Charles, 236, 261–2
Tilmatine, Mohand, 183
Tiran (Red Sea island), 58–9
Transparency International, 122, 143
Tripp, Aili Mari, 212, 222
Trump, President Donald, 20, 59, 60, 63, 95, 237, 239
Tunisia
  agriculture, 124, 126
  allies, 2
  Arab Spring, 208
  Ben Arous, 110, 111
  Bourguibists, 103
  centralisation, 103; *see also* decentralisation
  colonialism, 103, 198–9
  corporitist model, 104
  COVID-19 pandemic, 2, 101, 115, 116–18, 120
  decentralisation, 101, 103, 109, 118–22; *see also* centralisation
  democracy, 2, 200
  Democratic Constitutional Rally (RCD) *see* Neo-Destour party
  economy, 2, 105, 106, 109, 117, 124
  education, 109, 110, 112f
  and Egypt, 244
  elections, 119, 125
  elites, 106, 107
  employment and unemployment, 107, 111, 112f, 115, 117
  Ennahda party, 123, 217, 242, 243
  and European Union, 235
  extremism, 105
  feminist movement, 200
  Gafsa, 108, 123
  Gafsa Phosphate Company (GPC), 106–7
  gas, 113, 114, 115, 116
  gender equality, 198–200, 218–19, 220, 222
  gender quotas, 216, 217
  gendered violence, 209, 213
  governance, 111–13, 126; *see also* centralisation; decentralisation
  and Grand Ethiopian Renaissance Dam, 64
  and Gulf Cooperation Council, 242
  human rights, 200
  internet subscriptions, 112f
  Islam, 199
  Jemna, 108
  justice process, 123–5
  Kairouan, 110
  Kasserine, 108, 110, 111, 124
  Kebili, 110, 111
  Kesra, 113
  and Libya, 34
  Local Authorities Code, 119–20
  marginalisation, 101–9; *see also* positive discrimination
  medical care, 110–11, 112f, 116–18
  migration from, 106, 116–17
  minority groups, 107–8
  Monastir, 110
  Nawaat (blog), 127
  Neo-Destour party (later

Democratic Constitutional
Rally (RCD)), 199
oil, 113, 114, 115, 116
positive discrimination, 122–5, 126
post-revolution, 75
protests, 107, 109, 111, 113–16
revolution (2010–11), 101, 102, 108–9
and Russia, 258
and Saudi Arabia, 2, 242, 243
Sfax, 108, 110, 111
Sidi Bouzid, 105, 108, 110, 111, 113
and Sub-Saharan Africa, 250, 251–2
TGV line, 126
Tataouine: Kamour protests, 113–16; medical care, 110
tax fraud, 126
tourism, 106, 258
Tozeur, 111
Truth and Dignity Commission (Instance Vérité et Dignité, IVD), 124–5, 126
Tunis, 108, 110, 111, 127
Tunisian General Labour Union (UGTT), 115, 116
and United Arab Emirates, 2, 242–3
United States and, 5–6
water supply, 127
wealth gap, 109–10
Youssefists, 103
Zraoua, 108
Turkey
and Egypt, 60–1, 249
influence of, 3
and Libya, 18, 19, 60
and Qatar, 241–2, 248–9

United Arab Emirates (UAE)
and Algeria, 247
and Arab Spring, 241
and Bahrain, 244
and Egypt, 18, 58, 64, 246
and Ethiopia, 64
and Israel, 59
and Libya, 3, 18–19, 20, 24, 60, 61, 246
and Mauritania, 247
and Morocco, 244, 245, 248
and oil, 30
and Qatar, 59
and Sudan, 63, 64
and Tunisia, 2, 242–3
and Turkey, 249
and United States, 59
see also Gulf Cooperation Council; Gulf States
United Nations
Beijing Conference (1995), 211, 213
and Egypt, 47
and Grand Ethiopian Renaissance Dam, 64
and Libya, 19, 20, 250, 257
UN process (1951), 15–16
and Western Sahara, 90–1
United States
Abraham Accords, 59, 95, 248
and Egypt, 5–6, 45–6, 63, 64, 238
and Ethiopia, 63
and Europe, 261–2
influence of, 5–6, 234, 236–8, 259, 261, 263
and Libya, 13, 16, 18, 20, 22, 23, 24–5, 29
and 'Middle East Security Alliance' (proposed), 60
and migration, 239
and Morocco, 74, 95
and Syria, 13
trade and investment by, 240
and Tunisia, 5–6, 118, 259
and United Arab Emirates, 59

United States (*cont.*)
   and Western Sahara, 238–9
   women's suffrage, 212
uti possidetis doctrine, 93

Vall Ould Mohamed, Colonel Ely, 137
Villasante-de Beauvais, Mariella, 151

weapons of mass destruction (WMDs), 13
Weddady, Abderrahmane, 149
Western Sahara conflict, 90–5, 147, 238–9, 250, 260
   human rights, 92
Wiley, Katherine Ann, 207
women
   and Arab Spring, 208–9
   and corruption, 195
   Egypt, 45–7, 48, 49
   empowerment of, 210–23
   legal rights, 196–7
   Mauritania, 152–3, 155–6
   and political participation, 212, 213–14, 217, 223–4
   role of, 195
   sexual harassment of, 221, 223, 224
   violence against, 209, 213, 217, 219–20, 221, 223, 224
   see also gender equality
World Bank
   and feminism, 205
   and infrastructure investment, 253
   Women, Business and Law Index, 196–7
World Economic Forum: Global Gender Gap index, 196

xenophobia, 28

al-Yahyaoui, Khaled, 244
Yemen, 23, 60, 61, 75, 245, 247
Yerkes, Sarah, 6
Youngs, Richard, 234, 239–40
al Yousouffi, Abderrahman, 205

Zbiri, Colonel Tahar, 171
Zefzafi, Nasser, 82, 84
Zeghal, Malika, 145
Zeidan, Ali, 29
Zeroual, General Liamine, 173

EU representative:
Easy Access System Europe
Mustamäe tee 50, 10621 Tallinn, Estonia
Gpsr.requests@easproject.com

www.ingramcontent.com/pod-product-compliance
Lightning Source LLC
Chambersburg PA
CBHW050201240426
43671CB00013B/2202